Consumer Tribes

Consumer Tribes

Edited by

Bernard Cova

Robert V. Kozinets

Avi Shankar

AMSTERDAM • BOSTON • HEIDELBERG • LONDON • NEW YORK • OXFORD
PARIS • SAN DIEGO • SAN FRANCISCO • SINGAPORE • SYDNEY • TOKYO

Butterworth-Heinemann is an imprint of Elsevier

Butterworth-Heinemann is an imprint of Elsevier
Linacre House, Jordan Hill, Oxford OX2 8DP, UK
30 Corporate Drive, Suite 400, Burlington, MA 01803, USA

First edition 2007

Notice
No responsibility is assumed by the publisher for any injury and/or damage to persons or
property as a matter of products liability, negligence or otherwise, or from any use or operation
of any methods, products, instructions or ideas contained in the material herein. Because of rapid
advances in the medical sciences, in particular, independent verification of diagnoses and drug
dosages should be made

British Library Cataloguing in Publication Data
A catalogue record for this book is available from the British Library

Library of Congress Cataloging-in-Publication Data
A catalog record for this book is available from the Library of Congress

ISBN: 978-0-7506-8024-0

For information on all Butterworth-Heinemann publications
visit our web site at http://books.elsevier.com

Typeset by Charon Tec Ltd (A Macmillan Company), Chennai, India
www.charontec.com

Transferred to Digital Printing in 2010

Working together to grow libraries in developing countries

www.elsevier.com | www.bookaid.org | www.sabre.org

ELSEVIER   BOOK AID International   Sabre Foundation

Contents

    to fan club formation and continuance   163
    Paul Henry and Marylouise Caldwell

    Introduction   163
    Method   164
    Findings   165
    Conclusion   171
    References   172

PART IV   TRIBES AS PLUNDERERS   175

12 **Harry Potter and the Fandom Menace**   177
    Stephen Brown

    This just in   177
    Authorpreneurship   178
    Back story   178
    Real story   180
    The triwizard iTribes   181
    Get a life   183
    The auror, the auror   185
    When good fans go bad   189
    References   191

13 **Inno-tribes: *Star Trek* as wikimedia**   194
    Robert V. Kozinets

    A brief history of *Star Trek*   196
    Star Trek as wikimedia   197
    Prosuming's final frontier   198
    Gays, grays, and ego plays   200
    Death by canon, or the death of canon?   202
    Star Trek fans as inno-tribes   204
    Considerations   206
    References   209

14 **Seeking community through battle: understanding the**
    meaning of consumption processes for warhammer gamers'
    communities across borders   212
    David J. Park, Sameer Deshpande, Bernard Cova and Stefano Pace

    Introduction   212
    Consumption tribes   213
    Warhammer   214
    Understanding gaming brand community: a case of warhammer
    gamers in the US and France   217

List of contributors

Caroline Bekin is a PhD candidate at Birmingham Business School, University of Birmingham, England from where she obtained her MSc in Marketing. She has worked in consumer research and advertising. Her research interests include community consumption, consumer resistance and ethical consumption.

Stephen Brown is Professor of Marketing Research at the University of Ulster, Northern Ireland. He is no relation to Dan Brown, though he wishes it were otherwise. He is hopeful, however, that *The Marketing Code*, his latest blockbuster, will benefit from its shameless attachment to Dan Brown's coat-tails. Written as a thriller, it reveals that *The Da Vinci Code* was a marketing conspiracy from start to finish. He has also written loads of other books and journal articles (see: www.sfxbrown.com).

Douglas Brownlie teaches and researches in marketing subjects in the Department of Marketing at the University of Stirling, Scotland. He previously did this at the University of Strathclyde, the University of Glasgow and University College Cork. He has published widely on topics including consumer culture theory, marketing management and technology forecasting.

Marylouise Caldwell is a Senior Lecturer in Marketing at the University of Sydney, Australia. She has published in various journals including *European Journal of Marketing, International Journal of Arts Management, Psychology and Marketing, Advances in Consumer Research, Qualitative Market Research* and *Consumption Markets and Culture*. Her primary research activity centres on creating films and articles that focus on consumer (dis)empowerment, happiness, well-being and gender.

Robin Canniford would rather be on a beach. When not, he is gainfully employed as a Lecturer in Marketing and Consumer Culture at the University of Exeter, England. His research interests include sociological interpretations of advertising and branding campaigns; historical approaches to understanding consumer culture; and the marketing of sports. He is currently conducting historical and ethnographic investigations into the kinds of communities and social networks fostered in consumer culture. He has published in the *European Journal of Marketing, European Advances in Consumer Research* and *Qualitative Market Research*. If he were a caterpillar he would be ready to pupate.

Marylyn Carrigan is a Senior Lecturer in Marketing at the Birmingham Business School, University of Birmingham, from where she gained her PhD (Commerce). She has published extensively in the field of marketing ethics and ethical consumption, and is on the editorial boards of the *International Marketing Review*, and the *Journal of Marketing Communications*. Her research interests include marketing ethics, ethical consumption, sustainability and family consumption.

Fabrizio Cocciola is Demand and Customer Service Manager for Sanofi-Aventis, a worldwide pharmaceutical company. He graduated in Economics and Business Administration from L'Aquila University, Italy. His post-graduate activities focus on E-Business and especially Internet based communities. He was a co-developer of a tool dedicated to the capture of word-of-mouth on below-the-web channels like mailing lists and newsgroups.

Bernard Cova is Professor of Marketing at Euromed Marseilles, School of Management, France and Visiting Professor at Università Bocconi, Milan, Italy. Ever since his first papers in the early 1990s, he has taken part in post-modern trends in consumer research and marketing, while emphasizing a Latin approach (e.g., Tribal marketing). He has published on this topic in the *International Journal of Research in Marketing, European Journal of Marketing, Marketing Theory* and the *Journal of Business Research*. He is also known as a researcher in B2B marketing, especially in the field of project marketing.

Sameer Deshpande is an Assistant Professor of Marketing and faculty member of Centre for Socially Responsible Marketing in the Faculty of Management at the University of Lethbridge, Canada. His interests primarily lie in studying social marketing and consumer culture. Previously, Sameer has published in journals such as *Journalism and Mass Communication Quarterly, International Journal of Public Opinion Research* and *Social Marketing Quarterly*.

Kristine de Valck is an Assistant Professor of Marketing at HEC School of Management, Paris. She earned her PhD from the RSM Erasmus University. Her dissertation research investigated the influence of virtual communities of consumption on consumer-decision making. Her research continues to focus on interpersonal influence, word-of-'mouse' and the role of new communication technologies (blogs, podcasts, mobile phones, etc.) in marketing.

Luciano Fratocchi is an Associate Professor of Business Management in the School of Engineering at the University of L'Aquila, Italy. His main research interests are related to the internationalization processes of small and medium firms with a special focus on the use of Information and Communication Technologies (ICT) to support foreign market entry and development.

Markus Giesler is an Assistant Professor of Marketing at York University's Schulich School of Business, Toronto, Canada, informs the socio-dynamic study of market and consumer systems. He can be reached at http://www.markus-giesler.com.

Christina Goulding is Professor of Consumer Research at the Business School, University of Wolverhampton, England. Her research interests lie in cultural consumption, sub-cultural consumption and consumption and identity. She has published her work in a number of international journals including *Psychology and Marketing, European Journal of Marketing, Consumption Markets and Culture* and *Journal of Marketing Management*. She is the author of the Sage book entitled 'Grounded Theory: Practical Applications for Managers and Market Researchers' and is co-editor of the forthcoming book 'Critical Marketing".

Paul Henry is Senior Lecturer in the School of Business at The University of Sydney, Australia. He has written extensively on marketplace inequality, disempowerment, social class and a variety of associated consumption behaviours. His work appears in journals such as *Consumption, Markets and Culture, European Journal of Marketing, Psychology and Marketing, Journal of Consumer Research, Journal of Sociology* and *Qualitative Market Research*.

Paul Hewer is a Senior Lecturer in the Department of Marketing at Strathclyde University, Scotland. Previously he held academic positions at Stirling and Loughborough Universities. Prior to this he read Sociology at Leeds University, completed an MA in the Sociology of Contemporary Culture and a PhD in the Sociology of Men's Consumer Behaviour at York University. His current research interests lie in the area of unpacking contemporary consumer culture, from exploring its visual representations to understanding consumers' everyday practices.

A member of many tribes, **Robert V. Kozinets** is an Associate Professor of Marketing at York University's Schulich School of Business in Toronto, Canada. His tribal affiliations include anthropology, film, Star Trek, Star Wars and X-Files fan, coffee connoisseur, Burning Man phreak, online and offline videogame, consumer activist, technophile, blog and venomous virtual community member – and he has managed to quench his own interest in all of them by turning them into stultifyingly ordinary research. Some of this tribally tinged twaddle can be found hidden in the rearmost pages of the *Journal of Marketing*, the *Journal of Consumer Research*, the *Journal of Marketing Research*, the *Journal of Contemporary Ethnography, Consumption, Markets, & Culture* and the *Journal of Retailing*. He developed and continues to seek brave souls to join him in developing the highly flammable techniques of netnography and videography, to tipping sacred cows in fields, and to saving our planet before it is too late.

Roy Langer is Professor of Organizational and Marketing Communication at Roskilde University, Denmark. His research interests include post-modern marketing and consumption, stealth and undercover marketing and qualitative research methods. Roy has published widely in journals such as *Psychology and Marketing, Corporate Communications – An International Journal, Corporate Reputation Review*, and *Qualitative Market Research*.

Marius Luedicke is an Assistant Professor of Marketing at Innsbruck University School of Management. He earned a doctorate from the University of St. Gallen in Switzerland and is a frequent visiting researcher at York University in Canada and the University of Arizona in the US. His research explores the social fabric and virtue of brands in contemporary consumer culture.

Pauline Maclaran is Professor of Marketing and Consumer Research at Keele University, England. Her research interests focus on cultural aspects of contemporary consumption, and she adopts a critical perspective to analyse the ideological assumptions that underpin many marketing activities. In particular, her work has explored socio-spatial aspects of consumption, including the utopian dimensions of fantasy retail environments, and how the built environment mediates family relationships. Her publications have been in internationally recognized journals such as, the *Journal of Consumer Research, Psychology and Marketing, Journal of Advertising* and *Consumption, Markets & Culture* and she has co-edited a book entitled Marketing and Feminism: Current Issues and Research. She is also Co-editor in Chief of *Marketing Theory*, a journal that promotes alternative and critical perspectives in marketing and consumer behaviour.

Michel Maffesoli is Professor at the University of La Sorbonne, Paris, France. He is also the Director of 'Sociétés', a scholarly journal in the humanities and social sciences, and Director of the *Centre d'Etudes sur l'Actuel et le Quotidien* (*CEAQ*) and Secretary General of the *Centre de Recherche sur l'Imaginaire* (*Maison des Sciences de l'Homme*). His book *La Transfiguration du Politique* obtained the *Grand Prix des Sciences Humaines of the Académie Française* in 1992. His book *Le Temps des Tribus* (1988) – translated in English in 1996 under the title *The Time of the Tribes* – is today considered the building block of the research on community and tribal marketing.

Diane M. Martin is Senior Associate in Ethos Market Research, LLC and an Assistant Professor of Marketing at The University of Portland in Portland, Oregon. Prior to her academic career Diane founded and ran Oregon

Attractions Marketing from which she managed marketing for the Mount Hood Railroad and consulted with clients such as the Oregon Zoo, Oregon Museum of Science and Industry and Portland Art Museum. During anchorage, Alaska's bid for the Winter Olympics she also performed as Seymour the Dancing Moose.

James H. McAlexander is a Founder and Principal of Ethos Market Research, LLC and a Professor of Marketing at Oregon State University where he founded and directs the Close to the Customer Project. Jim has worked as a Scholar in Residence at Harley-Davidson, Inc. A former air traffic controller and PATCO striker, he also enjoys the distinction of having been fired and banned for life from his career by a President of the United States.

Albert M. Muñiz, Jr. is an Associate Professor of Marketing at DePaul University. His research interests are in the sociological aspects of consumer behaviour and branding, including consumer generated content and user innovation in online communities. He has researched extensively in the area of consumer brand communities for over a decade and his work has been published in the *Journal of Consumer Research* and the *Journal of Interactive Marketing*. Professor Muñiz received his BS, MS and PhD from the University of Illinois, Urbana-Champaign. Before coming to DePaul, Professor Muñiz taught at the University of California at Berkeley.

Clive Nancarrow is Professor in Marketing Research at Bristol Business School, University of the West of England. He was Research Director for a major marketing research agency in London, Research Director for L'Oreal UK and has been retained by Seagram, Dell Computer Systems and more recently TNS. He is a Trustee for the League Trust – the charitable arm of the League Against Cruel Sports.

Pamela Nancarrow has a first degree in history from the University of Manchester, England, and a Master of Arts degree in Popular Culture from the Open University. She has worked in television and magazine publishing (working on Cosmopolitan and other major titles). More recently she has worked as a marketing research consultant with a particular interest in contemporary culture.

Jacob Ostberg is an Assistant Professor of Marketing in the School of Business at Stockholm University, Sweden and holds a PhD from Lund University, Sweden. His research interests cover such areas as brands as cultural resources, Scandinavian consumer culture and the anxiety over food consumption in late modernity. His work has appeared in *Advances in Consumer Research* and *Consumption, Markets and Culture* as well as in several book chapters. To capture the visual element of contemporary consumer culture he has worked with videography and presented award-winning films at the ACR film festival and in CMC.

Cele Otnes is a Professor of Marketing in the Department of Business Administration at the University of Illinois at Urbana-Champaign. Her primary research interest is in the area of ritualistic consumption. She is the co-author with Elizabeth Pleck of Cinderella Dreams: The Allure of the Lavish Wedding (University of California Press), and co-editor with Tina M. Lowrey of Contemporary Consumption Rituals: A Research Anthology (Erlbaum). She has published articles on gift giving, magical consumption, the ambivalence surrounding wedding planning and the relationship between advertising and ritual in the *Journal of Consumer Research, Journal of Contemporary Ethnography, Journal of Advertising*, and other publications.

Stefano Pace is an Assistant Professor in Marketing at Università Bocconi, Milan, Italy where he also obtained his PhD in Business Administration and Management. He was visiting student at the Wharton Business School, Philadelphia, USA. His research interests include brand communities, Internet marketing, service marketing. He published on these topics in such journals as the *European Journal of Marketing* and the *European Management Journal*.

David J. Park is an Assistant Professor in the Communications Department at Xavier University, Louisiana, USA. He holds a PhD (2003) in Mass Communication from the University of Wisconsin-Madison. He has published in *Global Media Journal, Journal of Communication Inquiry, American Behavioral Scientist* and other journals. He has been a Fulbright Scholar to the Caribbean, a Tinker-Nave Scholar to Argentina, and a Rotary Scholar to Belgium. Currently Park is working on a book manuscript titled 'Conglomerate Rock: The Music Industry's Quest to Divide Music and Conquer Wallets', which is under contract with Lexington Books.

Diego Rinallo is an Assistant Professor of Marketing at Bocconi University, Milan, Italy. A few years ago, he would have stated 'I'm a fashion scholar, not a fashion consumer'. Now things have changed, even though he is not a fashion victim yet. Prada shoes are a possible exception.

Michael Saren is Professor of Marketing in the Management Centre at the University of Leicester, England. Prior to this he was Professor of Marketing at the University of Strathclyde, Scotland. He is currently working on a number of research projects including investigation into sub-cultural consumption, branding and identity and is UK area editor of the journal *Marketing Theory*.

Hope Jensen Schau is an Assistant Professor of Marketing at the University of Arizona. Her research focuses on the impact of media and technology on marketplace relationships and the co-creation of value, with special emphasis on consumer generated brand-oriented content. Her research has been published in the *Journal of Consumer Research* and the *Journal of Retailing*. She earned her PhD at the University of California, Irvine.

John W. Schouten is a Founder and Principal of Ethos Market Research, LLC and an Associate Professor of Marketing at The University of Portland in Portland, Oregon where he also co-founded Moonstruck Chocolates. John is a poet and yet-to-be-published novelist. His 1991 poem 'Life Among the Winnebago', published in Highways and Buyways: Naturalistic Research From the Consumer Behaviour Odyssey, discusses the tribalism among consumer ethnographers.

Avi Shankar is a Senior Lecturer in Marketing and Consumer Research, in the School of Management at the University of Bath, England. He has eclectic research interests that can be broadly subsumed within three categories: critical analyses of contemporary consumer culture; consumer identity projects; and tribal consumption. Whilst the holy grail of the *Journal of Consumer Research* has thus far eluded him, he lives in hope. Meanwhile his ramblings can be found in, amongst others, the *European Journal of Marketing, Consumption, Markets and Culture, Marketing Theory* and the *Journal of Marketing Management*. When not writing these articles that no one seems to read, he is fully occupied with keeping his own tribe in order and has a keen interest in the production and consumption of vegetables and herbs, foraging for wild food in the valleys surrounding his riverside cottage and cooking the results of his exploits.

Stephen Treanor was one of the shining lights of the class of 2004! He achieved a 1st class degree in Marketing and Sociology at Stirling University, Scotland, prior to an MSc in Applied Social Research. His work has been published in the journal *Finanza Marketing e Produzione*. He is currently in the market for a post-graduate studentship and would welcome any offers.

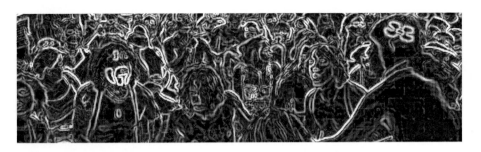

Part I
Conceptual
foundations

1

Tribes, Inc.: the new world of tribalism

Bernard Cova, Robert V. Kozinets and Avi Shankar

Introduction

You hold in your hands a book that spans current thought about the role of the tribal in contemporary commercial society. Its chapters cut across the continents ranging from the philosophical to the grounded, from critical conjecture to ethnographic evidence, sampling a range of tribal identities, activities and practices along the way. In this chapter, we seek to add another conceptual piece to the contemporary jigsaw puzzle that is the current world of tribal consumption by considering some of the powerful tensions between commercial culture and communal collectivities that this book's topic and its chapters raise.

Consumer Tribes, the title of this book, is difficult and problematic. In the first place, the groups of people we examine in this book are doing far more than what is commonly glossed by the terms 'consumer' and 'consumption'. In common parlance and dictionary definitions, consumers are those who 'use up', 'destroy' or 'deplete' economic goods. But the Consumer Tribes in the chapters of this book are doing far more than that. They do not consume things without changing them; they cannot 'consume' a good without it becoming them and them becoming it; they cannot 'consume' a service without engaging in a dance with the service provider, where the dance becomes the service. Participatory culture is everywhere.

No doubt there are some people who may take exception to the creativity and agency ascribed to consumers in this book's chapters. For a start they may say the term 'consumer' has become naturalized and normalized, not just within everyday business speak but also in everyday political speak too. From this view, 'people' have been turned into 'consumers' and are passive victims of the current, dominant mode of the capitalist system – an ideology of neo-liberalism – and its global, corporate juggernauts. To be sure, Marxian inspired theories of hegemony and ideology, although increasingly out of favour these days even within sociological and cultural studies circles, are an important addition to the critical examination of contemporary business practice. Marxian concepts such as commodity fetishism, reification, and commodification still provide perceptive insights for our understanding of a market society. But this passive absorption model of consumers is not what we see in the chapters of this book. Active and enthusiastic in their consumption, sometimes in the extreme, tribes produce a range of identities, practices, rituals, meanings, and even material culture itself. They re-script roles, twist meanings, and shout back to producers and other groups of people while they fashion their own differentiation strategies. They both absorb and resist the pre-packaged, off-the-shelf, brand-and-product meanings of marketers.

So, in the first instance, let's be clear that Consumer Tribes rarely consume brands and products – even the most mundane ones – without adding to them, grappling with them, blending them with their own lives and altering them. Consumer Tribes *do* things. Consumers are people, yes, but people who live in a specific social and historical situation. This places them in a co-dependent relationship with commercial culture, one where industrial and post-industrial information economies create not only things, but critical elements of cultural, social, and self-identity, and where those identities are at both the bottom and the top of the proverbial economic–industrial–political pyramid. So let's be content for the moment in stating that consumers are consumers primarily in that they take commercial identities as important aspects of themselves and their collectives, that they use these identities to relate to themselves, to other people, and to the world around them through lenses that incorporate a vast range of commercial and commercially produced pursuits, objectives and definitions of the self.

And although it is currently in vogue, the term 'tribe' opens up yet another a hornet's nest of unwelcome associations. Perhaps most alluring of all is the notion that by calling a phenomenon 'tribal' we have somehow explained it. Like a semantic undertow, Consumer Tribes constantly draws us back to a Rousseauian version of contemporary society: a primitivist longing for better bygone days; a nested and natural nostalgia for a more pristine and closer world, where nature enclosed and emplaced humanity; where small kin-like groups of people bore tighter social bonds and loving links to the Earth;

where people were unburdened of repressive social l... themselves freely and in harmony; where daily life wa... with natural animal sexuality; where humans were free t... animist and transcendent spirit of the world; and finally where ...sed to find their True Selves.

Jacques Barzun (2000) reminds us that the idealist vision of ... a place of powerful primitive retreat, is a constant cultural compon... Modern Age (for marketer's take on the retro, see Brown, 2001; Brc... Sherry, 2003; Brown, Kozinets, and Sherry, 2003; Cova and Cova, 2002). ... volume, Robin Canniford and Avi Shankar's chapter on surf culture exan... the construction and allure of the tribal metaphor. They identify how colo... discourse constructed surf culture through tribal tropes and later how commer-cial culture re-appropriated this tribal symbolism to imbue products and serv-ices with a sense of 'otherness,' excitement and danger. This otherness, the idea of a wild or *natural* human state to which we can return, or at least taste a little bit, is a myth whose potency has diminished little over the past 200 years. It refers us to some very important aspects of the phenomena we study here – the hunger of community, expression, transcendence, a natural state (see e.g., Goulding, Shankar, and Elliott, 2002) – and yet it is certainly not the whole story – the Consumer Tribes in this book are less rigid and fixed than their anthropo-logical counterparts.

For the past decade or so, and inspired in part by the application of the theories of one the contributors to this book, Michel Maffesoli (see his chapter in this book), a new understanding of Consumer Tribes has emerged within marketing and consumer research theory. This perspective rejects an atomistic, overly individualistic, information processor view of people as individuals who are to some extent sealed off and separated from their experiential worlds – in short, assumptions underlying the type of research that still dominates the text books, journal articles, and LISREL models of our discipline.

Rather, a variety of studies from both a North American anthropological tradition and a European micro-sociological tradition accept as axiomatic that human life is essentially social. Social life is a rich, complex, kaleidoscopic confusion that cannot ever be represented by 'causes' and 'effects'. Such stud-ies reject analyses of market-based phenomena through the imposition of abstract modernist structures (class, age, gender, and so on), what we can call a top down modernist sociology, in favour of what might be termed a bottom up postmodern sociology. In this view, the building blocks of human social life are not to be found in abstract categories applied to the analysis of social life, but in the multiplicity of social groupings that we all participate in, knowingly or not, through the course of our everyday lives. These *tribus* or little masses (popularized as neo-tribes) are fundamental to our experience of life in general. They differ from traditional tribes in an anthropological sense in one import-ant way; we belong to many little tribes and not one tribe. From this perspec-tive the consumption of cultural resources circulated through markets (brands, leisure experiences, and so on) are not the *sine qua non* of contemporary life, rather, they facilitate what are – meaningful social relationships. As

va (1997) has argued the 'links' (social relationships) are more
than things (brands, products, experiences, ideas).

clear to say that when taken as some sort of explanation of contem-
practice, Consumer Tribes, our title, obscures more than it reveals.
Henry Jenkins (e.g., Jenkins, 2006) teaches us, our mass mediated world
filled with participatory personalities whose interests coalesce with commercial culture, such as in his example of consumers' interest in following
an American Idol candidate blending extemporaneously and temporarily
into tribal affiliations with Coca Cola bottlers around the world. These are
relationships of passion and, as Marianna Torgovnick (1996) reminds us, the
allure of the primitive, of the tribal, lies in its ability to arouse our desires and
passions.

In this chapter, we seek to delve deeper into the rotating cultural currents
swirling around these ideas of consumption and production, primitivism and
postmodernism, the commercial and the communal, nature and culture, past
and present, oppression and liberation, conformity and transcendence, and to
see what hybrid forms are born within them. As our headings, we offer statements about Consumer Tribes that form four coherent themes running through
the chapters of this book: that Consumer Tribes are activators, double agents,
plunderers, and entrepreneurs (see Figure 1.1). Through example and assertion, this introductory chapter circulates through meanings of consumers and

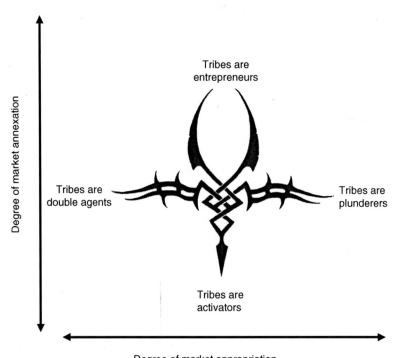

Figure 1.1 Mapping Consumer Tribes.

tribes as it tracks moments of resistance, co-construction, and transcendence, and finds within them new ways to see the relation of producers consumed, and consumers produced.

In Figure 1.1, we seek to encapsulate the various identities and associated practices that Consumer Tribes adopt. These range along two continua. The horizontal axis portrays the appropriation axis, the active tendency of Consumer Tribes to poach their creative material from the commercial marketplace, a practice that often gets tribes into trouble. This can range from the minimal appropriation of the double agent identity where, the Tribe enjoys being the target subject, passing on information to brand owners for example, and the distributor of marketplace objects, messages and meanings, to the pirate-like plunderers, who actively play with and shape objects whose rights may belong to other groups, invert and invent meanings, and spread their own messages. On the vertical axis, we have the amount of market annexing or building practices engaged in by the Consumer Tribe. On the low end, this holds the playing-within-the-market identity of the Tribe as an activator, wherein market-based norms and standards are respected, and the Tribe is firmly identified with the role of Consumer. At the high end of the annexation axis is the Consumer Tribe as entrepreneur, actively involved in entering into and expanding the marketplace, on a common footing with commercial producers as a creator of not only cultural and social value, but also economic wealth. Consumer Tribes and their members can move between these different active modalities and identities fluidly, shifting from one form of market interaction to another effortlessly.

Consumer tribes are activators

There are clear tensions revealed by our title of Consumer Tribes. Are people acting in some sense as self-regulating armies of robotic commercial drones or are they vividly alive, dancers on a stage? Are they retreating into an idealized past, or are they intrepid bricoleurs melding and collaging their way through a postmodern present? The reality of course lies somewhere in between these extremes; it is not 'either or' but elements of both. They are players as in performers, as in contestants, as in improvisers, supernumeraries, suzerains, overseers. Play activates. Tribes are activators.

Before we can truly explore these notions of play, we need to grapple for a moment with a question of control and freedom. Many contemporary studies of consumers are structured by a polarizing question. This question asks whether consumption involves consumers choosing between two theoretical alternatives. In one, they let themselves be immersed within and submerged by the system of commercial consumption. In the other alternative, consumers are dodgy dissidents who resist the market.

Based on the vision of Consumer Tribes, we would argue that this dichotomy is a poor representation of what consumption actually entails. Of course, these theoretical positions are not only extreme and ideal-typical but also strongly marked by notions of power and opposition (Aubenas and Benasayag, 2002) that pose everyday questions in absolutist terms. We, of course, prefer Absolut markets to absolute ones. Embedded in logics of manipulation and control, the lens given by this dichotomous posing blurs the perception that 'consumer experience' is a complex, moment-by-moment, situated occurrence. Lived experience is never simple and binary, but ever-shifting, full of adjustments and hybridizations. To see consumer experience as a choice between slavery and freedom, structure and agency, passivity and rebellion is to use an analytical frame that equates the increasingly subtle techniques of postmodern marketing with the excessive manipulation of consumers.

However, we wish in this volume and beyond to argue for the delineation of ever more subtle, nuanced, dynamic, and complex systems that are at work in the commercial world. In these systems, consumers are not manipulated but engage in tacit compromises (Rémy, 2002). Consumers, in other words, are not naïve about living in their commercial–material world: like Madonna, they are commercial–material boys and girls. They know the game plan; they read the playbooks; they know the strategy. Conscious of a partial manipulation, they decide to what extent they will be manipulated and they manipulate too.

Consumers decide to what extent they will appear to be misled, to be truly misled, to remember and to forget, and then mislead, and then manipulate these manipulations in ways that enliven their daily lives and life (Badot and Cova, 2003). 'The neo-consumer model does not involve an individual who has been manipulated and hypnotized but one who is mobile' (Lipovetsky, 2003, p. 88) and can play, often simultaneously, at coupling hyper-commercialization with de-commercialization. What we are trying to understand is a process that lacks subjects, whether companies or consumers. Instead, we should be thinking in terms of processes where subjects like companies and consumers exist within the confines of a situation that no one truly controls. This is play, improvizational play, playing by the rules and playing with the rules, playing with the playbook and the other players, all elements that have been noted as important by several consumer researchers over the last decade (e.g., Deighton, 1992; Deighton and Grayson, 1995; Kozinets, Sherry Jr., Storm, Duhachek, Nuttavuthisit, and DeBerry-Spence, 2004).

The central tensions of consumption and production seem almost to contain within them the links to rituals of resistance and opposition, yet these rituals all too often turn out to be playful, hollow or bereft of real animosity or vigour. This disappoints some (perhaps many) researchers, whose own ideological stands tend to lead them to seek rebellious consumers, activists who will change the system. Yet the dialectics of tribes and tribalism are often equal parts playful and liberatory, a place where struggles against the system are cloaked less in ideologies of resistance and more in identities of liberation. They often take place in the context of a complex social process ever unfolding whose significance lies not in the value of its players' transactions but in the transaction of its play values.

We can see the metaphor of Consumer Tribes as players who activate and enliven a social process of commercial meanings and identity production–consumption. This theme runs strongly through many chapters in this book.

In their chapter on the British Royal Family, Cele Otnes and Pauline Maclaran unpack what seems at first to be obsessive fan behaviour into a tribal reconnection with history and tradition. In this reconnection, the mass media as societal proxy and socially constructionist creator of past and present plays a crucial role. Co-created through these institutional dynamics, followers of the British Royal Family build and play with their own sense of belonging and heritage.

These topsy-turvy liberatory (or were they oppressive?) dynamics of commercial culture are especially evident in the chapter by John Schouten, Diane Martin and James McAlexander. Their chapter charting the evolution of consumption meanings within the Harley-Davidson subculture or tribe questions our extant notions of meanings such as 'freedom' or 'machismo' and then shows how these meanings possess considerable semiotic flexibility when constructed by different social groups. Another important and very complementary look at the plasticity of masculine meanings is covered in the chapter on metrosexuality by Diego Rinallo, who looks at industrial- and consumer-oriented Italian fashion tribes. In notions of oppositional acceptance of mainstream 'hegemonic' masculinity – that constrain male action but also give metrosexuals something to individualize from and resist against – this chapter demonstrates how semiotic ambiguity underscores and supports the playful tribal venture. Meanings of masculinity and femininity are related fluidly to fashion and both tribalize into smaller groups and detribalize, as smaller group tastes become mainstreamed for wider acceptability.

In yet another related chapter, Jacob Östberg shows how the Stockholm Brat's tribalism is about carefully assembling, displaying and using various consumption objects to create just the right ambience of coolness. All of these chapters offer us a critical take on consumption meanings that illustrate beautifully how important a deep contextualization of meaning is when we seek to understand particular Consumer Tribes, with their immense proclivity for accepting/resisting play and for acting within a complex social process as activators.

Consumer tribes are double agents

Like Walt Whitman's metaphor of self, but literally true, tribes contain multitudes. It is no wonder then that they are constantly contradicting themselves; they are paradox incarnate. We emphasize with this construct the important limitations that come with viewing all tribal or communal consumer behaviour as oppositional or resistant. Many collective experiences tend to re-appropriate products and services from the consumption system without consciously associating any oppositional attitude with this act. For example, there is little opposition in the fannish activities of aficionados who dig up and revive vintage products like old Citroën cars (e.g., *Génération 2 CV*) or pre-war bicycles (e.g., *Confrérie des 650*). In their own way, these groups are imbuing such products with meanings and usages that differ from the ones they originally conveyed. They use them as physical forms that are like *tabula rasa* – but not quite, as the patina of age has not been completely worn clean of meaning – and are made new again by the inscription of additional meanings. Building meaning through shared experiences and emotions constitutes a daily episode in the creation, consolidation, and preservation of a communitarian sentiment within these groups.

Moreover, certain re-appropriation actions are relatively spontaneous in nature. Consider the way that 'street persons' have hijacked Bavaria's deluxe beer, an 8.6 beverage that has now become a 'street beer'. Or the horror felt by deluxe champagne manufacturers Moët and Chandon when the working class 'Chav' subculture appropriated their luxury brand and bent its meanings. Another example is offered by 'flash mobs' (spontaneous get-togethers for no ostensible purpose; see Rheingold, 2003) where email round robins are used to organize gatherings of individuals with no shared past or future but who are happy to temporarily invade some commercial premises on the spur of the moment. For example, such a 'flash mob' materialized in a Rome bookshop. Between 200 and 300 people crowded the aisles, asking shopkeepers for non-existent books. They broke into a round of spontaneous applause. Then they dispersed. In the same neo-Situationist vein, Reclaim the Streets (www. rts.gn.apc.org) is an anti-capitalist movement whose aim is for 'local social–ecological revolution to transcend hierarchical and authoritarian society'. They use tactics like Street Football to protest outside gas (or petrol) stations. However, in an interesting twist the idea of Street Football has been hijacked by the largest lager brand in the UK, Carling, and featured in their latest television advertisement. What all of these actions have in common is that they are experiences that help products or services to transcend their status as mere merchandise, mere things. The consumption object becomes the agent or the double agent.

The experience of transcendence enables people to enact a ritual of decommercialization even as they continue to operate within a market framework, that is, to work within the staging that brands and companies have built. In Dougie Brownlie, Paul Hewer and Stephen Treanor's chapter on Car Cruisers we see the creative ways that commercial culture, in this case that surrounding cars, is re-integrated into the lives of Car Cruisers. Moreover, the staging of The Cruise temporarily invades spaces, like the deserted car parks of out-of-town shopping centres at night. In this way the predominantly young men are able to express their creativity and shared identity providing them with a sense of community and belonging.

The success of a beer called Pabst Blue Ribbon (PBR) is also significant in this respect.[1] Since the 1970s, this venerable but watery brand, a flag carrier for Pabst breweries, had struggled in the US markets. It hit its nadir in 2001 when fewer than 1 million barrels were sold, 90 per cent below the 1975 peak. All of a sudden, sales began to explode, with growth reaching 5.3 per cent in 2002. Even more significant is the fact that Pabst Blue Ribbon (PBR to its fans) is omnipresent in San Francisco, New York or Chicago's trendy bars today. PBR is now the fifth biggest seller in Portland, America's capital of micro-breweries, right behind giants like Coors Light, Budweiser, Bud Light and Corona.

[1] Based on the data published in 22 June 2003, *The New York Times Magazine* and October 2003 *Business Digest*, No. 134.

This breakthrough is all the more remarkable because it owes little to marketing done by the company that owns PBR. Pabst has done very little advertising over the past two decades, operating as it does in a market where giants like Budweiser or Miller think nothing of spending tens of millions of dollars to increase market share. So how can we explain PBR's sudden return to popularity? The most interesting thesis is that, paradoxically, the absence of marketing around the product may have contributed to its success. By the late 1990s, PBR was suffering from poor distribution, a cheap reputation and an almost see-through image. These traits, associated with the unfounded rumour of Pabst's impending bankruptcy, may have contributed to the beer's being adopted by so-called alternative circles, such as New York bike couriers, who inscribed their own meanings on the brand. Pabst was so out it was in. So uncool it became cool.

Cool people, *people in the know*, began consuming PBR without Pabst's executives having strategically targeted or even envisioned the possibility of them drinking it. Because the brewery was originally based in Milwaukee, and the Wisconsin brewery later shut down, PBR's fans view their consumer behaviour as a gesture of solidarity with workers from America's heartlands. Part of the story may be an act of resistance to the market economy and unfettered globalization. Part of it might be, as Alex Wipperfürth (2005) argues, sheer dumb luck, the 'serendipity' of having your brand be at the right place at the right time with the right set of (tired, square, or non) meanings. The key for Pabst was not their marketing of the brand, but their not marketing of it.

Faced with this re-appropriation by consumers, Pabst's executives (surprisingly enough, or perhaps with only the savvy that comes from being a commercial giant like Miller) developed a marketing strategy diametrically opposed to the customary managerial recipe for a fast moving consumer product. The new strategy is based on no aggressive marketing, no new packaging, no widescale media campaign and no spectacular contracts with sports or music stars. Instead, Pabst is to have a low profile, as discrete a presence as possible in underground circles, plus a few hundreds micro-projects like small mountain biking competitions held on vacant lots, point-of-sales distributions of badges or tee-shirts, financial support for local musicians, and so on.

A cynic might say that this low-key strategy is intended to help Pabst fly under the collective cultural radar, to make people forget, or at least ignore, that Pabst's Wisconsin workers were all fired during the 1990s when the brewery delocalized to Texas. At the same time, it would be wrong to view the strategy as an example of contradiction, or even worse, as a manipulation. The beer's success is much more strongly rooted in a rejection of aggressive marketing than it is in the distraction away from a corporate social responsibility reckoning. Above all, PBR's anti-capitalist image has been entirely formulated by consumers themselves, and it would be difficult for them to complain now if this image does not correspond entirely to reality. All they can do is ignore the reality, as long as the company does not remind them of it. This will be their compromise with the commercial world.

These consumers will have been complicit with, but not tricked by, the way PBR's current image was built. In short, they are not trying to escape the market (Kozinets, 2002a) but to play with it. And this play has magical overtones. 'Re-enchantment occurs through distancing consumption and production from the structuring productivity and rational rules normally in effect . . . as if consumption, freed from its normal and adult status as a duty, can return to playfulness; the material world can become seat of the sacred again; consumption can become (re)ensouled' (Kozinets, 2002a, p. 32). Consumer Tribes breathe magic breath into dead and dying things, but they also suck the life from thriving brands. They work both sides.

The metaphor Consumer Tribes as Double Agents runs through Clive Nancarrow and Pamela Nancarrow's chapter on how Seagram, the world's largest alcoholic drinks company tried to understand the 'cool' people of a 'cool' inner city area of London. The dance between 'producers' and consumers' casts the cultural intermediaries, the cool people, in an uneasy relationship, caught between the narcissism of being identified as 'cool', yet potentially tainted because of their association with and bit-part in the marketing process – the identity tension between being a sell out or a cool urbanite.

How to face a world in which Consumer Tribes are Double Agents? We maintain that enlightened marketing professionals should be humble and almost self-effacing in nature. They will be concerned to avoid being guilty of poor taste, to not push too hard, to avoid being seen as trying to structure the experience of consumers and cramp their style, but also to spark and fan the ever-flickering flames of transcendent enchantment. A related theme courses through the chapter on a 'non-marginal, non-stigmatized' brand community by Hope Schau and Al Muñiz. Drawing on autobiographical experience, this ethnography of the Tom Petty fan community focuses on fans' uneasy maintenance of distance, the balancing act of kratophany that, the chapter's authors suggest, distinguishes mainstream devotion from marginalized fanaticism. Although the music and entertainer inspired devotion that felt and looked religious, this was subject to a rational temperance, a reordering of a social world in which the commercial commingles with sacred realm.

Along similar lines are Paul Henry and Marylouise Caldwell's exploration of the Cliff Richard Meeting House. In this chapter, we learn how fans develop a type of para-social relationship with Cliff Richard that involves careful psychic negotiation by tribe members. To be a proper and appropriate fan requires the support of feelings of not being a fan. To avoid losing her soul, the fan of the brand must be a double agent who can both care and critique, think and love, reach and resist at the same time.

Building-related realizations of delicate balance into marketing is light years away from the sledgehammer models that powered the repetitive advertising of the 1980s. Today's marketers monitor their actions, and those undertaken by their company, to ensure that they never fall prey to overkill. Salomon understood this clearly when it wrote a charter stipulating the need to avoid any misdeed that could lead to its being accused of behaving like some vulgar 'world company' (Cova and Cova, 2001). The firm banished all frontline actions that failed to entail a passion for sports. For example, local competition winners no longer receive mobile phones as their prize but the right to demonstrate their skills to an audience of champions. Salomon has also created new operations instead of transplanting them onto existing ones. A single logic is at work here, one aimed at sustaining the passion for (and practice of) sports through the organization of major meetings for fans' benefit. The company is careful not to co-opt its tribes, ensuring that all communications, including direct mail programs, are as unaggressive as possible. The goal is no longer to highlight Salomon's image in a particular market but to help the company become a fully fledged member of different tribal movements, much as an individual fan can become, with all of the non-commercial connotations that follow from such a positioning.

Consider the opposite example. Companies and their marketers need to avoid affirming their capitalist vocation as loudly and overtly as Frank Riboud, the CEO at Danone, a French food giant, did in 2001 with an ultra-commercial discourse that shocked consumers and torpedoed their attempts to achieve the double-agent's ever-unsteady compromise with large corporations. That year, a management study about possibly cutting back capacity in Danone's European biscuit operations was leaked to the press, where it was described as an ineluctable reality. A consensus hostile to the firm soon took shape and Danone was accused of sacrificing workers to the demands of the financial markets. Frank Riboud said that the restructuring was necessary in order to guarantee the future success of the company and to make it competitive versus major rivals. Riboud was accused of being overly focused on protecting the interests of Danone shareholders. A critical website (www.jeboycottedanone.com) became a huge success, sporting justifications such as '*A boycott is the last remaining form of political action in a society where money has profoundly perverted the democratic system.*' Indeed, once all other forms of interaction are excluded, all that remains for consumers is to revert to the old solution of rejection and politically shaped activism.

Whether in their experiences with Pabst, Salomon, Tom Petty, or with other products like Red Bull or Nutella (Cova and Pace, 2006), consumers are not being misled by marketers and corporations. They are fully aware that what they dealing with are products emanating from companies that operate in a commercial world. At the same time, they are free to choose the extent to which they want to be tricked in their consumption experience. On empowering Web2.0 media like CurrentTV and YouTube, they are free to 'make their own (non-commercial) film' about a product, brand or company, as long as the latter is careful to offer signs that are congruent with this image and do not take on other, more commercial overtones. Walking a tightrope of resistance and passion, the tribe acts as a double agent.

Consumer tribes are plunderers

Tribes are not squeaky clean, by any means. They are often charged with acting like pirates, and are often guilty as charged. Not only are they pirates, but also they are marauders, pillagers, plunderers, hooligans, gangsters and hijackers. We argue that some of the charged ideas flowing from the polarizing internal contradictions and complexities of Consumer Tribes can help to reveal and delineate more nuanced and dynamic understandings. Two important senses of their leaning towards plundering or 'hijacking are critical here – one academic (de Certeau, 1980) and one pragmatic (Wipperfürth, 2005).

Michel de Certeau's (1980) construct of hijacking followed from his cogitation of the various primitive aspects of consumers over a quarter of a century ago. Today's consumers hijack things in a way that differs from the variant that Situationists used to defend (Vanegeim, 1967), as explained by Michael Borras,[2] an Underground Internet Artist who manages the *Systaime* website (www.systaime.com) which specializes in artistic hijacking: 'The principle underlying the name "Systaime" [*Trans. Note: A title incorporating the root word "aime", meaning love in French*] is the idea that to by-pass a system (an IT system, a political organization, etc.) or to hijack or subvert it, a person must first be in love with it.' We can see in this statement the same ambivalence, the same paradoxical qualities that inform our conception of the Consumer Tribe as a Double Agent. Why would I steal something I didn't care about? Something is only worth plundering if it truly captures the heart.

Some of the same reasoning applied to consumption plunderings happens on a collective basis. For example, activist consumer groups like *The Media Foundation* (which publishes Adbusters; see Kozinets and Handelman, 2004; Rumbo, 2002), *The Billboard Liberation Front* and the *No Logo* groupies of Naomi Klein (2000) use their affection for the marketing system to subvert it. *The Media Foundation* produces false advertisements call 'subvertising' and has even started manufacturing and marketing its own brand of anti-brand 'blackspot' shoes. These activist groups are not plentiful or powerful: they are not legion, nor do they necessarily have the support of broad swathes of the general population, even among young persons or web activists. The extreme nature of 'Adbusters' discourse, which tends to revel in revealing corporately sponsored murder, linking America to the world's consumption and environmental ills, and decrying the consolidation of the media industry, is a poor reflection of the complex and contradictory relationship people have to the commercial world and its brands. However, without the extremely intense focus on the ghouls of the corporate world and its dark legions of brands, Adbusters' writers, Naomi Klein, and other activist journalists would have little to write about.

The joy of plundering what one loves is found throughout the chapters of Consumer Tribes, blended inextricably with the joy of creation and origination evident in the chapter by Dave Park, Sameer Deshpande, Bernard Cova and Stefano Pace on the Warhammer tribe. Members of this tribe feel a sense of accomplishment from personally creating figurines, painting them, and assembling warrior replicas. Their research highlights how this tribal production is not freed of structural constraints such as age, gender, and cultures.

The plundering and pillaging processes are evident in Stephen Brown's boisterous chapter on the *Harry Potter* tribe. So passionate are the Potter Tribes

[2] Interview published in *Technikart*, No. 77, November 2003, p. 102.

that, amongst many activities, they write their own stories – hundreds of thousands at the last count – produce their own podcasts, create their own games like Live Action Role Plays, all distributed and mediated via the World Wide Web. As Brown's chapter illustrates, the waltz between brand owners and brand community is often an uneasy one.

Robert Kozinets returns to his roots to examine a related phenomenon in the *Star Trek* world, where *Star Trek* becomes both stolen property and gift. As pro-suming productive consumers, *Star Trek* fans have a history of shoplifting the text, then blowtorching their own elements into the mythic mix. The latest and arguably greatest incarnation of this is fans' creation of new episodes of the show, written and starring themselves, broadcast to the world over the Internet. Kozinets theorizes what happens when corporate pull yields to citizen push: the vaunted and vaulted media property opens like a budding flower, becoming wikimedia. The tribe becomes like a hive of active bees, collecting, organizing, creating, reproducing, distributing, making networks, closing deals, being entrepreneurial (as we shall soon see): they become inno-tribes.

The phenomena are related to what the psychoanalyst Serge Tisseron (2003) was demonstrating when he analysed the behaviour of today's teenagers and deduced that modern adolescence manufactures playful individuals, that is, *homini ludens* (Huizinga, 1951). What we have is a playful humanity that disobeys but does not rebel. Instead of confronting things, it bypasses and plunders them. It lacks any illusion of utopia. Plunder and pillage is interesting because it is temporary, a type of bracketing of a tribe just a 'movin' through'. Just as the feral participants at Burning Man plunder corporate colours, logos, and codes to welcome people to the 'Black Rock Café' (Kozinets and Sherry, 2005), these people are engaging in dipping and diving into various social worlds, with their various rules and relations to social and market logics endlessly shifting and morphing. Products, brands, companies, cultures, and identities constantly change as one form morphs into another, and those forms are altered individually and collectively shared.

For consumers, plundering may be an act of resistance, but there is little doubt that this resistance has changed form, if not substance, over the past few years. The purpose is no longer to do battle with markets and companies construed as core institutions, but to play around with the markets even as one plays them. This means that confrontation *per se* is not an essential activity. 'We don't need to ask ourselves whether we are free or enslaved . . . since we become completely free once we experience freedom' (Aubenas and Benasayag, 2002, p. 74). In the play spaces of ESPN Zone Chicago, Kozinets et al. (2004, p. 671), found that 'the wills of consumers and producers tend to be far more overlapping, mutual, and interdependent than commonly recognized.'

In other words, plundering is less and less of a conscious, revolutionary countercultural action, and more of an aestheticization of the daily experiences (see Featherstone, 1991). Consumers hijack commercial reality when they work in a group and with relative unawareness of exactly what they are doing, devising a zone of ephemeral and limited autonomy inside of the market system (Desmond, Mc Donagh, and O'Donohue, 2000). It is a *stylistic* move. In the commercial interstices of temporary autonomous zones (Bey, 1991) and in hypercommunities (Kozinets, 2002a), what is created is not only community, meaning, or matter, but also pop vox, bleeding edge, lead user style, and fashion: art.

For Alex Wipperfürth (2005), this 'brand hijack' occurs when a group of consumers takes a brand away from its marketing professionals in an attempt to enhance its further development. Such brand hijack phenomena are accentuated when interactions with the brand tribe occur on-line (Kozinets, 2002b; O'Guinn and Muñiz, 2005). Recent research has highlighted many problems a company can have when interacting with this kind of hard-to-control collective actor whom the net has spontaneously helped to foster and nurture (Broderick, MacLaran, and Ma, 2003). On-line consumers would appear to be more active, participative, resistant, militant, playful, social and communitarian than ever before (Kozinets, 1999). They want to be influential participants in the construction of experiences (Firat and Shultz, 1997). The shared passion that certain consumers have for a cult brand will translate, through a range of collective learning systems, into expertise and competency, imbuing on-line tribes with greater legitimacy in production and marketing matters (O'Guinn and Muñiz, 2005). As a result, companies are finding in this era of collective intelligence that they have to adjust to the presence of tribes comprised of impassioned, united and expert fans. Because of technology, there is a re-balancing of company–consumer power relations occurring on a massive scale, one that has only just begun and some of whose implications we explore further in our next section.

Consumer tribes are entrepreneurs

When we look at a particular act of brand plunder, the re-balancing of power between tribes and companies constitutes little more than a passing phenomenon. It would be easy (and it is easy) to exaggerate the importance of single instances of plunder. But the evidence points to a more dynamic view. Plunder transpires as part of a Consumer Tribe movement that is itself in the midst of a broader process of development. Tribes are poised to become collective actors in the marketplace, much in the same that way that companies already are. The marketing competencies of tribes will soon rival those of companies. Indeed, just as Napster once looked like the Grim Reaper for a bloated and rapacious music industry, so too should the thought of *Harry Potter* fans making and sharing their own games, or *Star Trek* fans producing their own television shows and broadcasting them to the world through the Internet send a chill down every media executive's spine. In other words, we are already at the point where marketing is no longer the reserved domain of companies and corporations, but a set of practices, accesses, codes, and rituals that are available to all communities: this is the re-emergence of marketing 'as the empowering "tool" of the post-consumer (and) would tend to re-establish democracy in a form that is viable – based on the constitution of post-consumer communities or tribes' (Firat and Dholakia, 2004, p. 27; see also Gabriel and Lang, 1995).

Anders Bengtsson, Jacob Östberg and Dannie Kjeldgaard (2005) provide us with a fascinating case study of subcultural resistance. Their videography and ethnography show how a subculture resists tattooing's commercialization by detailing tribe members' and artists' perception that a boundary exists between the sacred, non-commercial sphere of tattooing and the profane, profit-maximizing realm of the commercial world. What we see at work here is a type of resistance that manifests through limiting the community's entrepreneurial capabilities. By limiting their own commercial capacities, they try to ensure the continued authenticity of a production that is supposed to remain pristine and not be subverted by any contact with the market (hence with the dominant cultural and economic system). Interestingly, the same debate is happening among hobbyist, consumer bloggers, like the Barq's Man. Here is what the Barq's Man (*aka* 'Michael Marx') says about being paid to promote a brand through his blog:

> I continue to blog about Barq's simply because I love the brand, I love the product, and I'd love to see the world drinking Barq's. You couldn't pay me to do it. If you did, I would lose my independence and independence is the best part of blogging. On the other hand, isn't getting paid to do what you love something that people aspire to? What about all those people who have monetized their hobbies? World class chefs, adventure tour guides, professional athletes? Is it still fun for them? Or is it more about the money? This issue can be argued both ways, but I do believe that where there is money, there is obligation. And with obligation independence is reigned in. And in the case of this Barq's blog, the fun is in the freedom.
> (*Source*: http://www.thebarqsman.com/, downloaded 9/13/2006)

The key to decoding these accounts is the romanticized and mysticized, yet culturally resonant assertion that, just as communities and markets do not mix, authenticity belongs to practices and personalities that are on the margins or as close to the outside of the market as possible. As Luc Boltanski and Eve Chiapello have shown (2006), if it is to regenerate itself, capitalism must look outside of the commercial sphere for the layers of authenticity in which it will be wrapping its product offerings.

As the ambivalence in the Barq Man's quote attests, however, today's tribal reality is much more complex. As Bruno Latour writes (1991, p. 167) 'In the middle, where there is supposed to be nothing, you find almost everything'. Between markets and communities is much hybridization. Collective tribes are increasingly capable of collective action and prepared to interact with the market in a way that is more and more entrepreneurial. Indeed, as recently discussed by Thomas O'Guinn and Albert Muñiz (2005), one key element in today's tribe-market interactions is that companies can lose part of their control over a brand, to be replaced by a Consumer Tribe that is trying to re-appropriate it. Alternatively, as Christina Goulding and Mike Saren highlight in this volume, Goth tribes form their own markets and engage with each other in the production and consumption of good and services. Here the market transactions are marked by tribal affiliation and the reconnection of 'producers' and 'consumers,' the very antithesis of globalized, corporatized and socially distanced relationships that characterize many market relationships. In Roy Langer's chapter on the Fetish community in Denmark, he also highlights the entrepreneurial activities of its members. The on-going tension between sub- and mainstream culture is highlighted and the ensuing problems and challenges that this creates for the tribal marketer is identified, as they seek to maintain boundaries of distinctiveness between tribal and mass marketing.

The engagements tribal members have with one another can be marked by conflict. Kristine de Valck's chapter in this book examines the contested meanings and practices of members of a food consumption on-line community. The on-line war of an e-tribe underscores that the apparent tribal uniformity of a differentiated group can cloak brewing conflict and disagreement within the tribal fabric itself. We see conflict and differentiation in other tribal settings. The devoted Hummer tribe explored in Marius Lüdicke's and Markus Giesler's insightful chapter is in a perpetual state of conflict with the mainstream. Constantly seeking new justifications for the basis of their brand identification, the members of the Hummer tribe reveal the potent pressures that brand tribe members can never completely avoid, and the discursive strategies that they must adapt and adopt.

Let's add to these examples by exploring two clear-cut and demonstrative cases of tribal entrepreneurship that are characterized by different gradations of this phenomenon. Consider first The Paris Roller Case. This example is based on the interaction between roller skater tribes and companies/brands in France, as explained by Boris Belohlavek, VP of Paris Roller, an association created by roller skating fans in 1998 to manage and supervise Friday night mass skate tours in Paris, some of which have witnessed as many as 25,000 persons skating from one end of the city to the other. Belohlavek feels that 'Brands have a role to play in the tour but must be entirely under the Association's control'.

It is critical to note that these tours grew organically from the streets; they are not the product of someone's calculated initiative but simply reflect the libertarian wishes of a few skaters for a new way of enjoying their city. As the tours grew in size, companies and their brands began to take an interest and tried to sponsor the tours. This of course is the traditional co-optational marketing approach. But it didn't work. Remember the Barq man's comment, that 'if you pay me, I would lose my independence'? Tribe members were very quick to understand that for the tour to retain its cultural purity they would have to develop certain competencies not only to resist the companies and brands but also to co-operate with them based on sets of rules that were defined by the tribe itself and not by the business world. This was a remarkable undertaking to witness. The community said no to sponsors, and then told them what it would take for them to say yes. What Robert Kozinets (1999, p. 258) said about e-tribes applies equally well to all tribes: the existence of groups of united consumers 'implies that power is shifting away from marketers and flowing to consumers,' as consumers are increasingly saying '"no" to forms of marketing they find invasive or unethical.'

As a result, the roller skating tribe mutated from a group of fans organized on an associative basis into a tribal enterprise capable of engaging in dialogue and even forcing companies and brands to accept its ideas and perspective. As Boris Belohlavek says, 'It is much easier (for a firm or a brand) to speak to a tribe when it feels respected, as this makes it natural to want to return the favour'. To help firms' in-house marketers, who are more accustomed to acting upon segments than to tribal interactions, Paris Roller wrote the following rules to govern companies/brands' tribal marketing approaches:

- Skaters should be respected for who they are.
- The understanding is that a skating tour is very different from the commercial ventures associated with cycling's Tour de France.
- Skaters must not be viewed as traditional marketing targets.
- Nothing may be sold during the actual skate tour.
- The distribution of flyers by themselves is discouraged.
- Excessive branding is prohibited. The ability to host any partners will belong to the Association, whose predominance must remain visible.
- Resources should be offered to skaters (samples, free games) and to the Association (funding, membership privileges, materials, etc.).

According to Boris Belohlavek, 'Respect for the tribe's independence helps partners to discover that less basic marketing solutions are in fact a possibility.' Of course, any such solutions require the modification of certain rules, with the Association transferring its tribal marketing competencies to firms that are severely lacking in them.

Mozilla Firefox provides a second case. In the world of OSS (Open Source Software), it is widely recognized that collective effort, social interaction and group influence are all crucial to the development and use of software like Linux. Tribal volunteering is very important for this kind of enterprise: 'OSS projects not only entail unpaid contributions of code by developers, but also unpaid assistance and advocacy by existing volunteer users to enlist and help new users' (Bagozzi and Dholakia, 2006, p. 1100). This phenomenon of volunteering has provided a basis for the development of tribal initiatives that, from the very outset, act upon the market by operating outside of the borders of a reduced community.

Mozilla Firefox is a case where individual consumers become tribe members and subsequently become marketing agents trying to use the net's power to attain certain marketing goals (Krishnamurty, 2005a). Firefox's success derives from 63,000 volunteers having spread the word by putting up links to the main download site (including in their email signature file), discussing Firefox in blogs, posting its icon to their personal websites, collecting testimonials and visiting technical sites where they vote for their favourite browser. In addition, over 10,000 volunteers donated $30 each to help launch a full-page advertisement in the *New York Times*. Krishnamurty (2005b) identifies the central tenet for this type of tribal entrepreneurship as the idea that consumers should be exerting their power in the marketplace through constructive and not destructive collective action, with the Consumer Tribe producing, marketing and servicing an offer that competes favourably with corporate products in the marketplace.

In both examples (Paris Roller and Mozilla Firefox) as in many others, we see how a tribe is no longer trying to resist economic actors or the market but instead has itself become a legitimate economic actor in its marketplace, without losing any of its communitarian nature or forms. In particular, note that these tribes' tribal knowledge has given them a significant competitive advantage over their corporate rivals (Moore, 2006). This is clearly not your mother's tribalism: bones in the hair and sacred drum circles. Modern primitivism is primal partnership, tribal trading and collective capitalism.

Stephen Brown's *Harry Potter* tribes are acting as entrepreneurs and inventors, as are the inno-tribes of Robert Kozinets' new *Star Trek* episode film-makers and webcasts. In fact, the fan-film-makers that Kozinets wrote about recently posted a message on their web-page stating that 'It is our dream that CBS/Paramount will someday license and/or support these fan films' (Cawley Entertainment Company, 2006). In other words, we are a Consumer Tribe but we want our work to be licensed: share the wealth, profit from us, help us make money from this. What could be more entrepreneurial? We believe that these examples are the crest of the Consumer Tribal Wave, harbingers of things to come.

A kind of social entrepreneurship is evident in Isabelle Szmigin, Marylyn Carrigan and Caroline Bekin's look at how New Consumption Communities create alternative market ethics that facilitate alternative producer–market– consumer relationships thus ameliorating their reliance on what they see as repressive market ethics. The tribes examined in this chapter view their activities not as resistance to mainstream production and exchange, but as positive alternatives that can complement and have a positive impact on society and exchange relations. Stefano Pace, Luciano Fratocchi and Fabrizio Cocciola highlight the passion of a craftsman of fine briar smoking pipes, a more typically entrepreneurial individual who shares ideas and emotions with other individuals with the same interest thus forming a tribe. From this sharing and this participation stem entrepreneurial and mutually beneficial commercial transactions that transpire at an international level. Throughout these chapters and examples, the entrepreneurial spirit of Consumer Tribes shines through.

Conclusion: tribes are open, aporic, and incorporated

Once upon a time, tribal knowledge was innate, usually unwritten, spoken only with a dedicated group of people. It was tantamount to an informal variant of group wisdom. As a term, 'tribal knowledge' is now used mostly in management circles when referencing information that other parties operating within a company may need to know. Unlike similar forms of artisan intelligence, tribal knowledge can be converted, albeit with some difficulty, into company property, as demonstrated by John Moore (2006) when he describes the thought process underlying decision-making at Starbucks.

However, whereas companies are working desperately to develop this type of knowledge, and often deploying ideas adapted form chaos theory to do so, the natural chaos of tribal groups of consumers seem *de facto* able to renew it quite effortlessly among their members. Tribes work differently: individuals enter social and economic relations knowing *ex ante* that giving–receiving is not dictated by some governing body, and that it can not be weighted using the usual rational methods. For example, the (economic) value of coordinating or being part of a tribe is based on perceptions, feelings and emotions – beneath the actual output of the tribe and its perceived value from each member. As word of mouth marketers are discovering, this calls for a complex set of inducements and understandings of cause–effect relations. Consumer Tribes are different: rather than offer 'a new form of organization' they are offering a new way of thinking about the problems of organizing.

In their radical departure, Consumer Tribes offer a viable solution to manage the duality between individuals and organizations. This gives them an undeniable advantage over companies, one they no longer use to simply resist the market but instead to play within and with it. Where once tribes were seen as transformative to their members, we are beginning to see how they are transformative to business and communicative practices and to society itself.

What is required to meet the challenge is a true shift in the underpinnings of marketing. The marketing 'revolution' is a term often debased by its application to insignificant changes in this field. 'KYC' (Knowing Your Customer) may be a crucial concept in marketing, but it is often given the restricted and manipulative denotation that marketers need to know absolutely everything about consumers to satisfy them and secure their loyalty. Seldom has the idea been proposed in marketing that consumers possess organizational knowledge that may be of interest to the management and strategizing of the company. We, however, are of the opinion that in the future companies will be obliged to incorporate other perspectives, like those put forward by consumers assembled alongside other consumers into tribes. The goal here will not be to exploit these Consumer Tribes but instead to see them as partners who can teach a kind of expertise and experience. That will require major advances in management and in the current climate may be impossible for many firms.

Another necessary shift is to understand that, contrary to received wisdom in marketing, companies do not need to send totally coherent messages to the marketplace. Consumers fill in the blanks, and they often do a better job of colouring in the picture than marketers would do. Recent studies (Giraud Voss, 2003) have even shown how positive it can be when gaps exist between a company's identity and the image it projects in the marketplace. Such gaps offer consumers more margin for freedom, giving them greater room to manoeuvre around the company and its brand. Similarly, consumers seem to prefer an ambiguous corporate image to one that is clear-cut (Giraud Voss, 2003). This creates room for a host of initiatives involving re-enchantment with consumption as well as hyper-reality – consumers do not automatically need or want everything to be true and coherent. As Stephen Brown (e.g., Brown, 2001) and his patron saint P.T. Barnum are endlessly reminding us, the so-called rational consumer has an insatiable hunger for reverie, mystery, and fantasy.

There is a magic here, a magic that rises in aporia, in the void of commercial pauses and stutters. We find consumers, in the moments when the brand pauses to inhale, breathing their life into it. And the collective breath is much more powerful. These inhalations draw us back to the market's origins. Anthropologist and archaeologists tell us that the early marketplace was 'marked out' as a boundary space, a line on the edge of forest, a place delimited in time and space on the edge where woods met dwellings met cities. The early market was an eldritch space of intrigue, shot through with more than a touch of dark trickery, of fetid and desirous potential hanging tightly coiled, ready to spring for good or ill. On those strange limbs, laden with the strange items and practices of the other, magic hung, an enchanting mystique that still inheres in the current consumer marketplace.

But after a century of Taylorized scientific management clouding the understanding of marketing as magic, the market's true workings have become cloaked beneath veneers of science and rationality. Today's consumers are not in the market because they want to feel that they are buying something mass produced, confirming conformist longing, commercial. They do not want to hear some CEO tell them how the market economy should run their lives. We need to cast a spotlight on situations where consumers adore a cult brand but hate the company that developed it because the firm lacked commercial taste, such as the fans of *Star Wars* who reject and despise George Lucas (Brown et al., 2003), or the followers of the Newton who reject Apple (Muñiz and Schau, 2005). Some consumers' shared passion for a brand can translate into a feeling of marketing legitimacy. They see themselves as guardians of a brand's authenticity and are unhappy when the firm organizes an overtly commercial hijack (notably where this is product related). They prefer, we would argue, a good plunder over a boring old hijack any day. Lucasfilm's treatment of the *Star Wars* series was criticized by fans for being overly commercial (Brown et al., 2003; Cova and Carrère, 2002). Instead, hordes of pillaging fans produced their own *Star Wars* films, lots of them, as digital cinematographers (Jenkins, 2003).

Michel Maffesoli's chapter in this book centres upon a type of mindful, in the present moment consumption style, which he likens to 'an eternal paganism'. The comparison is revealing and important, as magical thinking seems to lie at the heart of many of these phenomena. The most potent tribes, as Alex Wipperfürth (2005), Douglas Atkin (2004), and Kevin Roberts (2004) and other pop philosophers of the brand assert, are built in the interstices, in the margins, on the fringes. But these pop practitioners, locked into patterns of exploiting segments of consumers, have not yet begin to plumb the depths of the commercial commingling.

Why does tribal work occur on the fringe? Why does it grow, barnacle-like, around abandoned Apple Newton and deserted *Star Trek* brands, within semi-marginal gatherings of time has passed musical celebrities like Cliff Richards and Tom Petty, in the gaps of the outlaw Harley myth, among stig-matized Hummer drivers? What is it about these brands and products that draw tribal meanings to them like cat hair to an acrylic white sweater? Beyond simplistic notions of meaning creation and local authenticity, what is the rela-tionship between magic and the tribe?

We invite you, Gentle Readers and Web-Surfers, to begin your own specu-lation and investigations. Read this book. Look around. Hang out. Use your browser. Use Google groups. Watch television. Go to the mall. Consumer Tribes will welcome you. They await you without limit.

References

Atkin, D. (2004). *The Culting of Brands: Turn Your Customers into True Believers.* New York: Portfolio.

Aubenas, F. and Benasayag, M. (2002). *Résister c'est créer.* Paris: La Découverte.

Badot, O. and Cova, B. (2003). Néo-marketing, 10 ans après: pour une théorie critique de la consommation et du marketing réenchantés, *Revue Française du Marketing*, **195**, 79–94.

Bagozzi, R.P. and Dholakia, U.M. (2006). Open source software user communi-ties: a study of participation in linux user groups, *Management Science*, **52** (7), 1099–1115.

Barzun, J. (2000). *From Dawn to Decadence: 1500 to the Present: 500 Years of Western Cultural Life.* New York: HarperCollins.

Bengtsson, A., Östberg, J. and Kjeldgaard, D. (2005). Prisoners in paradise: subcultural resistance to the marketization of tattooing, *Consumption, Markets & Culture*, **8** (3), 261–274.

Bey, H. (1991). *T.A.Z.: The Temporary Autonomous Zone, Ontological Anarchy, Poetic Terrorism.* Brooklyn, NY: Autonomedia.

Boltanski, L. and Chiapello, E. (2006). *The New Spirit of Capitalism.* London: Verso.

Broderick, A., MacLaran, P. and Ma, P.Y. (2003). Brand meaning negotiation and the role of the online community: a mini case study, *Journal of Customer Behaviour*, **2** (1), 75–103.

Brown, S. (2001). *Marketing: The Retro Revolution.* London: Sage.

Brown, S. and Sherry Jr., J.F. (2003). *Time, Space, and the Market: Retroscapes Rising.* New York: M. E. Sharpe.

Brown, S., Kozinets, R.V., and Sherry Jr., J.F. (2003). Teaching old brands new tricks: retro branding and the art of brand revival, *Journal of Marketing*, **67** (7), 19–33.

Cawley Entertainment Company (2006). Star Trek Lives! (accessed October 10, 2006), available at http://www.startreknewvoyages.com/800/home.php

Cova, B. (1997). Community and consumption: towards a definition of the linking value of products or services, *European Journal of Marketing*, **31** (3/4), 297–316.

Cova, B. and Carrère, V. (2002). Les communautés de passionnés de marque: opportunité ou menace sur le Net, *Revue Française du Marketing*, 189/190, 119–130.

Cova, B. and Cova, V. (2001). Tribal aspects of postmodern consumption research: the case of French in-line roller skaters, *Journal of Consumer Behavior*, **1** (1), 67–76.

Cova, B. and Cova, V. (2002). Tribal marketing: the tribalisation of society and its impact on the conduct of marketing, *European Journal of Marketing*, **36** (5/6), 595–620.

Cova, B. and Pace, S. (2006). Brand community of convenience products: new forms of customer empowerment. The case of the my Nutella Community, *European Journal of Marketing*, **40** (9/10), 1087–1105.

de Certeau, M. (1980). *L'invention du quotidien. 1. Arts de faire*. Paris: Gallimard.

Deighton, J. (1992). The consumption of performance, *Journal of Consumer Research*, **19** (December), 362–372.

Deighton, J. and Grayson, K. (1995). Marketing and seduction: building exchange relationships by managing social consensus, *Journal of Consumer Research*, **21** (4), 660–676.

Desmond, J., Mc Donagh, P. and O'Donohue, S. (2000). Counter-culture and consumer society, *Consumption Markets and Culture*, **4** (3), 207–243.

Featherstone, M. (1991). *Consumer Culture and Postmodernism*. London: Sage.

Firat, A.F. and Dholakia, N. (2004). Theoretical implications of postmodern debates: some challenges to modern marketing, Working Paper 2004/2005, No. 4, College of Business Administration, University of Rhode Island, Kingston.

Firat, A.F. and Shultz II, C.J. (1997). From segmentation to fragmentation: markets and marketing strategy in the postmodern era, *European Journal of Marketing*, **31** (3/4), 183–207.

Gabriel, Y. and Lang, T. (1995). *The Unmanageable Consumer: Contemporary Consumption and its Fragmentation*. London: Sage.

Giraud Voss, Z. (2003). Les effets des ruptures d'authenticité sur la rentabilité de l'entreprise et la reaction du consommateur, Thèse es Sciences de Gestion, Université de Droit, d'Economie et des Sciences d'Aix-Marseille, IAE Aix-en-Provence.

Goulding, C., Shankar, A. and Elliott, R. (2002). Working weeks, rave weekends: identity fragmentation and the emergence of new communities, *Consumption, Markets and Culture*, **5** (4), 261–284.

Huizinga, J. (1951). *Homo ludens. Essai sur la fonction sociale du jeu*. Paris: Gallimard.

Jenkins, H. (2003). Quentin Tarantino's Star Wars? digital cinema, media convergence, and participatory culture, in Thorburn, D. and Jenkins, H. (eds.), *Rethinking Media Change: The Aesthetics of Transition*. Cambridge, MA: MIT Press, pp. 281–314.

Jenkins, H. (2006). *Convergence Culture: Where Old and New Media Collide*. New York: New York University.

Klein, N. (2000). *No Logo. Taking Aim at the Brand Bullies*. Toronto: Random House.

Kozinets, R.V. (1999). E-tribalized marketing? The strategic implications of virtual communities of consumption, *European Management Journal*, **17** (3), 252–264.

Kozinets, R.V. (2002a). Can consumers escape the market? Emancipatory illuminations from burning man, *Journal of Consumer Research*, **29** (June), 20–38.

Kozinets, R.V. (2002b). The field behind the screen: using netnography for marketing research in online communities, *Journal of Marketing Research*, **XXXIX** (February), 61–72.

Kozinets, R.V. and Handelman, J.M. (2004). Adversaries of consumption: consumer movements, activism, and ideology, *Journal of Consumer Research*, **31** (3), 691–704.

Kozinets, R.V. and Sherry Jr., J.F. (2005). Welcome to the black rock café, in Gilmore, L. and van Proyen, M. (eds.), *Afterburn: Reflections on Burning Man*. Albequerque, NM: University of New Mexico Press, pp. 87–106.

Kozinets, R.V., Sherry Jr., J.F., Storm, D., Duhachek, A., Nuttavuthisit, K. and DeBerry-Spence, B. (2004). Ludic agency and retail spectacle, *Journal of Consumer Research*, **31** (December), 658–672.

Krishnamurty, S. (2005a). About close-door Free/Libre/Open Source (FLOSS) projects: lessons from the Mozilla Firefox Develop Recruitment Approach, *Upgrade*, **6** (3), available at http://www.upgrade-cepis.org/issues/2005/up6-Krishnamurty.pdf

Krishnamurty, S. (2005b). The launching of Mozilla Firefox – a case study in community-led marketing, Working paper available at http://opensource.mit.edu/papers/sandeep2.pdf

Latour, B. (1991). *Nous n'avons jamais été modernes: Essai d'anthropologie symétrique*. Paris: La Découverte.

Lipovetsky, G. (2003). La société d'hyperconsommation, *Le Débat*, **124**, 74–98.

Moore, J. (2006). *Tribal Knowledge. Lessons Learnt from Working Inside Starbucks*. Chicago: Kaplan.

Muñiz Jr., A.M. and Schau, H.P. (2005). Religiosity in the abandoned apple newton brand community, *Journal of Consumer Research*, **31** (March), 737–747.

O'Guinn, T.C. and Muñiz Jr., A.M. (2005). Communal consumption and the brand, in Mick, D.G. and Ratneshwar, S. (eds.), *Inside Consumption: Frontiers of Research on Consumer Motives*. London: Routledge, pp. 252–272.

Rémy, E. (2002). Contribution à la valorisation et à la critique consumériste de la notion d'expérience, *Actes de la 7ème Journée de Recherche en Marketing de Bourgogne*, Dijon, Novembre, pp. 308–321.

Rheingold, H. (2003). *Smart Mobs: The Next Social Revolution Transforming Cultures and Communities in the Age of Instant Access*. New York: Basic Books.

Roberts, K. (2004). *Lovemarks: The Future beyond Brands*. New York: Powerhouse Books.

Rumbo, J.D. (2002). Consumer resistance in a world of advertising clutter: the case of adbusters, *Psychology and Marketing*, **19** (February), 127–148.

Tisseron, S. (2003). *Comment Hitchcock m'a guéri. Que cherchons-nous dans les images?* Paris: Albin Michel.

Torgovnick, M. (1996). *Primitive Passions: Men, Women, and the Quest for Ecstasy.* Chicago, IL: University of Chicago Press.

Vanegeim, R. (1967). *Traité du savoir-vivre à l'usage des jeunes générations*. Paris: Gallimard.

Wipperfürth, A. (2005). *Brand Hijack: Marketing without Marketing*. New York: Portfolio.

2

Tribal aesthetic

Michel Maffesoli

The specificity of a postmodern tribe is clearly its aesthetic. In the same way that politics were the sign of modernity, aesthetics may be the sign of postmodern society. Of course, we should apprehend this word in its etymological sense of people feeling emotions together. This is the sort of aesthetics that provide foundations for a community, offering a basis for what I have in the past called the postmodern 'tribe' (Maffesoli, 1988).

Tribal aesthetic conveys a passion for life that cannot help but shock settled minds that can do no better than identify and analyse average thoughts and lifestyles. Aesthetics remind us that human beings comprise an event, and even an advent. Turning to the opposition between modernity and postmodernity, we might say that for the former history is something that unfurls, whereas the latter involves an advent of events that intrude, impose themselves and cause uproar. Which is why they always appear so sudden, unexpected and surprising. This is another sign of the difference in tone between drama or dialectic (positing a solution or possible synthesis) and tragedy (which is aporic by construction).

An advent is something singular, although this singularity is embedded in an archaic and timeless substrate. Of course, what we are facing here are archaisms that have been re-designed as a function of the present and experienced in a manner that is specific yet remembers its roots. Something I've called an advent-event. What is certain is that things that are experienced qualitatively and with intensity strive to ensure the resurgence of that which is already contained within our individual or collective being. The reference here is to Heidegger, who engaged in post-metaphysical thinking when he tried to highlight the simple extra that serves as a substrate underlying human existence. Then there is Leibniz who with his 'undiscernable principle' tried to find a median path between absolute difference and the eternal return of the same (Vattimo, 1992). Between the two, the romanticism or philosophy of life accentuates the tragic aspect of the present, along with the demands, passion for life and sense of urgency that it generates. All of which can be summarized using two terms: creation–consummation.

It is characteristic of today's surprisingly aesthetic-based tribal attitudes that the persons holding such views are barely if at all concerned by the consequences of their acts. In the emotional arena, this is demonstrated by pluralistic families and successive and ephemeral loves. In public life, its signs are political versatility and ideological variation. In the disorder of our economic sphere, the proof lies in people's concomitant acceptance and extraordinary mistrust of anarchic laws of production. The net result of all this is an atmosphere of *insouciance* that does not encourage people to worry about tomorrow. What they want instead is to live in the present by referring to ways of being that have slowly taken shape over the years.

To define this atmosphere, we can try to compare it with the creative nature of an eternal paganism that strives to grapple with life and with everything life offers, to wit, the things presented to us. Pagan exuberance translates a desire for current pleasure and for an audacious and hardy life that is tinged with the freshness of the moment and offers something that is provisional, precarious and therefore very intense. Analysing the opposition between Machiavel and Christianism, Fichte spoke of 'general impiety' (Fichte, 1981, p. 48). It seems to me that we can extrapolate from what he said about his paganism. After all, at the core of Christianism we find a political project, an economic conception of existence and a search for the kind of security that different social institutions can offer. Let us not forget that the economy *stricto sensu* is in fact a Christian economy of salvation, where one seeks individual salvation in tomorrow's perfect society.

It is against this kind of Christianism that the postmodern return to tribalism rebels. The juvenile aspect of its effervescence, the freshness of its revolts, the exaggerated search for multiform present pleasures, all of this readily reveals its roots in the Ancient World that must of course be understood in a metaphorical sense, meaning everything opposing the various 'categorical imperatives' that modern moralism has formulated, be they sexual, economic or ideological in nature. It is in fact this return to the antique and archaic that lies at the core of postmodernity. As if, beyond the moderno-Christian interlude and for better or for worse, as part of our day-to-day lives or else in a paroxysm, softly or through destructive excesses – we have been reacquainted with the sublime and tragic beauty of the world.

If this is the only thing of importance, we might as well enjoy it for what it is, even if this means submitting to terrible and redoubtable laws that we have no choice but to accept. Here we cannot help but evoke the theme of *amor fati* whose significant social consequences can be evaluated from a Nietzschean perspective.

Waking from their Promethean dreams, more and more people have decided to adopt an attitude of stoicism, which when generalized provides us with an endless capacity for indifference. What *amor fati* means here is that destiny is not only something that happens to us but that we can also accept and even love it for what it is. This engenders a certain form of serenity that may appear paradoxical, even though it constitutes the basis of many tribal attitudes of generosity, mutual support and goodwill, as well as the different humanitarian actions that are so frequent in our social lives and which have tended in recent times to proliferate. After all, acceptance of what exists can coincide with a desire to participate therein. The idea here is not to master but to accompany a state of affairs, trying to get it to give the best of itself, thereby making one's life into a work of art and participating in its general creativity and 'expenditure'.

So that's aesthetic logic described in just a few words. What this means is that self-realization or a realization of the world can no longer be achieved by means of a simple economic action but must unfurl as part of an ecological interaction. This may be how we move from the Hegelian–Marxist 'control' that is intrinsic to modernity to what Bataille (1976) has called 'sovereignty', a construct that functions along the lines of structural reversibility and may be the mark of our pre- and postmodern periods.

When applied to today's situation, a propensity of this ilk cannot help but generate an undeniable wisdom that is non-active without being passive, and which brings out a tendency that at a certain point in time is embedded in the reality in question. As I once wrote (Maffesoli, 1996), moralism and its sense of duty have been succeeded by a 'code of conduct' where situations are taken seriously and people act in consequence. Moralism relies on the injunction to be one thing or the other. *A priori*, the individual must give in to the project that has been ordered, and society must also become what the intellectual, politician or expert thinks it should become. Everything else is a code of conduct that accepts the general trend, paying attention to the disposition of the moment, basically meshing with the opportunities of the present. Situations are the only things of any import. There is no indifference in this kind of immanentism, just a constant awareness, a presence in that which already exists, be it the world, the people you are close to or the social sphere. We could summarize this as a 'co-presence' to otherness in its various modulations (Giddens, 1987). Such co-presence varies in intensity but also integrates the globality of being, and no longer just a few of its parts or characteristics.

Returning to a well-known theme that Dodds (1959) has updated, remember the role of the *daimon* in Greek tradition. Socrates staged his *daimon*, of course, allowing us to interpret this as a generalized belief from which no one escaped. What is interesting to highlight within the framework of our present effort is the close link between the *daimon* and necessity, whose role was so important in the framework of ancient culture. In a word, we can say that many more things depend on necessity than on an individual's own character. Tragedies express the same thing in different ways: a person is more acted upon than s/he acts. This is our omnipotent and ruthless destiny, one that despite the will of the subject orients us in the direction of that which has already been written. Here again it is a form of predestination that we are facing. To only mention one example amongst many others, the entire Oedipus myth is built on such a necessity, with all of its well-known paroxystic consequences.

In actual fact, tribal aesthetic, the loss of oneself in another, what we might summarily call creation and its consummation, merely accentuates the rising power of the impersonal. What is at stake in this return of destiny is the negation of the philosophical foundation of today's Western World: free will; decisions made by individuals or social groups acting together to make History. The great fantasy of universality is the consequence thereof. Conversely, the affirmation or reaffirmation of cyclical systems means that free will of this sort is no longer operative (Dodds, 1959). The different mythical Eastern worlds that have intruded in postmodernity constitute a return to impersonal powers whose actions are tinged with inevitability. Whether this involves varying philosophies, religious practices (Buddhist, Hindu, Taoist, African animism and its direct contact with telluric forces or Afro-Brazilian cults of possession, without forgetting a host of New Age practices) or simply the fascination exerted by astrology, it all basically emphasizes the fact that individuals are at worst no more than toys and at best partners of superior forces they are forced to accommodate.

The expressions of contemporary mythology that are sci-fi films, video clips and sometimes advertizing itself all evoke this relativization of free will by a supra-individual force that is essentially tribal in nature. Pundits unsurprisingly mock such developments, despite their undeniable poignancy. They titillate the social imaginary, ensure the success of folklore shows and historical reconstitutions, launch crowds into pilgrimages and glorify initiatory novels. We can call this the 'ethic of aesthetic,' another way of reframing Medieval alchemists' questions about *glutinum mundi*, this glue of the world that ensured that whatever may happen there will always be a coherent something instead of nothing. In other words, the 'glue of the world' is an impersonal force, a vital flow in which everyone and everything participates in a mysterious attractive correspondence.

Many poets, artists and utopians have celebrated this kind of attraction, which is about to become an insurmountable juvenile reality and one we can identify in different musical gatherings and the success of reality TV programmes. What all of these instances express is the unconscious desire to act like other people, to only exist through others and in their sight. As such, it is something that can be analysed in a socio-anthropological manner, and I have suggested describing it as an 'orgy,' in the sense of a shared passion and social empathy. Giving a slightly different meaning to Durkheim's terminology, we can call it an 'organic solidarity,' one ensuring that everybody is part, voluntarily or otherwise, of a whole that constitutes what s/he is. In short, we only exist because the other, which is the social sphere, gives me my existence. I am what I am because the other recognizes me as such. This assertion may shock but it seems to be a good description of the empirical functioning of societies, from the smallest to the most vast. In her book 'How institutions think,' Marie Douglas demonstrated such 'structural effects' (Douglas, 1987). They help us to understand why anyone who does not accept this kind of recognition is rejected, stigmatized or marginalized. His/her exclusion stems from the fact that s/he does not 'smell like the rest of the clan' and/or has not even tried to acquire such their smell.

Thus, above and beyond individualism (be it theoretical or methodo logical in nature), empirical social life is no more than the expression of a suc-cession of feelings of belonging. We are members, we are part of something, we fit into the whole, we participate, or more trivially 'we're in'. Although this is what occurred in modernity's better moments (involving the autonomy, distinction and affirmation of an individual or class identity), today it is no more than an illusion or pretence. It is what I've called the sociology of orgy (Maffesoli, 1982), meaning an order of fusion and even of confusion signifying that everyone lives according to a principle of heteronomy *stricto sensu*: the Other is the one who gives me the law.

It is by keeping this in mind that we can understand the powerful and poignant return of emblematic figures and other daily archetypes. The phe-nomenon of groups of fans in young generations is no more than the paroxys-tic form of multiple adhesions that people experience without paying any attention to what is taking place. Thus we participate magically alongside some rock singer, sporting idol, religious guru, intellectual or political leader. Such participation generates a quasi-mystical communion, a common senti-ment of belonging. In a nuanced comment, Gilbert Durand (1981) has evoked great tragic figures like Don Giovanni to show how they have become pure 'objects'. In fact, they are more objects that subjects insofar as they only exist in other people's minds and have become 'ideal-types' (Durand, 1981).

We can further this analysis by noting that these 'great abstractions', these archetypes, have tended to proliferate and democratize, increasingly involv-ing great figures who have in fact become smaller and smaller. Soon each postmodern tribe will have its own emblematic figure, much in the same way as each tribe *stricto sensu* used to possess a totem and be possessed by it. In any event, identity, free will, decision or individual choice may be affirmed or demanded but the reality is that all of these factors remain tributary of the identities, decisions and choices of the group to which their protagonists belong. Note also the resurgence of tribal archetypes of this kind, despite reaffirmations of a moment's tragic atmosphere. This is a correlation that merits attention.

Instead of steadfastly opposing this trend and allowing oneself to be over-whelmed by its dialectic and dramatic mechanism or soothing synthesis, we are still capable of experiencing freedom and necessity via a 'contradictorial' tension I've called conflictual harmony. This is redolent of the mystic trad-ition or Hindu philosophy but also of the process of individualization that Jung (1978) described so well, where the id serves and lives itself as the object of the Subject that englobes it. This is an experience of the Self that does not destroy the empirical individual, with an id that to the contrary glorifies it, raising it so that it becomes part of a greater whole. This is the intensity and jubilation of a tragic situation, reminiscent of a Nietzschean *amor fati*: becoming free because of a full need for love (Aurigemma, 1992, p. 250). In short, a form of dependency that is full of quietude, with individuals fulfilling themselves in a 'better being' that reveals a person to him/herself.

All of which shows us what such instances of 'better being' might entail nowadays. Big meetings, large gatherings of all kinds, group trances, sporting events, musical excitement and religious or cultural effervescence – all raise the individual to a form of plenitude that s/he cannot find in the grayness of economic or political functionality. In each of these phenomena, there is a sort of magic participation in strange things and strangeness, a globality that supersedes individual singularity. This globality is sacred in tone, and each and everyone can commune with it. What we have here is a tragic irony, a 'ruse' in our collective imagination, one that injects into our social channels the numinous dimension that modernity had tried to evacuate from social life. Is this a re-enchantment with the world? This seems to be the case, given the undeniable abandonment of simple utility or *ustensilarité* that we are witnessing, at both the individual and social levels.

In this sort of perspective, the world and the individual do not progressively become what they are supposed to be as a function of some planned finality but instead 'advent' to what they really are. Archetypes simply help out with this creative unveiling. They are revelators trying to bring out what already exists, and it is in this sense that a close link exists between an archetype's tragic dimension and the accentuation of a cyclical conception of time.

This structural proximity between the archetypal procedure, the collective unconscious and the cycle stems, to take a Jungian expression, from the fact that every 'vital process follows its own internal laws'. As an example, the unconscious cannot march to the beat of someone else's drum. It pops up when the time is right – like a well that gushes or dries out at its own rate, our predictions of an unconscious flow's emergence can never be certain.

The best comparison is with the way alchemists think. As is the case in the dynamic of the unconscious, there is something circular (or even better, spiral-shaped) in the production of images. The idea here is not to adhere to the mechanistic linearism of simple reasoning – instead, it is to fit in with a set of convolutions, even though they singularly complicate interpretation. Both the unconscious and the world of images are characterized by a labyrinth structure. Whereas the former has been largely overrun by intellectual interpretation, the same does not apply to the latter, which has been scorned or marginalized by thinkers, or at least by those who defend a strictly rationalist viewpoint.

Convolutions and (as per Jungian theorization) 'circumambulations' are good ways of describing the slow and circular work that everyone must undertake to slowly accede to what I called a 'better being' above. This is the work of a lifetime (Jung, 1978), a creation *stricto sensu*. A good illustration in the Eastern tradition is the Tibetan *mandala*, something expressed in the West by the myth of Holy Grail. In all these cases there is a repetition, a cyclical movement and a tragic conception of life. The archetypal figures always proceed by repetition, always referring to a mythical time that cannot be dated using our modern tales and legends: 'back in the time when,' *illud tempus*.

This is one striking feature of the mythical illustrations that abound in literature, cinema, theatre or song. It remains that this phenomenon of intemporality, cyclical or tragic accentuation can also be identified in the staging of modern stardom that occurs on a daily and *a fortiori* spectacular basis. The *puer aeternus* represented by Michael Jackson, the repentant depraved woman that Madonna plays so well or, more prosaically, the divine rascals embodied by financial traders, without forgetting the belligerent hero figures that are our sporting icons, all are embedded in a re-enchantment with the world that resonates throughout our collective unconsciousness. These figures do not create anything specific, they merely repeat and re-state anthropologically embedded characters and manners. They recreate what already exists. Moreover, it is because of this cyclical aspect that they have reached a pinnacle, and it is by communing with their repeated stagings and identifying with them that we all (after a long initiation period that is usually experienced unconsciously) transcend ourselves and explode creatively, breaking free from our enclosures and throwing off the shackles of our small individual ids. Here again we find the close link between creation and consummation that Jeffrey (1998) has illustrated and exemplified in his research in varying ways – so many juvenile phenomena to marvel at!

It is important to note the existence of a fundamental repetition, whether in the empirical expressions of modern art or else in the contradictions of myths (something that is not necessarily very different). Levi-Strauss and Gilbert Durand have strongly stressed this aspect: repetition and its correlative DIY approach are the main elements at work in some of humanity's spiritual *magnus opi* (Durand, 1981). To a certain extent, this repetitive aspect, whether it involves a Nietzschean 'return of the same,' the obsession–creating idea of an author, the phrase typifying a musician, a painter's footprint, a thinker's endless theoretical digression or even a singer's personal *ritornello*, emphasizes the presence of timelessness in history and a sort of immobility in movement.

It is by remembering a myth's repetitive nature and the existence of repetition in daily creations (without forgetting the repetition marking our daily lives, of course) that we can understand the extent of the intimate emotion generated by the familiarity of regularly returning phenomena, situations, ideas, etc. Moreover, this is a characteristic specificity of tribal aesthetic. The *habitus* that Thomas Aquinas analysed stresses the structuring aspect of established customs. The 'fold' metaphor that Deleuze (1988) offered for reflection is a modern way of expressing the poignancy of habit. All of these things show that individual or collective perfection is not necessarily the same thing as boundless progress (as modern education postulates), but that it does on occasion mesh with those things that arise time and again: morays, myths and rituals, the habits of a given society – basically, creation as recreation. This is what pre-modern society has offered us, and in postmodern tribalism it may well regain its importance.

References

Aurigemma, L. (1992). *Perspectives Jungiennes*. Paris: Albin Michel.

Bataille, G. (1976). *La souveraineté*. Paris: Gallimard.

Deleuze, G. (1988). *Le Pli, Leibniz et le baroque*. Paris: Ed. de Minuit.

Dodds, E.R. (1959). *The Greeks and the Irrational*. Berkeley: University of California Press.

Douglas, M. (1987). *How Institutions Think*. London: Routledge.

Durand, G. (1981). *L'âme tigrée, les pluriels de psyché*. Paris: Denoël.

Fichte, J.G. (1981). *Machiavel et autres écrits philosophiques et politiques de 1806–1807*, French Trans. L. Ferry & A. Renaut. Paris: Payot.

Giddens, A. (1987). Time and Social Organization, in Giddens, A. (ed.), *Social Theory and Modern Sociology*, Cambridge: Polity Press, pp. 140–165.

Jeffrey, D. (1998). *Jouissance du sacré. Postmodernité et religion*. Paris: Armand Colin.

Jung, C.G. (1978). *Aion: Researches into the Phenomenology of the Self*, Collected Works, Vol. 9, Pt. II, 2nd ed. English Trans. R.F.C. Hull. Princeton: Princeton University Press.

Maffesoli, M. (1982). *L'Ombre de Dionysos, Contribution à une sociologie de l'orgie*. Paris: Méridiens.

Maffesoli, M. (1988). *Le Temps des Tribus*. Paris: Méridiens. English Trans. (1996), *The Time of the Tribes*. Sage: London.

Maffesoli, M. (1996). *Éloge de la Raison Sensible*. Paris: Grasset.

Vattimo, G. (1992). *The Transparent Society*, English Trans. D. Webb. Baltimore: Johns Hopkins University Press.

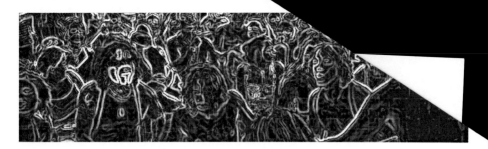

3

Marketing the savage: appropriating tribal tropes

Robin Canniford and Avi Shankar

Introduction

This chapter discusses how surf-culture has been constructed and appropriated by various media and marketing discourses that are constitutive of contemporary consumer culture. We explore how literature, film and advertising have represented and articulated surfing as a *savage* or *primitive* pursuit in order to imbue various products with a sense of otherness and excitement. More specifically, we will consider why *primitive* tropes have proved so seductive in various marketing contexts.

Torgovnick (1990) believes that the primitive is largely a construction of the Western colonial imagination that recognized and emphasized difference between colonial and colonized cultures. She stresses that the primitive remains a powerful ideal in Western cultures by providing a counterpoint to urban, civilized social orders and subjectivities. For example, in opposition to discipline and foresight, the primitive is non-materialistic, utopian and embodied (Torgovnick, 1990). Through practices that meet these criteria, urban subjects may encounter an exciting cultural territory through which they may explore the frontiers of the normal, the urbane and the civil.

Why should this opportunity be important? A large body of literature discusses the increasing levels of social regulation, rationality and foresight required by people following the emergence of the commercial society

, Elias, 2000; Keiser, 1998; Newton,
ple have inhabited increasingly net-
rationalized and disciplined working
eisure have emerged as cathartic antidotes
created by these environments (Rojek, 1995).
note, however, that these exciting activities do
ed chaos. Rather, they observe that apparently exces-
practices may serve as channels through which libidinous
ted into increasingly safe and mimetic social spaces. In many
spaces result in marketable leisure forms that support the fragile
social life in industrialized economies.

n particular, this chapter will consider how these theoretical approaches can inform our understanding of marketized representations of surf-culture. By means of various examples, we show how surfing has been constructed as an exciting remedy to some of the alienating qualities of urban life. Previous work by Fiske (1983) and Fisher (2005) has viewed surfing as an activity through which aspects of urban life may be renegotiated. This is to say the subject can experience a sense of release from the artificial or alienating urban environment, and return instead, to a more *primitive* or *natural* state.

Nevertheless, as Booth (2005) explains, surf-culture continues to support a huge commercial market that continues to grow. In this chapter we emphasize how entrepreneurial ventures have exploited the adventurous, sexual, care-free, natural and oceanic values associated with surfing. The symbiotic relationship between surf-culture and marketing relies, to a large extent, on the appropriation and reconstruction of various *primitive* tropes derived from colonial representations of surfing. Products fetishized in this way are instilled with ideals of subversion and pollution in order to offer excitement, deviance and escape sought by consuming subjects.

The chapter is divided into four sections. First, we identify how missionaries and industrialists constructed surfing as an immoral pursuit during the nineteenth century and discuss how this representation was exploited in literature, advertising and film during the nineteenth and early twentieth centuries. Second, we reflect on post-Second World War depictions of surfing that continued to construct surf-culture as a site for contained deviance, a move that supported numerous entrepreneurial ventures in music, film and advertising. In the third section the filmic portrayals of the embodied act of surfing are identified as a central feature of surf-culture that were undeveloped in previous productions. Moreover, this section discusses how surfing was used as a means to express some of the cultural contradictions of American society during the 1970s. Finally, we conclude by considering the importance of the *primitive* in marketing discourses as well as the changing order of primitive tropes.

The fall and rise of surf-culture

At the time of the colonization of the Pacific Islands in the late eighteenth century, surfing was an integral part of political, religious and sexual life in

Hawaii and Tahiti (Finney and Houston, 1996). The early accounts of surfing recorded by Captain Cook and his entourage praised the activity as noble and exciting (Finney, 2002). Nevertheless, the consolidation of European colonial power during the nineteenth century led to Hawaiian and Tahitian cultures being eradicated and traditional forms of surfing being discouraged (Finney and Houston, 1996; Sahlins, 1981). Surfing and the cultural connotations reproduced in its practice were considered to be at odds with the productive imperatives of colonial and industrial political economies, as this quote from an early twentieth century history of the Hawaiian Islands shows:

> The evils resulting from all these sports and amusements have in part been named. Some lost their lives thereby, some were severely wounded, maimed and crippled; some were reduced to poverty, both by losses in gambling and by neglecting to cultivate the land; and the instances were not few in which they were reduced to utter starvation. But the greatest evil of all resulted from the constant intermingling, without any restraint, of persons of both sexes and of all ages, at all times of the day and at all hours of the night.
>
> (Dibble, 1909, p. 102)

Surfers, at this time, experienced a two-pronged attack on their activities through a politico-industrial and a religious-moralistic discourse. At the turn of the nineteenth century, surfing had vanished in Tahiti and had become marginalized in Hawaii. Perhaps this kind of difference and domination led authors of the period, such as Defoe and Robert Louis Stevenson to draw on stories of the South Seas as means to express the excitement and *otherness* of the world beyond their homelands. R.M. Ballantyne's adventure story *The Coral Island* (1858) does just this. He describes surfing as a form of amusement invented by savage, dangerous and sub-human natives who sacrifice children to their eel god. Ballantyne has two European visitors discuss the practice:

> Well, ye see, I 'spose they found swimmin' for miles out to sea, and divin' fathoms deep, wasn't exciting enough, so they invented this game o' swimmin' on the surf. Each man and boy, as you see, has got a short board or plank with which he swims out for a mile or more to sea, and then, getting on top o'yon thunderin' breaker, they come to shore on the top of it, yellin' and screechin' like fiends.
>
> (Ballantyne, 1858, p. 198)

An illustration that accompanies the text shows the large figure of a tribal chief, face painted, lips pulled back over his teeth, stripped to the waist, exposing his well-defined, tanned body, as he rides a wave into the shore. Other naked natives are seen in the background with arms, torsos and legs sticking out of waves and sand. The European observers, Bill and Ralph, on the other hand remain detached, phlegmatic, dry, pale-skinned, and fully clothed observers. Their reserve and dignity are preserved by their separation from the action. In the background, the stolid presence of their ship – white sails set on a mast that reaches to the clouds – serves as an icon of imperial, colonial civilization. The visual metaphor is made complete by the breaking waves that enclose the natives: civilization over primitivism, imperial subject over primitive other.

Through reference to surfing, Ballantyne distinguishes European from Polynesian and constructs a sense of the excitement and danger of the South Seas. Simultaneously he considers the role of the Europeans in controlling and taming these kinds of behaviour: 'Wherever the savages take up Christianity they always give over their cruel ways, and are safe to be trusted' (Ballantyne, 1858, pp. 185–186). Surfing in this context is used as a metaphor to express and explore the ungoverned, exciting and primitive pleasures that were barred in European society. We would suggest that the appeal of this literature may, in part, be ascribed to the prompts provided by these *other* behaviours, through which both author and reader can consider the boundaries of civilized or acceptable conduct (see Roper, 1994). In other words, surfing is a site around which issues of civilization and colonialism versus excitement and primitivism may revolve in the imagination of the reader.

Interestingly, the power of this effect may have been a factor that prevented surfing's decline. At the end of the nineteenth century, before industrial and religious zeal could extinguish surfing completely, the activity began to feature increasingly in literature, tourism advertisements and in film. For instance, at the beginning of the twentieth century, Mark Twain described surfing in *Roughing It* (1904) and Jack London wrote of surfing's esoteric qualities in *The Cruise of the Snark* (1911 [1971]). These authors participated in the emerging tourism economy that had grown in Hawaii during the latter years of the nineteenth century and extolled an ethic of excitement and renewal through adventure tourism.

Opportunities of this kind were increasingly regarded as important during the latter years of the nineteenth century (Lewis, 2000) at a time when Simmel (1971) constructed his notion of the *adventurer*, a personality type who found remedy to the alienating qualities of society through exciting leisure and sublime environments. This kind of adventurous activity may be observed as an embodied refusal of the kinds of discipline and regulation espoused by moral and industrial forces that had taken hold of European society at this time.

Stranger (1999) calls on this notion of the *adventurer* to explain how surfing – the activity that had recently been repressed for its depraved, counterindustrial values – was apt to become an increasingly popular feature of the Western imagination. In particular, he considers that surfing's appeal derived from its association with ideas of excitement and release that had developed in various literary and artistic fields during the nineteenth century. Some of these had particularly emphasized the ideals of the *noble savage* and a return to a more *natural* state of being.

It is important to note that these constructions, whilst reviving surfing through reference to tribal and primitive metaphors, such as those incorporated in South Seas adventure stories, reconstituted surfing as a secular and hedonic form dissociated from indigenous religion, politics and sexuality.

Instead of returning to its original status as a locus of political, religious and sexual life, surfing was attached to romantic celebrations of nature, health, physical activity, excitement and outdoor adventure (Ford and Brown, 2006). This observation supports ideas of leisure as providing contained forms of deviance that do not disrupt the fabric of industrial society. However, despite this sanitized version of Hawaiian culture, we should not consider the deviant, licentious properties of surf-culture to have vanished. Instead, from this early stage onwards, deviance and conformity appear to be closely linked.

Heinmann (2004, p. 3) notes how, 'depictions of island life, including images of surfing, were instrumental in luring tourists' to Hawaii. It appears that a care-free, spur of the moment experience was available to tourists who travelled to Waikiki's beaches where men and women could mix topless at a time when bathers remained segregated and disciplined in Western nations (Booth, 1995). Surfing was presented as an ideal kind of activity to meet this requirement for it provided elements of danger, physical ability, and escapism, all in a natural theatre (George, 2001). Such features became a medium through which beach culture and sea-bathing were promoted at the turn of the century (Thoms, 2000). Surfing featured in advertisements, brochures, and films designed to promote tourism in Hawaii (Heinmann, 2004; Thoms, 2000). Furthermore, the beach proved to be a popular subject for film-makers who found that audiences enjoyed its spectacular qualities in travelogues and adventure pictures. These regularly featured well-built, semi-naked, often tanned men and women as they rode waves in tropical playgrounds. Thoms (2000) stresses that these marketing strategies emphasized the sexual escapism associated with the beach and with surfing: 'Throughout the Jazz Age, Hawaii and the South Seas continued to fascinate Hollywood producers, for whom they symbolized both romance and illicit sex' (Thoms, 2000, p. 32). We turn now to how these aspects of surf-culture were appropriated following the Second World War by considering how morality and deviance are played out through a variety of surfing films.

Hollywood beach films

According to Schroeder and Borgerson (2005, p. 11) 'a Hawaiian craze swept the US after World War Two. . . . Tiki culture – complete with backyard luaus, tiki bars, hula hoops, Hawaiian shirts and the hula dancing craze – emerged in the 1950s.' Another feature to have been imported from Hawaii to mainland America was surf-culture. Surfing experienced massive growth in California during the 1950s (Irwin, 1973) and the marketing potential of surf-culture was recognized in Hollywood. The level of appeal that surfing created is evident in the growth enjoyed by products associated with surfing. Music, fashion and film all drew on surf-culture's visual styles to successfully position and sell products. Borgerson and Schroeder (2003) help to clarify the appeal of these products by noting the appropriation of *primitive* tropes, largely severed from the Hawaiian context that provided paradisiacal connotations.

A successful series of Beach Films were produced during the late 1950s and early 1960s that expressed the carefree fun surfing could offer (Booth, 1996), and provided a tangible embodiment of a lifestyle dream (Ford and Brown, 2006). These values portrayed in the Beach Films continued to draw on a sense of a more primitive lifestyle and subjectivity than that generally espoused by 1950s US society. The first of these films was Colombia's *Gidget*, the true story of a young Californian girl who decided to learn how to surf. The film characterized surfers as penniless, amoral layabouts: the friends that Gidget makes at the beach are hedonists; rebels with no other cause than the joy of sliding along a wave. Between surfs, they loiter, womanize, drink and party to the sound of beating drums and surf music that Thoms (2000) reads as allusions to traditional Hawaiian rhythms. These features present surfing as a means through which youths may escape from society and foster alternative values. For example, one of the central characters, *Kahuna*, declares that he is fed up with, 'too many hours, and rules and regulations'. He overtly rejects and challenges society's values, announcing: 'I ride the waves, eat, sleep, not a care in the world . . . I'm a surf bum' ('Kahuna' in *Gidget*, 1959).

The film represents surfing as a lifestyle through which social norms surrounding work, time, familial roles and responsibility can be rethought, perhaps even refused. The beach culture is a place of physical and sexual excitement divorced from mundane reality and based on similar metaphors to those extolled in the various productions considered above. This is to say that, once again, surfing is presented as a practice associated with various kinds of deviance and abandon. However, *Gidget* represents a different set of discords in society to those played out in the adventure literature of the nineteenth century or the tourism literature and film of the early twentieth century. Conflict no longer exists between native and colonial authorities, but between youths and various dominant institutions in society such as educational bodies, employment, the conjugal household, gender roles and consumer lifestyles.

Ultimately however, *Gidget* upholds dominant societal values over those created by youths through surf-culture. By means of a romantic sub-plot, *Gidget* falls for one of the Malibu surfers. This event is pivotal, for following this development, the surfers come to their senses, re-emerge from their previous guises sporting clean clothes and close-shaved faces, whereupon they return to family responsibilities and school careers. This being the case, it could be argued that this, and other films of the genre, neutralized some of the deviant and primitive features that were developed by rebellious youths following the Second World War. Thoms (2000) and Booth (2001) both note that these films tended to depict the lighter sides of surfing, reducing the surfing life to little more than a summer fantasy. Indeed, Rutsky (1999, p. 15) observes:

> Most analyses of surfing or beach films . . . subordinate the surfing scene and culture to bourgeois notions of work, sexual morality, and monogamous relationships. The playful party atmosphere of the beach is therefore typically presented as a mere vacation, or as a last summer fling before adulthood.

Perhaps the kind of delinquency that the surfing lifestyle represented was just too radical at this time, and the challenging themes were accordingly resolved in order to overcome the threat to the moral order. If this is the case, how can the producers of these films be charged with drawing upon ideas of deviance and primitivism in order to sell their products? We could instead, regard these films as propaganda *against* primitive and illicit values. Rutsky (1999), however, is disparaging of critics who assume that *Gidget's* popularity can be explained in terms of a comforting portrayal that negated the subversive energy of a youth scene and upheld the more powerful force of white, middle class American values. On the contrary:

> To see these films solely in terms of conformity, reassurance, or escapism is, I believe, to give far too much credence to the power and the pleasure of conformity. It overlooks the degree to which the appeal of these films also depends upon elements of sexual, cultural, and ideological difference that can never be simply or entirely normalized. However much these films seem to affirm sexless romance and conformity to white middle class values and morality, it is also the case that sexuality, parodic irreverence, and nonconformity are crucial to their appeal.
>
> (Rutsky, 1999, p. 13)

In other words, the two themes – nonconformity/otherness versus conformity/familiarity exist as two sides of the same coin. These films rely on the titillating exposure of young flesh, good looking, pert bodies in tight shorts and in particular, bikinis. Deviance remains written into these narratives; the beach is sexualized as both an attractive and risky cultural space that is popular amongst youths. So despite the apparent domestication of surf-culture, Rutsky (1999) points to the means through which the exotic and deviant excitement may have continued to establish a sense of *otherness* key to the appeal of surfing:

> . . . the attraction of the surfing films, and of surf subculture, is much less a matter of the reassuring pleasures of bourgeois conformity than of the thrill of non-conformity, the attraction of a certain difference, both sexual and otherwise.
>
> (Rutsky, 1999, p. 14)

In short, the Beach Films retained sufficient sexual and subcultural appeal in opposition to the propriety of mundane, adult society, to prompt increasing levels of popularity and shared awareness of surfing amongst America's youth (Rutsky, 1999). Much like the effects observed in Ballantyne's narrative, where surfing appears at the border of civility and primitivism, 1950s/1960s youth surf-culture is constructed as an arena where deviance and nonconformity could offer youths access to the exciting, dark-side of consumer-culture. Simultaneously however, the narratives did not seek to undermine productive ethics in society. Surfing's otherness is presented as a temporary feature, a strategy that may have inadvertently rescued the scene from those who preferred to cast it as a dangerous kind of subversion (see Booth, 2001). This was likely to have prevented exclusion or moral panic in general society, and resulted in stronger economic links between the surfing scene and the wider US economy. Indeed, these films were a huge commercial success. Booth (1996) notes that *Beach Party* alone grossed 3.5 million dollars and propelled surfing and surfers' styles into the United States' popular cultural consciousness.

Endless summers and cultural napalm

Having said this, it should be recognized that not all surfing film productions fulfilled the roles assumed by the Beach Films. In 1964, the release of *Endless Summer* marked the popular acceptance of a film genre that showed how portrayals of surfing could be exciting in and of themselves. Instead of the narrative 'sexing-up' of surf-stories, Bruce Brown's film followed a group of 'real' surfers as they travelled Africa in search of waves. Since this watershed, *Endless Summer* has become an iconic and archetypal example of the *Pure Surf Film* genre that surfers created in order to express the embodied styles of surfing (see Booth, 1996; Fisher, 2005) over the sweetened, sexualized features of the Beach Films. Pure Surf Films expressed nomadic, simple lifestyles of surfers; they stressed the eschewal of work and family commitments espoused by many of surf-culture's hard-core types during this period. Moreover they privileged aesthetic performance; the embodied styles surfers developed through constant intercourse with waves.

A number of films followed this formula throughout the 1970s. These productions gradually altered the emphases of surfing films from a post-Second World War youthful optimism to the darker political realities of the Cold War (Booth, 1996). In particular, Booth views the Pure Surf Films of the 1970s, to have expressed an increasingly political *apocalyptic hedonism*, engendered by the threats of the Cold War, consumer culture and environmental degradation. This resulted in films such as Paul Witzig's *Sea of Joy* (1971), which according to Thoms (2000, p. 115) 'is a film about beauty instead of ugliness, freedom instead of chains, life instead of death, peace instead of war, love instead of hate'.

Sea of Joy and other films such as Albie Falzon and David Elfick's *Morning of the Earth* (1972) are cut with scenes showing surfers in *far-out* situations. Indeed, for Thoms (2000, p. 115) 'its bearded, longhaired surfers in full-length wetsuits seemed a breed apart, far from the fun-loving adolescents of Bruce Brown films and more akin to Zen masters in their devotion to pure surfing'. *Morning of the Earth*, marked this statement by cutting between surfing shots and lifestyle scenes of surfers getting back to nature; living rurally, raising chickens, enjoying the healthy life, meditating, and sating their copious appetites for the happy weed. It is reasonable to suggest that these features represent a culture that sought to distance itself from the mainstream and establish a new way of life; one seated in less urban, more primitive values, consonant those of the general countercultural critique.

Booth (1996) observes these films as important media through which surfers could think about the boundaries of their culture. Surf-films were likely to have been a site around which countercultural rebellion, and the primitive, nature-oriented lifestyles could be planned out and communicated. However Booth (1995, 2005) also expresses the contradictions present in this surfing culture. He considers that these films created new roads for commercial capital to exploit surf-culture as well as promote professional surfing. This state of affairs represented a paradoxical counterpoint to the values of those surfers who might be regarded as developing a primitive lifestyle as part of the *back to nature* movement expressed in these films. This position is in line with many authors to have considered the issue of counterculture as a means to commercialism (Hall and Jefferson, 1976; Heath and Potter, 2005). Particularly, Booth (2001) considers that commercial ventures were motivated by the hedonic desires of surfers as these economic strategies represented a path towards eternal self-indulgence, which probably always came ahead of political activism.

Such representations of surfing as a political statement, however, were not isolated to Pure Surf Films. As the 1970s drew to a close, Francis Ford Copolla's *Apocalypse Now* (1979) bluntly stressed the cultural contradictions that shook surfing during this period. On one hand, the film helped surfing re-enter the mainstream following the countercultural period discussed above (Kampion and Brown, 2003). On the other hand, the deviance and nonconformist excitement of the countercultural period continued to be writ large. In line with his literary muse – Joseph Conrad's *Heart of Darkness* – screenwriter and surfer John Milius, constructed a contested colonial circus in which Willard – the character charged with killing the deviant Kurtz – meets crazy Colonel Kilgore of the *Air Cavalry*. In this classic scene we learn that Kilgore happens to be an obsessive surfer. As bullets and shells shriek overhead, Kilgore excitedly greets a new conscript and fellow waterman named Lance:

> It's an honor to meet you Lance. I've admired your noseriding for years – I like your cutback too. I think you have the best cutback there is.
>
> (Colonel Kilgore – *Apocalypse Now*)

Lance and others are forced to go surfing under the most extreme of circumstances, an event that acts as metaphorical allusion to important political shifts. Questions about savagery, recklessness, American colonialism and freedom abound. The scene conflates surfing with an assault on the Vietcong. Milius knows that surfers are surfers, even under the most extreme circumstances, and the attack is twisted into another way of finding good surf. However, Kilgore's stand can also be understood as one of intense rejection of American foreign policy and a means through which to negate military duty.

It appears that surfing – in much the same way as in adventure stories, tourism films, advertising and the Beach Films – continues to represent an embodied practice around which values of primitive deviance and the questioning of imperial/colonial/urban conformity are enacted: 'The tragedy of this war is a dead surfer,' reflects Lance.

Nevertheless, we may also read contradictory undercurrents into this scene. Surfing is extolled by a madman and a merciless warmonger: Kilgore appears no less concerned with the aesthetics of riding waves as the lives of his soldiers or the success of Willard's mission. In a carnival of competing rationalities, military strategy and duty collide with the ethics of surf-culture. This is to say, despite Kilgore's apparently muddled and deviant priorities, the wave-riding assault on 'Charlie's Point' remains an expression of freedom and the American way of life. Surfing in this sense represents a means of *Othering* the Viet Cong: 'Charlie don't surf,' shouts Kilgore proudly. This cultural assault somehow reaches further than the F4 Phantoms that raze the physical environment with napalm. As with the previous examples, deviance and conformity are closely related, surfing may simultaneously appear to offer a means of escape from our culture, whilst also reinforcing that culture.

Twelve years later, *Point Break* (1991) marked another Hollywood success in which the contradictions between urban discipline and a more primitive way of life are unleashed once again through reference to surfing. In a ridiculous but enjoyable story line, under-cover cop 'Johnny Utah' infiltrates a Los Angeles surfing subculture to catch a group of criminal surfers, 'the Ex-Presidents'. They hide behind rubber masks that depict Reagan, Nixon, Johnson, and Carter whilst they 'rip off banks to finance the endless summer' (Utah, *Point Break*). These surfers are characterized as deviant criminals who live day-to-day, existing only for the next adrenaline rush. This story calls upon the myth of the hard-core surfer, a subject who embodies hedonism and rock n' roll deviance.

The leader of these surfers, 'Bodhi', is a 'modern savage . . . a real searcher', who, according to his surfer girlfriend, 'Tyler', has devoted his life to 'the ultimate ride' (Tyler, *Point Break*). This is a spiritual pursuit as much as it is about *getting radical*. Bank robbing is not about the money; rather it's a means to keep surfing, and a means to hide from the realities of the urban-jungle and a nine-to-five job. Bodhi explains their creed by stating:

> We stand for something – To those dead souls inching along the freeway in their metal coffins, we show them that the human spirit is still alive.

The film invites viewers to decide who the good guys are. As in *Apocalypse Now*, opposing ideologies are set on a collision course and surfing is the theatre through which we are invited to assess our own values and desires. It is fair to assume that we are supposed to ask 'Who are the robbers?' Are they Reagan, Nixon, L.B Johnson, and Carter: the crooks who created this impersonal, technocratic world? Or are they the deviant surfers? This problem with which the viewer is presented, calls on a similar principle to all of the productions discussed so far.

This is to say that surfing represents a practice that may fulfill *quests for excitement* in pacified, networked societies. In the South Seas adventures of the nineteenth century, we have shown that surfing could represent a means to consider the boundaries of urban culture and more primitive lives. During the early twentieth century, tourism advertisements associated surfing with an adventurous ethic of escape and renewal from urban alienation. Following the war, film productions constructed surf-culture as a site that could offer a rejection of mundane life and the development of deviance. This opportunity became increasingly imbued with political values throughout the 1970s. These references to alternative ethics, based in primitive refusals of urban culture have remained popular throughout this time, we now consider why this should be the case.

Appropriating tribal tropes

> Primitives are our untamed selves, our id forces – libidinous, irrational, violent, dangerous. Primitives are mystics, in tune with nature, part of its harmonies. Primitives are free. Primitives live at the 'lowest cultural levels'; we occupy the 'highest'.
>
> (Torgovnick, 1990, p. 8)

What is it that has proved so popular about surfing such that it has featured in popular literature and film for more than two centuries? This chapter has observed surfing as an example of the potential for marketing to exploit *primitive* metaphors. Surfing has provided a set of cultural referents through which such tropes may be inscribed into products. In the preceding quote Torgovnick regards primitivism as fundamental to our identity by providing a sense of the *other*. In opposition to the metropolitan repression considered by Elias and Dunning (1986) and Roper (1994), primitive values provide an alternative set of ethics around which deviance can be considered and communicated against ideas of what is civilized and conformist. Lewis (2000) and Stranger (1999) highlight the kinds of subjects who re-attune themselves with the natural environment in response to urban alienation. Putting this another way, Irwin (1973, p. 138) considers that going surfing affords a 'primeval way of life . . . the complete antithesis of a too mechanized, too routinized, too tame civilization'. Furthermore, Fiske (1983) and Fisher (2005) emphasize the role of surfing as a kind of carnival space through which to seek out alternative interpretations of modern culture. Similarly, Ford and Brown (2006, p. 160) consider that romanticized aesthetics and the risky and sublime leisure practices through which they are enacted, reflect 'preoccupations with the senses, mystical experience, the sublime and the lone individual estranged from civilization yet at one with nature'.

Putting this another way, we suggest that the entrepreneurial products considered in this chapter have drawn both upon these kinds of images, as well as those kinds of exotic tropes discussed by Schroeder and Borgerson (2005). We believe that the various portrayals of surfers as *noble savages* and *modern savages*, and the products that have constructed these portraits have succeeded by marketing ideals of freedom, simplicity, escape and excitement. As we have shown, early twentieth century tourism promised the possibility for people to shake-off the kinds of moral and industrial subjectivities required of them in mundane life. Instead they were free to experience the exposure of bodies, close contact with the sea, each other and the Hawaiian beach boys who took tourists for rides on surfboards. During the 1950s and 1960s this freedom was related to issues of bodily exposure, teenage sexuality, work, leisure, and identity. Later still, surfing offered a site to consider moral orientations: freedom in drug use, freedom to express subversive political opinions concerning work and foreign policy. Finally, surfing has more recently expressed the dissatisfaction with the mundane workaday life demanded in an urbanized, marketized consumer society.

It should be made clear that the kinds of release considered in the context of the examples presented in the course of this chapter represent different kinds of freedom and deviance. It is worth stating that notions of the primitive are constantly changing in response to the changing kinds of repressions and challenges required in the social orders we inhabit through history. Booth (1996) argues that surf films have reflected the general zeitgeist of the period during which they were produced, albeit in multiple, contradictory and inconsistent manners. More specifically, we would stress that productions that draw on surfing have often revealed the kinds of dissatisfaction present in societies at any time. Films, books, and various other products, market forms of illicit and exotic pleasure to consumers by constructing tropes that emphasize freedom, release and various forms of a mystical return to nature. In short, the portrayals of surfing considered in this chapter *make up* notions of the primitive in order to enable consumers to consider their untamed selves, their libidinous and irrational desires, in safe and productive spaces (cf. Elias and Dunning, 1986).

The packaging of surfing as a means of release from the mundane lives that people lead relies on a desire to people to renegotiate the alienating and boring qualities of capitalist society. In recent years this has continued to represent a successful formula upon which organizations as diverse as Billabong, RipCurl, Quiksilver, Toyota, Ford, Guinness, Vauxhall, Exeter University, Budweiser, Marks and Spencer, Price Waterhouse Coopers, Tommy Hilfiger, and Old Spice, have to various degrees, appropriated images of surfers or surfing in order to supply some sense of escape, difference or excitement, 'other' to the mundane and everyday. These marketing discourses draw on practices that inhabit an interstitial space between conformity/civility and thrill/primitivism to meet the need for excitement through the inconsistencies they support.

Paradoxically however, these mainstream, and often costly, market offerings that are advertised in this way, serve to tie images of freedom back into to the alienating institutions from which they proffer escape. With a few rare exceptions (see Fisher, 2005), representations of surfing in film, literary and advertising productions extol ethics of freedom alongside dominant values. These representations of surfing transform acts of deviance, petty illegality or delinquency into various productive practices. In the South Sea adventures, the natives are transformed and *civilized* by missionaries; in the Beach Films, teenagers eventually abandon surfing for *normal* lives; equally, those countercultural expressions supplied by the Pure Surf Films during the 1960s and 1970s were eventually subsumed by commercial ventures (Booth, 1996). Furthermore, in *Apocalypse Now*, Lance loses his mind and Kilgore has his board stolen. Finally, law and order are restored to Los Angeles when *Point Break's* Ex-Presidents come to various messy ends. Ultimately therefore, these branded escape attempts fail to subvert the fabric of Western society and doom consumers to reproduce the technocratic imperatives of dominant social institutions over those ideals associated with indigenous Polynesian cultures or late-modern surfing subcultures from which tribal metaphors continue to be misappropriated.

References

Ballantyne, R.M. (1858/1994). *The Coral Island*. London: Puffin.

Booth, D. (1995). Ambiguities in pleasure and discipline: the development of competitive surfing, *Journal of Sport History*, **22** (3), 189–206.

Booth, D. (1996). Surfing films and videos: adolescent fun, alternative lifestyle, adventure industry, *Journal of Sport History*, **23** (3), 313–327.

Booth, D. (2001). *Australian Beach Cultures: The History of Sun, Sand and Surf*. London: Frank Cass.

Booth, D. (2005). Paradoxes of material culture: the political economy of surfing, in Nauright, J. and Schimmel, K. (eds.), *The Political Economy of Sport*, London: Palgrave, pp. 104–25.

Borgerson, J.E. and Schroeder, J.L. (2003). The lure of paradise: marketing the retro-escape of Hawaii, in Brown, S. and Sherry Jr., J.F. (eds.), *Time, Space and the Market: Retroscapes Rising*. London: M.E. Sharpe.

Dibble, S. (1909). *A History of the Sandwich Islands*. Honolulu: T.G. Thrum.

Elias, N. (2000). *The Civilising Process*. Oxford: Blackwell.

Elias, N. and Dunning, E. (1986). *Quest for Excitement*. Oxford: Blackwell.

Finney, B. and Houston, J. (1996). *Surfing: A History of the Ancient Hawaiian Sport*. California: Pomegranate.

Finney, B. (2002). Whoa dude, surfings that old? in Colburn, B., Finney, B., Stallings, T., Stecyk, C.R., Stillman, D. and Wolfe, T. (eds.), *Surf Culture: The Art History of Surfing*, California: Laguna Art Museum in Association with Gingko Press.

Fiske, J. (1983). Surfalism and sandiotics: the beach in Oz culture, *Australian Journal of Cultural Studies*, **1** (2), 120–149.

Fisher, K. (2005). Economies of loss and questions of style in contemporary surf subcultures, *Junctures*, **4** (June), 13–21.

Ford, N. and Brown, D. (2006). *Surfing and Social Theory*. Abingdon: Routledge.

George, S. (ed.), (2001). *The Perfect Day: 40 Years of Surfer Magazine*. San Francisco: Chronicle.

Hall, S. and Jefferson, T. (1976). *Resistance Through Rituals: Youth Subcultures in Post War Britain*. London: Hutchinson.

Heath, J. and Potter, A. (2005). *The Rebel Sell*. Sussex: Capstone.

Heinmann, J. (2004). *Surfing: Vintage Surf Graphics*. London: Taschen.

Irwin, J. (1973). Surfing: the natural history of an urban scene, *Urban Life and Culture*, **2**, 131–160.

Kampion, D. and Brown, B. (2003). *A History of Surf Culture*. California: Evergreen.

Keiser, A. (1998). From freemasons to industrious patriots: organising and disciplining in 18th century Germany, *Organization Studies*, **19** (1), 47–71.

Lewis, N. (2000). The climbing body, nature and the experience of modernity, *Body and Society*, **6** (3–4), 58–80.

London, J. (1971). *The Cruise of the Snark*. London: Seafarer Books.

Newton, T. (2003). Credit networks and civilization, *British Journal of Sociology*, **54** (3), 347–372.

Rojek, C. (1995). *Decentring Leisure: Rethinking Leisure Theory*. London: Sage.

Roper, L. (1994). Drinking, whoring and gorging, *Oedipus and the Devil: Witchcraft, Sexuality and Religion in Early Modern Europe*. London: Routledge.

Rutsky, R.L. (1999). Surfing the other: ideology on the beach, *Film Quarterly*, **52** (4), 12–23.

Sahlins, M. (1981). *Historical Metaphors and Mythical Realities: Structure in the Early History of the Sandwich Islands Kingdom*. Ann Arbor: University of Michigan Press.

Schroeder, J.E. and Borgerson, J.L. (2005). Packaging paradise: organising representations of Hawaii, *Paper Presented at Critical Management Studies Conference*, Cambridge, July 2005.

Simmel, G. (1971). *On individuality and social forms: selected writings/edited and with an introduction by Donald N. Levine*. London: University of Chicago Press.

Stranger, M. (1999). The aesthetics of risk – a study of surfing, *International Review for the Sociology of Sport*, **34** (3), 265–276.

Thoms, A. (2000). *Surfmovies: A History of Surf Films Since 1897*. Queensland: The Blue Group.

Torgovnick, M. (1990). *Gone Primitive: Savage Intellects, Modern Lives*. Chicago: University of Chicago Press.

Twain, M. (1904). *Roughing it*. New York: Harper.

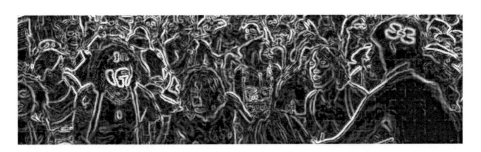

Part II
Tribes as activators

4

The consumption of cultural heritage among a British Royal Family brand tribe

Cele C. Otnes and Pauline Maclaran

All at once heritage is everywhere – in the news, in the movies, in the marketplace . . . It is the chief focus of patriotism and the prime lure of tourism. One can barely move without bumping into a heritage site. Every legacy is cherished. From ethnic roots to history theme parks, Hollywood to the Holocaust, the whole world is busy lauding – or lamenting – some past, be it fact or fiction.

(Lowenthal, 1998, p. xiii)

How do consumers come to understand and actively engage in their own cultural heritage(s) – defined as products of individuals or groups that include tangible objects, human actions, ideas, customs and knowledge that we value from the past (Davison, 1991)? Clearly, marketers understand that individual and collective heritages are significant to consumers. As evidenced by the excerpt above, consumers support industries that enable them to participate in heritage tours, understand their origins, and gain access to peoples that may be personally or historically significant to them. But given the mobility and fragmentation that define the postmodern world, consumers who wish to remain connected to their individual or collective heritages must often make concerted efforts and devote significant amounts of money and energy to do so.

With the exception of studies that examine how consumers engage in disposing and acquiring tangible items from one generation to the next (e.g., Price, Arnould, and Curasi, 2000), and the consumption of history at a 'living' museum (Goulding, 1999, 2001), consumer researchers have largely ignored the intersection of heritage and consumption. This is the case even as they have immersed themselves in heritage-laden contexts to explore broader topics that pertain to consumption (e.g., consuming fantasy, Belk and Costa, 1998; the synthesis of worship and shopping and religion, O'Guinn and Belk, 1989). Furthermore, heritage and history are distinct, because as 'history explores and explains pasts grown ever more opaque over time [,] heritage clarifies pasts so as to infuse them with present purposes' (Lowenthal, 1998, p. xv). Focusing on heritage, therefore, will enable scholars to examine important questions pertaining to how consumers conceptualize their individual and cultural pasts, and how they incorporate these pasts into their present and future lives.

In this chapter, we explore the following research questions: (1) what are the specific ways members of a tribe consume heritage as it relates to the British Royal Family (BRF)? and (2) how do these tribe members shape BRF-related consumption experiences of a wider audience outside of the tribe? In exploring these questions, we focus on how people who meet Maffesoli's (1996) definition of a Consumer Tribe – that is, a group that is loosely connected, inherently unstable, and held together essentially through emotion and passion – collectively engage in consuming the BRF brand, and how they interact with cultural producers who create and disseminate narratives about this brand to a wider public.

Our rationale for conceptualizing the BRF as a brand stems from Balmer, Greyser, and Urde's (2004) argument that the monarchy should not be regarded solely as a political institution, but is conceptually comparable to a corporate brand that offers consumers tangible benefits. These include providing consumers with a respected and shared symbol of nationalism, helping them engage in national 'togetherness' and fostering a sense of identity based on shared history, culture, and traditions among consumers. Moreover, conceptualizing the BRF among all extant monarchies is especially appropriate, because although it no longer plays any real political role in the UK, 53 countries still claim allegiance to the British Commonwealth (wikipedia.org, 2006). Furthermore, many manufacturers in a plethora of industries (e.g., tourism, film, publishing, china, and ceramics) produce goods, services and experiences specifically designed to enhance consumers' knowledge and enjoyment of the BRF.

Methods

This study is grounded within a larger project on the meaning of the BRF brand to consumers. Our data collection began in April 2004 and has extended (so far) to June 2006. At the beginning of our research, 'Elizabeth' emerged as a key informant. A white, middle-class Englishwoman, Elizabeth is a recent retiree (or 'pensioner' in the UK) and divides her time between her two main interests in life: her children and grandchildren, and her passion for the BRF. This passion includes a collection of over 7,000 pieces of BRF-related memorabilia insured for over £40,000 in her bed and breakfast (B&B) in North London (see Figures 4.1 & 4.2). Wall-to-wall shelving, with china, crockery, pictures, and other colourful memorabilia abound throughout the living spaces of her home. Floor space is at a premium, with a sea of items spread densely across the carpets, including fourteen life-size concrete corgi dogs, four giant cardboard cutouts (two of Diana, one each of Charles and the Queen Mother), and a large wooden replica of the coronation throne. Each room features a quasi-shrine to particular royal family members (e.g., the Queen and Prince Philip, their children, the Queen Mother, and, most recently, Charles and Camilla). Elizabeth's pride and joy is her Diana Room, an extension to her home commemorating the late Princess of Wales, her favourite member of the BRF.

This collection has made Elizabeth a minor celebrity in her own right, and provides her with the impetus to organize many social BRF-related events

Figure 4.1 One room in Elizabeth's collection.

Figure 4.2 Elizabeth's dining room (with royal cutouts).

for consumers and the media alike. These activities, and her faithful attendance at many BRF-related events, justify our interpretation of Elizabeth as the linchpin of this particular BRF tribe. Over the two year period, the authors interacted with Elizabeth and members of the tribe, as well as with cultural producers who disseminate information to the public (e.g., reporters, museum curators who borrow items from Elizabeth's collection) and retailers who carry BRF merchandise (not discussed here). Interactions occurred primarily through interviews and in-depth immersions. For example, one of us stayed at Elizabeth's B&B during the week that culminated in Prince Charles and Camilla Parker-Bowles's wedding, while the other attended a party orchestrated by Elizabeth to mark the Queen's 80th birthday in April 2006. These immersions helped us supplement our interview data with direct observation of gatherings, places, trends, and day-to-day practices – key elements of Consumer Tribes (Cova and Cova, 2002). Although preliminary questions were compiled and used, the interviewers largely allowed informants to direct the flow of interactions. The data used for this chapter consists of over 280 pages of interview text as well as photographs and videotape. In interpreting our text, we read the interviews several times, consulting the literature on tribes, heritage, collecting (e.g., Belk, 1995), and other key constructs (e.g., rituals; see Otnes and Lowrey, 2004). We engaged in member checks with Elizabeth and Dan, two key informants with whom we interacted several times.

Findings

The structure and function of the BRF tribe

Before we address our specific research questions, we offer a brief summary of the structure of this tribe and the function of its members. We delineate this tribe conservatively as comprising the 22 people whose origins in the tribe stem from their relationship with Elizabeth or someone in her inner circle, and who attended at least one of three BRF events that were thoroughly reported in the data – a TV viewing party of Charles and Camilla's wedding held at Elizabeth's home, her party celebrating the Queen's 80th birthday, and the anniversary of Princess Diana's death that takes place annually on August 31st at Kensington Palace. The researchers were present at the first two events and relied on extensive narratives by Margaret and Dan of Princess Diana's anniversary celebration. In total, we interacted with 17 of the 22 people listed in Table 4.1, as well as the media members and retailers mentioned above.

When we classified these consumers according to Kozinets'(1999) typology of member types (see Table 4.1), two key points about the function of these tribe members emerge. First, because we limit ourselves to identifying the four types Kozinets describes, we refrain from discussing people outside of the tribe who clearly help its members (and specifically, Elizabeth) maintain their passion for the BRF (e.g., the media who pay her for interviews, 'scouts' who help her acquire items, her children, paying guests). Second, only eight members are actually hard-core BRF consumers or collectors; the rest are loosely affiliated through their relationships with others (primarily Elizabeth and her friend Jane). Thus, the structure and function of this group affirm Cova's (1997) statement that contemporary tribes often support 'the postmodern leitmotif [that] the link is more important than the thing' (1997, p. 311).

Consuming heritage within the context of the BRF tribe

Our first research question explores how this BRF tribe collectively consumes heritage, or collective aspects of their past that subsequently make their current lives meaningful. Our analysis reveals three main ways this tribe does so: (1) creating rituals and establishing traditions; (2) airing grievances and grieving; and (3) sharing fantasies about desired BRF experiences. We illuminate these with excerpts from our text.

Creating rituals / establishing traditions

Balmer et al. (2004) note one of the key benefits of the monarchy for consumers is that it serves as a source of national traditions. In examining the rituals surrounding the BRF that emerged from the Victorian Era to the reign of Elizabeth II, Cannadine (1983) argues that the rituals enacted by the Royals themselves have progressed from those characterized by ineptitude to those

Table 4.1 BRF tribe members and roles

Roles[*]	Name	Demos	Rel. to Elizabeth	Membership motivation
Insiders	Elizabeth[**]	Div, 60, Eng		Love of BRF
	Victor	S, 40s, Eng	Friend	Love of Diana
	Tony	S, 50s, Eng	Diana Anniv.	Love of BRF
	Monica	M, 50s, Eng	Diana Anniv.	Love of Diana
Devotee	Colleen	S, ??, Irish	Diana Anniv.	Love of Diana
	GermanGirl 1	????	Diana Anniv.	Love of Diana
	GermanGirl 2	????	Diana Anniv.	Love of Diana
	GermanGirl 3	????	Diana Anniv.	Love of Diana
Mingler	Dan	S, 60s, Eng	Friend	Rel. w/Eliz
	Amy	S, 50s, Eng	Neighbour	Rel. w/Eliz
	Ellen	S, 20s, Eng	Neighbour's daughter	Rel. w/Eliz
	Jane	M, 50s, Eng	Friend	Rel. w/Eliz
	George	M, 50s, Eng	Jane's Husband	Rel. w/Jane
	Donald	S, 30s, Eng	Jane & George's son	Rel. w/Jane
Tourist	Martha	F, ??, Eng	Friend of a friend	Curiosity
	Tia	S, 10, Eng	Jane's granddaughter	Rel. w/Jane
	Serena	S, 10, Eng	Tia's friend	Rel. w/Tia
	Jay	S, 60s, Eng	Monica's brother	Rel. w/ Monica
	Audrey	??, 40s, Eng	Victor's sister	Rel.w/Victor
	Rosa	??, 60s, Eng	Eliz's neighbour	Rel. w/Eliz
	Lucy	M, 60s, Eng	Eliz's neighbour	Rel. w/Eliz
	Geoff	M, 60s, Eng	Lucy's husband	Rel. w/Lucy

[*]The four roles Kozinets (1999) identifies are: Insider: strong ties to both consumption and social activities of the tribe; Devotee: stronger interest in consumption over social activities; Mingler: stronger interest in social over consumption activities; Tourist: weak interest in both social and consumption activities.
[**]All names are pseudonyms.
Eng: English; Rel.: Relationship; Anniv.: Anniversary, ??, ????: information not known.

designed to reflect the international importance of the BRF. Furthermore, those same rituals that were often shoddily performed in their initial attempts have been perfected, and now stand for continuity, splendour, and the reaffirmation of the importance of the British Commonwealth on the international political stage. While the members of our BRF tribe are consciously aware of standard ritual elements such as ceremonial music, carriage-laden processions and specific vestments and artifacts, in truth the tribe often creates brand-related traditions and rituals without considering how these align with the types or tenors of these existing royal rituals, or how the general public might regard them.

The annual gathering at Kensington Palace to commemorate Princess Diana's death demonstrates how this tribe develops and maintains 'trademark' traditions distinct from those of other tribes also present. Elizabeth and Dan comment on the roles of particular members in upholding these traditions:

> E: Tony, who dresses in red, white, and blue, he sort of keeps wires and scissors and stuff and helps people put them [flowers/ photographs] on the [gates], and people have these pictures plastercised [laminated] and put those up . . .
>
> D: We know everybody there because Elizabeth is the star, when Elizabeth walks up, they say, 'There she is', don't they?
>
> E: They all know me, yes. We're all part of it, we make it for each other. It's almost like a party and yet it's not . . .
>
> D: [Victor] is quite the personality, especially down at the gate . . . he's the man in the white suit . . . I'm the one that takes photographs.
>
> E: Yes, but Dan has to take them with my camera, and then with Victor's, he sort of doubles it up.

These excerpts demonstrate that within the broader cultural context of this anniversary, four core members of this tribe perform fairly fixed ritual performance roles (Rook, 1985). Specifically, although there is no request from the general public for them to do so, Victor acts as greeter, posting himself in a white suit and white jewelled shoes (for which he reports paying £90) at the gates, Elizabeth acts as minor celebrity and hostess for when interacting with people she 'sees once a year,' and Dan serves as assistant to both Elizabeth and Victor. Although Insiders do not use these traditions and rituals to deliberately try and increase enthusiasm for the BRF or for their tribe, such events do create opportunities for more loosely affiliated members to connect with both in a more leisurely and playful manner (Hirschman and Holbrook, 1982).

Furthermore, although these tribe members are undoubtedly aware a larger audience is observing them enact their ritual performance roles, unlike other groups they do not exist specifically to be noticed by these larger audiences, or to make a political statement. That this BRF tribe regards its traditions as distinct from those that other groups create is clear when Elizabeth and Dan discuss their disapproval of 'The Diana Circle' at Kensington Palace, and rationalize why their friend Monica chose to join:

> [They're] more sort of cliquey and they've got T-shirts with 'Diana Circle' on them and all that. So you're either in or you're out . . . They're very 'stand up and be shouted' . . . and you're supposed to toe the line. So even if you don't agree with what they're saying, you're supposed to pretend you agree and I'm not one to join groups, really, I'm a one-off. But I wouldn't say Monica is a big member of the Diana Circle . . . her husband died of cancer and I suppose she really joined . . . because of that.

In short, although the members of this BRF tribe are keenly aware that the monarchy 'survives by being noticed, over and over again' (Billig, 1982, p. 1) they consume heritage by creating loosely bounded rituals and traditions both for their own recreational enjoyment, and to enable them to express

aspects of their individual personalities, rather than to fulfil a more public need. These loosely bound rituals include parties to commemorate or
co-create BRF events such as Charles and Camilla's wedding, adopting
specific and identifiable ritual performance roles that socialize and educate
others with respect to the BRF, and gathering in small subgroups on particular
days at key BRF locations (e.g., Althorpe, where Princess Diana was raised)
in order to both dilute some of the effects of more negatively charged groups
such as the Diana Circle, and to demonstrate their reverence and respect for
BRF members.

Negative emotions: grievances and grieving

Billig (1982, p. 11) notes that although 'there is no general problem about the
[monarchy] itself . . . there are all manner of specific controversies about the
conduct of its business and the character of its members.' Although publicly the Insiders and Devotees of this tribe avidly support the BRF (and in
Elizabeth's terms, 'never say anything anti-' about the monarchy), within the
confines of the tribe members feel safe to air their disapproval and grievances
over particular actions of BRF members. Thus, the members consume the
monarchy by evaluating the activities of the Royals and opining on the ways
history has unfolded or how it unfolds before them.

Given the controversy surrounding the event, it is not surprising that
airing grievances among the tribe was most prevalent at Elizabeth's TV viewing
party of Prince Charles and Camilla Parker-Bowles's wedding. Donald states
he appreciates the fact that the UK has a monarchy because he believes the
Queen's efforts mean 'there's great stability for Britain on the international
stage.' However, he later comments he is absolutely not in favour of Prince
Charles's marriage and believes he is 'speaking for the majority of the English
people when he says, "Do we have the trust for the future of this?" ' Likewise,
the unhappiness about this wedding is evident when a Danish television crew
wishes Elizabeth and her friends to stage a toast to the new couple: 'Donald
takes the champagne bottle . . . after he pours and distributes the champagne,
no one here raised a toast to Charles and Camilla; someone just said something vague like, "To the day" ' [FN (Field Notes), April 2005].

In addition to unhappiness about the goings-on in the BRF, members of
this tribe often engage in grieving behaviour, specifically mourning the loss of
Princess Diana at Kensington Palace on August 31st. Elizabeth observes that
on that day, she seems to serve the role of 'agony aunt,' as 'people cry all over
the place, it's amazing,' and Dan notes people say, 'Oh Elizabeth, what do
we do?' This mourning for what was for many a beloved (and even saintly;
Richards, 1999) member of the BRF brand enables the group members to participate in catharsis, even eight years after Diana's death. However, the airing of
grievances and sadness exists more as undercurrent in this tribe than as a core
activity, perhaps because the existence of the BRF is not really threatened.
This situation is in contrast to the virtual community surrounding the Apple
Newton, whose members are vocal in complaining about the lack of corporate
and social support for the brand (Muñiz and Schau, 2005).

Sharing consumption fantasies

On a more positive note, members of this tribe often share their desires to consume the BRF in ways that currently exist only in their imaginations. Elizabeth describes how she and three members who run a Diana Club in Germany wish to see Princess Diana more formally commemorated:

> They . . . meet about once a month . . . And they would like to – in fact I've said the same thing – to have a Diana Day but I don't think it's ever going to happen because Camilla isn't going to put up with that, is she, nor Charles, nor the Queen. So it isn't going to happen but we would like a Diana Day. What I would like is a channel on the television for the Royals . . . I think that would be nice. [June 2006]

Likewise, Dan and Elizabeth discuss the fantasy they share with Victor about going to Paris and seeing the tunnel where Diana was mortally injured:

> D: You've always wanted to go to Paris.
> E: Yes, I think I will one day, I've got a passport.
> D: We could do a B&B.
> E: I don't know whether I'm quite ready for that, to see where she [crashed], I mean Victor says that he's going to go one day, get a taxi to go through the tunnel and stop where [it happened]. I said, 'Victor, I don't think they'll let you.' He said, 'Well, I'll tell them to stop' and he wants to get out, he'll get killed . . . But that's what he wants to do.

Although in both cases there is an underlying tone of pessimism as to whether these fantasies will come true, sometimes tribe members assist Insiders by acting as compensators (Otnes, Lowrey and Kim, 1993) and providing them with gifts that may not completely fulfil their fantasies, but may become cherished nonetheless. For years, Elizabeth had mourned the fact that she was unable to fulfil her fantasy of owning one of Diana's dresses when they were auctioned at Christie's, noting 'If I'd have known then what I know now, I think I would have re-mortgaged the house and bought a dress.' Although these sacred objects remain financially out of reach, her friend Jane was aware of her desire to own something that was authentically linked to Diana:

> E: [Jane] worked at the [hotel]. And she got me the carpet in the Diana room, the green carpet.
> D: Which Diana walked on.
> E: Walked on because they [Kensington Palace] used to have their staff parties there, so Diana would have walked on that . . . when [Jane] got it home she hated it . . . and when she heard I was having the Diana room built she said, 'I'd like you to have it.' So it will always be there.

In summary, the members of this tribe consume heritage by creating sometimes kitschy, personal rituals that may run counter in temperament to those in which the BRF itself engages, by griping and grieving about the BRF, and by sharing BRF-related fantasies. Furthermore, Insiders and Devotees consume the BRF by orchestrating or fantasizing about encounters with the BRF or related items they wish they could own, while Minglers and Tourists loosely consume the BRF by enjoying themselves on a more social level, and helping the wishes and hopes of the true devotees come to fruition.

Shaping the heritage consumption experiences of a wider audience

Our second research question explores how these tribe members shape BRF-related heritage consumption experiences of an audience outside the tribe. Again, three salient themes emerged from our analysis, namely: (1) socializing and educating peripheral tribe members; (2) managing relationships with the media; and (3) adapting/spurring the evolution of rituals and traditions.

Socializing / educating peripheral tribe members

With over 7,000 pieces of BRF memorabilia, Elizabeth's home is a focal point for many socialization and education processes that occur both internally and externally to the tribe. Within this environment, Elizabeth's parties serve several socialization functions: to reinforce the tribal bonds of core members (Insiders and Devotees); educating peripheral tribe members (Minglers and Tourists) and, with the help of the media, to bring the activities of the tribe to a wider audience. On the day of Elizabeth's party to celebrate the Queen's 80th birthday, her house takes on a life of its own, as members of the tribe intermingle with members of the press. Insiders conduct many tours of the house and its exhibit for members of the media, or for first-time visitors or peripheral tribe members.

In the following exchange, Monica (an Insider) educates her brother Jay (a Tourist), by taking him on a tour of the displays. Pointing to a small travel food hamper full of traditional English foods, she explains: 'This is what came from the Windsor Exhibition. Look Jay, this is what the Queen does when she travels – look at the picnic things. This is what she takes on her travels abroad.' Through facilitating such exchanges, Elizabeth's homes acts as a type of living history museum, where snippets of information about the BRF are continually being shared and passed around, through the social interactions taking place. As Muñiz and O'Guinn (2001) highlight, such storytelling is an important way of establishing and maintaining community bonds.

Invitations to Elizabeth's parties are informal, and attendance is somewhat random, with the ultimate guest list often depending on whom she meets in the lead-up to the event. Furthermore, members of her tribe bring their friends and relations. Referring to the recent 80th birthday party, Elizabeth confesses she did not know everyone that was there:

> There was a lady here I didn't know at all. She came quite late and I still don't know who she is. Her name was Pam, she was a friend of a friend . . . I think somebody had told her to come along and whether or not she was coming with somebody else and they didn't come, but I haven't got a clue, and even when she went out the door, I still didn't know who she was.

True to her role as BRF ambassador (Otnes and Shapiro, 2007) Elizabeth is very proud of the fact that she never refuses entrance to anyone, and sees this as part of her role in supporting and perpetuating the BRF brand. Whether her visitors are international (often arriving by the busload) or local who have heard of her collection by word-of-mouth, Elizabeth welcomes all who are interested. She is happy to freely share her knowledge and her displays, and this accessibility is a key factor in socializing and educating those outside the tribe, a factor that also gains her the respect of other tribe members, including Dan:

> D: She's an ambassador because she's so available for everybody to come . . . It's like an open house.
> E: Yes, people tell people about it. I mean the next morning, you know, when GMTV were here there was a sort of noise out in the hall and I thought, that's funny because the front door was open, and it was a little girl from down the road and she said, 'I want to go round to Elizabeth's house because it's the Queen's birthday.' So her Mum brought her round before school and she was only about 5 or 6. I thought that was so sweet. It's nice when you see children take an interest.

Managing relationships with the media

As we can see in the above quote, the media that flock to Elizabeth's door are a huge attraction, not only for the tribe members, but also for outsiders curious to see what is going on at her home. Led by Elizabeth, the tribe's relationship with the media is an important factor in their ability to shape the BRF consumption experiences of a wider audience. Through the media, Elizabeth and her tribe have come to represent what the BRF brand means to ordinary English folk. Elizabeth's media appearances are actually encouraged by the BRF publicity team at Buckingham Palace, who sometimes point journalists and programme makers to her. This action reveals that even though 'the Palace' may not explicitly be aware of Elizabeth's articulation to 'never say anything anti-' about the BRF, they implicitly trust her enough to reciprocate her devotion to the Royals, even if on a minor scale.

Consequently, Elizabeth has gained considerable media expertise and savvy through her numerous media appearances over the years. Known as 'Britain's Loyalist Royalist,' she is in such demand that she often forgets by whom, and for what, she has been filmed. Recently, she bought a set of DVDs sold through a *Daily Express* promotion to commemorate the Queen's birthday, only to find that, unbeknownst to her, she and her collection were featured in one of them:

E: So I'm sitting here reading it [the promotional offer] and it says, go 'round the home of Britain's Loyalist Royalist, a Royal super fan, and marvel at the splendors of Windsor. And I thought, either someone else is calling themselves this, and it's their home, or it's me . . . It's only about three or four minutes.

D: It's very good.

E: But I'm on with the Royals, do you know what I mean? I've sort of been elevated and what did it say I was? I forget what they said I was.

D: Eccentric.

E: Yes, eccentric and charming or something like that, it's very sweet.

The relationship Elizabeth has with the media is important for the entire BRF tribe for two reasons. First, it maintains her status internally with other tribe members who see the media interest as validating her interests and, in turn, their own. Second, it enables their activities to be shared with a much wider audience. Thus, Elizabeth works hard to maintain her expertise and knowledge on all matters to do with the BRF, and to reinforce her role as the tribe's opinion leader (Venkatraman, 1989). She does this through constantly building her collection, keeping abreast of the latest royal events, and, assisted by her tribe, avidly following all the rumours and gossips. In order to ensure that she always has an opinion on current happenings, Elizabeth buys every newspaper on a daily basis that carries any article about the BRF, and has done so for 25 years:

E: So when somebody says to me, 'What paper do you take?,' it's a bit of a dumb question really!

D: You take the lot don't you?

E: Yes, I do, anything with the Royals in.

True to her belief that Royal Family items are sacred items, Elizabeth often engages in possession rituals (Belk, Wallendorf, and Sherry, 1989) with these newspapers, ironing them, refusing to cut them up to save only the BRF-related articles in them, and stacking them intact in high piles around her house. The piles bear silent testimony to all who cross her threshold that Elizabeth is quite literally the font of all knowledge about the BRF brand.

Members of the tribe support and underpin Elizabeth's relationship with the media, attending her events and making themselves readily available to help in whatever ways they can, to the point where she remarks: 'They all think they're celebrities now.' During the 80th birthday party, a German TV crew arrives to film. Members of the tribe show no hesitation in welcoming the presenter and making him feel at home with a cup of tea, and they chat unselfconsciously to him while Elizabeth prepares for filming. As filming commences, they happily accommodate any requests he makes of them, patiently and often humorously tolerating the numerous takes and retakes that occur throughout the afternoon. The filming becomes part of the fun, and communal bonds are strengthened through their shared sense of moral responsibility (Muñiz and O'Guinn, 2001) to assist Elizabeth in retaining her high profile to the rest of the world. In this way the media also become a normalized aspect of their tribal rituals, a facet of this tribe experience we explore in more detail in the next section.

Adapting / spurring the evolution of rituals and traditions

Earlier in this chapter, we highlighted how this tribe commemorates many events with its own rituals and traditions. An interesting finding to emerge from our data is that members of the BRF tribe often adapt those rituals that begin unselfconsciously as expressions among themselves, in response to external influences such as the media. Indeed, the reason Elizabeth chooses to have her party the day before the Queen's official birthday is to accommodate the media and press attention she knows it will receive, and to enable the media to release pictures or film of the party on the birthday itself. Constantly aware of the media-gaze, Elizabeth is continually adapting the contents of her parties to have more media appeal:

> E: Last time I had a party for the Queen's Jubilee, I had Australian television filming it, and who else? – CNN from America filming it. Filming my neighbours munching sandwiches! And I thought 'I've got to get something going here.' So I got a Pearly King and Queen[1] to come along because that was visual. Next year [referring to 80th party] I think I'm going to try and get . . . what do you call it when they do country dancing with sticks?
>
> I: Oh, you mean Morris dancers[2].
>
> E: Yeah, yeah. Because they're pretty, aren't they? And you need something visual.

In this excerpt we can see potential, and rather arbitrary, intersections of two long-established English traditions (Pearly Kings and Queens, and Morris dancing) with those of a BRF tribe. Elizabeth's desire to connect her tribe's activities to these other traditions, with their own sets of ritual practices, is made entirely on the grounds of their visual impact for the media. Yet, in doing so, she is also confident that these traditions can be easily incorporated into those of her tribe's, a fact that testifies to the loosely bounded nature of their rituals, as we have previously discussed. This echoes Maffesoli's (1996,

---

[1] A colourful part of London's history, the Pearly Royals date from Victorian times when they were street vendors of fruits and vegetables. Each area of London has its own King and Queen who dress in elaborate suits, hats, and dresses decorated with pearly buttons and sewn with mystic symbols.

[2] Morris dancing is a traditional English Dance performed with colourful costumes, ribbons, bells, and sticks.

p. 76) contention that neo-tribes are 'characterized by fluidity, occasional gatherings and dispersal.'

Furthermore, this fluidity is well illustrated in the adaptability of the BRF brand tribe to the media. For example, tribe members willingly adapt their singing rituals to accommodate the requests of German TV during the birthday party. Key members rally around to help put on a good show for the cameras. Wearing a gigantic, carnivalesque, red, white, and blue hat, Dan passes union jack flags and hats to everyone around the table. As they finish their first rendition of Britain's national anthem, 'God Save the Queen,' Victor spontaneously adds 'three cheers for the Queen,' and receives an enthusiastic response. This is then incorporated into the next takes. Monica draws attention to discrepancies in wording of the anthem's last line ('our' versus 'the' Queen) to ensure the tribe is singing in unison. After discussion among the tribe, Elizabeth rules it is 'our' in the first line but 'the' in the last. On the third take, the tribe gives a polished performance (complete with Victor's three cheers) as waving the flags, they participate merrily in this highly mediated ritual that goes out to the German audience. This iterative process of staging preparations, rehearsals, and final performance that occurs solely because of the media presence ensures this ritual becomes more formalized, and may be henceforth added to the tribe's repertoire of ritual practices.

In summary, this BRF tribe shapes the heritage consumption experiences of those outside the tribe by quite literally bringing history to life. Similar to the role of a living museum (an analogy that certainly applies to Elizabeth's house), the tribe draws people to it who are fascinated by the pageants its members perform, and curious about the past that they keep alive. In creating a celebrity culture around Elizabeth and, in turn, the tribe, the media play a crucial role, not only in reaching its wider audience, but also in helping to develop the performative aspects of the tribe's activities.

Discussion

Our analysis points to several ways to extend research in brand tribes. First, a key emergent finding in our text is that while some people do not participate in tribal activities, or profess interest in the focal consumption activity of interest, they may nevertheless prove to be integral to the way individual members or subgroups within a tribe interact with their beloved brand. In short, our conservative criterion for membership in the tribe (e.g., attend at least one of three BRF-related events discussed in-depth in the data) means we do not include the myriad supports who call Elizabeth when they see BRF memorabilia at antique fairs, who transport items for her, or who, like her builder, provide the facilities for her to house her collection. Furthermore, we excluded Elizabeth's four grown children from this tribe because they are not present at the BRF-related events Elizabeth hosts or attends, and because she has indicated they did not share her interest. Nevertheless, all of her children provide both financial support for her collection in the form of gifts (including some of her most treasured and expensive pieces), and much-needed emotional support at times of crisis (e.g., Elizabeth's son Arthur broke the news to her mother that Princess Diana had been killed). We therefore argue for an expanded conceptualization of types of tribe members beyond the four Kozinets advocates, to include the outsider role of Supporter. This role includes people in tribe members' social networks who do not participate in the key tribal practices Cova and Cova identify, but who nevertheless provide invaluable assistance to members. In the future, we hope to interview individuals whom we believe act as supporters for this BRF tribe, to unpack their roles and relationships to the tribe more fully.

Second, this research points to the importance of the interaction of celebrity with brand tribes. Because Elizabeth's status as a minor celebrity proves to be a magnet for some with regard to participating in her parties and events, tribe members may be participating for the sake of seeing themselves as part of the celebrity culture. Given that many celebrity-based tribes interact to some degree with their idols, and that some who follow celebrities fervently through collections or pilgrimages become opinion leaders and celebrities in their own circles (e.g., to *Star Trek* events; Kozinets, 2001), the intersection of celebrity and brand tribes is certainly worth pursuing.

Finally, the BRF actually has more active consumers outside of the UK than in (e.g., 80 per cent of the subscribers to *Royalty* magazine reside in the US; Houston, 2005). Given that the BRF is obviously integral to British heritage, it would be interesting to compare the motivations and activities of any BRF tribes in the US or in other countries (such as Australia and Canada) where the monarchy may have different meanings. Such logic could be extended to any heritage-based brand tribe where the following of the brand is more intense in markets other than where the brand originated.

References

Balmer, J.M.T., Greyser, S.A. and Urde, M. (2004). Monarchies as corporate brands. *Harvard Business School Working Papers Series*, No. 05-002.

Belk, R.W. (1995). *Collecting in a Consumer Society*. New York: Routledge.

Belk, R.W. and Costa, J.A. (1998). The mountain man myth: a contemporary consuming fantasy, *Journal of Consumer Research*, **25** (December), 218–240.

Belk, R.W., Wallendorf, M. and Sherry Jr., J.F. (1989). The sacred and profane: theodicy on the Odyssey, *Journal of Consumer Research*, **15** (June), 1–38.

Billig, M. (1982). *Talking of the Royal Family*. New York: Routledge.

Cannadine, D. (1983). The context, performance, and meaning of ritual: the British monarchy and the 'invention of tradition,' c. 1820–1977, in Hobsbawm, E. and Ranger, T. (eds.), *The Invention of Tradition*. Cambridge: Cambridge University Press, pp. 101–164.

Cova, B. (1997). Community and consumption: towards a definition of the 'linking value' of products or services, *European Journal of Marketing*, **31** (3/4), 297–316.

Cova, B. and Cova, V. (2002). Tribal marketing: the tribalisation of society and its impact on the conduct of marketing, *European Journal of Marketing*, **36** (5/6), 595–620.

Davison, G. (1991). *The Meanings of Heritage*. North Sydney: Allen and Unwin.

Goulding, C. (1999). Contemporary museum culture and consumer behavior, *Journal of Marketing Management*, **15**, 647–671.

Goulding, C. (2001). Romancing the past: heritage visiting and the nostalgic consumer, *Psychology and Marketing*, **18** (6), 565–592.

Hirschman, E.C. and Holbrook, M.B. (1982). The experiential aspects of consumption: consumer fantasies, feelings, and fun, *Journal of Consumer Research*, **9**, 132–140.

Kozinets, R.V. (1999). E-tribalized marketing? The strategic implications of virtual communities of consumption, *European Management Journal*, **17** (3), 252–264.

Kozinets, R.V. (2001). Utopian enterprise: articulating the meaning of *Star Trek*'s culture of consumption, *Journal of Consumer Research*, **28** (June), 67–88.

Lowenthal, D. (1998). *The Heritage Crusade and the Spoils of History*. Cambridge: Cambridge University Press.

Maffesoli, M. (1996). *The Time of the Tribes*. London: Sage.

Muñiz, A. and O'Guinn, T.C. (2001). Brand community, *Journal of Consumer Research*, **27** (March), 412–432.

Muñiz, A. and Schau, H.J. (2005). Religiosity in the abandoned apple brand community, *Journal of Consumer Research*, **31** (September), 737–747.

O'Guinn, T.C. and Belk, R.W. (1989). Heaven on earth: Consumption at Heritage Village, USA, *Journal of Consumer Research*, **16** (September), 227–238.

Otnes, C.C., Lowrey, T.M. and Kim, Y.C. (1993). Gift selection for 'easy' and 'difficult' recipients: a social roles interpretation, *Journal of Consumer Research*, **20** (September 1993), 229–244.

Otnes, C.C. and Lowrey, T.M. (2004). *Contemporary Consumption Rituals: A Research Anthology*. Mahwah, NJ: Lawrence Erlbaum Associates.

Otnes, C.C. and Shapiro, E.N. (2007). How brand collecting shapes consumers' brand meanings, in Belk, R.W. and Sherry, J.F. (eds.), *Consumer Culture Theory*, forthcoming.

Price, L.L., Arnould, E.J. and Curasi C.F. (2000). Older Americans' disposition of special possessions, *Journal of Consumer Research*, **27** (September), 179–201.

Richards, J. (1999). *Diana, The Making of a Media Saint*. London: I.B. Tauris.

Rook, D.W. (1985). The ritual dimension of consumer behavior, *Journal of Consumer Research*, **12** (December), 252–264.

Wikpedia.org, Commonwealth of Nations. wikipedia.org/wiki/British Commonwealth.

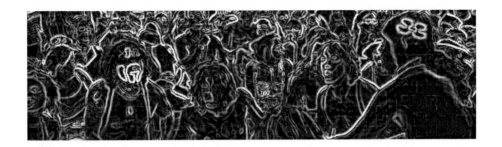

5

The evolution of
a subculture of
consumption

John W. Schouten, Diane M. Martin
and James H. McAlexander

Introduction

The power of an elegant theory lies partially in its contextuality. Each new idea, each turn in our understanding is situated in time, space, and our evolution as scholars. Meanings and the knowledge associated with them change over time. The modernity project continues to exact different behaviours from humans, and our understanding of those behaviours must keep pace. As our wider culture evolves, subcultures of consumption also evolve, taking on new shapes and forms, leaving behind old meanings and developing new ones.

In this chapter, we examine the evolution of one such subculture. The authors have been engaged ethnographically with Harley-Davidson owners continuously since the beginning of the seminal work on subcultures of consumption (Schouten and McAlexander, 1995). During those years we have expanded the scope of the ethnography to include many contexts outside of the times and spaces of the original inquiry. More importantly perhaps, we began to reexamine our own underlying assumptions as embedded in the hegemonic perspective of the straight white male.

We address the evolution of the Harley-Davidson subculture in three stages. First, we briefly describe the original research (1990–1994) and the foundational insights at the heart of a theory of subcultures of consumption. We then describe how on-going ethnographic engagement in a subculture of consumption (2004-present) reveals evolutionary change. We address changes we have observed and the forces behind them. Next, we recount how a critical turn (Martin, Schouten, and McAlexander, 2006) enriched our understanding of the subculture by uncovering knowledge and perspectives that previously had eluded us. Finally, we invite a fresh and contemporary look at foundational theories of consumer behaviour, critically examining the contextual assumptions in practice at the time of their emergence.

The original study in retrospective

Part of what made the new bikers, that is, the post-outlaw subculture of Harley-Davidson owners, interesting from a consumer behaviour perspective was their apparent homogeneity and their extraordinary brand loyalty. Even more interesting to us was the fact that no one to date had ever fully acknowledged and studied the remarkable power of consumption to organize consumers into social collectives.

The activities and findings of our original 3+ years ethnography are a matter of record (Schouten and McAlexander, 1995). Briefly, we posited that a subculture of consumption exhibits a homogeneous ethos of core values and expressions, and that it displays a hierarchical social structure based on authenticity and commitment to a well-understood ideology of consumption. In the Harley-Davidson subculture we highlighted the core values of personal freedom, patriotic Americanism, and machismo. We examined socialization processes by which new members entered the subculture, gained legitimacy within it, and experienced varying degrees of identity transformation. We concluded that certain characteristics of a consumption subculture, such as its apparent stability and longevity, and the robustness with which it co-creates product and brand meanings with the firm, made it especially interesting from a marketing standpoint.

The relatively monolithic subculture we observed and embraced as ethnographers was partly the product of larger cultural and demographic movements, such as the emptying of baby-boomer nests and collective mid-life crisis. It was not, however, a mere accident of social forces. Harley-Davidson, Inc., through its participation in rallies and events and its adept management of the Harley Owners Group (HOG), helped to consolidate and cultivate the subculture in a fashion that was completely consistent with management of the relationships detailed in 'Building Brand Community' (McAlexander, Schouten, and Koenig, 2002).

Market forces and subculture change

Subcultures of consumption present obvious opportunities for marketers. Their members take active roles in the co-creation with marketers of brand meanings, of styles, of product categories and modifications, and of social and technical support systems. The effects of a subculture on a market are just half the story. The other half is the effects of the market on a subculture of consumption. Because they are essentially artefacts of the marketplace, subcultures of consumption feel the effects of market forces more so than other subcultures, such as those with ethnicity or religion at their foundations.

The rise to prominence of the Harley-Davidson subculture, the rescue of the company from financial ruin, and the renewal of the brand all helped to fuel a renaissance in American motorcycling. As the cultural and material contexts of motorcycling have changed, the Harley-Davidson owner base has evolved with them. Some of the more important change agents include market growth, increased familiarity of the general public with Harley-Davidson, improved competition from other motorcycle manufacturers, increasing diversity of riders, changing motorcycle fashions and the effects of popular culture, and aging rider demographics.

As ethnographers, with the support of Harley-Davidson, Inc., we have catalogued many of the effects of these market forces. Collectively during the past decade we have ridden many thousands of miles on different kinds of motorcycles. We have engaged in participant observation at scores of events. We have conducted hundreds of hours of depth interviews and focus group discussions. We have focused our attention beyond the predominantly white, male, baby-boom population that fueled the growth of the Harley-Davidson market to include more women, more Gen-Xers, more echo-boomers, and more ethnic minorities. In these intervening years we have witnessed the death of the relatively monolithic subculture of consumption that we first encountered. In its place we have observed the emergence of something larger and richer, something we are more comfortable thinking about as a complex brand community or a mosaic of microcultures.

Market growth has played a central role in subculture evolution. Harley-Davidson sales have grown dramatically and steadily over the past 15 years. In the early 1990s, when we began our ethnographic work, the Motor Company was shipping about 70,000 motorcycles annually. Harley-Davidson production and sales passed 100,000 units in 1998, and in 2005 the Motor Company shipped more than 325,000 Harley-Davidson branded motorcycles. While hundreds of thousands of new riders have acquired Harley-Davidson motorcycles in the past decade, many others have purchased look-alike bikes from Honda, Yamaha, Kawasaki, Suzuki, and Polaris.

One result of this massive sales growth is ubiquity and a fundamental shift in how the non-riding public views bikers. In the early 1990s, most people didn't personally know anyone who dressed in black leather and rode a Harley-Davidson. Their points of reference were primarily mass-mediated, and the dominant media portrayal was the outlaw biker. Now, however, it seems like everybody knows somebody who rides a Harley-Davidson, and that person is likely to be their dad, their uncle, their neighbour, their boss, or increasingly their mom or the lady next door. The outlaw biker stereotype has become a cliché, the biker image has lost its sharp edges, and the intimidating biker no longer serves as the public's dominant frame of reference.

Improved competitor products have also had an impact on the subculture. In our original ethnographic work we found the Harley-Davidson subculture to be a rather insular group within the motorcycle riding community. Part of this insularity was reinforced by the Motor Company. HOG, the official corporate-sponsored owners club, largely limits participation at its events to Harley-Davidson owners. That stance, though, also reflected the attitudes of Harley owners. We observed that Harley owners generally rode only with other Harley owners and routinely derided non-Harley motorcycles as crotch rockets, rice burners, or wannabes. A refrain that we heard many times was 'There are two kinds of motorcycle riders: Harley owners and those that wish they had a Harley.'

Japanese 'Harley clones' or 'metric cruisers' have so closely approximated the Harley look and sound that even experts occasionally do double-takes to tell the difference. Japanese manufacturers have also filled an unmet need for smaller, less expensive alternatives to the Harley line-up. The generation that grew up with imported automobiles and electronics has demonstrated a higher degree of acceptance of Japanese cruiser-style motorcycles. While pockets of xenophobia still exist, Japanese motorcycle bashing is no longer the norm. Now when we attend motorcycle rallies at Sturgis and Daytona we often find Japanese motorcycles parked next to Harleys, something that was previously a rarity. We have also participated in several Honda Hoots (a Honda-sponsored rally that invites motorcyclists independent of brand ownership) and found a considerable number of Harley-Davidsons parked in the lot and Harley owners enjoying the camaraderie of this inclusive motorcycle community event. As competitor bikes have gained market acceptance and legitimacy, the breakdown in the in-group/out-group barrier has multiplied the definitions of authenticity in the world of bikers.

The American motorcycling renaissance has attracted an increasingly diverse population of motorcyclists to the sport. That diversity has led to a broader range of meanings attached to motorcycles and to riders. In current popular culture, the heroes and outlaws who ride motorcycles are more likely to be seen in brightly coloured leathers and riding sport bikes than in black and riding Harley-Davidsons. Furthermore, they are more likely than ever to be female, such as Lara Croft or Charlie's Angels, or non-white, as seen in movies like *Biker Boyz*. As Hollywood has focused on a new kind of biker icon, Harley-Davidson seem to have become less fashionable among certain segments of style-conscious consumers. Among affluent baby boomers we have interviewed once-faithful Harley 'defectors' who have left the brand, either for more exotic bikes, such as Ducatis or custom choppers, or for non-motorcycle pursuits, such as sailboat racing.

The other real impact of changing fashion on the subculture is among youth. We find this notable because in our early ethnographic efforts we chronicled what we thought was a clear trans-generational appeal of the brand. In our experience as ethnographers it appears that American youth, especially among Whites, Asians, and African-Americans, have embraced sport bikes and racing styles and have largely turned an indifferent eye towards the traditional Harley-Davidson style of motorcycles and riding. In one notable exception, many young Latinos seem to be embracing the Harley-Davidson brand and style. Although we have seen no statistical evidence, we have interviewed several second-generation Latino males who have purchased or desire to own Harley-Davidsons, which they value as a symbol of American freedoms, affluence, and unambiguous masculinity. For somewhat different reasons, as we shall see shortly, many women, including young aspiring riders, also gravitate to the Harley-Davidson over the racier sport bike.

A critical turn

Our interest in women bikers began as a simple artefact of women's enormous market potential in the face of an increasingly saturated market of affluent male riders. Until recently our findings had been more or less immune to the critical turn in which ethnographers challenge hegemonic interpretive positions and seek voices and viewpoints not commonly recognized by an academy steeped in straight, white, male and Western traditions.

Challenged publicly for our own hegemonic stance (Thompson, 2002), we followed author Martin's lead in revisiting our ethnographic corpus from a feminist perspective in order to uncover gendered assumptions in the original work and to better explore the richness of women's motorcycling experiences. The study recounted here only briefly has been published elsewhere (Martin et al., 2006), and we invite the reader to refer to it for additional detail.

In approaching Harley-Davidson ownership as gendered consumer behaviour we began with the following questions: What does it mean to be a woman consumer in a hypermasculine consumption context? Do women riders embrace or resist hegemonic masculinity? Or do they somehow do both? What more can a critical turn reveal about feminine versus masculine ways of knowing and doing?

To address these questions we conducted participant observation at multiple motorcycle events, including a long-distance, multi-day, multi-state rally that included several women as riders of their own motorcycles as well as several woman passengers. As a participant observer Diane Martin completed two different rider-training courses with other woman students and purchased her own motorcycle from a female former owner. Finally, we conducted formal in-home depth interviews with 18 woman riders in two major metropolitan areas. In our analysis, we drew from three feminist perspectives: liberal feminism, women's voice/experience feminism, and poststructuralist feminism. We deconstructed the major themes from the original ethnography, examining them through the voices of women riders, and we allowed for the emergence of additional themes.

Privileging women's voices and experiences forced us to complicate our understanding of social structure in the subculture. While it remains true that member status is based on perceptions of commitment and authenticity, this study revealed those constructs to be much more richly layered than we previously believed. A woman undergoes a radical shift in status by moving from the passenger seat of a man's bike to the saddle of her own machine. The occasion is much more momentous than that of a man learning to ride and purchasing a bike. Against a backdrop of hypermasculine assumptions and posturing the woman's accomplishment is viewed as more remarkable, not only by the men in her social circle, but also by the woman herself.

In some ways women who ride have more options for participation in the subculture. For example, they tend to feel they can move at will between riding their own bikes and being passengers on men's bikes without lessening their status as women who ride. The same option is not open to self-respecting straight males, who would be chided mercilessly for 'riding bitch'. Women riders find that male riders often cut them more slack than other women riders do. We have encountered women riders who take offense at other women riders choosing to ride the passenger seat. It is as if the latter were 'selling out the revolution' by not exercising their rights and abilities to pilot their own bikes.

By listening to women's voices we learned that women riders have defined their own standards of authenticity in the subculture. Some women, depending on their sociocultural contexts, still borrow from outlaw bikers for their measures of authenticity. As women they cannot be fully participating club members, but as riders of their own motorcycles they escape the status of chattel accorded to all other women in outlaw biker clubs. Most riders, however, both male and female, no longer see outlaw clubs as necessary or relevant touchstones of authenticity.

Women riders establish their own authenticities in the context of women's ways of riding. Many reject hyper-male notions of speed, visceral intensity, and long distances between stops as marks of authenticity. Instead some favour slower paces, more sensory riding experiences, and more frequent and qualitatively different kinds of stops. For example, most men tend to orient themselves to riding hard and stopping only for gas and food, whereas for many woman riders a meandering ride connecting two or three antique shops and a café is a perfectly legitimate and authentic motorcycling experience.

Women also can gain status and authenticity through acts of resistance to the hegemonic male subculture. Ironically, they tend to do it through anti-male rhetoric that is almost macho in its provocative tone. One of our favourite helmet stickers reads, 'I got a Harley for my husband. It was a good trade.' The common theme running through such speech is resistance to masculine sites of power and authenticity, demonstrated here as access to put-down humour. The same helmet sticker on a female passenger would be incongruous.

The prevalence of resistance to male control serves to underscore the fact that motorcycling is still predominantly a boys' club. Most women's socialization to motorcycles came through a man, usually from riding on the back of a man's bike or, more rarely, riding their own bikes in the company of fathers and brothers in a rural setting. In only one case that we have encountered, an informant learned to ride due to the influence of her mother, a life-long motorcyclist. In recent years the incidence of women as leaders and role models is increasing rapidly. Several informants are actively trying to persuade peers or daughters to take up riding. In many HOG chapters women riders are taking over the affiliated Ladies of Harley organization and changing it from a women's auxiliary into a women's riding group. In Atlanta a woman who goes by 'Sunshine' operates a women-only riding school.

When we deconstructed the ethos of the subculture we found that women also claim the core values of personal freedom and machismo, but how they define and embrace these concepts is very different. The value of Americanism received much less emphasis.

Freedom is defined in terms of constraints. Women riders define personal freedom differently than men for the simple fact that they face different constraints in the first place. Learning to ride a motorcycle is a means of breaking free of constraining femininities that would confine women to subordinate categories such as 'arm candy', 'just a girl', or 'just a mom'. For example, one informant enjoys firing up her motorcycle in defiance of what she perceives to be the judgments of the snooty suburban neighbourhood tennis moms. Another learned to ride in part to spite her parents' limiting interpretations of appropriate girls' roles and behaviours. For many women, riding their own bikes is a means of exercising freedom and control over their own bodies. Being in control of the machine means taking responsibility for their own safety. It means having the prerogative to stop where and when they want. It means being fully engaged in the activity.

Machismo or hypermasculinity as a value serves women differently than it does men. Women engage it as a means of redefining, complicating, and expanding their own femininities. A woman riding a motorcycle attracts attention. Several informants feel that a bike enhances the power of their feminine sexuality, and they tend to accessorize their bikes and riding wardrobes with feminine touches to make an unambiguous statement about their gender orientations. For other informants, engaging in hypermasculine consumption behaviours functions as a counterbalance to traditional feminine roles. They do not resent their more traditional roles as moms or wives, but they feel strongly that they don't want to be judged as shallowly, boringly, or one-dimensionally feminine. For still other informants, hypermasculine behaviour is an acid test for personal competency and self-confidence. We have heard several variations on the theme, 'I thought if I could do this I could do anything.'

Conclusion

This is a story about evolution on two fronts. It is about social evolution within a subculture of consumption, but it is also about evolving as scholars of consumer behaviour. It underscores the need for sustained ethnographic engagement if we wish to keep current our understanding of a subculture that will and must undergo constant change. It also underscores the need for critical perspectives and approaches if we wish to understand a subculture at any level below or beyond that which is easily accessible from a single hegemonic viewpoint.

A subculture of consumption is about shared consumption values and decisions about commitment and authenticity. Meaning is negotiated by all participants in the subculture, whether from the consumer side or the marketing side, but in the past it was arbitrated from a viewpoint that is hegemonic, narrow, exclusive, and contextual.

As artefacts of the market, subcultures of consumption are particularly subject to market forces. The mystique of a subculture can contribute greatly to the popularity of a particular brand or activity. This, along with good marketing, attracts more players and fuels growth. Growth increases diversity. The empowerment of subcultural 'others', (i.e., non-male, non-white, non-straight, etc.) in social life tends also to increase the liberalization or democratization of subcultures of consumption. Diversity opens the symbolism of a subculture to other contexts and lived experiences, leading to multiple meanings and multiple authenticities. This also challenges and undermines the authority of the hegemonic perspective.

When contemporary researchers return to foundational research with the clear-eyed perspective of time, history, and longitudinal engagement, patterns of change and development are immediately evident. In this chapter, we advance a working framework for a theory of subculture evolution. Moreover, adding gravity to the example of Thompson, Stern and Arnould (1998), who conducted a critical reexamination of Arnould's (1989) original ethnography of indigenous Nigerian women, this chapter also calls for a wider application of critical re-inquiry into the underlying assumptions and conclusions of the classics of consumer research.

How many of the theories that we hold dear and cite religiously are inherently limited by the hegemonic perspective of an academy that automatically and unquestioningly presumes maleness, whiteness, heterosexuality, able-ness, affluence, and Western-ness as default conditions of experience and perspective? Our own attempt at corrective critical research represents a small step in the direction of questioning hegemony, but it still falls far short. We have attempted to overcome the single assumption of maleness as the default interpretive standpoint, and may have succeeded partly. Yet we are still guilty of assigning 'other' status to large swathes of the Harley-Davidson owner base that are not of white European extraction, that ride with physical disabilities, or that perform gender from gay or lesbian orientations. We close with an open invitation to other researchers to critique, challenge, and expand our understanding from these and any other perspectives that we have inevitably failed to represent.

Acknowledgements

We express our deepest gratitude to our friends and colleagues at Harley-Davidson, Inc. Without their continuing support for ethnographic research none of the work reported here would have been possible.

References

Arnould, E.J. (1989). Toward a broadening of preference formation and the diffusion of innovations: cases from Zinder Province, Niger Republic, *Journal of Consumer Research*, **6** (2), 239–367.

Martin, D.M., Schouten, J.W. and McAlexander, J.H. (2006). Claiming the throttle: multiple femininities in a hyper-masculine subculture, *Consumption, Markets and Culture*, **9** (3), 171–205.

McAlexander, J.H., Schouten, J.W. and Koenig, H.J. (2002). Building brand community, *Journal of Marketing*, **66** (January), 38–54.

Schouten, J.W. and McAlexander, J.H. (1995). Subcultures of consumption: an ethnography of the new bikers, *Journal of Consumer Research*, **22** (June), 43–61.

Thompson, C.J. (2002). Re-inquiry on re-inquiries: a postmodern proposal for a critical-reflexive approach, *Journal of Consumer Research*, **29** (1), 142–146.

Thompson, C.J., Stern, B.B. and Arnould, E.J. (1998). Writing the differences: poststructuralist pluralism, retextualization, and the construction of reflexive ethnographic narratives in consumption and market research, *Consumption, Markets, and Culture*, **2** (2), 105–231.

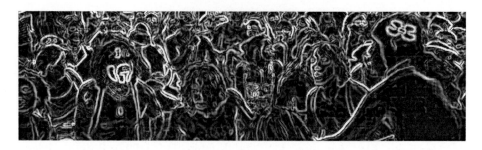

6

Metro/Fashion/Tribes of men: negotiating the boundaries of men's legitimate consumption

Diego Rinallo

Introduction

Today, fashion speaks to men. This development represents a cultural revolution respect to previous articulations of fashion discourse, that used to focus on women to the exclusion of men. For years, when targeting fashion-conscious men, marketers have produced representations of male beauty and appearance shaped by gay aesthetics. The resulting convergence in style between straight and gay men resulted according to some social observers (e.g., Colman, 2005) in the decreased reliability of the 'gaydar', the emic term employed in the gay subculture of consumption to refer to the ability to identify sexual orientation from style-related consumption (Kates, 2002).

When read in terms of subcultural theory, the filtering of gay aesthetics into the mainstream is problematic. The commodification of the stylistic choices of a subculture into mainstream fashion is said to result in active resistance by members of the subculture, who adopt new styles (Clarke, 1986; Gottdiener, 1985; Hebdige, 1979). Marketers that co-opt and soften elements of a subculture to make them more appealing to mainstream consumers incur 'the risk of alienating hard-core members, corrupting the subculture, and diluting its original appeal' (Schouten and McAlexander, 1995, p. 59). With explicit reference to gay consumers, Kates (2002) highlights the oppositional nature of their subcultural consumption practices, which are renegotiated through boundary work in relation the heterosexual, mainstream culture. Under this perspective, marketers' metrosexualization of straight consumers 'should' result in gay consumers' active boundary maintenance. However, the research findings here proposed do not support this idea and suggest alternative outcomes of subcultural style commodification.

In a world of fragmentation, an increased similarity between straight and gay men – at least with respect to attitudes towards fashion and appearance – is hardly surprising. Postmodern tribes are defined as 'a network of heterogeneous persons – in terms of age, sex, income, etc. – who are linked by a shared passion or emotion' (Cova and Cova, 2002, p. 602). While only a minority of consumers, the so-called 'fashion victims', could be considered as a tribe à la Maffesoli (1996) in a strict sense, marketers of fashion products could benefit from the application of one of the basic tenets of tribal marketing, that is the fact that consumers value goods mostly for their contribution to establish or reinforce bonds between individuals (Cova, 1997; Cova and Cova, 2002). Fashion, after all, is about the creation of social bonds, as it ensures consumers that they will fit into a given social setting (Thompson and Haytko, 1997).

This book chapter examines recent developments in the marketing discourse around masculinity centred upon the so-called 'metrosexuals', that is male consumers living in or near metropolitan areas who adopt the aesthetic sensibility often associated with gay men (Simpson, 2002), and contrasts them with the lived experience of fashion-conscious straight and gay men in Italy. My approach is similar to the one adopted by Holt and Thompson (2004, p. 425), as I analyse the construction of masculine identity 'as it moves through two moments of cultural production – mass culture discourse and everyday consumption practices'. Unlike previous studies in consumption culture theory on men's consumption and media representations of masculinity (Belk and Costa, 1998; Holt and Thompson, 2004; Kates, 2002; Patterson and Elliott, 2002; Schouten and McAlexander, 1995; Schroeder and Zwick, 2004; Sherry et al., 2004), however, I investigated both straight and gay men following developments in the sociology of masculinities. Gender dynamics, it is argued, can be usefully analysed *within* as well as *between* genders (Connell, 1992; Carrigan, Connell and Lee, 2002).

This chapter is structured as follows. Firstly, I examine the cultural production of the metrosexual by advertising agencies, marketers and other marketplace actors in the context of the traditional discourse of men's fashion. Secondly, I provide methodological details about my informants, data gathering and analysis procedures. In the sections that follow, I report my research findings regarding:

(i) reading strategies of media representations of men by straight and gay consumers;

(ii) the symbolic horizon of straight men's consumption and the renegotiation of the boundaries of gender-legitimate consumption;

(iii) gay consumers reactions to the filtering of gay aesthetics into straight men's consumption.

I conclude by theorizing on alternative outcomes of the commodification of subcultural style and by arguing that the approach adopted by most marketers to entice straight men are flawed as they do not take into consideration the basic principles of tribal marketing.

Marketplace actors and the cultural production of fashionable masculinities

Fashionable representations of masculinity have to face centuries-old cultural taboos. As sharply noted by Craik (1994, p. 176), the discourse of men's fashion has long been centred upon a set of denials:

> that there is no men's fashion; that men dress for fit and comfort, rather than for style; that women dress men and buy clothes for them; that men who dress up are peculiar (one way or another); that man do not notice clothes; and that most men have not been duped into the endless pursuit of seasonal fads.

The idea of fashion-unconscious men may be traced back to early fashion theorists, who observed the diffusion, in the decades following the French Revolution, of the so-called 'Great Masculine Renunciation' (Flügel, 1930), that is the principle that men should dress in the same, dark uniform as other men in order not to call attention to themselves as objects of beauty, and leave the more varied and elaborate forms of ornamentation that were prevalent among the aristocracy to the use of women. The construction of fashion as a woman's preoccupation has made men's interest in fashion and appearance at the very best 'suspect' of effeminacy or, even worse, of homosexuality (Crane, 2000; Davis, 1992); a fair suspicion, as fashion has long been a primary method of reciprocal identification for gay man (Cole, 2000). In more recent years, however, mass media representations of masculinity have fostered a renegotiation of gender boundaries (Bordo, 1999; Patterson and Elliott, 2002).

In the 1980s, men's lifestyle magazines proposed to their audiences (and advertisers) a 'new man', more in touch with his feminine side and not afraid of caring about his physical aspect (Mort, 1996; Nixon, 1993, 1996). In the 1990s, as the 'new man' was criticized for being unrealistic, a new generation of men's lifestyle magazines proposed a new representation of masculinity, the less feminine and soft 'new lad' (Crewe, 2003). In the first years of the new millennium, history repeated itself with the media hype surrounding metrosexuals (Simpson, 2002). In June 2002, journalist Mark Simpson authored an article on the online magazine *Salon.com* in which he introduced his audience to the 'metrosexual', a term he had previously coined (Simpson, 1994) to refer to male consumers living in or near metropolitan areas, who spend significant amount of time and money on their appearance and lifestyles and who, although most often straight, tend to embody the aesthetic sensibility frequently associated with gay men. The tone of Simpson's writing on the subject reminds the so-called 'compensatory consumption thesis' (Holt and Thompson, 2004) popularized by many scholars and social observers (e.g., Kimmel, 1996): men, whose identity is threatened by major economic and social changes in society, seek to 'symbolically reaffirm their status as real men through compensatory consumption' (Holt and Thompson, 2004, p. 425). In Simpson's words, metrosexuality refers to a man 'less certain of his identity and much more interested in his image . . . A man, in other words, who is an advertiser's walking wet dream' (Simpson, 2002, p. 1).

In light of Simpson's sarcastic remarks, it is ironical that the term metrosexual was soon after employed by the multinational advertising company Euro RSCG, which issued in June 2003 a research report that represented metrosexuals as an existing and viable market segment. Interestingly, while in Simpson's original definition the sexual orientation of a metrosexual is irrelevant, Euro RSCG's (2003) report and the subsequent media hype have constructed metrosexuals as straight men. In a curious case of synchronicity, in the same months the newly launched television show 'Queer eye for the straight guy' started representing the consumption practices stereotypically associated to gay men as 'disarticulated from its referent and resignified as metrosexuality' (Miller, 2005, p. 112).

Sustained by Euro RSCG's publicity and the media craze surrounding it, metrosexuality enjoyed substantial worldwide visibility. Mass culture representations of metrosexuality have recently included countless articles on the news media all around the world (e.g., Hackbarth, 2003; St. John, 2003), a few books (Flocker, 2003; Hyman, 2004), a tarot deck, and a 2003 episode of the television show South Park. Fashion designers, including Dolce and Gabbana and Giorgio Armani, were among the first of countless marketers to launch metrosexual-inspired new products and collections. The term metrosexual was voted by the American Dialect Society the 2003 word of the year for its domination of the US discourse, and now accounts for more than 1,800,000 hits in popular internet search engines as google.com. Several tests are now available on the Internet to help men measuring their degree of metrosexuality.

After a couple of years of undisputed attention, the metrosexual was deposed by his self-nominated successor, the übersexual. According to the term's creators, the descriptor 'über' was chosen 'because of its connotation of being the greatest, the best'. Übersexuals are thus 'the most attractive (not just physically), most dynamic, and most compelling men of their generations. They are supremely confident (without being obnoxious), masculine, stylish, and committed to uncompromising quality in all areas of life' (Salzman,

Matathia and O'Reilly, 2005, p. 76). Similarly to what happened in the 1980s and 1990s when the new lad substituted the softer new man, here again the metrosexual was substituted by the harder – but equally style addict – übersexual. As fashionable masculinities rise and fall, marketplace actors remain behind the media halo surrounding 'cool' definitions of masculinity. Ms. Salzman is one of the authors of Euro RSCG International's (2003) report on the metrosexual and both of her co-authors are involved in the advertising business at multi-national agencies that investigate/construct trends in consumer society to better serve their corporate customers.

Today, marketplace organizations employ the media arena to 'sell' their own version of masculinities, and are doing so at an accelerated pace. For marketers in many consumer goods industries, straight men are the other half of the sky, as female consumers represent a mature market unlikely to show dramatic growth in the years to come and gay men, in spite of their increased visibility in society and great potential as a market segment, are still a minority. This is not a new development: 'new men' and 'new lads' were both a creation of glossy men's magazines that aimed to sell their advertisers a valuable target group (Crewe, 2003). Today, the cultural production of masculinities is a diffused process that see the cooperation of countless marketers, advertising agencies, market research companies, news media and magazine publishers that, as moved by an invisible hand, conspire to reassure straight consumers of the appropriateness of caring about their look. To use Simpson's (2005, p. 1) sharp comments, marketers 'imagine the way to persuade billions of men to buy more product is to keep telling them there's nothing faggy about being . . . faggy'.

When we move through the circuit of culture from mass media representations of masculinities to the consumption practices of real men, the developments here described appear problematic. According to some, a number of today's men have an attitude of indifference to having their sexual orientation misinterpreted, as they embrace consumption practices neither straight nor gay but lying in between, in a grey area of 'gay vagueness' (Colman, 2005). While continuously reassured by marketers of the manly nature of, say, wearing pink shirts, shaving their bodies or going to spas, straight men have, however, to face centuries-old prejudices against these consumption practices. The risk they incur is the same faced by dandies in the eighteenth century: being perceived as effeminate or homosexual. The heterosexual characterization of metrosexuality by Euro RSCG may be seen as an antidote to the difficulties in promoting these 'risky' practices to straight male consumers. Similarly, the launch of the übersexual may be seen as a move towards further reassuring straight male consumers of the gender-appropriateness of the same consumption practices.

Method

To analyse the construction of the male identity in the sphere of consumption, I generated textual data from both straight and gay male consumers through

Table 6.1 Age and occupation of informants

Straight informants		Gay informants	
Age	**Occupation**	**Age**	**Occupation**
22	Undergraduate student	21	Undergraduate student
24	MSc student	23	MSc student
25	MSc student	24	MSc student
25	MSc student	25	MSc student
26	Research analyst	27	Sales representative
29	Sales representative	30	Fashion executive
33	Teacher	34	Public relations executive
37	Bank executive	38	Photographer

long, phenomenological interviews (McCracken, 1988; Thompson, Locander and Pollio, 1989). My informants were 16 fashion-conscious men, aged 20 to 38 years old, living in or near metropolitan areas in Italy, equally split between sexual orientations. While informants where selected having in mind the metrosexual's profile, none of them actively identified himself as one and, in a few cases, were not even aware of the meaning of the term. Background varied in terms of upbringing, education, occupation and level of fashion consciousness. Gay informants also varied in terms of the visibility of their sexual orientation to significant others (family, friends, co-workers). All participants in the study were assured of anonymity and are here identified through pseudonyms. Table 6.1 provides a list of informants together with key background information.

Interviews were semi-structured and lasted from a minimum of 90 min to – in two cases – more than 4h. 'Grand tour' questions regarding the informant's background were followed by open-ended questions regarding the topics of the present study: media representations of masculinity and informants' consumption practices related to fashion and, more in general, physical appearance. At appropriate moments during the interviews, a photoelicitation technique (Heisley and Levy, 1991) was employed: to enrich narratives and overcome difficulties in speaking of gender-related issues, I exposed informants to selected representations of masculinity taken from men's lifestyle magazines. All interviews were videotaped, transcribed and subsequently analysed and interpreted following the methodological procedures outlined in Spiggle (1994).

When men look at other men: reading strategies of straight and gay consumers

A central concept in scholarship about the practices of looking is the gaze, which was brought to prominence by Laura Mulvey (1975). The feminist film-maker and writer employed psychoanalysis to suggest that the convention of popular narrative cinema position women as the passive object of a 'male gaze'. The female body, in other words, is offered as a spectacle for the pleasure of male, heterosexual viewers. The resulting objectification of women thus reproduces the disadvantaged positions of women in patriarchal societies. Mulvey's ideas are echoed by art historian John Berger (1972) who, in his analysis of the classic Western tradition of images, suggests that men tend to be depicted in action and women as object to be looked at.

Changes in mass culture representations of women and men led, however, to reconsider the concept of the gaze, to account for the male body as object of the gaze and the pleasure of female spectators (Sturken and Cartwright, 2001). Among others, Bordo (1999) astutely noted that men are now portrayed as passive objects of a sexual, desiring gaze offered to an undefined other: male of female, straight or gay. In consumer culture theory, Patterson and Elliott (2002) referred to this phenomenon as the 'inversion of the male gaze' and proposed that men can adopt multiple subject positions in the consumption of media representations of masculinity, resulting in processes of negotiation and renegotiation of the male identity. Adding to this debate, Schroeder and Zwick (2004) suggested that certain upper-class men have always paid attention to their appearance and contended that the gaze has expanded, rather than merely inverted, to include new possibilities for male identity within the boundaries of gender opposition.

Men may thus consume visual representations of masculinities in many manners. Figure 6.1 synthesizes my informants' most common reading strategies in dealing with the idealized images of male beauty proposed by men's lifestyle magazines and other cultural products. An interpretive strategy

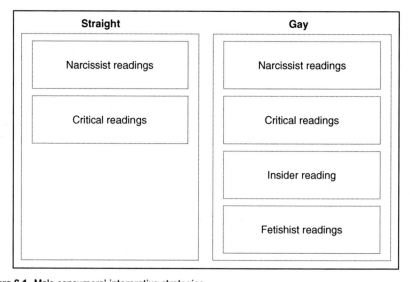

Figure 6.1 Male consumers' interpretive strategies.

shared by straight and gay men consists of *narcissistic readings* (Patterson and Elliott, 2002). A narcissistic reading of male imagery entails desiring what one would like to become:

> Well, his [an ad model's] physique is very sculpted . . . but I'm becoming like that myself, just give me time . . . His tattoos are too cool, I'd like to have one . . . Of course, If I had the physique he has, tattoos would look much different on me . . .
>
> (Davide, 24 years old, straight)

Davide admires the statuesque beauty of the advertising model's sculpted physique. He compares his own body with the model's – a contest that cannot be won – and admits he is not built enough for tattooing. The model however embodies an aspiration ideal which (perhaps unrealistically) is not considered impossible to attain (Hirschman and Thompson, 1997). Davide's words evoke the image of a statuesque physique adorned with tattoos which becomes the object of somebody's admiring gaze. Such gaze may be female, but not necessarily as other (straight) men may be an equally possible audience:

> The gym's locker room . . . is the place where a men shows the Narcissus inside himself . . . because locker rooms are full of mirrors, you know? Because there you undress, step out of the shower and look at yourself . . . you gaze at yourself, you admire yourself, you look at how you are and how you could improve . . . I spent a lot of time in front of these mirrors . . . Often, we stand in briefs and tell each other 'look at the arms . . . the thighs . . . the quadriceps'. [In these moments] everybody likes himself and wants to be appreciated by the other guys . . . Even among guys . . . It may seem odd but . . . Do you understand? Even among guys . . . [They tell you] 'Look, what a nice chest you have' and inside yourself you say: 'Wow!'.
>
> (Massimo, 26 years old, straight)

Massimo and other informants' narratives speak about narcissistic pleasures: looking at the mirror, they see a body in transformation as their muscles grow bigger and their physique becomes increasingly similar to those of distant advertising models and more approachable gym mates. Informants realize that there is something queer in the way they look (and occasionally touch) each other in this male-only environment. Massimo explicitly notes the 'oddness' of a situation where men admire each other's physiques and feels the need to specify that he and his gym mates are not naked when involved in this activity, as to exorcise a homosexual interpretation of his words.

Another reading strategy of male imagery in advertising shared by both gay and straight consumers consists of *critical interpretations* (Hirschman and Thompson, 1997; Patterson and Elliott, 2002). Ads' models are rejected for being 'unreal', 'made of plastic', 'identical to each other' and even pitied for an 'empty' existence devoted to maintaining their beauty. In the words of informants a semiotic opposition is created between the majority of 'normal', 'real' men and the few ones who can act as models for adverts:

> Oh my! This is a man unattainable by men . . . If you watch television, if you look at magazines they [models, actors] are all over-muscled, over-buff, thin, and beautiful, painfully beautiful. These guys are far from reality because they spend all their day at the gym, follow a super balanced diet . . . They don't do anything else in their life! They take care of themselves . . . And, honestly speaking, I don't like the fact that they shave themselves . . . they pluck their eyebrows . . . this kind of things . . . I don't find that necessary at all.
>
> (Gabriele, 22 years old, straight)

The rejection of models' lifestyle, made of endless hours at the gym and dietary restrictions, is strengthened through an ideological inversion of their status within an ideal hierarchy of masculinity. Models occupy top positions with respect to beauty: 'normal' men may only aspire to be 'in the middle'. Supporters of the 'compensatory consumption' thesis would argue that marketers' cultural production of masculinity compels male consumers to partake in such hierarchy and motivates them to move upward through narcissistic consumption. Through critical interpretations, however, male models are knocked off their pedestal by consumers who invoke the male gaze to objectify – and feminize – the excessive pursuit of beauty, particularly when it involves doubtful practices such as shaving one's chest or plucking one's eyebrows.

Critical and narcissistic readings often coexists in the same informants and denote consumers' ambivalence towards mass-mediated masculinities. Like in the myth of Narcissus, men look at the media to see reflections of their own male identity. But media representations are distorted mirrors: as the 'impossibly thin' female models may cause low self-esteem and eating disorders in women, the equally impossibly muscular and beautiful male models may cause feelings of discomfort and inadequacy in men.

Gay consumers' relationships with media images of masculinity (see again Figure 6.1) are characterized by interpretive architectures generally more complex than those of their straight counterparts. For gay informants, a possible interpretive response consists of *insider readings* (Kates, 2004): adverts are perceived as directed at gay audiences without appearing to do so. Unlike ads with explicit homoerotic elements, these ads interpellate gay men in ways which are not evident to most straight consumers. Insider readings by gay informants are frequent in the case of ads featuring two or more male models:

> Look at this image . . . There is a lot of attention to the physical aspect of the guys . . . The choice is peculiar . . . It's a situation of strong intimacy . . . It is not openly gay . . . but it suggests an intimacy between the guys.
>
> (Alex, 34 years old, gay)

Insider readings are personalizing interpretations (Hirschman and Thompson, 1997) that reflect gay consumers' experiences and needs. Gay consumers employ the gaydar, that is the capability to understand from subtle signs whether a person is gay or not, to detect gay subtexts in advertising messages. This does not imply that advertisers actually inscribe such subtexts in their ads. On the contrary, the commodification of gay aesthetics in the production of fashion imagery often produces 'biased' insider readings. Another reading strategy of gay consumers dealing with images of male beauty consists of *fetishist readings* (Patterson and Elliott, 2002) that, in most (but not all) respects, mirror those of straight men dealing with media representations of women:

> Sincerely . . . I'd like to have his address . . . or rather I'd like him to have mine! . . . What do you want me to say? He's beautiful, beautiful, beautiful . . . He is a sex god . . . Good for a night of fire.
>
> (Paolo, 30 years old, gay)

Media masculinities are looked by gay consumers with a desiring gaze and may be the starting point for erotic or romantic fantasies or 'mental film making'. An ad's model may thus be objectified as 'sexual toy' – playing the role of the gazer's 'hunter' or 'prey'. In the words of gay informants, however, fetishistic and narcissistic readings often intertwine as models are both object of the gaze and recipients of the gazer's identification. For gay consumers, images of men are thus blank screens that evoke a variety of subject positions within the realm of voluptuousness. A variety which is denied to most straight men.

The risky consumptionscape of straight men

When speaking of fashion and physical appearance, informants highlighted the clear existence of do's and don'ts. The interpretive model proposed in Figure 6.2 makes sense of the imagined barriers that straight men dare not cross and the mechanisms that enforce respect of these barriers. As well as by the psychological perspectives on the gaze previously discussed, the model is informed by Michel's Foucault's (1977) ideas on the functioning of power in society. With reference to Foucault's work, Schroeder and Zwick (2004, p. 23) note that 'advertising imagery constitutes ubiquitous and influential bodily representations in public space, incorporating exercises of power, surveillance and normativity within the consumer spectacle'. Our look is subjected to the approval of beloved ones and important others: parents, partners, friends and acquaintances, co-workers and superiors. Surveillance thus entails the *panoptical gaze* of others: a gaze that reprimands those who do not conform to it and that we eventually interiorize.

Accordingly, for straight men, the consumptionscape is made of a 'safe area' – where the narcissistic gaze may be exerted in security – and of

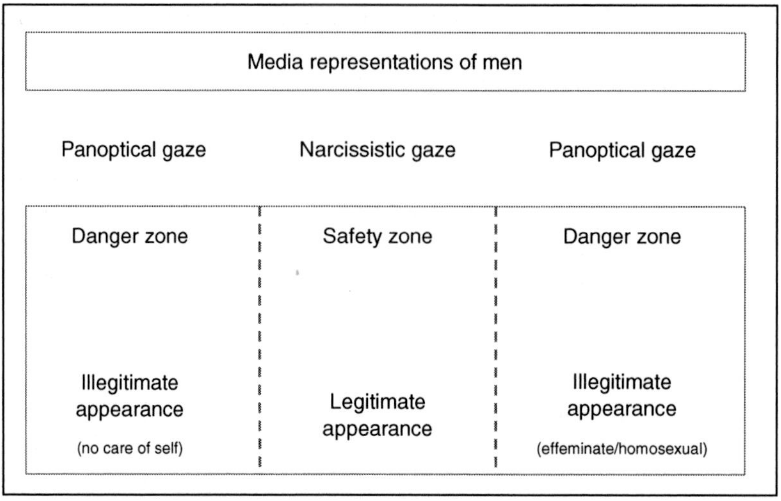

Media representations of men		
Panoptical gaze	Narcissistic gaze	Panoptical gaze
Danger zone	Safety zone	Danger zone
Illegitimate appearance (no care of self)	Legitimate appearance	Illegitimate appearance (effeminate/homosexual)

Figure 6.2 The cultural production of straight men's consumptionscape.

'danger zones' – where consumption is riskier as regimes of surveillance sanction illegitimate consumption.[1] Legitimacy is the 'generalized perception or assumption that the actions of an entity [here, a consumption practice] are desirable, proper, or appropriate within some socially constructed system of norms, values, beliefs, and definitions' (Suchman, 1995, p. 574). Consumption practices may be stigmatized for being untidy, sloppy, not refined, old fashioned. Other practices may on the other hand be too refined or fashionable, to the point of being gender-inappropriate for men. Most of the time the barriers between legitimate and illegitimate consumption are invisible, as they are deeply embedded in consumption habits and illegitimate products are normally avoided. Crossing the frontier however causes visible discomfort and, often, the need to justify 'questionable' consumptions:

> I employ a moisturizing cream . . . but I'd never use an eye contour cream. . . These are women's stuff. . . I associate them to women. . .
> (Gabriele, 22 years old, straight)

In the words of informants, the lower bound of the 'safe area' is rarely questioned: a minimum level of tidiness and aesthetic sense is taken for granted. The prominence of fashionable masculinities in mass culture induces however consumers to continuously renegotiate the legitimacy of consumption goods and practices beyond the upper bound. For Gabriele, using a moisturizing cream – a risky business for other informants – is a legitimate manly activity. An eye contour cream, on the contrary, is not. As suggested by Schroeder

---

[1] The idea of 'danger zones' in the context of working women's ideal business image was previously suggested by Kimle and Damhorst (1997). I am grateful to Susan Kaiser for bringing this reference to my attention.

and Zwick (2004, p. 23) 'masculinity is – semiotically – irrevocably connected with, opposed to and in relation to femininity'. Practices that violate norms of masculinity are thus viewed as effeminate:

> Come on! Gay guys are not the only ones who can wear jeans like those . . . or wear clothes which are peculiar . . . But once in a while I buy something a little fanciful and my friends say: You can't wear that . . . It's faggy . . . But as a joke . . .
>
> (Davide, 24 years old, straight)

Trespassing these imagined frontiers may cause consequences. Pushed by marketers, style innovators may sometimes experiment with 'peculiar' aesthetic choices. Negative sanctions by friends and acquaintances – even if limited to a disapproving gaze or, as in the case of Davide, irony – thwart their diffusion. Cultural barriers are however permeable and consumers often notice that practices which are fairly common today were unconceivable for men when their fathers were their age (e.g., pink shirts) or even a few years ago (e.g., shaving one's body, plucking one's eyebrows):

> I've always used an after-shave . . . but not creams . . . I've always kept creams away from me . . . Until I was 20, for me creams were women's stuff. Then, one summer my mom insisted I put a protection cream on before going out in the sun . . . 'Try it, try it', she said, and I: 'Leave me alone . . .'. Then she gave me a Shiseido after-sun. I brought it on vacation and my friends: 'how nice, how nice' – because it made the skin shine . . . if you were sun-tanned it made you shine . . . Now I'm starting using a cream for my face . . . not an anti-wrinkling cream . . . let's say a regenerating one . . . Because I always have these shadows under my eyes . . . My girlfriend wanted me to buy one that costs more than 20 euros . . . but I said 'wait, let's start buying a less expensive one . . .'
>
> (Massimo, 26 years old, straight)

With the exception of manly after-shaves, Massimo used to resist the use of creams (all creams) as they belong to the realm of female consumption. His process of acculturation takes several years, during which Massimo is exposed to positive sanctions by friends in the case of a sun protection cream, whose results nurture his narcissism. The more recent episodes show a process of boundary work, that is of renegotiation of the male identity to include certain forms of consumption in terms of product attributes, price levels, distribution channels – and not others. A cheap, 'regenerating' cream bought in a supermarket does not threat Massimo's gender identity the way an expensive, top brand anti-wrinkle cream bought in a cosmetics shop would. Lack of legitimacy may regard not only products and brands, but also their distribution channels, price levels, and modes of consumption.

The gaydar is dead: long live the gaydar!

For many gay informants, it is no more possible to infer a man's sexual orientation from his look. According to older informants, the 'problem' is heightened
in the case of younger men. The gaydar is thus less reliable than it once used
to be and subtler forms of radar have to be developed. As appearances may
be 'misleading', for many gay informants recognizing another gay men is
'a matter of glances' or a 'sense of sudden connection':

> According to me it is not possible to say whether a guy is gay or
> not from appearance only . . . not any more . . . Particularly young
> people . . . Look at them: they all look alike: same sunglasses, low-
> waisted jeans, colored t-shirt and sweaters . . . That is, you can't be
> 100 per cent sure when you say: he is gay, he is not . . . In short, gay
> guys who are 60, 70 years old are much more visible when they are
> in Ibiza with their white pants, their shirts, the gold chains this thick,
> things like that . . . . But not young people . . .
>
> (Dario, 38 years old, gay)

Previous research shows that gay consumers actively construct subcultural boundaries between gays and heterosexuals through consumption and
develop negative consumption stereotypes about the style of straight men
(Kates, 2002). However, appropriation of subcultural style by the heterosexual
mainstream, according to my informants, is not causing the active consumer
resistance suggested in other contexts (e.g., Hebdige, 1979). The adoption of
'gayer' style is possible but not as common as expected:

> Today there are fashion shows where men wear the gown . . . If one
> [a gay guy] wants to be more visible, he can . . . Yes, if one wants to
> put make-up on, he can, he knows that if he exaggerates people will
> take notice . . . If a queer wants to show himself up, all he needs is
> to put mascara on, you'll hardly find a straight guy who does that.
> This is a more extreme thing to do . . .
>
> (Alex, 34 years old, gay)

In the context I explored, gay consumers, rather than resisting the commodification of gay aesthetics, are enjoying the semiotic ambiguity of men's style,
which is now decoupled by sexual orientation. The gray area of 'gay vagueness' seems to be more appreciated by gay consumers than their straight
counterpart. Gay consumers, while still discriminated by society at large, have
long considered superior their own sense of style – and stereotyped straight
men for their inferior physical appearance (Kates, 2002). The diffusion of gay
aesthetics to the mainstream is thus applauded as a sign of 'civilization' of

straight men and an acknowledgement of the role gay subculture plays in society:

> Gay people have always been very creative. Look at the arts: Leonardo, Caravaggio and so many other Renaissance masters were homosexuals. In fashion, it's not a secret that most designers are gay . . . For centuries, the unique contribution of homosexual people to society has gone unnoticed, simply because people were afraid to come out and say: 'I'm gay'. Today, fortunately, this is not true anymore and the media credit us with being superiorly endowed individuals in the realms of creativity, art and fashion – not social misfits or sexual deviants . . .
>
> (Paolo, 30 years old, gay)

Discussion and conclusion

In this chapter, I analysed the production of masculine identity in two stages of the circuit of culture: mass-mediated marketplace discourse and men's consumption practices. Fashionable media representations of masculinities lure straight men into appearing beautiful according to inspirational models codified by advertising and to indulge in consumption practices long employed by gay men to build the symbolic boundaries of their subculture. To completely adhere to such beauty ideals, straight men should, for example, wear tight briefs, pluck their eyebrows, shave their bodies, employ creams and even cosmetics. Such practices, while encouraged by the discourse of fashion and advertising, are still considered of dubious legitimacy among straight men. Even the style innovators among them refrain from their adoption, as they are still subject to the regime of surveillance of the panoptical gaze in their social interactions.

Under these circumstances, subcultural theory would predict gay consumers' resistance to marketers and the heterosexual appropriation of important signifying consumption practices. However, quite the contrary appears to be happening. Straight men (i.e., the mainstream society) are resisting marketers' commodification of gay aesthetics and actively engage into boundary work to legitimize consumptions which are still 'suspicious' for men. The boundaries – or, better, the upper bound – of the 'safe area' of the consumptionscape (see again Figure 6.2) are thus subject to an ongoing process of negotiation and renegotiation as consumers invoke marketplace discourse on masculinity to placate the panoptical gaze. Gay men, on the other hand, seem to enjoy the diffusion of the 'gay vagueness' trend in society and appreciate it as a sign of 'civilization' of straight men and as a mechanism through which they can gain standing in society. These findings contribute to theory on subcultures of consumption as they propose alternative outcomes of the commodification of subcultural style. *Mainstream resistance* and what may be termed *subcultural revenche* are possible responses to marketer appropriation of the marker goods employed to express affiliation by discriminated subcultural groups.

How can we judge the collective marketing strategy employed to construct the metrosexual and other recent fashionable masculinities in terms of the principles of tribal marketing? Research has long shown the existence of two basic models in the diffusion of innovations (Strang and Soule, 1998): 'external source' or broadcast models, that refer to diffusion *into* a population; and internal or contagion models, that refer to diffusion *within* a population. Marketers' construction of masculinities seems to heavily rely on mass-mediated discourse, that is on external sources, neglecting at the same time the influence flowing within the adopting population of men. The panoptical gaze is however a powerful force to deal with, as it is interiorized and enforced by the net of relationships consumers are embedded in. To conquer straight men, marketers should take into consideration the risky nature of fashion adoption: for example, they should employ 'next door boys' in lieu of impossibly beautiful models in their adverts and propose 'safe' retail channels and price levels, in order to minimize the likeliness of critical readings. Moreover, the exploitation of opinion leadership phenomena and the reassurance of relevant others (women!) about the legitimacy of fashionable consumption seems to be of utmost importance. As Cova (1997, p. 311) reminds us, 'the link is more important than the thing', that is consumers value products or services to the extent that they facilitate social relationships. A lesson that the producers of the next fashionable masculinity should hold dear.

Acknowledgements

I would like to thank Susan Kaiser and participants to the 2006 ACR Conference on Gender, Marketing and Consumption for insightful comments on earlier versions of this chapter. My thanks also to Matteo Aram Arslanian for his professional assistance during the fieldwork, and to my informants for speaking of gender to me – not an easy task for many of them.

References

Belk, R.W. and Costa, J. (1998). The mountain man myth: a contemporary consuming fantasy, *Journal of Consumer Research*, **25** (December), 218–240.

Berger, J. (1972). *Ways of Seeing*. London: Penguin.

Bordo, S. (1999). *The Male Body: A New Look at Men in Public and Private*. New York: Farrar, Straus & Giroux.

Carrigan, T., Connell, B. and Lee J. (2002). Toward a new sociology of masculinity, in Adams, R. and Savran, D. (eds.), *The Masculinity Studies Reader*. Malden, MA: Blackwell.

Clarke, J. (1986). Style, in Hall, S. and Jefferson, T. (eds.), *Resistance Through Rituals: Youth Subcultures in Post-War Britain*. London: Hutchinson.

Cole, S. (2000). *Don We Now Our Gay Apparel: Gay Men's Dress in the Twentieth Century*. Oxford: Berg.

Colman, D. (2005). Gay or straight? Hard to tell, *New York Times*, 19 June.

Connell, R.W. (1992). A very straight gay: masculinity, homosexual experi-ence, and the dynamics of gender, *American Sociological Review*, **57** (December), 735–751.

Cova, B. (1997). Community and consumption: towards a definition of the 'linking value' of products or services, *European Journal of Marketing*, **31** (3/4), 297–316.

Cova, B. and Cova, V. (2002). Tribal marketing: the tribalisation of society and its impact on the conduct of marketing, *European Journal of Marketing*, **36** (5/6), 595–620.

Craik, J. (1994). *The Face of Fashion: Cultural Studies in Fashion*. New York: Routledge.

Crane, D. (2000). *Fashion and its Social Agendas: Class, Gender, and Identity in Clothing*. Chicago: University of Chicago Press.

Crewe, B. (2003). *Representing Men: Cultural Production and Producers in the Men's Magazine Market*. Oxford: Berg.

Davis, F. (1992). *Fashion, Culture, and Identity*. Chicago: University of Chicago Press.

Euro RSCG (2003). *The Future of Men: US*. Unpublished Research Report. New York: Euro RSCG.

Flocker, M. (2003). *The Metrosexual Guide to Style: A Handbook for the Modern Man*. New York: Da Capo Press.

Flügel, J.C. (1930). *The Psychology of Clothes*. London: Hogarth Press.

Foucault, M. (1977). *Discipline and Punish: The Birth of the Prison*. New York: Vintage Books.

Gottdiener, M. (1985). Hegemony and mass culture: a semiotic approach, *American Journal of Sociology*, **90** (5), 979–1001.

Hackbarth, A. (2003). Vanity, thy name is metrosexual, *The Washington Post*, (November 17).

Hebdige, D. (1979). *Subculture: The Meaning of Style*. London: Methuen.

Heisley, D.D. and Levy S.J. (1991). Autodriving: a photoelicitation technique, *Journal of Consumer Research*, **18** (December), 257–272.

Hirschman, E.C. and Thompson, C.J. (1997). Why media matter: toward a richer understanding of consumer's relationships with advertising and mass media, *Journal of Advertising*, **26** (1), 43–60.

Holt, D.-B. and Thompson, C.J. (2004). Man-of-action heroes: the pursuit of heroic masculinity in everyday consumption, *Journal of Consumer Research*, **31** (2), 425–440.

Hyman, P. (2004). *The Reluctant Metrosexual: Dispatches from an Almost Hip Life*. New York: Villard.

Kates, S.M. (2002). The protean quality of subcultural consumption: an ethnographic account of gay consumers, *Journal of Consumer Research*, **29** (December), 383–399.

Kates, S.M. (2004). The dynamics of brand legitimacy: an interpretive study in the gay men's community, *Journal of Consumer Research*, **31** (September), 455–464.

Kimle, P. and Damhorst, M.L. (1997). A grounded theory model of the ideal business image for women, *Symbolic Interaction*, **20** (1), 45–68.

Kimmel, M.S. (1996). *Manhood in America*. New York: Free Press.

Maffesoli, M. (1996). *The Time of the Tribes: The Decline of Individualism in Mass Society*. London: Sage.

McCracken, G. (1988). *The Long Interview*. London: Sage.

Miller, T. (2005). A metrosexual eye on *Queer Eye, GLQ: A Journal of Lesbian and Gay Studies*, **11** (1), 112–117.

Mort, F. (1996). *Cultures of Consumption: Masculinities and Social Space in Late Twentieth-Century Britain*. London: Routledge.

Mulvey, L. (1975). Visual pleasure and narrative cinema, *Screen*, **16** (3), 6–18.

Nixon, S. (1993). Looking for the Holy Grail: publishing and advertising strategies of contemporary men's magazines, *Cultural Studies*, **7** (3), 466–492.

Nixon, S. (1996). *Hard Looks: Masculinities, Spectatorship and Contemporary Consumption*. London: UCL Press.

Patterson, M. and Elliott R. (2002). Negotiating masculinities: advertising and the inversion of the male gaze, *Consumption, Markets and Culture*, **5** (3), 231–246.

Salzman, M., Matathia, I. and O'Reilly, A. (2005). *The Future of Men*. New York: Palgrave Macmillan.

Schouten, J. and McAlexander, J. (1995). Subcultures of consumption: an ethnography of new bikers, *Journal of Consumer Research*, **22** (June), 43–61.

Schroeder, J.E. and Zwick, D. (2004). Mirrors of masculinity: representation and identity in advertising images, *Consumption, Markets & Culture*, **7** (1), 21–52.

Sherry Jr., J.F. et al. (2004). Gendered behavior in a male preserve: role playing at *ESPN Zone Chicago, Journal of Consumer Psychology*, **14** (1/2), 151–158.

Simpson, M. (1994). Here come the mirror men, *The Independent*, 15 November.

Simpson, M. (2002). Meet the metrosexual, *Salon.com*, 22 July.

Simpson, M. (2005). MetroDaddy v. Übermummy, *3AM Magazine* (December).

Spiggle, S. (1994). Analysis and interpretation of qualitative data in consumer research, *Journal of Consumer Research*, **2** (December), 491–503.

St. John, W. (2003). Metrosexuals come out, *New York Times*, 22 June.

Strang, D. and Soule, S.A. (1998). Diffusion in organizations and social movements: from hybrid corn to poison pills, *Annual Review of Sociology*, **24**, 265–290.

Sturken, M. and Cartwright, L. (2001). *Practices of Looking*. Oxford: Oxford University Press.

Suchman, M.C. (1995). Managing legitimacy: strategic and institutional approaches, *Academy of Management Review*, **20** (June), 43–61.

Thompson, C.J. and Haytko, D.L. (1997). Speaking of fashion: consumers' uses of fashion discourses and the appropriation of countervailing cultural meanings, *Journal of Consumer Research*, **24** (1), 15–42.

Thompson, C.J., Locander, W.B. and Pollio, H.R. (1989). Putting consumer experience back into consumer research: the philosophy and method of existential-phenomenology, *Journal of Consumer Research*, **16** (September), 133–147.

7

The linking value of subcultural capital: constructing the Stockholm Brat enclave

Jacob Ostberg

Are markets capable of nurturing genuine communities? If so, what do these communities look like, what functions do they serve, and what consumption phenomena do they revolve around? These questions have occupied consumer researchers over the past decade (e.g., Cova, 1997; Cova and Cova, 2001, 2002; Kates, 2002; Muñiz and O'Guinn, 2001; Schouten and McAlexander, 1995; Schulz, 2006). For a long time, the received view was that anomie, dislocation, and disconnectedness were the results of modernity's fatal assault on the pre-modern community. Recent consumer research has increasingly acknowledged that the marketplace seems to be a place where new types of communities spring to life. In this chapter, one such community – the Stockholm Brat enclave, an exclusive group of young, affluent consumers living their lives in the fast lane, and frequenting the trendiest nightclubs in Stockholm – will be looked at in more detail.

The Stockholm Brats' consumption ethos is about carefully assembling, displaying, and using various consumption objects to create just the right ambience of being 'in the know', or perhaps being cool (Nancarrow, Nancarrow, and Page, 2002) even though they would scoff at such a description themselves. If one had to settle for one term to describe the cultural organization of social logic by which the Brats operate, it would have to be 'style'. Style, or at least the Brats' specific rendition of this ephemeral quality, is what holds the *linking value* (Cova, 1997; Cova and Cova, 2001, 2002) around which this specific market tribe congregates. In order to grasp how a specific rendition of style gets imbued with linking value, the chapter emphasizes how the community continually uses external factors from media and popular culture to structure its internal social organization. The purpose of this chapter is to add to the recent theoretical developments of the tribal aspects of consumption by looking at why and how certain consumption objects and activities have the potential to exert linking value, and how this linking value is valorized by its recognition of sources external to the specific tribe. In explicating this, the concept of subcultural capital will be introduced.

The outline of the chapter is as follows. First, the chapter will be positioned theoretically within consumer culture theory on communities and consumption. Then, the concept of subcultural capital will be explicated by drawing from relevant literature in consumer research and the social sciences more broadly. Next, the fieldwork and the sites underlying the empirical study will be described. Following, the ways in which the Brats embody both elements from popular culture and contemporary media commentary on their lifestyle by turning it into subcultural capital will be illustrated. In doing this, a number of illuminating examples of how the Brats are portrayed, chronicled, criticized, and debated in media and other cultural texts will be provided.

Theoretical positioning

Many studies within consumer research have hitherto focused on establishing whether it is feasible to talk of market-driven communities or subcultures. A theoretical common ground for this research is Maffesoli's (1996) work on neo-tribalism. Maffesoli looks at how the macro-forces of globalization and post-industrial socio-economic transformation have eroded the traditional bases of sociality. In the wake following this erosion, a dominant ethos of radical individualism has arisen, oriented around a perpetual search for personal distinction and autonomy in lifestyle choices. In Maffesoli's view, consumers respond to these potentially alienating and isolating conditions by forming more ephemeral collective identifications that are grounded in common lifestyle interests and leisure pursuits (cf. Cova, 1997; Maffesoli, 1996).

Prior research on community and consumption has either focused on a particular brand as the tie that binds consumers together (e.g., Kozinets, 2001; Muñiz and O'Guinn, 2001; Schouten and McAlexander, 1995), certain consumption activities that serve this unifying function (e.g., Arnould and Price,

1993; Belk and Costa, 1998; Celsi, Rose, and Leigh, 1993; Cova and Cova, 2001; Goulding, Shankar, and Elliott, 2002), or certain groups' consumption patterns, such as gay communities (Kates, 2002) or immigrants (Penaloza, 1994). Cova (1997) has added to this literature by emphasizing that the linking value of a brand, product, or activity is even more important than the brand, product, or consumption activities *per se*. There are, however, a number of aspects related to community and consumption that have hitherto been more or less neglected. Most prior studies have focused on the consumption of *one* brand, product, or activity despite the fact that a call for an increased focus on 'ensembles of objects' have accompanied consumer research for almost two decades (Belk, 1988). Consequently, looking at communities where the linking value is made up of more complex consumption patterns is important. The focus on *one* brand, product, or activity is inherent in Cova and Cova's definition when they write that a linking value is '[a] product's, or service's, contribution to establishing and/or reinforcing bonds between individuals' (2001, p. 70). The community under investigation in this chapter is focused on style rather than a specific consumption object or activity. What constitutes style is constantly changing but the group congregates around common perceptions of what is stylish at each given point in time (cf. Ewen, 1999). Hence, consuming in a stylish manner is what holds the linking value. Furthermore, considerably little attention has been given to how consumption communities are contextualized in a particular socio-cultural milieu. In the brand community studies, the relationships with users of other brands have been explicated (Muñiz and O'Guinn, 2001), and in the studies of subcultures of consumption (Schouten and McAlexander, 1995) and market tribes (Cova and Cova, 2001) the relationship between community members and broader social currents are discussed. What has been overlooked so far, however, are the nitty-gritty details of how a community constantly negotiates and re-negotiates with its surroundings about the boundaries of the community as well as the internal social organization governing the members of the community. This study tries to fill these theoretical gaps by focusing on a group whose linking value is not made up of a singular brand, product, or activity but rather a carefully composed concoction of them all. Also, the emphasis is on the dialectical process between the group and the media and sources from popular culture, whereby the community defines its limits and its internal structure.

Subcultural capital

To illuminate how this group of consumers actively engages in this dialectical process, the concept of subcultural capital will be used (Thornton, 1996, 1997). This concept helps to show the mechanisms through which the members of the community embody the cultural codes necessary to maintain one's membership. Responding to the media and knowing, as well as performing, relevant elements from popular culture are important parts of the subcultural capital. The concept was coined by Thornton (1996, 1997) in her analysis of

British club culture. The concept of subcultural capital, of course, draws on the work of the French sociologist Pierre Bourdieu. In the book *Distinction: A Social Critique of the Judgment of Taste* (1984) he describes a system of distinction in which cultural hierarchies correspond to social ones and people's tastes are first and foremost a marker of class. He makes a distinction between material wealth and cultural assets of a particular class, the first one is described as economic capital and the second as cultural capital. Bourdieu reasoned that culture adds to the wealth of a particular class and largely defines cultural capital by formal education and social background. The framework also includes discussion of a third category, social capital, which emanates not from what you own (economic capital) or know (cultural capital), but from *who* you know (and who knows you).

Bourdieu's framework, has been used in consumer research to investigate the processes by which consumption choices and behaviours are shaped by social class hierarchies (Holt, 1998). The strength of Bourdieu's schema is that it moves away from rigidly vertical models of the social structure, for example ones based on income. Instead, social groups are located in a highly complex multi-dimensional space rather than on a linear scale or ladder. Thornton (1997, p. 202) asks the crucial question whether it is possible to observe subspecies of capital operating within other less privileged domains. In answering this question she suggests the concept of *subcultural capital* as a more localized type of cultural capital that have bearing in more limited spatiotemporal domains, or fields, than Bourdieu's original concept. Her empirical investigations show that rave clubs are refuges for the young where their rules hold sway; inside, as well as outside, these spaces, subcultural distinctions have significant consequences. Subcultural capital affects the standing of the young in many ways like its adult equivalent. Just as books and paintings display cultural capital in the family home, so subcultural capital is objectified in the form of fashionable haircuts and carefully assembled record collections in the club cultures. In this way, subcultural capital is transformed into practice and both objectified, as in owning the right consumption objects, and embodied, as in expressing a certain style. It is important to acknowledge that subcultural capital confers status on its owner in the eyes of the relevant beholder. This beholder needs to be in possession of some degree of subcultural knowledge to be able to decipher the relevant codes. A primary factor governing the circulation of subcultural capital is the media. In fact several writers have remarked upon the absence of media analysis in Bourdieu's framework (Thornton, 1997). According to Thornton, it is impossible to understand the distinctions of youth subcultures without some systematic investigation of their media consumption.

Methodological procedures

The data material for this project has been collected over a two year period as part of a research project focusing on the consumption patterns of the

Stockholm Brat enclave. As suggested by prior researchers focusing on market communities (Cova and Cova, 2001, p. 71) multiple methods have been used. The fieldwork consists of three main parts:

1 a study of the group's whereabouts on the Internet, this is the main part of the study;
2 a study of the group's presence in the media and popular culture;
3 participant observations at venues where members of the group congregate.

The members of the Brat community use the Internet as their key media channel. Several web-pages specialize in chronicling the Brats' whereabouts and the web is also an important place where the individual Brats make their voices heard. Accordingly, the Internet has provided one important empirical site for this project. Consumer research using ethnographic methods on the Internet 'enables researchers and their clients to see the world through the eyes of consumers in the context of their everyday lives' (Maclaran and Catterall, 2002, p. 321). Although this project focuses on the Brats' Internet presence and how they are represented in a Computer-Mediated Environment (CME), the Brats are not an online community, they exist in Real Life (RL). Their Internet presence, though serving a strongly communicative function, is not what binds this group together; rather, the RL activities, later posted on the Internet, display the membership core. There has been no direct communication with the Brats online. Instead, the research team has engaged in extensive 'lurking', that is gleaning information by 'listening in' on text-based discussions without announcing one's presence (Catterall and Maclaran, 2002).

The core of the online research has been conducted at three free-access web-pages (G life, 2006; Piccaboo.com, 2006 [formerly known as SthlmVIP.com]; Stureplan.se, 2006 [formerly known as YoSthlm.se]) that specialize in publishing pictures and documenting the lifestyles of the Brats. The Brat web-pages are financed through advertising of various kinds, especially luxury brands (e.g., Longines, Prada, Helmut Lang), as well as high-end high-tech equipment (e.g., Bose, Audi), and, most notably, alcoholic beverages (Hennesy, Moët and Chandon, Skyy Vodka). These sponsors are also featured in editorial material on the web-pages where the products are placed in the context of the high-end stylish life the Brats are aspiring to. To gain an understanding of the Brat community, the different Brat web-pages were scanned for new content on a weekly basis. In an average week, pictures from 5 to 10 new parties are added with 15 to 60 pictures posted from each party. People visiting the homepages are invited to comment on the pictures and engage in debates on various topics. The pages also provide editorial material in the form of columns discussing topics of importance to the Brats, chronicles about the latest parties, and features on, what seemingly are, the coolest people.

The second part of the fieldwork consists of a study of the group's presence in the media and popular culture. Various types of media have been

systematically scanned for the duration of project to follow what is communicated about the Brat subculture in those venues. An overview of relevant
media and other popular culture outlets looks as follows. The large
Stockholm-based Swedish newspapers comment on and often criticize the
Brats for their behaviours; an edited book with contributions from top-
journalist in Sweden was recently published (Lundell, 2006); several books
have been published with the story set in a Brat milieu and Brats as either the
main characters or as important supporting characters; magazines directed at
young urbanites frequently comment on, or feature, Brat-related phenomena;
magazines distributed for free in Central Stockholm show pictures from Brat
events and keep the public up-to-date on the Brats' whereabouts; a number of
documentaries have been shown on national TV depicting the lifestyle of the
Brats; recently the first ever play about Brats premiered in Stockholm; finally,
the Brat subculture have even spurred the creation of their own rap-group FFL
(Ruined for Life), a name that alludes to the fact that when you are brought up
with parents that always follow your slightest wish, you will never be able to
survive in the outside world. While not all these outlets will be dealt with in
this chapter, due to length restrictions, it is vital to get a sense of the width of
Brat coverage in media and popular culture.

Finally, to gain a deeper understanding of the Brats' RL activities, a third
step of fieldwork has been initiated consisting of participant observations at
venues where members of the group congregate. The logic is that by studying
how consumers consume in their natural setting, an understanding of the
cultural codes at play within the community can be gained (an inspiration
has been Holt (1995), who gained valuable insights about how consumers
consume at baseball games by participant observations). The participatory
element has consisted of observing and listening in on conversations held by
the Brats. No formal interviews have been conducted but plenty of casual conversations with members of the community have taken place. The Brat venues
cater to a wider variety of customers than the Brats and the researchers have,
as far as they can tell, had no difficulties blending in and getting close to the
Brats without disturbing the natural course of action. The noisy environment
and the wish for unobtrusiveness has prevented the recording of these conversations, instead field notes have been taken in immediate connection to the
observations.

The material collected from the Internet and the field notes from the observations were coded for instances of media and popular culture reflexivity and
contrasted and compared to the media and popular culture analysis. In a first
stage, the material was assembled to gain an emic understanding of the Brats'
whereabouts. In the next step, an etic understanding was aimed for by connecting the data material to relevant theoretical frameworks from consumer
culture theory. A guiding principle during the analysis has been the discourse
analysis framework suggested by Catterall and Maclaran (2002, p. 234), as this
methodology looks at how language is used to make sense of and construct
the social world.

Results: the reflexive construction of subcultural capital

In the following section, the Stockholm Brat enclave will be described in order to show how media and sources from popular culture co-construct the Brat identity by providing fodder for the construction of subcultural capital. These consumers are usually referred to as 'Brats', both by external observers, including the media, and by the participants themselves; the Brat terminology is therefore used throughout the chapter. In the English language, the word brat is used to denote a spoilt child who gets its way in most things. In Sweden, this original denotation is lost and the English word brat is used only in the meaning described in this chapter. Drawing on Muñiz and O'Guinn's (2001, p. 215) criteria, it is reasonable to say that the Brats have enough things in common to qualify as a community; they exhibit a shared consciousness, they have certain rituals and traditions that should be followed, and in rough times, they show a sense of moral responsibility. The Brat community can be viewed as a form of enclave (Firat and Dholakia, 1998) or *ad hoc* community (Thornton, 1997, p. 200) with fluid boundaries. Some members might spend just a few months as part of the group whereas the core seems to endure for several years.

Historical roots

At a first glance, the Brats might seem like typical über-consumers, sometimes referred to as postmodern consumers, living a shallow and superficial life and inhabiting a world of free-floating signs, fragments and fads (cf. Löfgren, 1994, p. 47). They are undoubtedly focused on appearance and desirable looks, assembling appropriate outfits and cultivating a certain style. However, viewing the Brats in this way might lead us in the wrong direction. Instead of viewing the Brats as a new phenomena of supposedly postmodern consumers, we are better of regarding them as the latest variation of an old theme of young, rich urbanites consuming in a conspicuous manner. Similar motivations to consume for the sake of consuming were first introduced by Veblen's 'conspicuous consumption' (1899). Veblen focused on how consumption functions to set consumers apart from others by displaying wealth and power. Moreover, the Brats might be suggested to participate in a kind of 'potlatch' practice, ritually, and conspicuously, disposing of accumulated excess in return for status, and other potential benefits (Mauss, 1997). Löfgren (1994) directs our attention to how every generation seems to give birth to a new breed of over-consumers. These have been called different names over the years ranging from nouveaux riches, parvenus, and 'goulash barons' (Löfgren, 1994) to the 'robber barons' of Veblen's time (Solomon, Bamossy, and Askegaard, 2002, p. 395) but many of their characteristics remain the same.

Some of the reasons for the Brats' conspicuous manner of consumption can be traced in the consumption patterns of their parents. Belk (1986) provides a useful historical overview of the consumption logic of the last decades that potentially sheds light on why the Brats are so keen on conspicuousness. Although Belk talks about the American context, the general overview is valid in Sweden too. In the mid-sixties and extending into the early seventies there was an ascendancy of counter-cultural consumer values that increasingly challenged the middle class materialism that had flourished since the end of World War II. The world was increasingly critical of what was seen as the selfishly acquisitative lifestyle of Western consumers. Instead it became fashionable to scale down on consumption. This was the time of the Hippies who rebelled against middle class values and consumption patterns. One of the ways in which this rebellion took place was by adopting blue-collar clothing such as jeans and work shirts. In the late sixties, as protest against US involvement in Vietnam grew stronger the hippies were portrayed in popular press as the trendiest youth movement. The Hippie movement had a distinct impact on the Swedish upper class as young members of the old aristocratic families flirted with the leftist ideas fashionable at the time. For example, some of the nobility decided to leave the house of nobles, sometimes changing their last names that connoted their noble family history. They hence downplayed their role as aristocracy in favour of a more politically correct view of all people as equal. While not all aristocrats choose to downplay their privileged position, the traditional role of the upper class as definers of style for society as a whole was lost during this era.

The Brats' inclination towards conspicuousness should be read against this relative downplaying of the style leadership of their parents. Whereas their parents' generation abolished their sense of classic style and their hegemonic position as stylistic agenda setters, the Brats see themselves as defenders of stability and providing a timeless, classic (and classy) environment as an alternative to all available fast-moving consumer fads. They do not regard themselves as representing something new, or as following contemporary trends. Instead, they are characterized more by conservatism and a willingness to uphold – what they perceive to be – the traditional values their parents' generation eliminated. This can also be seen in light of the larger backdrop of Sweden's longstanding political tradition of relative economical and gender equality. The Brats are, more than anything else, rebelling against this ethos of equality and standing up for their right to conspicuously flaunt their stuff; a right that their parents swindled them of. The worst accusation for the Brats is to be accused of being just one of 'the Joneses', or 'a Svensson' as they would have it in Sweden.

Youth constellations typically described in subcultural research (e.g., Hebdige, 1979) usually display some kinds of rebellious traits oftentimes directed towards the mainstream or the parent generation (Thornton, 1997). This rebelliousness portrays the parents as 'squares' who are too conservative or sucked into the market system. The Brats show a distinct difference on this dimension as they rebel by being more conservative than their parents. Also, they are not, as opposed to many other consumption communities described (e.g., Kozinets, 2002; Thornton, 1996), opposing the market. Rather, their whole existence is dependent on the market. With respect to economical issues, style issues, and gender roles their subcultural capital prescribes that they should be rebelling by resurrecting conservative values.

In many ways the Brats see themselves as bearers and upholders of the consumption ethos laid down by the Yuppies in the 1980s (see Belk, 1986). One sign of this genealogical connection to the Yuppies is detectable in the Brats' fascination and admiration for a number of popular culture sources that the Brats seem to regard as relevant historical accounts that set a standard for extravagant consumption. The first one is the novel *American Psycho* by Bret Easton Ellis. The book is usually portrayed as one of the great chronicles of the Yuppie era. When the book was launched it stirred up a great deal of controversy due to its violent and radically consumption-oriented nature. The Brats forget all these dimensions, and instead hail Patrick Bateman, the leading character of the book, as a superhero whose consumption style should ideally be mimicked. A sign of this is a recent invitation to an 'American Psycho Party' posted on the SthlmVIP homepage. The invitation states a strict dress code for men: suit, tie, suspenders, and business cards; and for women: hot/dress-to-impress. The best Bateman-look-alikes will be invited to an exclusive VIP party together with the women of their choices. The objectification of women as the ultimate accessory portrayed in the book is clearly adopted by the Brats. Although *American Psycho* is a fairly recent book (originally published in 1991) it represents history to the Brats. By adapting the 'classic' style of Bateman one shows one's knowledge of the appropriate codes. Another important historical points of references for the Brats is Tom Wolf's *The Bonfire of the Vanities*, where the leading character Sherman McCoy is held up as a style icon. In the book, McCoy views himself as a 'Master of the Universe', a person that, because of his social standing and his affluence, does not have to comply to the rules that govern the rest of the society. The Brats clearly aim at gaining such a privileged position. Both *American Psycho* and *The Bonfire of the Vanities* were originally published as books but have since been converted to motion pictures. It seems like most of the community members have watched the movies but only a fragment have actually read the books. Rather, they are alluded to as some kind of mythical sources that only a few have been able to digest in their entirety. Or, as explained by a Brat during a fieldwork conversation: It is kind of like the bible, most know the basic plot but few have bothered to read the whole thing (fieldnotes, 2004-08-16).

The Oliver Stone motion picture *Wall Street* is another celebrated moment in Brat 'history'. Especially Michael Douglas' character Gordon Gecko's classic comment 'Greed is good!' is celebrated as an important historical moment where the consumption ethos of the Brats was established. It is common to hear the comment used by young male Brats who, in moments of Champagne intoxication, want to show the world that they have the right attitude towards money. To buy another 90-dollar-bottle of champagne and sign the credit card bill with a winning smile while stating 'greed is good' is a typical way to show 'class' (fieldnotes, 2004-08-16). The Gordon Gecko name is also used as an alias by a member of the Glife web-community and Michael Douglas was recently named a style icon by magazine *King* (June 2006), due to his stylish rendition of the Gecko character.

In this way, subcultural capital drawn from quasi-historical pop cultural references is embodied in the form of being 'in the know', using (but not over-using) current slang and looking as if you were born to perform. This is very similar to how classical cultural capital is personified in 'good' manners and urbane conversation. It should be pointed out, though, that both cultural and subcultural capital put a premium on the 'second nature' of knowledge. Nothing depletes capital more than the sight of someone trying too hard (Thornton, 1997, p. 202), when someone is caught doing that they are quickly stigmatized as 'a wannabe' (fieldnotes, 2004-05-14). In what follows, more examples will be drawn from the empirical material to show how the Brats build and use subcultural capital through consumption and a reflexive knowledge of relevant popular culture. The analysis is organized around the themes style and media reflexivity.

Style

A basic feature in Brat consumption patterns is to play the consumption game with *style*. On the web-pages, references are many times made to how they, the Brats, do things with style, whereas others lack the capital, both economical and subcultural, to be stylish. For example, two non-brats caught on camera on the Brat web-pages were mocked for wearing tight jeans and snug fitting v-neck t-shirts, with derogatory comments of the type: 'ha-ha, so 15 minutes ago' (SthlmVIP, 2004-08-27). The very same week, there were several other pictures of people wearing the same type of clothing. From a purely objectivist viewpoint one could then be tempted to conclude that they were sending out the same signals with their clothing (cf. McCracken, 1988, Chapter 4). This would be too grave a simplification however. The people depicted on the photographs who are already members of the Brat community, that is their pictures are frequently published on the pages, are accepted in wearing the outfits whereas the people wearing it to, seemingly, try to fit in are exposed as wannabees.

A common denominator for what is stylish is that it should be connected to what other, imagined, groups of similar consumers around the world are engaging in. In this way, the Brats are consciously tying their consumption patterns to some kind of cosmopolitanism (Thompson and Tambyah, 1999) that they envision is lived out in other, more glamorous consumptionscapes inhabited by 'global players.' Oftentimes references are made to how consumption occurs among so-called players in cooler places than Stockholm, such as London, New York, Paris, and St. Tropez. The content on the web-pages suggests that the Brats see themselves as part of a global community of young, affluent, stylish people – 'global Brats' – who consume in a highly aestheticized manner. The Stockholm enclave clearly demarcates themselves from the 'ordinary Swedes' who lack in sophistication, and instead search for inspiration from imagined soul mates around the globe. Frequently, parties are organized where the theme is to mimic one of these glamorous places such as 'A Verbier-style after-ski party' (SthlmVIP, 2004-11-13), 'Miami Extravaganza' (SthlmVIP, 2004-08-14), or a 'Night of St. Tropez lounging' (YoSthlm, 2004-05-21). The Internet media thus sets up an (imagined) international benchmark of style to which the members of the community try to measure up. The literature focusing on the Brats also help in co-constructing this international ideal by describing how young, successful, affluent Swedes spend time in exotic locations, such as the French alps (Rudberg, 2003). The Swedish Brats are hence taking, what they perceive to be, a global lifestyle, and adopting it to certain local conditions. This global lifestyle is to a large degree made up of the consumption of different global luxury brands such as Möet et Chandon, Gucci, and Prada. Knowing which brands are appropriate at a certain time is an important part of the subcultural capital. Ordering a bottle of Italian Nastro Azzuro beer can be extremely stylish if done while sitting outside in the afternoon, perhaps after skiing; ordering the same beer at a nightclub while sitting at a table is brutish, such an occasion calls for champagne or a mixed drink (fieldnotes, 2004-05-14). The key to stylishness, then, lies not in objectification, that is in just buying and having the right stuff, but in embodying the consumption of goods in precisely the right manner.

Media reflexivity

From time to time, a phenomenon within the Brat community receives enough attention from the outside to provoke a response from the group. The Brats are hence feeling a moral responsibility towards the community (cf. Muñiz and O'Guinn, 2001). For example, journalists in the main Swedish newspapers frequently make references to the Brats and their extravagant consumption patterns. Sweden's largest newspaper, *Dagens Nyheter*, recently commented on how the refurbishing of a classic Stockholm nightspot risked making it yet another venue for the Brats (Dagens Nyheter, 2003-10-17), and their allegedly pig-like behaviours (Dagens Nyheter, 2003-10-03), and the second largest newspaper, *Svenska Dagbladet*, lamented over how the Brats' bad influence was responsible for the poor work ethic of young people in Sweden (Svenska Dagbladet, 2003-08-02). In such instances, the Brat web-pages provide a forum for upset Brats' alternative explanations for their behaviour and their rejections of stereotypical views of the Brats as spoiled youngsters with too much money. One of the features among the Brats that spur the most criticism is their very strict and conservative gender division. Roughly, the male Brats are 'real men' and the female Brats are there for the males to enjoy (Ostberg and Borgerson, 2004). According to the web-page portrayals, the women appear content with this gender division, playing only supporting roles in the males' identity game. This stands in stark contrast to accounts of other contemporary nightscapes that have been characterized as 'feminized', where young women are adopting 'predatory' sexual attitudes traditionally reserved for men (Chatterton and Hollands, 2003, p. 155). There has been a fair share of criticism in the media towards this behaviour and a column on the SthlmVIP homepage (2004-03-31) responded by defending the Brats' gender roles.

The result is a fascinating concoction of biologism and racism. Nevertheless, the comments on the column, both from men and women, stand as a unitary celebration of someone standing up for the Brats' core values.

In these instances, the Brat community is quick to state that they stand over the 'common people' and dismisses any derogatory comments passed at them. Nevertheless, they never miss a chance to soak up any positive occurrences in mainstream media. An example is the chief editor of the magazine *Stureplan* and related web-page www.stureplan.se Alexander Schulman, who proudly publishes all positive feedback received. Examples include national radio proclaiming: 'Schulman's witty ways with words sets his pen on fire' and one of the main cultural magazines, *Bon*, announcing: 'Schulman is the 9th most powerful person in media!' (www.stureplan.se, 2006-06-28).

Concluding remarks

Consumption-oriented communities, under one of the competing labels within consumer culture theory, has been a richly employed concept the last decade. Much of prior research has striven to establish whether it is viable to talk about consumption-driven communities; what brands, objects, or activities are likely to spur the creation of communities; and to what extent companies can facilitate community building. The Stockholm Brats are not about consuming *one* particular object but about style, that is about carefully assembling, displaying, and using various consumption objects to create just the right ambience of being 'in the know'. The first contribution of this chapter is that it sheds light on the ways in which a consumption community is dependent on the external world in constructing its internal codes. The linking value of the Brats' particular rendition of style is valorized by the recognition of the Brats by sources external, such as the media and popular culture. This appreciation, in both negative and positive ways, is what seems to forge the social link between the members of the Brat community. The second contribution is that the research taps into the performative aspects of subcultural capital necessary to forge the communal bond. This is done by contextualizing the communal consumption and looking at the dialectical process with the media and popular culture whereby the community defines its limits and its prescriptive behavioural codes. By employing the concept of subcultural capital, and showing how this is transformed into practice and both objectified, as in owning the right consumption objects, and embodied, as in expressing a certain style the chapter furthers out knowledge of community and consumption.

References

Arnould, E.J. and Price, L.L. (1993). River magic: extraordinary experience and the extended service encounter, *Journal of Consumer Research*, **20** (June), 24–45.

Belk, R.W. (1986). Yuppies as arbiters of the emerging consumption style, in Lutz, R.J. (ed.), *Advances in Consumer Research*, Vol. XIII. Provo, UT: Association of Consumer Research, 514–519.

Belk, R.W. (1988). Possessions and the extended self, *Journal of Consumer Research*, **15** (September), 139–168.

Belk, R.W. and Costa, J.A. (1998). The mountain man myth: a contemporary consuming fantasy, *Journal of Consumer Research*, **25** (December), 218–240.

Bourdieu, P. (1984). *Distinction: A Social Critique of the Judgement of Taste.* Cambridge, MA: Harvard University Press.

Catterall, M. and Maclaran, P. (2002). Researching consumers in virtual worlds: a cyberspace odyssey, *Journal of Consumer Behaviour*, **1** (3), 228–237.

Celsi, R.L., Rose, R.L. and Leigh, T.W. (1993). An exploration of high-risk leisure consumption through skydiving, *Journal of Consumer Research*, **20** (June), 1–23.

Chatterton, P. and Hollands, R. (2003). *Urban Nightscapes: Youth Cultures, Pleasure Spaces and Corporate Power*. London: Routledge.

Cova, B. (1997). Community and consumption: towards a definition of the 'linking value' of product or services, *European Journal of Marketing*, **31** (3/4), 297–316.

Cova, B. and Cova, V. (2001). Tribal aspects of postmodern consumption research: the case of French in-line roller skaters, *Journal of Consumer Behaviour*, **1** (1), 67–76.

Cova, B. and Cova, V. (2002). Tribal marketing: the tribalisation of society and its impact on the conduct of marketing, *European Journal of Marketing*, **36** (5/6), 595–620.

Dagens Nyheter (2003-10-03). Åsiktsmaskinen: Cochon oblige, 10/03/2003, 3.

Dagens Nyheter (2003-10-17). Åsiktsmaskinen: Nya Sture, 10/17/2003, 3.

Ewen, S. (1999). *All Consuming Images: The Politics of Style in Contemporary Culture*, Revised Ed. New York: Basic Books.

Firat, A.F. and Dholakia, N. (1998). *Consuming People: From Political Economy to Theaters of Consumption*. New York: Routledge.

G life (2006). G life home page http://www.glife.se [2006-04-21].

Goulding, C., Shankar, A. and Elliott, R. (2002). Working weeks, rave weekends: identity fragmentation and the emergence of new communities, *Consumption, Markets and Culture*, **5** (4), 261–284.

Hebdige, D. (1979). *Subculture: The Meaning of Style*. London: Methuen & Co. Ltd.

Holt, D.B. (1995). How consumers consume: a typology of consumption practices, *Journal of Consumer Research*, **22** (June), 1–17.

Holt, D.B. (1998). Does cultural capital structure American consumption? *Journal of Consumer Research*, **25** (June), 1–25.

Kates, S.M. (2002). The protean quality of subcultural consumption: an ethnographic account of gay consumers, *Journal of Consumer Research*, **29** (December), 383–399.

Kozinets, R.V. (2001). 'Utopian enterprise: articulating the meanings of star trek's culture of consumption, *Journal of Consumer Research*, **28** (December), 67–88.

Kozinets, R.V. (2002). Can consumers escape the market? Emancipatory illuminations from burning man, *Journal of Consumer Research*, **29** (June), 20–38.

Löfgren, O. (1994). Consuming interests, in Friedman, J. (ed.), *Consumption and Identity*, Vol. 15. Singapore: Harwood Academic Publishers, 47–70.

Lundell, S. (ed.) (2006). *Stureplan: Det vackra folket och de dolda makthavarna.* Stockholm: Lind & Co/Stranger than fiction.

Maclaran, P. and Catterall, M. (2002). Researching the social web: marketing information from virtual communities, *Marketing Intelligence and Planning*, **20** (6), 319–326.

Maffesoli, M. (1996). *The Time of the Tribes*. Thousand Oaks, CA: Sage.

Mauss, M. (1997). *Gåvan*. Lund: Argos Förlag.

McCracken, G. (1988). *Culture and Consumption: New Approaches to the Symbolic Character of Consumer Goods and Activities*. Bloomington, IN: Indiana University Press.

Muñiz Jr., A.M. and O'Guinn, T.C. (2001). Brand community, *Journal of Consumer Research*, **27** (March), 412–432.

Nancarrow, C., Nancarrow, P. and Page, J. (2002). An analysis of the concept of cool and its marketing implications, *Journal of Consumer Behaviour*, **1** (4), 311–322.

Ostberg, J. and Borgerson, J.L. (2004). Living la dolce vita: embodied figurative tropes among the Stockholm brat enclave, in Scott, L.M. and Thompson, C.J. (eds.), *Proceedings from the ACR Gender, Marketing and Consumer Behavior Conference*, Madison, WI: Association for Consumer Research.

Penaloza, L. (1994). Atravesando fronteras/border crossings: an ethnographic account of the consumer acculturation of Mexican immigrants, *Journal of Consumer Research*, **21** (June), 32–54.

Piccaboo.com (2006). Piccaboo home page, www.piccaboo.com [2006-02-15].

Rudberg, D. (2003). *o.s.a.* Stockholm: Bokförlaget Fischer & Co.

Schouten, J.W. and McAlexander, J.H. (1995)., Subcultures of consumption: an ethnography of the new bikers, *Journal of Consumer Research*, **22** (June), 43–61.

Schulz, J. (2006). Vehicle of the self: the social and cultural work of the H2 hummer, *Journal of Consumer Culture*, **6** (1), 57–86.

Solomon, M.R., Bamossy, G.J. and Askegaard, S. (2002). *Consumer Behaviour: A European Perspective*, 2nd Ed. Harlow, England: Prentice Hall.

Stureplan.se (2006). Stureplan – La publication glamoureuse, superfashion et tres exlusif! www.stureplan.se [2006-01-12].

Svenska Dagbladet (2003-08-02). Bratsen bidrar till ohälsoproblemet, *Zsiga, Erik*, 4.

Thompson, C.J. and Tambyah, S.K. (1999). Trying to be cosmopolitan, *Journal of Consumer Research*, **26** (December), 214–241.

Thornton, S. (1996). *Club Cultures: Music, Media, and Subcultural Capital*. Hanover, NH: Wesleyan University Press.

Thornton, S. (1997). The social logic of subcultural capital, in Gelder, K. and Thornton, S. (eds.), *The Subcultures Reader*. London and New York: Routledge, pp. 200–209.

Veblen, T. (1899). *The Theory of the Leisure Class*. New York: The Modern Library.

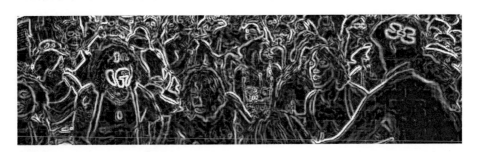

Part III

Tribes as double agents

8

Sociality in motion: exploring logics of tribal consumption among cruisers

Douglas Brownlie, Paul Hewer and
Steven Treanor

Introduction

This chapter discusses consumption as cultural formation and the part played
by exemplary artefacts in performing identity work within complex webs of
social relations. Accounts of the dynamics of distinction-making are situated
through acts of spectacular consumption and bricolage. We discuss how fluid
patterns of collective association and 'sociality' are nurtured through particular forms of materiality and interaction with specific objects of desire – in this
case, cars. We also explore the value of understanding car cruising as a collective or distributed strategy for spreading the burden of representation through
the generation of symbolic resources and the management of self-constructed
forms of identity. In doing so, we consider the value of adopting a cultural
approach to understanding consumption as unstable patterns or flows of

affiliation and identity which characterize the 'sociality' of 'differentiated cultural citizens' (Willis, 1990).

Considerable influence is attributed to the work of the Centre for Contemporary Cultural Studies (hereafter CCCS: cf. Clarke, Hall, Jefferson, and Roberts, 1993; Hall and Jefferson, 1993; Hebdige, 1991, 1993). However, after Bennett (1999) we call for a reworking of the concept of subculture in the light of recent Maffesolian insights (1996a,b) regarding the elusive determinacy of shifting patterns of commitment and ways of life organized around creative interaction with commodity aesthetics and their conspicuous consumption. On the topic of car culture, the study draws on a small, but insightful extant literature base (Miller, 2001; Moorhouse, 1991; O'Dell, 2001). It also draws on data generated through interviews and participant observation among car cruisers to explore how they distinctiveness is produced through the performativity of the cruise, while at the same time maintaining a shared identity. The cruise becomes a site where collective understandings and group allegiances are sustained and reworked through practices such as creative debranding practices.

Tribes in motion

The language of tribes is everywhere. Switch on your HDTV or DAB radio and any numbers of social groupings will be labelled as 'tribes'. Tribes are also big business, especially in the economies of culture and sport. In other words, 'tribes' is the latest in a long line of buzzwords appropriated by the media to bracket the complexity of contemporary social reality and make it malleable. In this chapter, we explore one particular tribal group – that of a cruiser community for whom the modified car is an iconic object in which it sees reflected its values and collective self-image. We will show that during the performance of the cruise, modified vehicles occupy centre-stage in an unfolding drama of aesthetic contest and creative reworking through which particular consumption practices distribute a sense of authenticity and sub-cultural capital.

The cruise is a fluid grouping of car enthusiasts who, on the first Thursday of every month, drive in 'convoy' to the site in central Scotland, marketed by Visit Scotland as 'The Falkirk Wheel'. On such evenings the car park of this very imposing and innovative canal lock becomes, not merely another tourist attraction, but the site for a gathering known as the 'Falkirk Cruise'. Similar gatherings can be witnessed in cities and towns throughout the UK, where cars sporting thousands of pounds worth of modifications are temporarily brought together for the display, spectacle and ritual performance of what is termed *the cruise*. Despite the significance of such spectacles to those involved and the context-specific practices they engage in, little is known about them beyond the charged tone of the media coverage which seeks to 'other' them through portraying them as troublesome, secretive gatherings of 'joy riders' and 'boy racers' intent on inflicting their deviant practices on an unsuspecting and innocent general public (Campbell, 1993; Evening Times, 2002a–c, 2003; Mulford, 2000). The effect of such interested media representations, as previously noted by Thornton (1997), is not merely to stigmatize cruising as anti-social, but to construct participants as committed members of a menacing collective expression of the unacceptable face of the 'reality' of youthful resistance, irresponsibility and subversion.

For two important and related reasons it strikes the authors that beyond the froth of such manipulated media accounts there lurks a topic in need of closer inspection. First, there is the issue of understanding the cultural significance of the car in contemporary society. And second, there is the issue of how young people interact with cars and how their lives are organized and made meaningful through those interactions. For it seems that until we are able to offer a better understanding of both those issues, we will not be in a position to frame the broader issue of car consumption.

Others have similarly argued that the study of the culture of the car has received limited attention (Miller, 2001; Moorhouse, 1991; Urry, 2000). With only a few particular exceptions (Banik, 1992; Solomon, 1992; Stern and Solomon, 1992), the same could be said of consumer research which has failed to get beyond the understanding of cars as simply extensions of the self (Belk, 1988). We argue that consumer research needs to better understand how cars and sociality interact to understand the material cultures of consumption produced through such interactions.

Indeed as Miller (2001) discovered, the car has become so central and 'second nature' that its significance has been overlooked to the detriment of an accurate understanding of the extensive role it plays in people's lives. He argues that the car has been viewed as the 'taken for granted mundane that hides the extraordinary found in this material expression of cultural life' (ibid., p. 2). Bull suggests that we think of the car as an extension to the home in which individuals, 'physically cocooned' (Jacobsen 2000 cited ibid.), inhabit a 'free dwelling' in motion on the road (2001, p. 185). As he explains, the car has become a metaphor for dominant western values of individualism through which people adhere to the rule of an individualized society, namely, 'to each his own bubble' (Baudrillard, 1993 cited in Bull, 1999, p. 185). For us this individualized approach is insufficient since it fails to address what Riggins (1994) refers to as the 'socialness' of such material objects. In writing about the social value of cars, Dant (1996) sets out to avoid the fetishism of the object through understanding the car as an inherently social object, a point of connection or 'vector of communion' (Maffesoli, 1996b) through which people are able to share their enthusiasms and passions to produce what Maffesoli might refer to as ephemeral, local emotional communities (Maffesoli, 1996a).

A (sub)cultural approach to consumption

Studies of bikers (Schouten and McAlexander, 1995) to those on goths (Goulding, Saren, and Follett, 2004; Miklas and Arnold, 1999), rave cultures

(Goulding, Shankar, and Elliott, 2002), gay men (Kates, 2002), mountain men (Belk and Costa, 1998), trekkies (Kozinets, 2001) and X-Philers (Kozinets, 1997), have all sought to understand the situated nature of consumption practices. In doing so, they have highlighted the value of what Arnould and Thompson (2005) refer to as a cultural approach to the study of consumer complexity that involves 'study[ing] *in* consumption contexts to generate new constructs and theoretical insights and to extend existing theoretical formulations' (ibid., p. 869).

Our pathway into the cultural studies literature has revealed the deep influence of structuralist ideas in the early work of the CCCS (cf. Gelder and Thornton, 1997; Hall and Jefferson, 1993; Hebdige, 1991; Hodkinson, 2002, 2004; Malbon, 1998; Skelton and Valentine, 1998; Willis, 1978). It offers a useful approach to cultural analysis framed through the lens of subculture. The study of so-called subcultural groups such as Mods, Rockers, Teddy Boys, Goths and Punks depicts such groupings as tight, coherent cultural formations organized around forms of interaction and ways of life that are distinct, and typically in opposition to other, usually dominant, structures of oppression (Bennett, 1999; Gelder and Thornton, 1997; Goulding et al., 2002; Hall and Jefferson, 1993; Hebdige, 1991).

In the case of studying the subculture of skinheads, Clarke writes that 'Skinhead style represent(ed) an attempt to recreate, through the "mob", the traditional working class community as a substitution for the real decline of the latter' (1993, p. 99). He argues that groups of similar minded youths were able to resist the 'people on our backs' within their 'community', with solidarity expressed through the symbolic construction of taste and style (1993, p. 99). In this way, the subculture is manifested through a collective response to changes taking place in wider social conditions, organized around style-based allegiances, especially to fashion and music. Early debate around the value of the CCCS notion of subculture centred on the idea of taste and style as articulations of symbolic capital and as the basis for strategies of resistance enacted through the conspicuous consumption of style-inscribed commodities. In one study Clarke et al. (1993) asserts that 'despite visibility, things simply appropriated and worn (or listened to) do not make a style. What makes a style is the activity of stylization – the active organization of objects with activities and outlook, which produce an organized group-identity in the form and shape of a coherent and distinctive way of "being in the world"' (1993, p. 54).

Through solidarity and conformity to argot, appearance and taste, the CCCS (Clarke et al., 1993; Hall and Jefferson, 1993; Hebdige, 1991, 1993) theorized that individuals were brought together in a stylized ensemble to form a 'tight', coherent social group (Clarke et al., 1993; Hebdige, 1991). Yet, as Bennett (1999, p. 605) explains, the idea of 'subcultures [as] subsets of society, or, cultures within cultures . . . imposes lines of divisions and social categories which are very difficult to verify in empirical terms . . . [and] there is little evidence to suggest that even the most committed groups of youth stylists are in any way as coherent or fixed as the term subculture implies'. So studies of youth culture which are located within a theory of subculture have attracted criticism based on the assumed stability of the categories defining the collectives and the limited role of consumer creativity and autonomy in constructing identities.

In consumer research, the work of Schouten and McAlexander (1995) imports a subcultural framework into their research among a community of bikers, albeit with little reference to prior ethnographic studies of bikers (Willis 1978), or the work of the CCCS (e.g., Clarke et al., 1993; Hall and Jefferson, 1993). In producing an ethnographic account of the new biker community, they also introduced the term 'subculture of consumption' as a means of characterizing individual and group organizing structures, such as clearly defined hierarchical fields, systems of formal and informal membership, a unique ethos or shared set of beliefs, rituals, jargon and modes of symbolic expression.

Although these characteristics, in particular shared rituals and modes of symbolic expression, seem extremely similar to those which mark neo-tribes (Cova, 2002), there are fundamental differences. For instance, a 'subculture of consumption' recognizes that subcultural groupings are defined by clear hierarchical social structures that may identify the status of individual members. Expanding on the work of Fox (1987), Schouten and McAlexander (1995) explain how subcultural groupings can be characterized by a concentric social structure and related consumption practices, signifying three levels of involvement based on commitment to the ideology of the group. 'Hard core' members exhibit a 'commitment and ideology that is full time and enduring' (ibid., p. 48). This group acts as opinion leaders to the 'soft core' members, who demonstrate less commitment and willingness to submit to the ritualized practices of the group, especially where discomfort or hardship is involved. In turn their role is subordinate to and dictated by the 'hard core'. Finally, 'Pretenders' show great interest in the subculture but only 'delve superficially' into the ethos serving as an audience and material support to the hard core and soft core members (ibid.).

Tribal membership practices

Another crucial distinction between neo-tribes and subcultures as ways of framing cultural collectives relates to formal and informal membership practices. Maffesoli (1996a) argues that neo-tribes are distinctive on the basis of their ephemerality: that is, they do not have any permanent membership other than through the duration of rituals. It also appears possible to belong to more than one neo-tribe through switching allegiances, where one mask is dropped and another is worn (Malbon, 1998). Within a subcultural framing then, identity is theorized as being unified and fixed: membership is seen to be static, one mask being permanently worn, in that distinct dress codes and a specific stable way of life permeates everyday activities. As Schouten and McAlexander (1995) discovered, the biker culture could be represented as a rigidly defined and stable way of life. Or as Miklas and Arnold (1999, p. 568) observed, Goth culture inscribes a 'sort of religion', apparently underlining the stability and intensity of commitment and belonging.

On the other hand, membership framed through the concept of neo-tribes is represented as being temporary, unstable and shifting, making possible simultaneous membership of several sites, so that the individual can live out a temporary role or identity in one site, before relocating to another to assume a different role or identity. And those roles or identities are not simply class-based. As Maffesoli argues, '. . . it is less a question of belonging to a gang, a family or a community than of switching from one group to another' (1996a, p. 76). Recent research into 'rave cultures' (Bennett, 1999; Goulding et al., 2002; Malbon, 1998) has been critical of the relevance of subcultural theory to our understanding of contemporary tribal groupings on the basis of its static focus on structures at the expense of agency. Bennett maps out some of the key objections, namely that it may be inappropriate to utilize 'structuralist accounts to explain what are, in effect, examples of consumer autonomy and creativity' (1999, p. 599).

Drawing on the work of Goulding et al. (2002), we suggest that subcultural activities may be better understood as moving expressions of self-identity and creative solidarity, rather than resistance against domineering forces in what is becoming a progressively classless society. As a raver in this research stated 'Going to a rave is like going to a massive party where everyone is in the same wavelength. Dancing kind of draws people together, not in any kind of sexual way, it's just like you're sharing something exhilarating, dancing till you nearly drop' (ibid., p. 273). Bennett (1999) employs the neologism of 'neo-tribe', arguing that membership of such groupings is based not on conformity nor exclusivity, but an ambience, a state of mind that binds fellow individuals, even strangers, together into one tribal moment (Bennett, 1999; Goulding et al., 2002; Malbon, 1998). In his research on music-making, Stahl (2004) opts for the analytical concept of 'scene' to account for the loose affiliations and 'webs of connectivity' that may define participants' everyday practices in moments of communal activity.

Car practices

Turning to studies of car consumption we find that most have tended to adopt the subcultural approach rather than that of the tribal framework. For example, Moorhouse (1983, 1991) investigated the 'hot-rod' enthusiasm of post-war America and was able to identify a specific subculture with its own values, interests, vocabulary, magazines and rituals. He argued that the most important practice, entailed customizing modifications as a means of creative self-expression, varying from 'simply bolting a few shop-bought accessories onto your car, to creating, through one's own labour over many years, a streamlined special' (1991, p. 17).

In describing the enthusiasm that bound the group, Moorhouse (1991) writes that 'through action and activity "commodities" like the car become the basis for various fields of interests, even identities for individuals and, relatedly, become the basis of various enthusiasms . . . I believe that a large amount of personal consumption and, especially, the explanations, ethics, and ideologies which surround consumption, are regulated through involvement in such enthusiasms' (1991, p. 18). In a similar fashion, O'Dell (2001) documents how the car served to bring individuals together forming the *Raggare*, a subcultural grouping in Sweden where the car became both 'a forum for self-expression' (ibid., p. 114) and 'a mobile family room or kitchen – a semi public sphere in which friends congregate and socialize' (ibid., p. 125). Through acts of bricolage the cars of the *Raggare* were customized and decorated outlandishly with two-tone paint and as much chrome as possible, becoming 'something of a vulgarity' to the general public (ibid., p. 114). Lipsitz (1997) notes how the result of customizing bricolage in LA is to modify cars in such a way as to flaunt their impracticality or otherness, for instance where widely understood fast cars are modified to go slowly, even decorated with chandeliers instead of overhead lights.

We argue that the value of such studies lies not in their adoption of the language of tribes, but in the attention they draw to the practices of customization and the consumer empowerment that flows from them. By this reckoning we employ the lens of practice (Warde, 2005) as a device to help frame social relations circulating around the cultural form of the 'car', as particular manifestations of consumer culture in the making. We interrogate questions of identity making and the affiliative work of objects, in this case cars, through employing the language of tribes and also of subcultures. This helps unravel the complex processes by means of which consumer culture is instantiated in the particular milieu of the car as bricolage, a site where cruisers improvize collective responses to their environment. Logics of appropriation can then be seen to be the means by which tribes seek to capitalize on difference and pursue strategies of authenticity through creative reworking of available resources. We suggest that this approach also avoids the trap of developing a static focus on the structures of social organization at the expense of the contingent flows of processes of identity formation and transition. In this way we identify pathways into the rich literature and various intellectual traditions available to consumer culture theorists (cf. Arnould and Thompson, 2005).

Methodology

Having mapped out the conceptual traditions that lay behind the chapter, it is useful to articulate the methodological underpinning for the research conducted. Cova and Cova (2001) emphasize that to study neo-tribes the marketer is 'well advised to cast aside the more traditional mono-disciplinary, systematic approaches and to favour practices based on detecting signs, foraging for faint hints and sighting glimmers of shadow' (2001, p. 71). In following this advice, data generation was organized around three key processes: first, to build an understanding of the jargon, rituals and aesthetic ambience shared by the group, a review of popular discourse was undertaken, involving websites, Internet discussions and newspaper coverage. The dedicated fanzines *Max Power* magazine and *Fast and Modified* provided accounts of 'key [cruise] events memorialized in words' (Fetterman, 1998, p. 92). Such textual resources were supplemented by recourse to 'consumer voices' (Stern, 1998, cited in Cova and Salle, 2003, p. 10) to generate accounts of the lived experiences and everyday practices of cruisers. As Elliott and Jankel-Elliott (2003) advise, interviews took the form of impromptu discussions between researcher and informants. This material was then coupled with a phase of participant observation, which involved an episodic 'deep hanging out' (Wolcott, 1999, cited in Elliott and Jankel-Elliott, 2003, p. 215) with tribal members over a six month period at a number of specific cruise events.

The cruise: as a way of being together

Car enthusiasts have existed in society for as long as cars have existed. As car manufacturing has evolved over the years, passion and interest in cars has increased exponentially. 'Cruisers' are not a new phenomenon but represent a contemporary form for an enthusiasm centred around the car. In this way, we can make links to previous groups such as American hod rod enthusiasts (Moorhouse, 1991). Our research reveals that central to their enthusiasm is the spectacle of the cruise itself, whereby cars meet periodically at a pre-arranged meeting place, usually a sizeable public car park, details having previously been circulated by internet, phone and email. The convoy exists as a form of being-togetherness which enables participants to express their solidarity by travelling in tandem along public roads. Or as Maffesoli might suggest: 'I will try to show that the object does not isolate, but that it is, on the contrary, a vector of communion. Like the totem for primitive tribes, it serves as a pole of attraction for postmodern tribes' (1996b, p. xv).

Comparisons here can be made to Hebdige's accounts of the Mods and their symbolic scooter charge on Buckingham Palace (1991, 1993). That is to say, the convoy and cruise represent the imaginative marking out of territory, a symbolic attempt to 'win contested space' (Clarke et al., 1993, orig. 1975). Moreover, they exist as ephemeral performances delivered on the public and commercial stage of the car park, what Cova (2002) refers to as 'anchoring sites', where upon the tribe marks its own 'unique' existence through rituals of display and performance. In terms of interpreting such cultural events we argue that such spectacles are not defined simply by their public visibility, but also as Kahn Harris (2004) and Butler (1997) prefer it is essential to view the cruise as a space for performance and ritual, through which the cruisers become visible to each other. Taking this line of argument further, we might suggest that the performance of the cruise functions to energize and vitalize the group, providing it not only with legitimacy, but also with a material presence to produce an ephemeral community where emergent socialities are produced. Namely through what Maffesoli might refer to as their 'undirected being together' (1996b, p. 86).

While we found it difficult to estimate the numbers involved, we concur with Cova and Cova's (2001) evaluation of the in-line skater tribe that hundreds of individuals may share in the vogue surrounding modified cars and cruising. Outward manifestations of this include the movie *Fast and Furious* and its sequel, as well as a variety of Internet sites and chat forums, what we might term neo-tribal spaces, where regular exchanges of information on modifications are facilitated but also where the identity of each regional cruise is marked out and a counter-discourse to the dominant media representations is produced. As the following response posted on one of the cruise forum conveys:

> Well the BBC certainly got one over us, what a fucking embarrassment to those that are genuine cruisers . . . This 'Inverness posse' bunch of twats climbing out car roofs and in through windows while on the move, smart! Good show for the camera's and exactly what the folk in Crail need to see when they get Crail shut down . . . . It was basically a bunch of neds selected to show us up, well done.
> (Edinburgh Cruise Forum, Tuesday March 23, 2004)

The Internet is in this way not simply giving rise to new forms of community, but operates as a cultural resource enhancing group solidarity through the affirmation of a 'them' and 'us' mentality mediated specifically in terms of local affiliations and differences.

Stylization and customization

The spectacle of the cruise is central to the collective display of the sensibilities of taste and style that mark out the imaginative territory of the cruise. In addition to this there is of course the 'look' of the car itself and the associated modifications made to this cultural object (see Figures 8.1 and 8.2).

We argue that it is not just the spectacle that cements and animates the group, but through the prior acts of modification and the codes which regulate and place value upon particular forms and styles of modification. Table 8.1 provides a synopsis of the main modifications of car cruisers gleaned from observation, revealing that designs of alloy wheels are the apparent 'calling card' for cruisers, where they, like the Mods before them (Hebdige, 1991, 1993) are not merely passive consumers of culture, but actively construct it. Bricolage involves a 'hyper-stylization' of the car, achieved for instance through the deliberate lowering of the suspension, or the addition of elements to attract the gaze of spectators such as bonnet vents or unique paint effects, debadging (Figure 8.1), neon lights, body kits and spoilers (Figure 8.2), smoothing, or I.C.E (see Table 8.1), illustrating that some commodities are constantly in flux and occupy shifting positions for consumers.

Figure 8.1 Debadged car.

Figure 8.2 Body kit, spoiler and neon lights.

By means of reworking their vehicles, removing original features and building-in or appropriating others, the vehicle is imaginatively removed from its original context. Through transcending the style boundaries imposed by the manufacturer's production design, the cruisers strive to express their

Table 8.1 A list of common tribal modifications

Mod	Description
Debadging	'Debadging' involves removing all the badges of the car manufacturer as to reveals a blank shell on which cruisers imprint their own brand creations.
Smoothing	Removing or inverting locks from car doors and boot as it is perceived that the smoother the car is, the better it looks.
Spoiler	Usually used for preventing lift on the car and increasing the downward force on the car. However, spoilers have largely been adopted as a style feature on their cars. These can vary in size and proportion. Prices range from £50 to £300.
Body kit	Body kits are moulded panels applied to the original shell of the car which makes the car, at times, unrecognizable according to shape and manufacturer. Prices range from £200 to £1,000.
Neon lights	Neon lights are fitted under the car to light up the underside of the car. Usually neon blue in colour these lights are perceived to add style.
Exhausts	Wider bore exhausts are purchased to replace standard exhausts. As well as for style and performance purposes, exhausts result in the car sounding louder and as a result is noticed more. Prices range from £100 to £700.
Paint effects and transfers	Paint effects can vary from smaller stencilled graphics to full bodywork coverings. The most popular style is multi-lustered 'flip' paint but more recently glitter paint effects have become widespread.
Tints	Tinting involves darkening the windows of the car so that it is difficult to see inside the car. Recent legislation has made some tinting illegal, depending on how dark the windows have been made. As a result many cruisers who previously modified windows have now discovered their windows are breaking the law.
Alloys	One of the first purchased modifications a cruiser is likely to make. Purely for style purposes. Ranging from £120 to £1,000s for a set of four, they can form a considerable expense. Sizes range from 10″ to 22″ and are available in a number of colours (white, black, powder coated, gun metal grey and most common, chrome). It is generally perceived that the larger the alloys, the more fashionable they are.
ICE (in car entertainment)	Given the time cruisers spend in their cars many have extensive in car entertainment. ICE varies in extent and variety. The most common ICE is a stereo system to listen to music. Frequently cruisers dedicate the whole boot to install their sound systems and 'sub whoofer' speakers that increase bass power and volume. Other examples observed in the field included flat screen DVD players in the passenger seat of cars and even Playstation consoles.
Custom lights and clear indicators	All lights on the car can be modified to suit individual tastes and styles. An example of custom lights are 'angel eyes' which are LED-powered light rings, forming a halo effect, that replace standard lights. Clear direction indicators involve replacing the conventional yellow indicator and making it clear.

(Continued)

Table 8.1 (Continued)

Mod	Description
Lowered suspension	Usually prioritizing style over practicality, lowering involves sinking the suspension. It is generally perceived that the lower the car is the better it looks. However, extremely low cars prevent anyone from sitting in the rear seats. Moreover driving over speed bumps is likely to damage the underside of the car, especially the exhaust usually lowered by 30 mm to as much as 150 mm.
Body vents	Used in rally cars to increase the flow of air and provide greater stability. However, cruisers use them for styling purposes.
Engine modifications	Used primarily for performance enhancement engine modifications take many forms. Examples include the following: conventional engine 'swaps' where one engine, is replaced by another; turbo charges and dump valves are installed to give more power. Such modifications not only increase performance of the car, but also serve to increase the subcultural capital ascribed to its owner. The intense sound of a highly tuned engine gives great pleasure to cruisers. More style-based engine modifications include colour coding the engine with different coloured leads and hosing, and installation of push button starters whereby the engine can be started at the push of a button.
Miscellaneous engine modifications	Given the amount of time cruisers spend in their cars it is unsurprising that the interior of the car tends to be stylized to the same extent as the exterior. A small selection of interior modifications include: stylized seats including bucket, leather, recliners, racing, etc.; replacing standard dials with custom images or coloured varieties; additional dials added to show extra elements of the car not provided by original manufacturer; replacement of floormats, steering wheels, handbrakes, pedals (available with neon lights) and gear shift sticks, with versions to suit personalized comfort and style ambitions.

individual creativity and autonomy and their affiliation with other cruisers. So, we understand the practice of customization, even where it involves removing the accoutrements of brand recognition (debadging) that many other consumers seem keen to cherish and display, as the formation of tribal capital, 'confer[ing] status on its owner in the eyes of the relevant beholder' (Thornton 1997, p. 11).

Individualism and affiliation

Central to understanding the relationship between cruisers and their cars is the problem of individualism (Maffesoli, 1996a, p. 9). At a superficial level it may seem adequate to define cruisers behaviour as a form of individualism as a number of individualistic elements did characterize the group. In this manner some of the respondents explained their passion for modifying cars in terms of the desire to be 'unique', to possess what they termed a 'one-off', but also '. . . to be as different as possible from anyone else'. However, this assertion is also framed in terms of what the CCCS (Hall and Jefferson, 1993) might define as the values of the parent culture. As some of the participants suggested:

> In a world where everyone had a grey coloured car, wore grey suits, had grey wallpaper and carpets would there be much to live for?

By this reckoning the name of the game is not simply a spectacle of escape and freedom (Goulding et al., 2002), but also appears geared to expressing resistance through symbolic means to broader cultural imperatives:

> The reason is to be different from standard. Standard is boring and you can see standard cars at any time of the week. It's all about individuality and standing out from the crowd.

It is as if in a drab humdrum world such groups are searching for the glamour of the spectacle, the glamour of display to express their identities and re-enchant themselves through communion with others. This being-as-a-group, or as they prefer 'standing out from the crowd', can be reaffirmed in their resistance or antipathy the logic of the market, what Willis refers to as the 'shit of capitalist production' (1978, p. 178), and their desire to inflect their own meanings from such commodities. Debadging being one such act of resistance or symbolic attempt to escape the market and it's characteristic brand-dominated culture. We must also understand; however, the extent to which the practice of debadging serves as an affiliative act enacted to produce a sense of belonging and community.

Debadging is also an aesthetic act, and the importance of the appearance of their cars cannot be underestimated (Hewer and Brownlie, 2007). Although no such codes existed around the 'look' of members, as no particular cruiser 'uniforms' appeared to exist as was the case with the CCCS work on mods, rockers and punks. Although one significant way in which membership was affirmed and reproduced was through the development of a unique argot. In this way, cruisers would use a lexicon of terms to not only endorse their own individual membership but also exclude non-members or outsiders. The language of 'Scooby', 'Evo', 'Cossie', 'Chinq', 'Feestie', 'fourteens', 'convoy', 'mods', 'peeps' and 'cruises' (see Table 8.2) may appear incomprehensible to non-members but they appeared to serve a unique function of mapping out the shared identity of the tribe.

Aloofness and fluid hierarchies

Although Cova and Cova (2001) do not describe any specific differentiating practices within neo-tribes, it was clear that a fluid form of style hierarchy

Table 8.2 The argot of Scottish car cruisers

Tribal term	Definitions
Mods	Modifications
Peeps	Endearing term for friends/other members
Fourteens/sixteens/ eighteens, etc.	14/16/18″ alloys
Scooby-doo	Subaru
Evo	Mitsubishi evolution
Cossie	Ford sierra Cosworth
Feestie	Ford Fiesta
Chinq	Fiat cinquecento
Slammed	Lowered cars
Dubs	20″ alloys
Beemer	BMW
Zorts	Exhaust
Rims	Alloys
Dusties	Fancy dustcaps
Tunes (choons)	In car entertainment (music)
Rims	Wheels
Smoked	To have been overtaken
Honnie	Handbrake turn
Donut	Drive rear-wheel drive car in a continuous circle

does operate within the cruiser community. Understood through the concept of tribal capital, it is based upon the possession of cars deemed to be outstandingly creative and stylish (see Figure 8.3).

Figure 8.3 Parading the work of art.

The question for the present study then becomes whether the tribal per-spective seems better suited to explaining shifting patterns of sociality within elective groupings, than stable structures based on ongoing conform-ity to the practices and ideology of the group, as explained by Schouten and McAlexander (1995). Within the studied community of cruisers, inter-action did appear unstable and fluid, more resolutely neo-tribal in charac-ter than a rigidly defined subcultural community. However, a tacit form of distinction-making was present, noted by a shifting two-tier social structure of 'cruiser chiefs', who possess what Simmel describes as 'works of art' (cited Nedelmann, 1991), and the rest. The position of these informal chiefs, like the group to which they belong, does appear to be constantly under threat and in flux. As Simmel argues 'works of art are destroyed in their uniqueness the moment they are reproduced . . . . [and] cannot exist in great numbers with-out losing their essential nature' (cited Nedelmann, 1991, p. 182). Indeed, according to informants there were several cruisers who attracted fame and notoriety due to their extraordinarily 'unique' cars. And the flux between the extraordinary creations and the ordinary creations of others did appear to ani-mate consumption activities and aspirations within the group. Discussions revealed that several style chiefs seemed successful in their efforts to acquire the distinction of 'coolness'. And one way in which this was managed and maintained was in their deliberate efforts to remain outside the socializing practices of the group, that is to say they would avoid speaking to or befriend-ing others or otherwise participating in face-to-face networking activities to maintain a sense of aloofness (Maffesoli, 1996a).

Discussion

In giving to the word culture its strongest meaning, that of the soil in which soil life takes root, one could speak of an aesthetic culture. This means a moment when aesthetic values contaminate the whole of social life, the moment when nothing escapes their influence . . . [when] Style become an encompassing ethic that slowly shapes the manner of being and different forms of representation.

(Maffesoli, 1996b, p. 37)

This chapter has sought to explore the value of adopting what we term a cul-tural approach to the understanding of car cruisers. This cultural approach relies heavily upon insights gleaned from the early work of the CCCS (Clarke et al., 1993), namely in the focus upon notions of stylization, creativity, 'winning space' and language. We have sought to rework their contribu-tion through a turn to the work of Maffesoli (1996a, b) which anticipates the demise of the distinction between structure and agency with the retreat of the classic institutions of family, state and class. We argue that the turn to Maffesoli helps frame the cruiser community in a way that captures the 'out-sourcing' of identity work through moments of movement, transition and disorganization. It also draws our attention to the social value of cars as culture in the making and the constitutive practices and platforms in play around this. Pivotal among these ideas is that of the reflexive nature of consumption practices which mediate social relations within the cruise community. Here tribal cars serve as a 'vector of communion', a nexus through which the group can cohere around like-mindedness while at the same time capitalizing on difference. The car in this sense not only operates as a 'pole of attraction' (Maffesoli, 1996b, p. xv), but also as a visual iconography, a totemic space in which emergent forms of sociality are negotiated.

The contribution to tribal marketing thus becomes clear, or as Cova (1997) makes explicit ' . . . postmodern persons are not only looking for products and services which enable them to be freer, but also products and services (employees + physical surroundings) which can link them to others, to a community, to a tribe' (1997, p. 311). For cruisers there appears a restlessness and impatience with the car in its mass-produced form. The cruise vividly dramatizes this in the variety of material forms that modifications take, capitalizing on the discursive marginality of the tribe while at the same time celebrating 'otherness'. We argue that it is through the refashioning of this social object the car, through practices of customization and the generation of symbolic social meaning, that a feeling of community and a sense of distinction is produced. This approach to marketing where 'the link is more important than the thing' (Cova, 1997, p. 311) sees consumers as important co-producers of value (Vargo and Lusch, 2004), coupling this with an appreciation of the social influence brand communities can exert upon individuals (Aglesheimer et al., 2005). This new logic places aesthetics, stylization and customization in centre stage, not only when trying to untangle social life, but also when seeking to understand tribal socialization and the desire to be with similar-minded people (Maffesoli, 1996b). What we are witnessing when we study the rituals, practices and performances of such cruisers is 'the emergence of a shared and tribal happiness' (ibid., p. 42) whereby they experience the pleasure and 'warmth' of a form of being-together. This eclipses the individual and transcends negative and manipulative media representations. It also reenchants daily life to produce a sense of belonging, a kind of sociality and a form of community within a fragmented, contingent and ever-changing consumer culture.

References

Aglesheimer, R., Dholakia, U.M. and Hermann, A. (2005). The social influence of brand community: evidence from European car clubs, *Journal of Marketing*, **69** (3), 19–34.

Arnould, E.J. and Thompson, C.J. (2005). Consumer Culture Theory (CCT): twenty years of research, *Journal of Consumer Research*, **31** (March), 868–882.

Banik, D. (1992). The all-American unobtrusive measure . . . or, you are what you drive, even if you're not from California, in Sherry Jr., J.F. and Sternthal, B. (eds.), *Advances in Consumer Research*, Vol. 19. Provo, UT: Association for Consumer Research, pp. 166–168.

Belk, R. (1988). Possessions and the extended self, *Journal of Consumer Research*, **15** (September), 139–168.

Belk, R. and Costa, J.A. (1998). The mountain man myth: a contemporary consuming fantasy, *Journal of Consumer Research*, **25** (3), 218–240.

Bennett, A. (1999). Subcultures or neotribes: rethinking the relationship between musical taste, *Sociology*, **33** (3), August: 599–620.

Bull, M. (1999). The dialectics of walking: walkman use and the reconstruction of the site of experience, in Hearn, J. and Roseneil, S. (eds.), *Consuming Cultures: Power and Resistance*. Basingstoke: Macmillan Press, pp. 199–220.

Butler, J. (1997). *Excitable Speech: A Politics of Performativity*. New York: Routledge.

Campbell, B. (1993). *Goliath: Britain's Dangerous Places*. London: Hutcheson.

Clarke, J., Hall, S., Jefferson, T., and Roberts, B. (1993) (orig. 1975). Subcultures, cultures and class: a theoretical overview, in Hall, S. and Jefferson, T. (eds.), *Resistance Through Rituals: Youth Subcultures in Post-war Britain*. London: Routledge, pp. 9–74.

Cova, B. (1997). Community and consumption: towards a definition of the 'linking value' of products or services, *European Journal of Marketing*, **31** (3/4), 297–316.

Cova, B. (2002). Tribal marketing: the tribalisation of society and its impact on marketing, *European Journal of Marketing*, **36** (5/6), 595–620.

Cova, B. and Cova, V. (2001). Tribal aspects of postmodern consumption research: the case of the in-line roller skaters, *Journal of Consumer Behaviour*, **1** (1), June: 67–76.

Cova, B. and Salle, R. (2003). When IMP-Don Quixote tilts his lance against the Kotlerian windmills: BtoB marketing deeply changed during the last 25 years, BtoC marketing too, *19th Annual IMP Conference*, Lugano, September 2003.

Dant, T. (1996). Fetishism and the social value of the object, *The Sociological Review*, **44**, 495–516.

Elliott, R. and Jankel-Elliott, N. (2003). Using ethnography in strategic consumer research, *Qualitative Market Research: An International Journal*, **6** (4), 215–223.

Evening Times (2002a). Time to crack down on lethal car cruise craze, *Evening Times* 8 February.

Evening Times (2002b). Call for ban on boy racer burnout cruise, *Evening Times* 12 November.

Evening Times (2002c). Cops call a halt to boy racer menace, *Evening Times*, 12 November.

Evening Times (2003). Banned boy racer jailed for one year, *Evening Times*, 11 March.

Fetterman, D.M. (1998). *Ethnography: Step by Step*. Thousand Oaks CA: Sage.

Fox, K.J. (1987). Real punks and pretenders: the social organisation of a counterculture, *Journal of Contemporary Ethnography*, **16** (3), October: 344–370.

Gelder, K. and Thornton, S. (1997)., *The Subcultures Reader*. London: Routledge, Kegan and Paul.

Goulding, C., Shankar, A. and Elliott, R. (2002). Working weeks, rave weekends: identity fragmentation and the emergence of new communities, *Consumption, Markets and Culture*, **5** (4), 261–284.

Goulding, C., Saren, M. and Follett, J. (2004). Virtue in darkness: a subculture of consumption from the margins to the mainstream, *Presented at the Academy of Marketing Conference*, Cheltenham, June 2004.

Hall, S. and Jefferson, T. (1993) (orig. 1975). *Resistance Through Rituals: Youth subcultures in Post-War Britain*. London: Routledge & Kegan Paul Ltd.

Hebdige, D. (1991) (orig. 1979). *Subculture: The Meaning of Style*. London: Methuen & Co Ltd.

Hebdige, D. (1993) (orig. 1975). The meaning of mod, in Hall, S. and Jefferson, T. (eds.), *Resistance through Rituals: Youth Subcultures in Post-war Britain*. London: Routledge & Kegan Paul Ltd, pp. 87–96.

Hewer, P. and Brownlie, D. (2007). Cultures of consumption of car aficionados: aesthetics and consumption communities, *International Journal of Sociology and Social Policy*, forthcoming.

Hodkinson, P. (2002). *Goth: Identity, Style and Subculture*. Oxford: Berg.

Hodkinson, P. (2004). The goth scene and (sub)cultural substance, in Bennett, A. and Kahn-Harris, K. (eds.), *After Subculture: Critical Studies in Contemporary Youth Culture*. Houndmills, Basingstoke: Palgrave Macmillan, pp. 135–147.

Kahn-Harris, K. (2004). Unspectacular subculture? Transgression and mundanity in the global extreme metal scene, in Bennett, A. and Kahn-Harris, K. (eds.), *After Subculture: Critical Studies in Contemporary Youth Culture*. Houndmills, Basingstoke: Palgrave Macmillan, pp. 107–118.

Kates, S.M. (2002). The protean quality of subcultural consumption: an ethnographic account of gay consumers, *Journal of Consumer Research*, **29** (December), 383–399.

Kozinets, R. (1997). 'I want to believe': a netnography of the X-philes subculture of consumption, in Brucks, M. and MacInnis, D. (eds.), *Advances in Consumer Research*, Vol. 24. pp. 470–475.

Kozinets, R. (2001). Utopian enterprise: articulating the meanings of Star Trek's culture of consumption, *Journal of Consumer Research*, **28** (June), 67–88.

Lipsitz, G. (1997). Cruising around the historic bloc: postmodernism and popular music in East Los Angeles', in Gelder, K. and Thornton, S. (eds.), *The Subcultures Reader*. London: Routledge.

Maffesoli, M. (1996a). *The Time of the Tribes: The Decline of Individualism in Mass Society*. London: Sage.

Maffesoli, M. (1996b). *The Contemplation of the World: Figures of Community Style*. Minneapolis: University of Minnesota Press.

Malbon, B. (1998). Clubbing: consumption, identity and spatial practice of everyday night life, in Skelton, T. and Valentine, G. (eds.), *Cool places: Geographies of Youth Cultures*. London: Routledge, pp. 266–286.

Miklas, S. and Arnold, S.J. (1999). The extraordinary self: gothic culture and the construction of the self', *Journal of Marketing Management*, **15**, 563–576.

Miller, D. (2001). Driven societies, in Miller, D. (ed.), *Car Cultures*. Oxford: Berg, 1–33.

Moorhouse, H.F. (1983). American automobiles and worker's dreams, *Sociological Review*, **31** (3), 403–426.

Moorhouse, H.F. (1991). *Driving Ambitions*. Manchester: Manchester University Press.

Mulford, S. (2000). 50 cars in illegal race meet at park, *Daily Record* 1, May.

Nedelmann, B. (1991). Individualisation, exaggeration and paralysation: Simmel's three problems of culture, *Theory Culture and Society*, **8**, 169–193.

O'Dell, T. (2001). *Raggare* and the panic of mobility, in Miller, D. (ed.), *Car Cultures*. Oxford: Berg, pp. 105–129.

Riggins, S.H. (1994). *The Socialness of Things: Essays on the Socio-semiotics of Objects*. New York: Mouton de Gruyter.

Schouten, J.W. and McAlexander, J.H. (1995). Subcultures of consumption: an ethnography of the new bikers, *Journal of Consumer Research*, **22** (June), 43–61.

Skelton, T. and Valentine, G. (eds.) (1998). *Cool Places: Geographies of Youth Cultures*. London: Routledge.

Solomon, M.R. (1992). Driving passions: vehicles and consumer culture, in Sherry Jr., J.F. and Sternthal, B. (eds.), *Advances in Consumer Research*, Vol. 19. Provo, UT: Association for Consumer Research, pp. 166–168.

Stahl, G. (2004). It's like Canada reduced: setting the scene in Montreal, in Bennett, A. and Kahn-Harris, K. (eds.), *After Subculture: Critical Studies in Contemporary Youth Culture*. Houndmills, Basingstoke: Palgrave Macmillan, pp. 51–64.

Stern, B. and Solomon, M. (1992). Have you kissed your professor today? Bumper stickers and consumer self-statements, in Sherry Jr., J.F. and Sternthal, B. (eds.), *Advances in Consumer Research*, Vol. 19. Provo, UT: Association for Consumer Research, pp. 169–173.

Thornton, S. (1997). The social logic of subcultural capital, in Gelder, K. and Thornton, S. (eds.), *The Subcultures Reader*. London: Routledge, pp. 200–209.

Urry, J. (2000). *Sociology beyond Societies: Mobilities for the Twenty-First Century*. London: Routledge.

Vargo, S.L. and Lusch, R.F. (2004). Evolving to a new dominant logic for marketing, *Journal of Marketing*, **68**, 1–17.

Warde, A. (2005). Consumption and theories of practice, *Journal of Consumer Culture*, **5** (2), 131–153.

Willis, P. (1978). *Profane Culture.* London: Routledge & Kegan Paul Ltd.

Willis, P. (1990). *Common Culture: Symbolic Work at Play in the Everyday Cultures of the Young.* Milton Keynes: Open University Press.

9

Hunting for cool tribes

Clive Nancarrow and Pamela Nancarrow

Hunting for cool

The quest for cool is today's alchemy and wouldn't we all like to extract its essence and apply it liberally to every aspect of our lives.

(Sunday Times Style)

Just as cool has become part of the language of popular culture, so it has become the preferred language of marketing for many companies targeting not only the youth market but also the now increasingly mature baby boomers who believe that a cool lifestyle is their birthright. Cool crosses cultures, age groups, socio-economic classes and national boundaries, existing as a tribal kind of identity, one which many marketers expend large resources trying to capture. However, the chameleon-like quality of cool and the exclusive nature of its tribes set the marketers a daunting challenge. In the hope of providing some enlightenment, this chapter will consider tribes in the context of Pierre Bourdieu's thoughts on *Distinction*, place cool in a historical context and attempt to define this elusive concept. It will also discuss the commodification of cool, the role of cultural intermediaries, the phenomenon of coolhunting and present a marketing research case study involving the search for cool.

Postmodern tribes

Whereas traditional tribes tended to focus on geographical or ethnic identification, shared heritage, conservative values and a sense of putting community interests above one's own, when the sociologist Michel Maffesoli wrote 'The Time of the Tribes' (1996) he specifically excluded this usual anthropological understanding of a tribe and referred rather to 'postmodern tribes'. Far from having any historical tradition, the tribalism he explored could be 'completely ephemeral, organized as the occasion arises'. As in postmodernity generally, stability gives way to fragmentation, a sense of belonging is superseded by multiple identities and style takes the place of substance.

Cova and Cova (2001, p. 67) elaborated further: 'These neo-tribes are inherently unstable, small scale, affectual and not fixed by any of the established parameters of modern society; instead they can be held together through shared emotions, styles of life, new moral beliefs and consumption practices.' Indeed they can be so ephemeral as to be 'just a feeling, a fancy, a fantasy' (Cova and Cova, 2001, p. 71), echoing Baudelaire's comment on bohemian life as 'transitory, fleeting, contingent' (Seigel, 1986, p. 122). On the worldwide web they can even be virtual. Nor does belonging to one tribe exclude the possibility of other tribal identities: 'individuals can belong to more than one neo-tribe whereas with earlier youth subcultures it would have been impossible' (Shankar and Elliott, 1999). But the sense of belonging, however fleeting, can be intense; for instance belonging to the tribe of England supporters during the World Cup – flying flags, wearing the colours, cheering at televised matches in public spaces – it may not last beyond the end of the tournament but for those few weeks it is a very real tribe. And of course it is a tribe that is based on making a distinction between supporters of the England football team and those of the other competing nations.

Tribal identity and cultural identity are closely linked. We belong to groups or tribes and we adopt the signifying images of such groups whether in clothing, hairstyle or accessories such as iPods or mobile phones. To confirm our social identity: 'we adhere to groups and we adopt the identifying images of social groups ... our tastes and our lifestyles have no intrinsic value but to serve to maintain the coherence of the group to which we belong' (Robbins, 1991, p. 174). Youth culture in particular tends to be tribal in nature and also to reflect many of the indicators most associated with postmodernism – a preoccupation with shopping, a preference for style over substance, the search for identity, recycling (retro) and pastiche, media-saturation, rapidly changing fashions, signifiers adrift from meaning, virtual reality and a desire for spectacle. There is also a strong desire to differentiate one's own group from the uncool mainstream. As Pountain and Robins (2000, p. 9) argue in *Cool Rules*, 'there is a tendency in cool that encourages the formation of tight peer groups and subcultures, unified by a shared definition of what is cool'. And excludes those lacking the necessary insider or tribal knowledge.

Tribes and distinction

Distinction, the thought-provoking work by the French sociologist, Pierre Bourdieu (1984) explores the relationship between 'taste' (in the cultural or lifestyle sense as well as the physiological sense) and social background, and how artificially constructed distinctions can be used to exclude the less privileged from influential positions in society and to maintain the hegemony of those who are already members of the elite.

Aside from all-important economic capital, Bourdieu argues that there are also various kinds of 'immaterial' capital that influence the way society is structured. As well as social capital (who you know, to whom you belong), symbolic capital (recognition as a leader, prestige in the community) and educational capital (qualifications) there is also 'cultural capital' or knowledge of the code of legitimate culture. Bourdieu sees cultural capital as playing a vital role in perpetuating the hegemony of the dominant group, in the case of France that he studied, the bourgeoisie. Cultural capital in this context is the appreciation of bourgeois culture – classical music, art and literature, a taste for fine food, knowledge of the great canon of literature, avoidance of the vulgar or ostentatious. It is sophisticated, refined and elitist. It excludes those who were not brought up from childhood to know this 'consecrated canon'. Thus he argues that 'supposedly natural or individual tastes' are actually socially constructed. *Distinction* emphasizes that taste is as much about what it excludes as what it includes.

For instance, in British society in 2006 'chavs' – young men and women from 'working class' backgrounds who dress rather ostentatiously in 'designer' clothes (fake or otherwise) in the manner of their cheerleaders, the WAGs (footballers' wives and girlfriends) – are treated by the mainstream media as something to be joked about or even reviled as lacking taste. This is in marked contrast to how the Hoxton Tribe of the late 1990s was treated by the media as a cultural elite. Hoxton, once 'a scruffy no-man's land of pie and mash and cheap market stall clothing' in the East End of London attracted a colony of artists in the late 1990s looking for airy, cheap workspaces – Damien Hirst, Tracey Emin, Alexander McQueen amongst them (Carter-Morley, 2003). It soon became 'the groovy district du jour' with retro fashions, hip new bars and gastro-pubs representing 'the cliff face of the cutting edge'. Of course it couldn't last and by 2003 the media were asking 'Where have all the cool people gone?' and declaring that 'overexposure has destroyed the sense of Hoxton as an exclusive club for the ultra-fashionable'. Even worse, 'the Bacardi Breezer drinking hordes' made it 'like walking into Essex' (*The Guardian*, G2, 21 November 2003).

Taste, it seems, is something that, by definition, most people can't have; like cultural capital, its exclusivity must be maintained. It is one of the key signifiers of social identity and in Bourdieu's (translated) words: 'taste classifies and it classifies the classifier'.

Subcultural or tribal capital

Bourdieu's ideas of the creating of distinction and of cultural capital can also be useful terms of reference when discussing the phenomenon of tribes.

Indeed Bourdieu's work has already been placed in the context of subcultures. It was Dick Hebdige (1979) whose pioneering work on British subcultures (such as mods and rockers) first proposed the idea of the adoption of a particular style or 'look' as a signifying practice, as a text to be read, not merely expressing cultural identity but also a form of resistance to the dominant culture, a way of remaining on the outside. Sarah Thornton (1995) subsequently synthesized Hebdige's subcultural theory and Bourdieu's concept of cultural capital in her work on club culture in 1990s Britain. Thornton argues that, within contemporary youth culture, cool is a form of 'subcultural capital'. According to Thornton the criteria for 'hipness' always fetish the exclusive – whether it is the alternative, the indie, the authentic, the esoteric. It is all about having underground knowledge, privileging the obscure and despising mass culture – thus making it very difficult for outsiders to take part. Just as the literary or artistic canon can be used to exclude those without a classical education from bourgeois society so lack of insider knowledge can effectively exclude the mainstream from being 'cool'. And, to update Thornton as she updated Bourdieu, this form of cultural capital can meaningfully be called tribal capital or *tribal knowledge* in the sense that it is most readily recognized by those tribal members with a shared definition of cool.

So what is cool?

Before attempting to define the elusive concept of cool we should like to put it into some kind of historical context.

Cool: some historical perspectives

Although cool has more than a little of the destructive heritage of Bohemia and poets like Rimbaud, Baudelaire and Byron, it is more realistic to say that the concept first became meaningful as part of the American jazz scene just after the First World War.

Hip and cool are both terms derived from the 'jive' talk of black jazz musicians and are virtually interchangeable in meaning. Both are characterized by a sense of detachment and of illicit 'knowledge' that stem chiefly from the drug culture of the jazz scene. Cool was, at least in part, an attitude of unspoken defiance on the part of black jazz musicians against the prejudice and difficult working conditions they often encountered. It was also linked to the drug-taking lifestyle that many of the musicians brought with them – marijuana from Mexico and cocaine and heroin (so prevalent in some US states that it formed part of every travelling medicine show). The need to stay awake until the early hours of the morning encouraged the taking of stimulants. Life in the ghetto was made more bearable by the taking of painkillers. Drugs also functioned as a point of artistic distinction – keeping the mainstream out of their world. This manifested itself in the detached persona that came to epitomize cool. It was a statement of separateness and it removed inhibitions (Shapiro, 1999). It was the culture of the oppressed.

Ironically it was the outlawing of alcohol during the Prohibition Years (1919–1933) that brought the pleasures of this illicit world to the attention of a very different audience. Prohibition not only inextricably linked alcoholic indulgence, bohemia and the criminal underworld, it positively encouraged the wealthy to take a walk on the wild side at speakeasys and jazz clubs. Like la bohème of Montmartre at the end of the nineteenth century, so the jazz scene existed as the exotic *Other* of conventional society.

Soon the hip values of this alternative culture began to filter into mainstream awareness, mediated through those middle class jazz enthusiasts labelled 'white negroes' by Norman Mailer. By the 1940s and 1950s these white bohemians, mostly middle class and mostly male, had become known as the Beats, most definitely recognizable as a tribe (Polsky, 1998). Revelling in jazz, blues and drugs whilst reinventing American literature, Kerouac, Burroughs and Ginsberg – collectively known as the Beat Poets – led the way towards 'self-discovery' and the 1960s counter-culture.

Here cool had a very new look– black influences were in retreat as white middle class baby boomers appropriated the cool concept for themselves. The illicit drugs remained with the addition of some newly available hallucinogenic ones and they spread further into the mainstream than ever before. Anti-establishment, hedonistic, unconventional, notably anti-(Vietnam) war; it seemed as though a whole generation of white middle classes students were making 'cool' their own. Adopting the language of mysticism and astrology, they began to view themselves as a 'hippie' tribe, quite literally adopting the signifiers of native Americans and hill tribes of the East – dream-catchers, incense burners and ethnic dress such as kaftans.

For arguably the first time the tribal 'look' became important. Although some elements of the black jazz musicians' gear had been picked up by the fringes of the mainstream – dark clothes, dark glasses and to some extent the zoot suit – this was the first time that an identifiable look became the mark of cool. And this hippie look was far from that of the jazz club. It was one which the mainstream could adapt and that the retailers could understand. Although it started in thrift shops and ethnic clothes stalls the hippie 'look' could soon be found in high streets across the globe. It has been argued that this saw the 'democraticization of bohemia' (Mignon, 1993, p. 181) as the availability of drugs on every campus, relaxed attitudes to work, permissiveness, global travel and the collection of ethnic artefacts tended to be inclusive, almost evangelical rather than exclusive and beyond the reach of the mainstream. Cool tended to replace bohemian as the name that represented hedonism, consciousness-expanding drugs, the carnivalesque and an alternative way of life.

Whilst American and European white youth embraced the counter-culture with its almost exclusively white music, black music seemed to lose its cool – the Supremes and the Four Tops, disco, soul were all too often considered to have become too commercial.

As the 1960s generation – the middle-class university-educated baby boomers – began to aspire to well-paid capitalist jobs, they still wanted to spend 'weekends immersed in a moral and cultural universe shaped by the Sixties' (Pountain and Robins, 2000, p. 7). This generation has been christened BoBos (bourgeois bohemians) by David Brooks (2000). However, whilst these BoBos maintain, in part at least, a cool lifestyle through their consumption not just of clothes but also of lifestyle products generally (food, restaurants, cars, holidays, interior décor), the ever elusive cool has moved on again and reverted to a style more recognizably rooted in the American jazz clubs.

By the 1990s, rap and hip-hop and other variants of the urban black music scene had put black culture firmly back on the cool map. The lyrics outraged the mainstream, it was overwhelmingly masculine and misogynist and it started fashions for sportswear, oversize clothes and then ghetto 'bling'. Drugs were omnipresent, guns and violent death were part of the culture, words like pimp and 'ho were part of their canon. This really seemed like taking a walk on the wild side. And if white celebrities wanted to emulate this 'cool' it often seemed as though behaving badly – a propos Kate Moss and Pete Doherty – was the fastest route to recognition as a cool icon, as this review of the Strokes makes clear: 'impeccably dishevelled in their dirty converse trainers and crotch-clinging jeans, the unassailably cool NY five pieces were embraced as rock gods and venerated as such' (Independent Music, 23 May 2006).

Cool and the ideology of authenticity

One of the most important ways in which members of a cool tribe distinguish themselves from mass culture is through an emphasis on authenticity. It has even been proposed as 'the truest hallmark of cool behaviour' (Southgate, 2003). Authenticity is in any case a deeply ideological discourse that denigrates popular culture and privileges the exclusive, whether in terms of literature, film, food, venues, sport. Music in particular, has been the focus of much disdainful media debate. Whilst commercial pop music is frequently considered 'feminine' and worthless by (male) music critics, indie music that either hasn't reached the mainstream yet or is destined to remain obscure is garlanded with praise. Best-selling artists like James Blunt are vilified, whilst niche acts like New Yorkers 'Antony and the Johnsons' reap music industry awards.

Authenticity is a very much a value judgement that is used to express distinction and is frequently gender-specific. The NME Cool List (www.nme.com), for example, is overwhelmingly male: Alex Turner, Liam Gallagher, Kanye West, Antony (Johnsons) and Brandon Flowers. It is the feminized mainstream of popular culture versus the masculine/genderless underground of DJs, club entrepreneurs, music journalists, esoteric knowledge and specialist genres. The feminization of popular culture has been a theme, a concern even, of cultural studies for a long time (see Andreas Huyssen, 1986). Authenticity is often cited as the opposite of this supposedly degraded mass culture. And, of course, in the postmodern world there is no need for this authenticity to have real heritage; it can be invented authenticity as with many alcoholic products, cigarettes, jeans brands and sportswear. Authenticity may have become just another style, but however contrived, styled and created it may be, it is still of immense importance to anyone trying to understand the cool world and its tribes.

Defining cool

The essence of cool is not easily captured; that is part of its seduction. There is no 'coherent philosophy of cool' (Gladwell, 1997). Cool is not something you can set out to acquire; it is something that is acknowledged in you by others. It involves originality, self-confidence and must be apparently effortless. It is often transgressive and anti-establishment. It is certainly narcissistic.

Some of its more universal signifiers are likely to include a refusal to conform, artistic involvement, a sense of detachment and a hint (or more) of the illicit. It is always about not being seen to try too hard. In the words of the undoubtedly 'cool' photographer, and publisher of *Dazed and Confused*, Rankin: 'If you have to try you've already failed; if you want it too bad you're just chasing your tail' (Knobil, 2002). This echoes Thornton's (1995, p. 12) thoughts on subcultural capital: 'nothing depletes capital more than the sight of someone trying too hard'.

Cool by its very nature is not caring what anyone else thinks. 'It's dispassionate, free-willed, self-confident and non-impressionable' (Smith, 2003). It also therefore tends to be 'intrinsically anti-social, anti-family, pro-drug, anti-caring and most of all anti-authority' (Pountain and Robins, 2000, p. 13). It is essentially urban or even metropolitan and, as we have noted above, there is also a strong tendency for cool to privilege the masculine.

The commodification of cool and the cultural capital of consumption

We would also argue that cool is now best described as an advanced form of knowledge about commodities and consumption practices: 'As for defining cool, although we see it as essentially rather elusive, we would define it partly as an attitude but also as a form of cultural capital that increasingly consists of insider knowledge about commodities and consumption practices as yet unavailable to the mainstream' (Nancarrow, Nancarrow, and Page, 2002).

The question of whether cool ideology really triumphed during the counterculture or whether it was thoroughly incorporated into the dominant consumer ideology has been the subject of much debate (see Brooks, 2000; Powers, 2000; Frank, 1997). Undoubtedly there was an engagement of countercultural values with the dominant ideology – hedonism, self-expression, sexual permissiveness, anti-authoritarian attitudes. But as Frank (1997, p. 119) argues convincingly in the *Conquest of Cool*, 'Hip consumerism marked a crucial step in the development of a new ideology of consumption'; cool entered the mainstream as a way of increasing consumption, co-opted by the world of advertising and marketing.

The counter-culture did not just represent a dissident subculture; they were educated middle-class voices and as time went by the increasing presence of graduate baby boomers in the media and culture industries gave them the opportunity to disseminate their own 'hip' ideology. As influential BoBos they still sought a cool lifestyle through the commodities they bought and through consumption practices.

Douglas Holt (1998, p. 3), writing in a USA context, calls this the Cultural Capital of Consumption, a cultural capital that 'consists of a set of socially rare and distinctive tastes, skills, knowledge and practices'. He argues that there is a strong desire amongst the 'hip' generations of the baby boomers and their children to consume goods and services in ways not available to those with less cultural capital – this partly relates to 'authenticity' (drinking tequila in the 'real' Mexican way) and, especially 'decommodified authenticity' – thrift shops, vintage clothing, ethnic artefacts, bricolage, customizing, eclecticism. Holt concludes that in a society where commodities circulate so freely and are copied so quickly by mass-market retailers, distinctive ways of consuming have become intrinsic to the concept of cultural capital.

Alternatively those 'in the know' may subtly change the criteria of taste, moving on from something being 'hip' to mocking late adherents for too obviously just following fashion. Often this exclusion works on the basis of understatement in the knowledge that outsiders are likely to over-compensate for their parvenu status (Bourdieu, 1984). Once again trying too hard is anathema to cultural capital.

Just as cultural capital can be commodified (a dinner menu, holiday destination, an evening out) so subcultural or tribal capital can be objectified or embodied – a haircut, a T-shirt, an item of cutting edge technology, an alcoholic drink. And as Gladwell (1997) writes of the cool tribe, 'their definition of cool is doing something that nobody else is doing'. It may even work in a negative sense: 'interestingly the social logic of subcultural capital reveals itself most clearly by what it dislikes' (Thornton, 1995, p. 12). So although the concept of cool continues to be built around never trying too hard, the pursuit of authenticity and distinctive consumption practices and always searching out new insider knowledge, now it also involves a considerable degree of market consciousness.

Messengers of cool

Of course not all tribes have any aspirations towards being considered cool, some are too proudly geeky to ever be considered 'cool' and many are more concerned with specialized interests. However, within tribes that have pretensions towards hipness or cool there are hierarchies of cool – there are the creatives, artists and designers who initiate new ideas, trends, fashions and new uses of technology and the followers who adopt, in varying degrees, these stylistic innovations. And then there those who, echoing de Certeau's 'art of being in between' (Klein, 2001, p. 78), are of immense interest to marketers and who we might call cultural intermediaries (after Bourdieu), or, perhaps, the messengers of cool.

Marketers are naturally concerned with the process of diffusion of innovation and, in particular with early adopters and opinion shapers. These highly sought after individuals may be known as 'style leaders', 'tastemakers', leading edge consumers or, as we choose to call them, messengers of cool. They are not the originators – the artists, designers and inventors whose work forms the basis of innovative technology, fashion and lifestyles, but they are the people who act as intermediaries, the people who can shape opinion and who are rather more accessible to marketers than the cool elite. They are a vital part of the cool tribe, constructing a cool world consisting of those few who initiate and those larger numbers who imitate. In many ways these intermediaries are the real arbiters of cool; tribe members at the leading edge who are able to decode the cultural significance of commodities and ways of consuming.

They are the successors of Bourdieu's (1984, p. 359) 'cultural intermediaries', the new middle-class who work in 'all the occupations involving presentation and representation (sales, marketing, advertising, fashion, media, decoration, etc.) and in all the institutions providing symbolic goods and services'. Writing in a French context Bourdieu (1984, pp. 363–366) saw them as 'upwardly mobile individuals who seek in marginal, less strictly defined positions a way of escaping their destinies' . . . who 'see themselves as unclassifiable, excluded, dropped out, marginal, anything other than categorized'. Most importantly these cultural intermediaries play 'a vanguard role in the struggles over everything concerned with the art of living'.

In the context of the cool community these intermediaries work in the media, fashion, music, advertising, the arts and in 'hip' shops and act as a channel between the innovative – whether it be the street, the clubs, the art colleges, designers – and the cooler part of the mainstream. They make a living out of spotting trends and re-interpreting them for a wider audience. As Featherstone (1991, p. 19) has noted these style leaders have 'the apparent contradictory interests of sustaining the prestige and cultural capital of these enclaves while at the same time popularizing and making them more accessible to a wider audience'. And herein lies one of the paradoxes of the 'cool' world; although insider knowledge is threatened by the mass media, many of those with the most subcultural or tribal capital become involved in the consumer media, perhaps initially in 'style' magazines but also in the mainstream.

Coolhunting

Marketers are naturally aware of the immense power that 'cool' has to sell products and services, not just to the often fickle youth market but also to the

wealthy BoBo market. For some time now and in the youth market in particular, insight, innovation and knowledge has 'trickled-up' from the street, with
all the major players in this market wanting 'a window on the world of the
street' (Gladwell, 1997). In the words of Sarah Smith (2003): 'Today we try to
bottle cool and turn it into a concept you can quantify.'

During the 1990s and particularly in the USA, global marketing giants such
as Nike, Adidas and Levis became heavily involved in seeking out and observing what the cool people were wearing. In their case this often meant adopting the voice of the street, and specifically black culture, to sell more products
to the mainstream. Aware that they were scarcely in a position to talk to cool's
inner circle themselves, these companies began to use so-called coolhunters
as intermediaries. The world of coolhunters often involved global companies paying for the transmitted thoughts of kids on the street, not just any kids
of course, but those considered to have the cool Midas touch (Gladwell, 1997).

Frightened at the thought that cool is not a controllable variable in their
marketing plans, many major companies rely on the cultural intermediaries
discussed above to act as cultural commentators, style runners or indeed, as
messengers of cool, for them. But as Gladwell (1997) points out, 'The paradox, of course, is that the better coolhunters become at bringing the mainstream close to the cutting edge, the more elusive the cutting edge becomes.'
Gladwell proposes three rules of cool for marketers to heed: 'the quicker the
chase, the quicker the flight', referring to the elusive quality of cool; 'you can't
manufacture cool out of thin air', in the sense that marketers can only acceler-
ate the diffusion process and 'you have to be cool to recognize cool', admitting
the essential role of coolhunters and the messengers of cool. He concludes,
somewhat ironically: 'if you add all three together they describe a closed
loop, the hermeneutic circle of coolhunting, a phenomenon whereby not only
can the uncool not see cool but cool cannot even be adequately described
to them'.

However, other writers in both the USA and UK have been far more derogatory about the way coolhunters might be considered to exploit both clients
and the less well-off sectors of society. Naomi Klein (2001, pp. 72–73) accuses
them of being in a relationship with their clients that is like 'a slightly S/M
symbiotic dance: the clients are desperate to believe in a just-beyond-their-
reach well of untapped cool and the hunters, in order to make their advice
more valuable, exaggerate the crisis of credibility the brands face' and refers
to them as the 'legal stalkers of youth culture'. Klein is angry at the coolhunters for the way brands like Tommy Hilfiger have 'turned the harnessing of
ghetto cool into a mass marketing science'. She writes that 'like so much of
cool-hunting, Hilfiger's marketing journey feeds off the alienation at the
heart of America's race relations: selling white youth on their fetishization of
black style and black youth on their fetishization of white wealth' (Klein 2001,
pp. 75–76). In a European context she also quotes avant-garde designer
Christian Lacroix's comment 'it's terrible to say, very often the most exciting
outfits are from the poorest people' (Klein, 2001, p. 63). She calls this 'culture
vulturing' and claims that 'coolhunters reduce vibrant cultural ideas to the

status of archaeological artefacts and drain away whatever meaning they once held for the people who lived with them' (Klein, 2001, p. 84).

Nick Southgate's critique (2003), however, is less concerned with the evils of global capitalism and more specifically with good marketing research practice. Southgate despairs of the 'pervasive influence of coolhunters' and their 'reputation for having the magic touch, as being marketing's first true alchemists after generations of charlatans and frauds'. Marketers, he argues, too often see themselves as uncool and the coolhunters as the high priests of cool. The coolhunters, in turn, are 'explicit about the inability of the uncool to function in the elevated and exclusive realms of the cool' and vague about the recruitment procedures with 'much talk of "instinct", "a sixth sense", "gut feelings" and "people who just know"'.

Overall, as marketers, we feel that Naomi Klein's analysis of the way today's superbrands exploit black culture, part of her 'strident call to arms' against capitalism (Sam Leith, cover notes, No Logo), is intelligently and passionately argued but seems to over-estimate the importance of coolhunters' gleaning information on the latest trainers from cool kids and perhaps to underestimate the value that this 'cool' cultural capital can have for otherwise disadvantaged youth. Southgate, after all, is quite adamant that not many coolhunters are really doing more than reporting what they see on the streets and read in the underground media.

We would argue that there is a marketing research role for some kind of coolhunting, and agree with Gladwell (1997) that 'the key to coolhunting is to look for cool people first and cool things later and not the other way round'; cool things come and go but 'cool people, on the other hand, are a constant'. Although the conquest of cool as a concept existing outside the marketplace may have been accomplished, its ever-evolving content remains the 'knowledge' of the cultural intermediaries. However, commodified cool (as in 'cool' trainers) becomes, it is people, rather than commodities who are 'cool'.

And the search for these cool people is not one that marketers or indeed, traditional market research agencies, can easily undertake without help from the coolhunters. Cool might be the holy grail of marketing but there is no Da Vinci Code to unlock its mysteries. Jazz musicians compared being part of the 'hip' world to membership of the freemasons; cool people recognize each other by style distinctions scarcely perceptible to those outside their world.

With these thoughts in mind, when Seagram, the global drinks company, undertook research into where and what the cool people of Metropolitan London were drinking, they were aware that the recruitment process was of vital importance. As a case study it demonstrates the successful use of some of coolhunting techniques grounded in the best marketing research practice.

A case study: looking for cool

In the definition of an innovation or trend it is assumed that a very small minority actually 'innovate'. Accessing these true innovators for marketing research is almost impossible and so the earliest the process can be tapped into is at the early adopter stage. As part of a wide-ranging study of the drinks market, Seagram UK was particularly interested in the thoughts, feelings and aspirations of 20-something early adopters in the alcoholic drinks market. Consumption of alcohol for this generation is in many ways a social and style statement so part of the study focused on the broad area of style leadership.

A group discussion format was chosen; although social posturing could have been a problem (we were talking 'cool', after all) it was decided that the benefits of a 'performing' group would outweigh this potential disadvantage, especially as the moderator was well qualified to handle any difficulty. Soho, London was chosen as a venue and a research agency with specialist recruiters in their 20s was briefed. They did not call themselves coolhunters but nevertheless knew where and how to find respondents who fitted the chosen criteria – by occupation (fashion/design/media), outgoing personalities, sociable lifestyles, in their twenties, drinkers of alcohol and having a certain 'look'.

The convened group consisted of eight 23–30 years old, equally split on gender and with a mix of nationalities and ethnic groups typical of central London. All were slim, dressed in an understated way and included a photographer, graphic designer, journalist, fashion buyer, web designer, fashion editor and a freelance film-maker. They could definitely be classified as 'cultural intermediaries'. Mostly their capital was cultural (or tribal) rather than economic (their work frequently being irregular and the cost of life in Metropolitan London being high) and they were using this cultural capital to make a living. Maybe they were not at the top of the innovation/diffusion ladder but their relative position tends to make them more useful in articulating what it is that makes a venue or a drink 'cool'; it is something they work at and think about.

Just as pubs played little part in this group's lifestyle so clubs, too, were often rejected in favour of more unusual venues. The problem with clubs was that the cool ones soon became too popular, attracting the unwelcome presence of businessmen and the *'desperate wannabes'* of the mainstream, and clubs in London tend to be expensive and involve the ignominy of queuing. One of the group moonlighted as 'door picker' and it would probably be true to say that *picking* was more congenial to them than waiting *to be picked*. There was a preference for bars in upcoming (but still shabby) areas still unknown to the business set and West End crowds, members-only clubs and bars (invitations coming through their media connections), parties and hotels. An air of consciously 'moving on', searching for something new, runs through their comments.

The young men and women in the group were very aware of their importance as innovators and 'taste-makers' and none expressed surprise that a marketing company should seek their opinion. They were both profoundly cynical and yet firm believers in the power of marketing. They are aware that history can be invented but still insist on the importance of authenticity, for instance, as in the case of a drink like Jack Daniels, a very masculine

'American icon'. Another drink they especially admired was Absolut vodka – not for its heritage but for its 'hardcore' values – strong, minimalist, exclusive, making it the 'the ultimate cool drink'. It was also admired for its low-key marketing strategy, sponsorship of arts events and limited distribution to select venues. Absinthe, a drink with illicit connotations and mythical powers, was another drink that had appeal to the group. High proof Caribbean rum that was not available in this country was another example of the cool choice being one that was difficult for the mainstream to imitate (until, of course, the manufacturer catches on and makes the product, possibly in a lower proof version, available on the high street).

It was agreed that to a certain extent 'you can be cool and drink whatever you like' – in other words, those at the higher levels of the cool hierarchy can get away with consumption practices that might be scorned in a 'wannabe'. There was certainly little tolerance for sweet 'girly' drinks or alcopops. It was noticeable that this style leader group was far less interested than the other mainstream groups in the project in consuming large quantities of alcohol as the basis of a good night out – losing control like the 'ladettes' was definitely not cool.

Deeply derogatory of those they do not consider 'in the know', these young men and women devote considerable time and effort to acquiring their own kind of cultural capital. They search out new venues, give credibility to what are essentially commercial ventures and then move on, ever fearful of being caught up by the mainstream. Their creed is that one shall 'never be seen to try too hard'.

Their concept of cool did indeed fit closely with the one we have attempted to define in this chapter. They were dismissive of the mainstream and especially anything 'girly', chose the authentic over the popular and sought insider knowledge rather than the easily accessible. They believed in understatement, liked the more esoteric consumption practices and even flirted with the illicit. It's also true that their concept of cool was a distinctly commodified one, reflecting considerable concern with the cultural capital of consumption.

This overview of the Seagram research project has concentrated on style dissemination and attitudes towards cool; however the project also provided valuable insights into the ways alcoholic drinks can be introduced to the market through exclusive distribution, word of mouth and 'virus' or 'whisper' advertising. The research methodology of using specialist recruiters and moderators and seeking out 'messengers of cool' was regarded as a success and a blueprint for future research. Chasing cool is not always in vain, though you do need to be fleet of foot. And to remember that what is cool today may be cold tomorrow (Knobil, 2002).

Conclusion

As a now longstanding part of contemporary culture, with roots stretching back to both bohemia and the American jazz scene, cool continues to weave its magic on both youth and many of the baby boom generation. Although it still exists as cultural capital and as insider or tribal knowledge, cool has now 'bought in' to the world of marketing and consumption practices; it has become the cultural capital of consumption. The ideology of cool is very much concerned with issues of authenticity (invented or otherwise) and with the creation of distinction; the cool will always be enticingly different from the rest of us.

Cool is also ever-changing; it evolves according to its place in time and space. It can mean one thing to a Japanese harajuku girl and something quite different to a Parisian 'BoBo'. It may even become known by a different term (as in the past it has been 'bohemian' or 'hip') but whether we regard it simply as another commodity or as an attribute belonging only to the very few, it is very likely that the concept itself will remain much sought after by the mainstream, both producers and consumers. And if the desirability of cool is so widely felt, then marketers will need to continue to track what cool means right here, right now (and preferably tomorrow too).

References

Bourdieu, P. (1984). *Distinction: A Social Critique of Judgment of Taste*, Nice, R. (trans.). London: Routledge.

Brooks, D. (2000). *BoBos in Paradise*. New York: Simon & Schuster.

Carter-Morley, J. (2003). Where have all the cool people gone?, *The Guardian*, G2, 21 November 2003.

Cova, B. and Cova, V. (2001). Tribal aspects of post-modern consumption research: the case of French inline roller skaters, *Journal of Consumer Behaviour*, **1** (1), 67–76.

Featherstone, M. (1991). *Consumer Culture and Postmodernism*. London: Sage.

Frank, T. (1997). *The Conquest of Cool*. Chicago: University of Chicago Press.

Gladwell, M (1997). The coolhunt, *The New Yorker*, 17 March.

Hebdige, D. (1979). *Subculture: The Meaning of Style*. London: Routledge.

Holt, D.B. (1998). Does cultural capital structure American consumption? *Journal of Consumer Research*, **25** (June), 1–23.

Huyssen, A. (1986). *After the Great Divide: Modernism, Mass Culture and Postmodernism*. London: Macmillan.

Klein, N. (2001). *No Logo*. London: Flamingo.

Knobil, M. (2002). What makes a brand cool? Market Leader, *Journal of the Marketing Society*, **18**, 21–25.

Maffesoli, M. (1996). *The Time of the Tribes: The Decline of Individualism in Mass Society*, Smith, D. (trans.). London: Sage.

Mignon, P. (1993). Drugs and popular music, in Redhead S. (ed.), *Rave Off: Politics and Deviancy in Contemporary Youth Culture*. Aldershot: Avebury.

Nancarrow, C., Nancarrow, P. and Page, J. (2002). An analysis of the concept of cool and its marketing implications, *Journal of Consumer Behaviour*, **1** (4), 311–322.

Polsky, N. (1998). *Hustlers, Beats and Others*. New York: Lyons Press.

Pountain, D. and Robins, D. (2000). *Cool Rules*. London: Reaktion.

Powers, A. (2000). *Weird Like Us*. New York: Simon & Schuster.

Robbins, D. (1991). *The Work of Pierre Bourdieu*. Milton Keynes: Open University Press.

Seigel, J. (1986). *Bohemian Paris: Culture, Politics and the Boundaries of Bourgeois Life, 1830–1930*. Baltimore: John Hopkins University Press.

Shankar, A. and Elliott, R. (1999). Consuming Popular Music: Critical Socio-Cultural Perspectives and Research Implications, Working paper of the Bristol Business School.

Shapiro, H. (1999). *Waiting for the Man*. London: Helter Skelter.

Smith, S. (2003). How to bottle cool, *Sunday Times Style*, 10 August, 24–25.

Southgate, N. (2003). Coolhunting with Aristotle, *International Journal of Market Research Society*, **45** (2), 167–189.

Thornton, S. (1995). *Club Cultures: Music, Media and Subcultural Capital*. Cambridge: Polity.

Thornton, S. (1995). *Club Cultures: Music, Media and Subcultural Capital*. Cambridge: Polity.

10

Temperance and religiosity in a non-marginal, non-stigmatized brand community

Hope Jensen Schau and Albert M. Muñiz Jr

'[Bob] Dylan told me recently I was a poet. Although I was impressed by what he said, I couldn't help feeling it was like being told you're an archer. Well, they may think you're an archer, but you know you don't own a bow'.

(Tom Petty from 'Tom Petty – in His Own Words' superseventies.com)

'I have people approach me on the streets and say, "Thanks for writing the soundtrack to my life." I can't tell you how good that makes me feel as a songwriter'.

(Tom Petty as quoted on gonegator.com)

'I love that about TPATH's music. It just sinks into your psyche and never leaves'.

(LizzyB, posted on TPATH Message Board 28 June 2006)

It is well understood that brand communities have a strong narrative component. Storytelling, by both the marketer and the consumer, fosters the construction of a larger than life brand mythology and allows consumers to insert themselves into this mythology. Recent inquiries have suggested that these mythologies frequently contain ethereal elements. Brand communities are the site of many magico-religious behaviours. Aspects of religiosity have been seen in brand communities centred on Apple Macintosh (Belk and Tumbat, 2002; Kahney, 2004), Apple Newton (Muñiz and Schau, 2005), Saab (Muñiz and O'Guinn, 2001), *Star Trek* (Kozinets, 2001), Star Wars (Brown, Kozinets, and Sherry, 2003), Xena: Warrior Princess (Schau and Muñiz, 2004), and the X-Files (Kozinets, 1997). Aspects of religiosity are also common in celebrity fan communities, such as those centred on Barry Manilow (O'Guinn, 1991) or Cliff Richards (Caldwell and Henry, 2006), and even in more generic entertainment communities, such as those centred on headbangers (Henry and Caldwell, 2006).

Now that the body of research on these closely related phenomena has grown, commonalities need to be considered. Looking across these brands, celebrities, and lifestyles listed above, some patterns emerge. The first thing that is evident is that most of the communities listed above are for small share, marginal brands or activities. For example, Saab's market share is less than 1 per cent in the US (Automotive News, 2000) and just over 1 per cent in the UK (Carpages, 2006), while Apple's share of the home computing market is just over 3 per cent (TWICE, 2005). There are, of course, exceptions to this observation. Star Wars, it could be argued, is a large market-share brand, as recent box office receipts would attest, and Kozinets (2001) presents data demonstrating that a large percentage of Americans watch *Star Trek*. However, both of those brands, like most of the others on the list, suffer from a certain amount of stigmatization, particularly for those who self-identify as fans. Brand communities, in general, may be said to be characterized by a sizeable degree of stigmatization. Kozinets (2001), Muñiz and Schau (2005), and O'Guinn (1991) all note the stigmas surrounding *Star Trek*, the Apple Newton, and Barry Manilow communities, respectively. Even Harley–Davidson still bears a stigma owing to the outlaw origins (Thompson, 1996) of its brand community (Schouten and McAlexander, 1995).

These traits have obvious benefits. Marginality and stigma can be an important source of tension. Tension can be a driving and unifying force within brand communities. A common struggle unites. It is well accepted that stigma-based tension has been used to market brand community brands, such as the self-deprecating ads for the original Volkswagen Beetle (Fox, 1984). This assertion, however, begs a few questions. Why is it that brand community so far has been strongest among low share brands? Is marginalization necessary for a strong brand community to form and sustain itself? Moreover, is marginalization (and the resulting stigma) necessary for a brand community to evince religiosity? To answer these questions, we turn our attention to a successful, mainstream, and non-stigmatized rock act, Tom Petty and the Heartbreakers (TPATH), and the broad fan community centred on that brand.

The way of the rockstar

The rockstar lifestyle has been immortalized in numerous songs. It is a wild fantasy of extreme excess and privilege, excess and privilege to a degree to which even most royalty cannot match. In today's vernacular, 'rockstar' has come to mean a high achieving person in any endeavour. Whether the rockstar lifestyle is fact or fiction (or most likely somewhere in between the partying and the liver transplant), the notion of rockstar is synonymous with success. Rockstars are adored and even worshipped by their fans. Some rockstars go far beyond their 15 minutes of fame, their one hit, and even their celebrity status to become rock legends.

Tom Petty is a Grammy Award winning musician with a career spanning over three decades. His setlist for any given performance is guaranteed to delight and disappoint. It will delight owing to the large number of excellent tracks from which it will draw. It will disappoint for the very same reason. Tom Petty cannot get through all of the songs his fans want to hear in 90 minutes. He cannot cover his greatest hits, tap underground favourites, and still plug a new CD within the confines of a single show. It is an enviable dilemma, but a dilemma nonetheless. To fill the void, TPATH has inspired, like many other rock legends living and dead, tribute bands (Klosterman, 2002), which perform as TPATH, covering their music and imitating their mannerisms for eager fans who need a fix of live TPATH off the official scheduled tours. By virtue of these measures, Tom Petty has easily achieved rock legend status. In 2002, this legend status was confirmed when TPATH was officially inducted into the Rock-n-Roll Hall of Fame and reaffirmed in 2003 when Tom Petty was recognized with the Legend Award at the Radio Music Awards.

Following and consuming this legend, we see a strong brand community, a brand community with magico-religious aspects. However, compared to the previous examples of fan and brand communities in which religiosity has manifested, the TPATH fan community is quite different. For starters, it is more mainstream, with a much larger share. Unlike many bands emerging in the 1970s, TPATH successfully managed and leveraged the music video art form, earning an MTV Music Video Award and a place on various compilations of the most influential music videos. TPATH has sold millions of albums and videos on various formats (records, 8-track, cassette, CD, MP3, VHS, DVD). Their 'Greatest Hits' album was certified 10xplatinum in 2003, while their debut release continues to sell globally; new fans emerge across generations and around the world. Tom Petty hosts a popular global weekly radio show on XM Satellite Radio called Tom Petty Buried Treasure in which Tom features his favourite deep cuts from various rock and blues artists. In 2006, ABC contracted with TPATH to use their song 'Runnin' Down a Dream' to promote the NBA Finals; the song was featured at the start of all playoff and finals games (www.ESPN.com). Moreover, TPATH is one of the few rock acts that has consistently garnered both mainstream popularity (enormous volume of record sales) and critical acclaim. Critics consistently give the band's output high marks (Erlewine, 2006) and other musicians (most recently Bob Dylan) consider Tom Petty to be a gifted musician, storyteller, and poet.

As a result of this widespread acclaim, TPATH fans are not stigmatized. There are no skits about obsessive TPATH fans needing to 'get a life' on Saturday Night Live, like there are about Trekies (Kozinets, 2001). TPATH fans aren't stereotyped as geeks or druggies or losers. Compared to Barry Manilow, Tom Petty is a non-polarizing persona. No one is ashamed to be a fan of TPATH. In fact, it is very respectable to be a TPATH fan. Their fans are omnipresent. If you mention you are a Tom Petty fan, chances are good that someone within earshot will declare themselves to be one, too.

Our approach

The data for this chapter are drawn from a long-term engagement with the Tom Petty fan community. The first author has been an avid fan of Tom Petty for over 20 years; it has been 22 years since her first concert. She admits that perhaps a day may go by without a TPATH or Tom Petty track accessed, but never a week. Pieces of her TPATH and Tom Petty collection are on her iPod, Rio, desktop, laptop, Garmin (GPS device), cellphone, CD players and satellite radio. She has enduring engagement with the band. This includes participation in multiple online forums devoted to Tom Petty. She follows several fansites and participates in several fan chat spaces. She has gone to fan parties and has hosted one herself for regional fans. She has spoken with hundreds of fans on and off 'the record'. She has collected fieldnotes of TPATH concerts (33 concerts over the course of 20 years) and has even published a short story of her experience at a TPATH concert in *Hawaii Review* (Schau, 2002).

She used a Tom Petty concert poster for an example in her advertising class in Spring 2006 and three students came up after class to disclose that they were hardcore fans. One, a young man from the UAE, shared that he has been to three TPATH concerts with his dad who is also a fan. He claimed he was anxiously awaiting the new single 'Saving Grace' and was trying to get Milwaukee tickets for 'Summerfest'. The other two students had inside information about the new single, had attended TPATH concerts, and were also planning to catch concert dates in summer 2006. In fact, it turns out that one of the students and the first author had attended the same concert a few years back. Both could recite the playlist. This kid is 23 years old! Perhaps even more amazing, she excused her class 30 minutes early to attend a TPATH concert on 4 October 2006 and discovered that in a class composed of 55 undergrads, four students also had tickets for the show and two more were planning to drive to the venue (90 minutes away) to buy tickets or at least 'party in the parking lot'. Incidents like this are not uncommon for the first author and explain a large part of her experiences in the community.

While her involvement may appear like a groupie, it has an important difference: she does not seek proximity. She has turned down invitations to 'party with the band' on numerous occasions and has never used a backstage pass. She has met the members of the band on one occasion. Tom Petty sang 'Make It Better Forget about Me' to her on stage. That night she talked with him and the band briefly afterward at the side of the stage, but declined to go backstage after two band members (Tom Petty and Stan Lynch) invited her themselves. She is a fan of the music and the art they produce not the men who produce it. The second author is a non-participant observer who enjoys TPATH's music, but does not self-identify as a Tom Petty fan, *per se*. He owns and enjoys several Tom Petty albums, but has never seen him in concert.[1] These differing viewpoints provide crucial interpretive perspective and tension in this endeavour (Denzin, 1998).

My life/your world: religiosity in the TPATH fan community

It comes as no surprise to find that the TPATH fan community is strong, and easily meets the criteria for brand community (Muñiz and O'Guinn, 2001). Consciousness of kind, rituals and traditions, and moral obligation are all present. TP fans congregate at concert venues, at private residences, and in chat-rooms and online forums. They meet to pay homage, to spin yarns, to share Tom Petty brand experiences and expertise, and to commune with other aficionados. In their devotion to Tom Petty, members display a 'passion for life' (Maffesoli, this volume). Some TPATH fans congregate more often than traditional religions mandate. During Tom Petty's active concert seasons, faithful fans make a vacation of following Petty on tour devouring brand experiences greedily in case it is the last opportunity (based on numerous rumours over the past decade). Indeed, the most credible threat of TPATH's 'last concert tour' comes from Tom himself in a *Rolling Stone* interview, where he claims that the 2006 tour will be his last 'for a very long time' (Strauss, 2006, p. 73). While at first blush this may seem somewhat similar to Deadheads or Parrot Heads (followers of the Grateful Dead and Jimmy Buffet, respectively), but TPATH fans are not known for their rowdy reverie or perpetual partying. They follow the band with temperance taking in one leg of the tour (West Coast, or Northern Sea Board) and planning it out as a vacation (two online forums are devoted to TPATH vacations). Multi-generational fan sets bring up their children or younger music fans in the Tom Petty fold. It is quite common to see children under 12 years at the concerts and to see multi-generational groups enjoying the show.

The TPATH brand community evinces religiosity (Muñiz and Schau, 2005). Traces of the magico-religious are widespread and abundant. Members tell a variety of stories that utilize religious discourse and demonstrate these motifs. The ways in which these tendencies manifest have their own idiom here,

[1] He knows he really needs to correct this oversight. And soon!

reflecting the particulars of TP and his fans. In the following, we will describe and analyse the culture of the TPATH brand community to further our understanding of brand communities and the source of their communal strength, with particular emphasis on religiosity.

Temperance in the TPATH brand community

O'Guinn (1991) notes, there are appropriate and inappropriate behaviours for members of the Barry Manilow fan community. In large part, these codes are derived from the values Barry Manilow promotes and publicly embodies. Similarly, the religiosity evident in the TPATH brand community is strongly influenced by Tom Petty's values, which hold God, family, friends, environment, and America in highest regard. Members of the TPATH fan community have a code of acceptable behaviours, influenced by the charismatic focal point of the community. Tom Petty is not known for wild antics, but rather bold acts of conscience. He has valiantly fought record labels over price hikes, ticket sellers for excessive ticket prices, and radio as an industry for their over-reliance on commercially derived playlists. Possibly due to his public statements against elements in the music industry, he was a victim of an arsonist who set fire to his residence in Southern California in 1987, destroying his home and possessions and nearly taking his life and the lives of his wife and two daughters. Undeterred by this act of violence against him, Tom Petty remains an independent critic of the music industry's commercialism with strong environmental and political convictions (Greenpeace endorser and outspoken anti-terrorist). Occasionally, these issues bring him into the media's eye but he is not a paparazzi darling.

The TPATH fan community shares Tom's convictions and his faith in God, family, America, and rock-n-roll as evidenced in popular songs like "Free Fallin'": 'She's a good girl/Loves her mama/Loves Jesus and America too/She's a good girl/Crazy 'bout Elvis.' In concerts, Tom Petty actively references and thanks God. He frequently uses gestures that dramatically invoke God as the source of his inspiration and the source of blessings like his fans' praise (i.e., placing his hands palms together outstretched upward toward the sky and outward toward the audience with bowed head). His latest single, 'Saving Grace' is about the search for redemption in life's ambiguity. This informal sense of God is part of the value system Tom represents. It contributes to his reputation as a 'good', 'regular', and 'nice' guy with a conspicuous moral barometer. Tom is perceived within the brand community as a grounded family man who happens to be a rockstar. TPATH fans relate strongly to him and his values, protecting the brand from anything they view as indecent (i.e., sexually explicit material and endorsement of some illegal substances).

Online, fans monitor, even police, postings on the official message board for content that is appropriate or 'good' which does not require an age restriction. When postings reference overtly sexual desires, established members of the community will chastise the poster, 'Hey now, we don't want this thread to be "18 and over" ' (posted by pettygrl on TPATH Message Board on 13 May 2005 in response to a poster who detailed a sexual fantasy about Tom Petty). Similarly, a guy posting about a romantic night featuring TPATH as the sound-track elicited the comment 'Did ya get lucky' by gonegator (on the TPATH Message Board on 28 June 2006). A rebuke quickly emerged from a fellow member, Bluegill, 'No use walking on the sidewalk when you can get down and roll in the gutter with GoneGator ☺' posted moments after the gonegator question. Similarly, images posted on TPATH's official MySpace site are monitored by the community and occasionally censored. Skweezme, a MySpace member, posted a picture of herself from behind wearing only a red thong. Immediately, members (male and female) posted comments disapproving, 'Nice ass hun, real classy to post it online. Hope your mom sees it' (posted by Steve03 on 27 September 2006). Another response to the same image, 'So, I'm not gonna show my ass, but I will say they ROCKED Hollywood Bowl last night' (posted by luna14 also on 27 September 2006). These sort of family–friendly constraints on the message board content are rather unique for a board devoted to a rockstar.

Interestingly, references to marijuana and alcohol are not strictly censored, but references to other substances (cocaine, crack, heroin) are. In the community, 'weed' and drinking are clearly accepted but only in moderation. Grant, a 32-year-old engineer, describes his experiences with other TPATH fans, 'Once in awhile we get together, get stoned and stay up all night. We party but that's not all we do' (personal interview, 15 February 2002). Here, Grant makes the distinction between a life of excess and occasional celebrations, which he deems to be within 'normal parameters of a productive person' (personal interview, 15 February 2002). In the late nineties, following his separation from his wife of 20 years, Tom lived like a hermit in a run down house in Southern California where friends and family feared he was using heroin, but the community held strong that his admission of severe depression was true, 'This talk of heroin is blatant anti-Tom propaganda – probably some [industry] insider tired of Tom's criticisms' (posted on Jake's Tom Petty fansite 2000). Similar community statements affirmed this sentiment, 'He's in the middle of a divorce, who wouldn't be depressed? Heroin is unlikely ... it's just not him' (posted by wild1 on the official TPATH Message Board on 16 December 2000). The community was willing to accept depression, a respectable result of separation and divorce, over heroin for his reclusive behaviour. For the community, depression was a logical outcome of a broken family bond. Temperance, or moderation, rather than excess are condoned and celebrated within the brand community. This jibes with Tom's music, his environmentalism, and his family-oriented lifestyle.

God by proxy: not proximity

Lest we be misunderstood, TPATH do have groupies, but these people tend not to be in the brand community. Groupie's goals differ markedly from TPATH community members. The community's interest in TPATH focuses on the music, the stories and the performance of both. The first author attempted to describe this phenomenon in a short story based on fieldnotes she compiled of her first concert:

> It isn't the truly magnificent that ignites, or reaffirms your faith in God, deities, or the spiritual supernatural; they can be too easily debunked. Take the cosmos (Big Bang), and human life (Evolution), both are grand and so easily dismissed by the scientific among us. It's the little things that steal your breath and strike a cord that resonates within you that make you believe.
>
> For me, it's Tom Petty. He's not God, but he provides sustenance for my faith that God exists. Some may say he's not conventionally handsome or not equipped with a wide vocal range. While I can and do take issue with the first, I must surrender on the second. But that's not the point. Tom's songs resonate with me. Perhaps on face value it doesn't make sense. I'm not male. I'm not a Southerner. I was a teenager in the late 80s, not the 60s. I don't idolize his heroes (Elvis and Dylan). I've gone down another life-way (no sequins or leather). Yet somehow, I connect with Tom's music.
>
> (Schau, 2002, p. 5)

. . .

> I suppose it doesn't make rational sense. It's not about Tom Petty the musician, or Tom Petty the man. It's about the possibility that someone exists who is not constrained by the insecurities that plague me. It's about Tom Petty the performance and Tom Petty the experience. It's his mix of vulnerability and open disdain for those who wronged him in his songs that steal my breath and make me believe there is something beyond what I know. It's about the Heartbreakers as quintessential American artifact. It's about long hair, jeans and defiance and a girl/woman who dreams of a peace within herself that comes fleetingly if at all. Tom Petty is God by proxy, not by proximity. He is a man, musician and legend who is (re)invented the moment I hit <play> or see him take the stage. He is my proof of something beyond my own subjective reality of anxiety and the never-ending search for someone else's approval. Tom is as I consume him, one disc, one video, one concert at a time, and a montage of my life playing in 3 minute segments.
>
> (Schau, 2002, p. 19)

TPATH and Tom Petty in particular are not ultimately the objects of lust/hero worship for most fans, but rather signify camaraderie embedded in songs that strongly relate to a broad set of experiences any person may encounter. Tom is at once a legend and a guy everyone can relate to. The Message Boards are filled with statements of resonance, of TPATH creating soundtracks of fans' individual lives. Fans relate to the music and the stories linking them intimately with their own personal life narratives. For example, Mark, a 37-year-old bartender, explains,

> Tom sings my life. He couldn't possibly know it, but I have lived my life playing and singing his songs. Each song has my memories of it and of what was going on in my life around that song. He sings about real people and real problems. Nothing gansta or sappy.
>
> (personal interview 22 July 2001)

Sarah, a 29-year-old registered nurse, explains, 'Lots of artists sing about bling and pimpin' or stuff that is very foreign to me . . . Tom's songs are about my life and my feelings' (personal interview, 16 August 2005). TPATH's appeal is that the music Tom writes depicts common human experiences in a manner that feels authentic. The authenticity stems from this tension between greatness and normalcy. Alan, a 33-year-old realtor summarizes:

> He's a real guy who made it. He could be you or me . . . if we were musically talented. He enjoys making music with Mike [Campbell – TPATH lead guitarist and Tom's lifelong best friend] and he has been super successful. We always say to do what you love . . . well he did and he never forgot who he is.
>
> (personal interview 28 July 2001)

While informants within the brand community repeatedly refer to Tom as 'just a normal guy' the hint of the ideal is never far behind; he is great and tempered by normalcy.

Touching greatness

The Tom Petty brand community also displays evidence of the Touching Greatness phenomenon (O'Guinn, 1991). Any kind of connection with Tom Petty that travels beyond the typical musician–fan (or groupie) relationship is enchanted and therefore cause for discussion. Any kind of personal connection to TP is valued highly and is a source of cultural capital within the confines of the community, except if it is perceived by members of the brand community to violate the norms and image of TPATH. Consider the following message posted to a TPATH community forum:

> 'My TP "claim to fame" (sort of . . .)' – Thread Title
>
> Just thought I would share my claim to fame with other TP fans. I'm almost middle-aged, with an 18-year-old daughter – we live in Ohio, but I grew up in Florida. My family still lives in Gainesville (Tom's hometown, as you well know). During my last visit to G'ville, I happened to mention Tom's name at the dinner table with my aging

parents present – I probably made some reference to his being from G'ville, etc. . . . My father pipes up and says, 'oh, yeah, Earl's boy'. . . . I dropped my fork and said, 'huh??? You know Earl Petty, Dad?' . . . Turns out that Tom's dad and my dad sold insurance together at the same regional insurance company. My father had the pleasure of meeting Earl in the late 1970s and early 1980s . . . he tells the story of how Earl once mentioned to him early on how his son was just breaking into the music business and how he hoped he would make it, given the difficulty of the business. Earl has passed on, but my father speaks of him warmly.

(Posted on TPATH Message Board by
MissinFlorida on 26 June 2006)

Given the gravity such claims carry, they are closely scrutinized by other member of the community. Consider the following exchange from a TPATH message forum:

'My Mom Dated Tom Petty!' – Thread Title
   In the 70s my mom went out with Tom Petty a few times. He was in Toronto at the time. I think that's pretty cool! Tom rocks!

(Posted on TPATH Message Board
by SexyKitten on 7 July 2005)

And would this have been before or after he married his high school sweetheart, Jane? And before or after he left our hometown of Gainesville, FL to go to California and start the Heartbreakers? Since he graduated high school in 1968, was forming the band in Gainesville in the early 70s . . . (I was at some of their free concerts here) . . . and left here in 75 or 76 for California . . . (and was already married) . . . that does not leave a lot of time for traveling or dating . . . lol. If it is true, great . . . but as 'fussman' said . . . we need details.

(Posted on TPATH Message Board
by LL Campos on 7 July 2005)

Look, I'm gonna level with you, Sexy. Every once in a while, someone comes on the board . . . from out of the blue, mind you . . . and makes some outrageous claim about Tom. We even had someone who joined the board just to claim that she had had Tom's 'love child'. Turned out, she was soliciting some . . . 'business' . . . something about internet porn. So, please understand our . . . um . . . *skepticism* . . . quite honestly, we've heard everything. If you can prove your claim, fine. But, seriously, we just aren't apt to buy it, either way.

(Response posted on TPATH Message Board
by little nel on 7 July 2005)

The members of the brand community are protective of Tom and claim about Tom. TPATH is a family guy and the accusations of infidelity, while believable for most rockstars, are preposterous to TPATH fans. There is significant tension between fans claiming to have had encounters with Tom (sexual, friendly, drug related) and other fans who publicly state their scepticism. Hardcore fans maintain Tom's image as a genuinely nice guy who happens to be a musical genius and a rock legend. He is thought to be faithful in his domestic relationships, devoted to his children, loyal to his friends, a patriot, a private person, and a guy everyone would like to be friends with.

> That talk about Tom going solo and leaving Mike and Benmont [Tench – TPATH keyboardist/pianist and lifelong friend] is crazy. That guy never met him. That's clear. He wouldn't toss away decades of friendship over creative differences or to make a few more bucks.
>
> (Kim, personal interview, 13 May 2006)

Here, Kim argues that the three solo albums Tom (with Mike) produced are not an indication that the band is breaking up or that friendships are falling apart. Spike echoes this incredulousness at some people's assertions about Tom:

> I'm not sure why these lunatics come on and claim to know him, claim to have slept with him, claim to have been beaten up by him, claim to be doing smack with him . . . It just isn't true. He's a decent guy who is a rock icon. Why is that so hard to believe? He is a rock-star without the excess. The truth is Bono *can* win a Nobel Prize, and Tom *is* nice guy who rocks.
>
> (Spike stated in chat November 2005)

Touching Greatness in this community means a proximal human relationship with the artist outside the confines of typical musician–fan interaction (music and performance appreciation) but within the boundaries of TPATH's ethos of 'good' behaviour.

Transformation

Brand communities are host to many transformative behaviours. They allow members to access parts of themselves that they might not normally access, to become more. Saab drivers tell of 'eventful, sometimes harrowing, but always meaningful journey[s] in their Saabs' (Muñiz and O'Guinn, 2001, p. 423). Jeep drivers attending Jamborees emerge changed from the communal experiences (McAlexander, Schouten, and Koening, 2002) and similar experiences are reported by participants in Harley posse rides (Fournier, McAlexander, Schouten, and Sensiper, 2000). The TPATH community is defined, in one sense, by a similar capacity. Consider the following exchange, posted under the un-ambiguous thread title 'Sign from God'.

> I just had one of my greatest TP experiences I've ever had! Of course, I listen to Saving Grace every day now since its release, but I hadn't heard it yet on the radio. So tonight I was driving with a girl (our first date) and I happened to turn the radio to 107.1 (a Canadian Rock Station) and there it was – the now classic riff and percussion of Saving Grace. Now she thought it was weird when I went nuts hearing it on the radio for the first time. But I looked at her and said 'I just want you to remember that the first time you heard this song and the first time I heard it on the radio we were together.' And I think she liked that. I'm only 17, but I think hearing this song for the first time on the airwaves at that moment could have been some kind of like omen. I don't know. That is when I felt the spark of connection to her.
>
> (Posted on TPATH Message Board
> by wake^time on 28 June 2006)

Here wake^time is detailing an omen. Hearing the song on the radio together with this girl sparks a connection or a foreshadowing of a serious relationship. This influences others to post similar stories in response, 'I love that story. I have almost the same story except it was 1981 and the song was "The Waiting". The cool part is we are still together. 25 years goes by in a flash. Treasure those moments' (posted by lacytom on TPATH Message Board in response to wake^time's above posting on 29 June 2006). The implication here is that Tom's songs bond people and transform relationships from trivial to meaningful. Here a 17-year-old boy (wake^time) and a 40 something year old woman (lacytom) talk about love and the resonance and impact of Tom Petty's music in their respective lives.[2] Likewise, Danielle, a 38-year-old school teacher, describes Tom's music as glue, 'When I'm mad at my husband I play *Hard Promises* and it puts it all in perspective. I guess it's the glue in our marriage' (personal interview, 26 July 2004). Danielle affords the album *Hard Promises* the power to hold her marriage together, or transform situations from intolerable to tolerable.

Tale of the miraculous

Muñiz and Schau (2005) described the tales of the miraculous visible in the Apple Newton brand community. There, miraculous tales centre on Newtons that had, as if magically, survived conditions that should have destroyed it or had their batteries regain efficacy. Tales of the miraculous are also evident in the TPATH brand community. Here, they centre on recovery, either emotional

---

[2] This intergenerational connection is rather unique for a shared interest in a rock band.

of physical, experienced by members via Tom Petty songs, concerts, and fellowship. Consider the following posted under the heading of 'Divorce Survival':

> I was going through a rough time. The roughest I've ever been through. I was breaking up with my wife after 16 years. I was alone. My friends didn't want to 'choose sides' so they dropped away. It was 1997 and life looked hopeless. I retreated from a lot of the world. I concentrated on my work and on music. I listened to Tom Petty constantly. It helped. I read an article about him separating from his wife, Jane, after 22 years. It struck a chord. In photos and video he looked haggard and drawn. He was alternately skinny and bloated. He had this scraggly grey beard and a paunch. I read he was having kidney issues. I took a hard look at myself. Clearly we were going through the same thing. I was a mess. I don't mean to say I took pleasure in his pain or that he has the power to heal me by some divine gift, but he saved my life. Knowing that a legend like Tom is human – not immune to the trials of ordinary men gave me hope. His music, esp. the songs written in the midst of his pain, Echo (1999), were inspirational to me. I think I might have just killed myself had I not had that strength from him. And as time went on that same strength from watching Tom move on and marry again gave me strength to try marriage again. I remarried last year [2002] and I know I wouldn't have had strength and inspiration to live life again after the divorce.
>
> (interview excerpt from Gavin 2003)

Gavin claims Tom's music and life saved his own, allowing Gavin to move on and remarry after a painful divorce.

Here is another miraculous story of a fan's healed knees:

> The boards were buzzing about Tom having some knee problem. I don't know if he did or didn't. I'm not him or his doctor. But, I knew my doc was telling me I have to change my runs. That surgery might be necessary. I'm 34 years old. I live to run. It's what I do every day for 20 years. I felt frail. I felt lost. I read the board postings with interest. I had my tickets for the concert. I went and Tom didn't show any signs of knee problems. He was hopping around the stage like he was 20 years. It was a great concert. The next day I got up and headed for my medicine cabinet but the pain was not there. It just wasn't. I ran my old run after 6 weeks of gym work (eeewww) and it was hard. I was out of shape. But, my knee was fine. It was fine. How could a concert do that? I dunno, but that's my story.
>
> (email excerpt from Chris 14 August 2005)

Somehow, Chris' knee was healed seemingly by proximity to Tom at a TPATH concert. The details are sketchy and Chris is a little disbelieving even as he testifies to it.

Lest you believe Tom Petty's 'power' only applies to human emotions and body parts:

> So my amp has been on its last leg for some time. I nurse it along because well I can't afford the one I want yet. Anyhow, so whenever it starts acting up, giving out, I play 'Refugee' or 'Honey Bee' and the amp comes back to life. It's good for maybe an hour afterward.
> (Terry, 26-year-old musician, personal interview,
> 8 November 2004)

Here, playing these TPATH songs cures the amp temporarily. These stories are similar to those found in the Apple Newton community where failing PDA batteries miraculously repair following a complex pattern of turning the device off and on (Muñiz and Schau, 2005).

Rituals and traditions

Brand communities are host to a variety of rituals and traditions that serve to reify the community and its culture. Methods and modes include celebrating the history of brand, sharing brand stories and myths, ritualistic communication and utterances, special lexicon, and communal appropriation of advertising, market icons, and commercial text. Obvious examples are the ways in which Saab wave, beep their horn, or flash their lights to other drivers of the same brand (Muñiz and O'Guinn, 2001). VW Beetle, Jeep, and Miata drivers, as well as riders of Harley–Davidson motorcycles, engage in similar activities.

The TPATH brand community is host to a variety of rituals and traditions, some unique to followers of Tom Petty, others reflecting the more general domain of rock performers. Rock concerts are, after all, the site of many general ritualized behaviour: from lighter/cellphone waving to concert t-shirt wearing, to ticket stub saving, to singing along. Individual TPATH rituals also exist. They include pre-concert parties that extend from private residences and public bars and restaurants to the parking lot – tailgate style. One ritual is that during the concert the entire audience sings 'Breakdown' with only pantomime and occasional vocals from Tom Petty. Other songs are as popular, but this song seems to have been embraced by the community as a sing-a-long that routinely embeds a cover of 'Hit the Road Jack'. Whereas acts like Tom Jones may inspire middle-aged women to shed and toss underwear at the stage, TPATH inspires camaraderie and environmental activism. Similarly, there is no mosh pit like you'd see at an old school metal (Judas Priest) or punk show (Beastie Boys) or new millennium Buckcherry concert. Fans sing along with Tom in a friendly communal atmosphere without the high drama of crowd aggression or legions of groupies trading sexual favours for the conquest.

TPATH fans tend to don casual cotton clothing in black or patriotic colours to concert, frequently including denim materials (jeans, skirts, jackets). These denim clothes most often paired with cotton shirts (tank tops and t-shirts) are likely to be emblazoned with TPATH logo (a heart with a guitar through it) as in official concert tour wear or homemade decorations. In concerts, fans display lots of hearts painted on faces, tattooed on bodies (permanent, henna, and temporary), displayed on clothes, written on signs or gifts (i.e., stuffed animals).

This particular conglomeration of behaviours is unique to TPATH: the communal singing, the casual cotton clothing, and the hearts. This is not to say that there is never a fight or that groupies don't hound the band, only that the brand community condones neither.

Tests of true fans

Muñiz and Schau (2005) reported nascent consumer rituals in the Newton brand community that created important knowledge, while demonstrating members' true devotion to the brand. Such tests are not uncommon in brand communities and the TPATH fan community is no different. There is cultural capital to be gained from choosing less commercially successful TPATH songs as your favourite songs. As mistereeman posts, 'What do you expect? His favourite song is 'Don't Do Me Like That'. No deep cuts. He just doesn't get it' (posted on TPATH official Message Board on 11 August 2004). And conversely, 'I knew he was cool when he told me his favourite TPATH song is "Spike". A deep cut guy! I fell hard and fast' (posted on the official TPATH Message Board on 16 July 2005).

Similarly, there is cache in knowing the band history including the following paraphrased '10 Things Every TPATH fan knows' (posted on Jake's personal website):

1 TPATH are from Gainseville, Florida.
2 Tom and collaborator (lead guitarist), Mike Campbell, are lifelong best friends.
3 Elvis and Dylan inspired Tom.
4 TP dropped out of high school at 17 to focus on Mudcrutch (precursor band to TPATH).
5 Tom married his high school sweetheart, Jane.
6 TPATH was considered a New Wave band in the early 1980s.
7 Tom fought price increases on recording and tickets.
8 TP is a member of the Travelling Wilbury's.
9 Tom's house in SoCal was burned to the ground by arsonists. He and his family survived but lost almost everything they had.
10 *The Last DJ* is critical of the recording and radio industry and was boycotted by radio stations that refused to give it air time.

While the band history is much richer, you get the idea – you need to know the band to engage in fan chatter. As Lillian, a 31-year-old physical therapist, comments, 'its fine to have an opinion [on TPATH's material] but an educated one means a whole lot more' (personal interview, 15 August 2006). Tim, a 37-year-old mechanic, echoes 'its clear who is in [the community] and who is not. Just listen to them talk' (personal interview, 24 July 2004). People who don't know the history are not deemed to be authentic (Arnould and Price, 2001) community members.

Journeys/Treks/Pilgrimages

Fans one-up each other in escalating displays of commitment to purchasing new releases, waiting in line for performance tickets, and travelling to attend concerts. Fans who access the music before it is commonly available are seen as more committed to the band and better community members. Jenny, a 31-year-old web designer, boasts,

> I got the 'Saving Grace' and 'Big Weekend' tracks off the web before anyone I knew. Everyone wanted to hear them and share them. I was the girl to know last Spring and now people on the forum think I'm some sort of expert.
>
> (personal interview, 12 September 2006)

Jenny's standing in the fan community went up due to her access to coveted new tracks.

Similarly, tales of getting tickets to the shows are informally ranked based on difficulty, with fans encountering more obstacles to the ticket sales being more serious fans. Fans who travel for the concerts achieve more social capital in the community than those who only attend local dates. For example, a 41-year-old New Jersey fan, Jon, 'won' a spirited TPATH commitment test when he revealed that he and his wife flew to San Francisco to catch the TPATH show at the Fillmore in 1999. Not only was he lauded for travelling so far to catch a show, but he also got coveted tickets to the concert series that was made into a DVD release. Todd, also a New Jersey fan, commented on Jon's tickets and trek, 'Damn, you lucky bastard. I wish I got those tickets. I'd have got some serious play outta my girl for weeks afterward.' Here scoring the tickets and taking the trip amounts to not only winning the commitment test for Jon, but also Todd laments that the tickets would've scored him some grateful reciprocity affection from his girlfriend. Stories of catching multiple live shows in a tour, following the band, and making pilgrimages to first concert sites or first concerts with loved ones sites are common. Consider Donovan's story,

> I saw my first TPATH concert with a then girlfriend. We had long since broken up, but stayed friends. I decided to get tickets to the show for us . . . a 20 year anniversary of our first TPATH concert. It was a great time. Now, we're living together and talking about getting married. Pretty cool, eh?
>
> (personal interview, 10 July 2004)

Donovan tells the story of reconnecting with his girlfriend to many TPATH fans who emphatically convey their respect for that story. Fans at concerts and

events discuss the above tests of fan commitment as early communal identi-
fiers and as status markers among established fans.

Concluding thoughts

Cultural critics both classic and contemporary have concerned themselves
with the death of enchanting experiences. Weber (1978/1922) felt that market
capitalism fostered the 'disenchantment of the world' (p. 177) and destroyed
the sense of connection between individuals and the world provided by myth,
magic, and religion. Modernity, via the increased cultural emphasis on reason,
disenchanted the world, disconnected the individual, and led to alienation
(Ellul, 1964; Freud, 1989/1930). More recently, Ritzer (1999) lamented the controlling nature of contemporary consumer culture and claimed that consumers
are becoming disenchanted with consumption. He claimed that contemporary
consumer culture succeeds only to the degree to which it lulls consumers into
dreamlike and uncritical states that engage them with consumption.

Among members of the TPATH brand community, we see consumers thoroughly engaged with consumption. However, contrary to what has been suggested by Ritzer and others, these consumers are far from uncritical. Fans of
TPATH are engaged, critical and actively involved in the creation and perpetuation of enchanting experiences centred on a contemporary marketplace
entity. Once again (Brown et al., 2003; Kozinets, 2001; Muñiz and Schau,
2005; O'Guinn, 1991) we are seeing a branded marketplace entity offering
consumers the opportunity for re-enchantment. Fans of Tom Petty are finding magic and fellowship in his creations. Tom Petty has achieved in life the
kind of power and immortality that most artists can only achieve after death
(Klosterman, 2005). The crucial difference this time is that the focal brand is
successful, non-abandoned, mainstream, and non-stigmatized. That we are
seeing manifestations of the magico-religious among the followers of such a
successful brand suggests that enchanting experiences in the marketplace
need not be limited to the few followers of fringe brands or entertainers.

Religions are powerful and pervasive social institutions that provide a
familiar discourse of greatness and morality. Members of the TPATH brand
community are simply applying pervasive and accessible leitmotifs and cultural scripts, primarily those of the magical, mythic, and religious to a marketplace phenomenon – most with understated cool and perhaps a little irony.
Their themes, motifs, and idioms are very portable. Part of the reason for this
portability is their applicability to a wide range of human phenomena. They
help us make sense of the world. In this case, they are helping us make sense
of a branded entertainer.

Religion, magic, and the supernatural can survive in a consumer culture.
These forces have proved themselves to be quite adaptable. As religions
have become savvier marketplace players, it should not be entirely surprising that other marketplace entities should also reflect this intermingling and
show traces of religiosity. Brands will increasingly play host to many of these

processes. Brands, even those that are mainstream, are increasingly the centre of the social world. They are assuming, for better or for worse, many of the functions once performed by other, older social institutions: moral arbiter, communal spirit, social acceptance, and social order.

While the strength of brand communities may indeed be enhanced by common threats and marginalization, we see in the TPATH fans a cohesive brand community for a mainstream brand without stigma attached and religiosity steeped in temperance. In essence, marginality is not a prerequisite for a successful enduring brand community to exist, nor is religiosity a response to stigmatization.

References

Arnould, E.J. and Price, L.L. (2001). Authenticating acts and authoritative performances: questing for self and community, in Ratneshwar, S., Mick, D. and Huffman, C. (eds.), *The Why of Consumption: Contemporary Perspectives on Consumer Motives, Goals and Desires*. London and New York: Routledge Press.

Automotive News (2000). U.S. car and light truck sales, model year 2000 vs. 1999, *Automotive News*, October 9, 59.

Belk, R.W. and Tumbat, G. (2002). *The Cult of Macintosh*. Salt Lake City, University of Utah: Odyssey Films.

Brown, S., Kozinets, R.V. and Sherry Jr., J.F. (2003). Teaching old brands new tricks: retro branding and the revival of brand meaning, *Journal of Marketing*, **67**, 19–33.

Caldwell, M. and Henry, P. (2006). Celebrity worship within affinity groups: adopting a multi-faceted perspective, Presentation to Association for Consumer Research, Latin America, Monterrey, Mexico.

Carpages (2006). Saab's market share flies to record levels in May, http://www.carpages.co.uk/saab/saab-record-sales-06-06-05.asp, retrieved July, 2006.

Denzin, N.K. (1998). The art and politics of interpretation, in Denzin, N.K. and Lincoln, Y.S. (eds.), *Handbook of Qualitative Research*, Thousand Oaks, CA: Sage, pp. 500–515.

Ellul, J. (1964). *The Technological Society*, trans. Wilkinson, J., New York: Vintage.

Erlewine, S.T. (2006). Biography of Tom Petty, *All Music Guide*, http://www.allmusic.com/cg/amg.dll?p=amg&sql=11:x95h8qptbtz4, retrieved July, 2006.

Fournier, S., McAlexander, J., Schouten, J. and Sensiper, S. (2000). Building brand community on the Harley–Davidson posse ride, *Harvard Business School* case 9-501-015.

Fox, S. (1984). *The Mirror Makers: A History of American Advertising and Its Creators*. New York: Vintage.

Freud, S. (1989/1930). *Civilization and Its Discontents*, in Strachey, J. (ed.), New York: Norton.

Henry, P. and Caldwell, M. (2006). Self-empowerment and consumption: consumer remedies for prolonged stigmatization, *European Journal of Marketing*, **40** (9–10), 2006, pp. 1031–1048(18).

Kahney, L. (2004). *The Cult of Macintosh*. San Francisco, CA: NO Starch.

Klosterman, C. (2002). The pretenders, *New York Times Magazine*, March 17.

Klosterman, C. (2005). *Killing Yourself to Live: 85% of a True Story*. New York: Scribner.

Kozinets, R.V. (1997). 'I want to believe:'a netnography of the X-Philes' subculture of consumption, in Brucks, M. and MacInnis, D. (eds.), *Advances in Consumer Research*. Provo, UT: Association for Consumer Research, 24, pp. 470–474.

Kozinets, R.V. (2001). Utopian enterprise: articulating the meanings of Star Trek's culture of consumption, *Journal of Consumer Research*, **28**, 67–88.

McAlexander, J.H., Schouten, J.W. and Koening, H.F. (2002). Building brand community, *Journal of Marketing*, **66**, 38–54.

Muñiz Jr., A.M. and O'Guinn, T.C. (2001). Brand community, *Journal of Consumer Research*, **27** (4), 412–431.

Muñiz Jr., A.M. and Schau, H.J. (2005). Religiosity in the abandoned Apple Newton brand community, *Journal of Consumer Research*, **31** (4), 737–747.

O'Guinn, T.C. (1991). Touching greatness: the central midwest Barry Manilow fanclub, in Belk, R.W. (ed.), *Highways and Buyways: Naturalistic Research from the Consumer Behavior Odyssey*. Provo, UT: Association for Consumer Research, pp. 102–111.

Ritzer, G. (1999). *Enchanting a Disenchanted World: Revolutionizing the Means of Consumption*. Thousand Oaks, CA: Pine Forge.

Schau, H.J. (2002). God by proxy, *Hawaii Review*, Issue **58**, 25(1).

Schau, H.J. and Muñiz Jr., A.M. (2004). Twenty years of consumer culture theory: retrospect and prospect, presentation to the 2004 Association for Consumer Research Conference in Portland, OR.

Schouten, J.W. and McAlexander, J. (1995). Subcultures of consumption: an ethnography of the new bikers, *Journal of Consumer Research*, **22**, 43–61.

Strauss, N. (2006). Tom Petty's last dance, *Rolling Stone*, Issue 1004/1005, 73–78.

Thompson, H.S. (1996). *Hell's Angels: A Strange and Terrible Saga*. New York: Ballantine Books.

TWICE (2005). 2004 U.S. PC sales strong, *TWICE*, **20** (4), 33.

Weber, M. (1978 [1922]). *Economy and Society*. Berkeley, CA: University of California.

11

Imprinting, incubation and intensification: factors contributing to fan club formation and continuance

Paul Henry and Marylouise Caldwell

Introduction

In recent times, researchers have expended considerable time and energy in understanding marketplace-based collectivities, alternatively conceptualized as consumption tribes (e.g., Bennett, 1999; Cova, 1997; Cova and Cova, 2002; Kozinets, 1999; Patterson, 1998) or brand communities (e.g., Algesheimer, Dholakia, and Herrmann, 2005; McAlexander, Schouten, and Koenig, 2002; Muñiz and O'Guinn, 2001). For a few reasons, these collectivities are of special interest. First, these groups typically comprise dense social networks of loyalists to particular brands, products or leisure activities. When properly nurtured, these concentrations of brand loyalists constitute a potent collective resource for marketing organizations, comprising customer retention, long-term profitability and positive word of mouth (Bhattacharya, Rao, and Glynn, 1995). Second, in the past, traditional marketing theory failed to adequately explain these phenomena, reflecting instead neo-classical notions of consumption as confined to instrumental and/or self-expressive motives. A more enlightened perspective recognizes that consumption can have strong social value, due to its ability to forge lasting social relationships that people value (Cova and Cova, 2002). In such instances the bonding that develops between participating individuals amplifies bonding with the focal consumption object and related activities. Significantly, such ideas had been already voiced by the institutional economists at the beginning of the twentieth century, notably Veblen, but since that time have been overshadowed by beliefs associated with advanced right wing capitalism. Finally, the emergence of these groups suggests that the rampant individualism supposedly believed to characterize late twentieth century affluent societies is arguably a myth. Rather the macro-subcultures of yesteryear, such as social class, age, gender and ethnicity have been replaced by micro-groupings (Featherstone, 1991; Van Raaij, 1993) defined by similarity of values, interests and life experiences (Cova and Cova, 2002).

In this chapter, we detail emergent theory with respect to how and why celebrity worship acts as a galvanizing factor in a specific type of marketplace-based collectivity known as a fan club. Significantly, fan clubs display the now well-recognized characteristics of marketplace-based collectivities. Notably members of these collectivities are as follows:

1 sustained admirers and advocates of a specific brand (in our case a branded person: i.e., a celebrity), product or activity that is mediated by mass media and/or commercial entities;
2 share a consciousness of kind and a sense of belonging to the group;
3 have common traditions, stories and lived experiences;
4 exhibit a sense of moral obligation to the community as a whole and each individual member (Cova and Cova, 2002; Muñiz and O'Guinn, 2001).

However, we suggest that compared to other marketplace collectivities, fan clubs possess certain idiosyncratic aspects.

Method

Our ideas derive from an extended ethnographic investigation of The Sir Cliff Richard fan club situated in Sydney, Australia. Cliff Richard is an aged celebrity (65 years old); his career spans 45 years. He is the largest selling recording artist in the UK, outselling the Beatles and Elvis. The fan club was formed in 1983 and still retains many of its original members. They meet every six weeks and maintain a busy calendar of extracurricular events and outings. During their meeting they chat about the latest Cliff news and/or their daily lives, plus exchange memorabilia they have purchased from commercial outlets or more

often than not, self-produced. Significantly, one member of the fan club in particular began making Cliff paraphernalia, etc., after Cliff's record company
ceased this activity. She produces Cliff imprinted battery-operated clocks, book-
marks, Christmas cards and Tee-shirts, and enjoys considerable status within
the broader Cliff focused social network as a result. The club has 20 members
who are generally aged 50 years plus. They are typically married with children,
mostly female, drawn from middle management positions and service industries and live in the outer suburbs of a large metropolitan city. They developed
an obsession with Cliff Richard during their teenage years, which obviously
continues to this day. Their obsession is characterized listening to Cliff's music
regularly, decorating their homes with prominent photographs of Cliff, check-
ing his website daily for news and participating in the associated chat rooms.

Over an eight month period, we attended meetings in club members' homes
and functions, such as the celebration of Cliff's birthday. Across this period, we
acquainted ourselves closely with the members. We met many of their families
and learned about their wider lives and individual histories. We initially interviewed them as a group. Then we conducted individual and couple interviews
after meetings or outside the club meeting times in their homes. We interviewed many members more than once and through our regular attendance at
functions informally conversed on a regular basis. We videotaped interviews,
club meetings and the accompanying environments. We collected a body of
photographic history about fan club, the individual members, and about Cliff
Richard himself. We listened to the music and watched video clips of Cliff's
concerts. We examined extensive newspaper scrapbooks, going back to the
1950s, that are maintained by club members. We reviewed a large variety of
Cliff Richard memorabilia and read several books about Cliff's life (e.g., St John,
1991; Turner, 2005). From this material, the researchers made a video-ethnogra-
phy piece called 'Living Dolls' which was screened at the 2005 Association for
Consumer Research Film Festival in Portland, Oregon.

Findings

Our research suggests that three phases associate with the formation and
continuance of fan clubs, notably: (1) imprinting, (2) incubation and
(3) intensification.

1 Imprinting

Life-long fandom is typically characterized by a moment in a fan's pre-adult life
when they are indelibly marked by exposure to a celebrity; thereafter they are
metaphorically compelled to follow in their footsteps. Researchers attribute this
behaviour to a variety of causes. First, it is well known that celebrities can act
as comforting role models of desired values and modes of conduct (Greene and
Adams-Price, 1990) when adolescents commence establishing an identity outside the family. For a small proportion of people, the obsession does not cease

with adulthood. In this instance, the obsession seems to be a critical ingredient to the stability of their adult identity. Indeed, the obsession can be so strong that such individuals are driven to marry other fans of the celebrity, or seek out people, who in some way resemble the celebrity, most commonly in physical appearance. Second, exposure to celebrities associates with the formation of non-family mediated preferences including fashion styles, personal appearance (Schindler and Holbrook, 1993) and objects of sexual desire (Holbrook and Schindler, 1994). For example men often voice a preference for the looks of a singer or movie star they encountered during puberty, even though this may have little to do with their day to day choices in romantic partners. Music preferences have similar origins, following an inverted U-shape that peaks in people's early twenties (Holbrook and Schindler, 1989). Hence it is not surprising that baby boomers are encountered listening to the music of the 1960s, such as The Rolling Stones, Credence Clearwater, and Dusty Springfield. Significantly such preferences often last a lifetime; not least of which because they potentially fuel nostalgia for times when life appeared simpler, and hopes were higher (Schindler and Holbrook, 2003).

Virtually all the club members first encountered Cliff Richard in their teenage years. This contact was highly memorable. The vivid descriptions upon recalling these events indicate these were defining moments in their lives: 'I can remember the first time he came on the radio. From that point on I couldn't get enough of him.' Delving back into this period – the 1960s – we found that Cliff Richard was a phenomenon comparable to The Beatles. Widespread fan hysteria surrounded Cliff. This phenomenon is vividly depicted in a BBC documentary in which Cliff Richard is featured being protected by police from huge surging crowds in London at a publicity event. At this time, he had a series of musical recording that topped the charts and he starred in a number of hit movies (e.g., *Summer Holiday, The Young Ones*). Many of our informants regard seeing the *The Young Ones* as their defining moment. These impressions were a consequence of liking more than the music, rather a product of the transition from teenage life to adulthood. One female informant put it thus: 'Cliff was my first introduction to music and all the things that go with it . . . the party gatherings, the boys and all the adolescent stuff.' Another female informant explained that she remembered falling in love with her husband while listening to one of Cliff's hit songs at a restaurant. Some male informants relished the belief they bore a similar physical appearance to Cliff, especially when younger.

Ideal self-consistency motives (Baumeister, 1998) contribute to explanations of pre-adult celebrity imprinting and continued fandom in adulthood. Fans tend to be attracted to celebrities endowed with characteristics that they desire for themselves (Caughey, 1994). For example Cliff Richard publicly portrays traditional notions of clean, wholesome living, and embraces schmaltzy romantic notions and traditional Christian values. An ideal self-consistency account would reveal that Cliff Richard's fans prize similar values and modes of life. Not surprisingly female fan club members evinced a preference for other clean living singing stars, such as Hugh Jackaman and Barry Manilow. Other self-concept/personality explanations focus on an individual's tendency to fantasize as a means of escape. They propose that some people are more likely to seek escape through fantasy if they lack control in core aspects of their lives or in some other way are disempowered (Maltby, McCutcheon, Ashe, and Houran, 2001). In a similar vein, Kozinets (2001, p. 71) found that obsessive *Star Trek* adherents are driven by the attraction of 'utopian refuge for the alienated and disenfranchised'. Desire for utopian refuge may contribute to celebrity fandom in cases where the celebrity portrays a better, brighter, fairer world.

Supporting the ideal-self-consistency motive our informants displayed a very conservative value set and behaviours. Their personal values and preferred lifestyles closely aped Cliff Richard's lifestyle. Most of the informants were practising Christians. Cliff's appeal is strongly rooted in his openly professed Christianity. 'We definitely admire him, a Christian man, not afraid to admit this. I revered him from afar, but when I met him he became just like my next-door neighbour. I respect him for his Christian beliefs; he cares for people in third world countries and just has a heart of compassion.' Part of their admir-ation is that in the 1980s Cliff publicly came out about his Christianity despite the fact that this was widely regarded as commercially risky for a rock musician. A male informant admired Cliff because 'he speaks up for the things that he believes in and I admire his courage, his honesty, straightforwardness, genuineness and the fact that he does not follow along with the mainstream, like a lamb'. Terms like 'clean' and 'wholesome' are commonly used to describe Cliff Richard. His music, video clips and entire public presentation are imbued with the traditional romantic fantasy images of the 'boy next door', 'clean shaven' appearance and 'white picket fence' family values. The fans' conservative values seem to imbue their fashion choices. They tended to wear clothing that was non-revealing or figure hugging, bland in colour and not noticeably fashionable.

The imprinting process is arguably fuelled by some fans' implicit acceptance of the concept of a para-social relationship (Cohen, 1997); that is, a person A believes they knows a lot about person B, but person B knows nothing about person A. In sum, a false sense of intimacy prevails. In such relationships, people experience a high degree of affinity and involvement with a person, often famous, with whom they have little if any direct contact. Boon and Lomore (2001) elaborate that strong feelings of attraction to the celebrity involve persistent positive thoughts related to the celebrity. This behaviour fuels growing identification and the perception that a special bond exists between the fan and the celebrity. In recent times, the use of Internet sites by celebrities, notably via blogs and embedded home-video clips has fuelled these types of relationships.

Despite never personally meeting Cliff, many of our informants appeared to exhibit close identification of a para-social nature. For example, one female informant said: 'You feel you know him . . . When we went to the airport to see Cliff arrive I took my young son. He ran up under everyone's legs right up to Cliff and asked him for a kiss and a cuddle. He just sees him as an extension of our family, because Cliff is always present in our home.' She further elaborated that when her home was threatened by bushfire, she had rushed outside with photos of Cliff, rather than other belongings. This case underscores the significance of Cliff in our fans' lives. Two informants when asked the question 'What if you didn't have Cliff in your life?' looked absolutely shocked and replied: 'I'd be devastated. Our lives would be poorer. We have so many memories. He's part of our life and he's part of us.'

The idea of a para-social connection is further underscored by the prominent display by fans of photos of Cliff in their living rooms, often taking greater prominence than photos of family and friends. They also reported sacrificing family outings and holidays, preferring instead to spend money and time going to Cliff concerts with other fan club members. In contrast, a few informants reported being less attached to Cliff, stating that they if didn't have Cliff, they'd adopt another hobby, 'like astronomy or building model aero-planes'. Another informant explained: 'When I was single mum, Cliff dominated my life, but now I'm married he's like a member of my extended family – always there, but not the main game. I have other things on my mind.'

Para-social relationships with Cliff are likely further supported by fan's ability to continue collecting of Cliff's music and memorabilia. Over his long career Cliff Richard has released several hundred recordings. Some of the club members have collected virtually everyone of them. Substantial collections of memorabilia were found in everyone of the homes that we visited. This ranged from Cliff Richard cups, plates, calendars, dolls, clocks, posters, pens, books and videos, through to pebbles that had been taken from his driveway and leaves plucked from the holly bush in his garden. Many fans retained all the tickets and programmes from the concerts they had attended, numbering in their hundreds. In addition, 'A lot of the members have a Cliff room . . . a whole room devoted to Cliff. Some wallpaper their bedrooms with his photos.' O'Guinn (2000) described similar phenomena in American fans clubs, likening these rooms to devotional shrines.

2 Incubation

Incubation comprises the time period that fans are more or less alone, prior to becoming members of the fan club. This period is characterized by a sense of alienation and stigma as a consequence of being an adult fan (regarded by most people as aberrant), coupled with being a fan of a Christian pop singer, such as Cliff Richard, in a highly secular society, such as Australia. The following quote from the long-time president captures the conflicting emotions experienced by consumers who worship Cliff Richard:

> So you like Cliff Richard? Is he a bible basher? Is he gay? Has he got a girlfriend? Why isn't he married? These are questions you face once you reveal that you are a Cliff Richard fan. You feel like a Christian thrown to the lions. I often wondered, I must be odd, because I'm the only one who likes Cliff. You ask record shops, they answer Cliff who? So can you imagine how I felt when I joined the Australian group.

We sense from this quote that not being able to interact with other fans can be extremely lonely. One informant described the exhilaration of her first fan club meeting, 'Knowing that you were able to share with like minds. It was so great to have people to talk to about Cliff. I felt so welcome and it was nice to talk about someone that you so admire.' Some informants described years of being a fan where they had no regular contact with other fans. 'I used to wonder if I was only one.' Most went to considerable trouble to find the fan club and expressed discernable relief when they succeeded. Their motivation appears to be more than just the need to interact, but extends into a desire for self-validation. 'I was nervous. I thought they'd know so much more about Cliff than me. But they were so accepting. I felt right at home.' The club gives them the sense that they are not aberrant; that they are not weird. 'It's great. I can just go to a meeting, not worry about what my family thinks. Often I can be more open in the fan club than at home. Anyway my family has got used to it. They don't object anymore.' Feeling an accepted member of a group particularly applied to the male fans, where sexual orientation issues in following a male celebrity can apply.

All of club members felt stigmatized by the term 'fan' and called their group the Cliff Richard Meeting House. The concept of celebrity worship was particularly obnoxious to them. 'We know not to cross the line. We like to see Cliff, to go to his concerts but that's it. We know of others, who believe one day he's going to marry them. He had to take action against her; she was so obsessed'. Despite acknowledging that others disapprove of their celebrity worship, some fan club members found it hard to understand why others think their love of Cliff as odd. 'I went into an English pub on my last trip. I said we were here to see Cliff in concert. They looked at me as if I was from outer space. I thought how dare they! Cliff's English, why shouldn't we like him?'

Incubation is also propelled by the celebrity's sustained career and arguably excessive need for admiration by others. After all, Cliff Richard is not a one-hit wonder. Long after their teen years, he has continued to produce successful records and very apparently from his interviews enjoys the limelight. Diehard fans have not an opportunity to grow out of him, due to a lack of activity in the charts or public life. Arguably Cliff's sustained narcissistic need for admiration of his own self-projection (Vaknin, 2001) fuels his continued drive to remain in the pop music charts. Further insight into his behaviour comes from a former producer of Cliff, who stated: 'How can someone so in love with himself ever fall in love with someone else?' (Turner, 2005, p. 362). When a celebrity's need for adoration fuels celebrity worship, the celebrity–fan relationship takes on a symbiotic character; fans and celebrity develop a dependency on each other. Each party becomes 'willing prisoners' of their expectations of each other.

This situation is particularly interesting in the case of Cliff Richard whose success was seeded in the 1950s and early 1960s when he swept up a generation of teenage fans. Since then he appears to have carefully catered for and adapted to this loyal fan base: 'I live for my fans.' In this case celebrity and fans play their respective roles in a scripted manner that both rigorously adhere to. There are no surprises or exceptions. Cliff Richard exhibits a stunning constancy in music, style and broader values. In this case continued delivery of what the fans desire helps to maintain the relationship. Cliff is notorious for pursuing the perfect performance through intensive practice and a careful eye for detail. For example, informants related the story of him missing a dance move in one performance and spending four hours the next day practising the one move over and over again. While many celebrities reduce their work-load once they achieve success and progress into middle age, Cliff continues to strive for recognition.

Despite liking Cliff, informants readily agreed that Cliff is vain and very self-assured. One stated: 'Oh he loves himself. He has no doubt about his own talents,' or 'He always tells us that [because we like him] we have good taste in men.' Another informant pointed to his obsession with his appearance: 'He always watches what he eats. He is always on a diet. He eats breakfast, never lunch and very little for dinner.' Photographs over the years suggest the occurrence of Cliff's frequent and major cosmetic surgery. Newspaper clips proclaim him as 'The Peter Pan of pop.' At 65 years of age, he has not a single grey hair, maintaining a deep brown hair colour. Cliff, himself, infers his excessive dependency on his fans adoration and narcissistic streak when he states in a 1960s film clip: 'My fans are everything to me. I will do anything to make them happy.' At one stage during his career Cliff adopted a hip funky more contemporary style in his appearance and the music he performed. When his fans indicated their dislike for this change of events, Cliff returned to his original image and music format immediately.

3 Intensification

Once becoming members of the fan club, members report greater freedom in their worship of Cliff arguably as they have willing fan club compan-ions. Every time Cliff tours Australia and New Zealand, the fan club mem-bers attend concerts together across the six main cities in the region; 'We go to every concert in Australia and spend every cent that we have, and some-times even resort to MasterCard. We even try to stay in the same hotel as him.' Although most the fan club members are circumspect about the degree to which they followed Cliff around, it seems it's a case of safety in numbers. The numerous times they reported encountering Cliff on fan club outings group further suggests that they are prepared to go to extraordinary lengths to be physically close to him or to meet him. For example, they described video-taping him sun-baking by a hotel pool; having multiple 'chance' meetings on aircraft flights and lurking outside his country home in England: 'We made a hell of a noise trampling on pebbles of his driveway; the gardener turned the garden hose on full blast. I think he wanted us to leave.' They described numerous instances of waiting long hours for Cliff at airports and/or at the entrance to hotels where he is staying; or pass by where he just happens to be playing tennis. During our fieldwork period, one pair of ladies travelled to England to attend eight consecutive Cliff Richard concerts at the Royal Albert Hall, London.

The fan club activity, on the surface at least, appears as a source of temporary escape or diversion from the stresses of everyday life, and hence may be a healthy activity. The group related a story in which they had all waited late at night after a concert at the entrance to Cliff's hotel. Upon finally arriving, he turned to them and asked: 'Haven't you got homes to go to?'. Initially they were a little offended by this response. However, one of them rationalized: 'We thought he must be terribly tired. Look you accept this from Cliff because fantasy is better than reality. If your husband came home leaving his dirty socks around and treated you like that, you wouldn't tolerate it. But with Cliff, well he's not there every day. It's just a diversion for us.'

Jenkins (1992) argued that we should emphasize the active positive benefits when fans created social networks. O'Guinn (2000) found that fan clubs act like a surrogate family for many members and that the personal relationships that developed often became amongst the most important in their lives. One of the most powerful mechanisms that maintain these fans' interests in Cliff are the strong, enduring friendships that have developed within the group. When interviewing two women their immediate response to the question: 'What if Cliff did not exist?' was 'Well we would not have met.' As one informant emphasized many of these friendships go back over 20 years: 'We have made so many really good friends, and over the years we have shared births, deaths, marriages, children growing up, and so many experiences. We have just sprouted these wonderful friendships worldwide.' Another informant asserts: 'It's (the club) like a part your family.' Instances of mutual support stemming from this community were manifold. For example, one informant described how 'For 5 years I was a single mother and it was really hard, but there was so much love from all these people. It was a huge support for me.'

An intensifier of fandom not mentioned in the literature, but which became obvious in our interactions with the fan club, was the physical attractiveness and sexual appeal of the celebrity. When the question of sexual attractiveness was put to female fans all positively affirmed this as their perception – 'He's yummy', 'he's the complete package, fit, good looking, very attractive in every way'. One informant stated: 'We'd pay just to sit and watch him eat his dinner on stage.' As noted earlier Cliff has put a lot of effort in maintaining physical attractiveness through exercise, diet and a variety of cosmetic enhancements. This contributes to the state of constancy. Male fans tend to shy away from the attractiveness topic. While they agree that Cliff is an attractive person, male fans verbalize more rational reasons for following Cliff. These reasons are around the quality of the musical performances, Cliff's talent, and the admirable values, ethics and personal characteristics of the celebrity.

Conclusion

Our findings suggest that marketplace collectivities, such as fan clubs, are possibly a consequence of consumers seeking sanctuary within their confines. They comprise environments in which consumers can experience social acceptance and a sense of belonging amongst 'like minds'. This can be a welcome relief after long periods of discomfort caused by the stigmatization and loneliness associated with adult celebrity worship. The bonds that consumers develop in fan clubs can strengthen their relationship with the brand (in this case a celebrity) and also act as important sources of emotional support with respect to other relationships in their lives (e.g., family, friends). Hence fan clubs enriches relationships within, and external to the market. Furthermore the numerous social groups and social networks in which our fans appear to successfully participate over long periods of time suggests such that these individuals are socially adept and more likely healthy psychologically. In this sense, Cova and Cova's (2002) idea of tribes (rather than segments or subcultures) appears appropriately applied to fan clubs; comprising one of the many tribes in which contemporary consumers participate.

References

Algesheimer, R., Dholakia, U. and Herrmann, A. (2005). The social influence of brand community: evidence form European car clubs, *Journal of Marketing*, **69** (July), 19–34.

Baumeister, R. (1998). *The Handbook of Social Psychology*. London: Oxford University Press.

Bennett, A. (1999). Subcultures or neo-tribes? Rethinking the relationship between youth, style and musical taste, *Sociology*, **33**, 599–617.

Bhattacharya, C.B., Rao, H. and Glynn, M. (1995). Understanding the bond of identification: an investigation of its correlates among art museum members, *Journal of Marketing*, **59** (October), 46–57.

Boon, S. and Lomore, C. (2001). Admirer–celebrity relationships among young adults, *Human Communication Research*, **27** (3), 432–465.

Caughey, J. (1994). Gina as Steven: the social and cultural dimensions of a media relationship, *Visual Anthropology*, **10**, 126–135.

Cohen, J. (1997). Para-social relations and romantic attraction: gender and dating status differences, *Journal of Broadcasting and Electronic Media*, **41** (4), 516–528.

Cova, B. (1997). Community and consumption: towards a definition of the 'linking value' of product or services, *European Journal of Marketing*, **31** (3/4), 297–316.

Cova, B. and Cova, V. (2002). Tribal marketing: the tribalisation of society and its impact on the conduct of marketing, *European Journal of Marketing*, **36** (5/6), 595–619.

Featherstone, M. (1991). *Consumer Culture and Postmodernism*. London: Sage.

Greene, A. and Adams-Price, C. (1990), Adolescents' secondary attachments to celebrity figures, *Sex Roles*, **23**, 335–347.

Holbrook, M. and Schindler, R. (1989). Some explanatory findings on the development of musical tastes, *Journal of Consumer Research*, **16** (June), 119–124.

Holbrook, M. and Schindler, R. (1994). Age, sex and attitude towards the past as predictors of consumers' aesthetic tastes for cultural products, *Journal of Marketing Research*, **31** (3), 412–422.

Jenkins, H. (1992). *Textual Poachers: Television Fans and Participatory Culture.* New York: Routledge.

Kozinets, R. (1999). E-tribalized marketing?: the strategic implications of virtual communities of consumption, *European Management Journal*, **17** (3), 252–264.

Kozinets, R. (2001). Utopian enterprise: articulating the meanings of Star Trek's culture of consumption, *Journal of Consumer Research*, **28** (June), 67–88.

Maltby, J., McCutcheon, L., Ashe, D. and Houran, J. (2001). The self-reported psychological well-being of celebrity worshippers, *North American Journal of Psychology*, **3** (3), 441–452.

McAlexander, J., Schouten, J. and Koenig, H. (2002). Building brand community, *Journal of Marketing*, **66** (January), 38–54.

Muñiz, A. and O'Guinn, T. (2001). Brand community, *Journal of Consumer Research*, **27** (March), 412–432.

O'Guinn, T. (2000). Touching greatness: The Central Mid-West Barry Manilow fan club, in Schor, J. and Holt, D. (eds.), *The Consumer Society Reader.* New York: The New Press, pp. 155–168.

Patterson, M. (1998). Direct marketing in postmodernity: neo-tribes and direct marketing, *Marketing Intelligence and Planning*, **16** (1), 68–74.

Schindler, R. and Holbrook, M. (1993). Critical periods in development of men's and women's tastes in personal appearance, *Psychology and Marketing*, **20** (4), 275–302.

Schindler, R. and Holbrook, M. (2003). Nostalgia for early experiences as a determinant of consumer preferences, *Psychology and Marketing*, **20** (4), 275–302.

St John, K. (1991). *Cliff in His Own Words.* London: Omnibus.

Turner, S. (2005). *Cliff Richard: The Biography.* Oxford: Lion.

Vaknin, S. (2001). *Malignant Self Love – Narcissism Revisited.* Prague: Narcissus Publications.

Van Raaij, W.F. (1993). Postmodern consumption: architecture, art and consumer behaviour, *European Advances in Consumer Research*, Association for Consumer Research, **1**, 550–558.

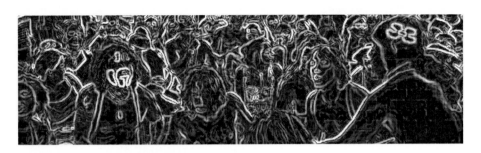

Part IV
Tribes as plunderers

12

Harry Potter and the Fandom Menace

Stephen Brown

This just in

The world wide web went critical in July 2006, as did Ye Olde mainstream media. Harry Potter, rumour had it, was being killed off, getting the chop, hanging up his Quidditch kit, going the way of all fictional flesh (Yeoman, 2006). According to J.K. Rowling, the boy wizard was unlikely to survive the final volume of her seven-book series, the first six of which had kept the world enthralled for the best part of a decade (Brown, 2005).

JKR announced Harry's impending fate on *Richard and Judy*, a book-led British television programme that has done more for the publishing industry than just about everyone bar Gutenberg and Oprah (Brown, 2006a). Cue pandemonium, blogageddon, Myspace meltdown. 'I feel as if I'm about to go to the funeral of a friend,' confessed Mary Catherine. 'I won't be able to get threw [sic] it,' said Clemence713. RavenclawWit wailed that Rowling's unspeakable behaviour was 'crossing the line from realism to outright cruelty'. Meanwhile, JohnB maintained that JKR was nothing less than 'a sadistic enchantress' (Yeoman, 2006, p. 8).

When the digital dust had settled, however, and the Harry Potterites had recovered their composure, such as it was, the real reason for the shocking, headline-grabbing revelation became clear. The paperback edition of the sixth book, *Harry Potter and the Half-Blood Prince*, was being published. Available in all good bookstores near you! For the attractively modest price of £7.99!! Buy one for all your friends!!!

It thus seems that far from being a sadistic enchantress, J.K. Rowling is a fantastic salesperson. Far from crossing the line from realism to outright cruelty, she was keeping a weather eye out for the bottom line. Get threw that, sucka. On your way to the funeral . . .

Authorpreneurship

To be sure, J.K. Rowling is nothing if not canny. Although she has repeatedly denounced the malefic machinations of Machiavellian marketing types – and once confessed that Harry Potter Happy Meals were the stuff of nightmares – the brute reality is that Rowling epitomizes the 'rebel sell'. As Heath and Potter (2006) rightly observe, anti-marketing is an effective marketing strategy. Using hostility to selling as a selling platform is a long-established sales tactic, one that's been employed by copious conveniently counter-cultural CEOs – Anita Roddick, Steve Jobs, Ben & Jerry, Richard Branson and so on – to say nothing of rock stars, movie makers and arts industry denizens generally (see Frank, 1997; Holt, 2002, 2004).

Rowling, if truth be told, is nothing less than an authorpreneur (Brown, 2006b). That is to say, a writer with a very strong sense of what the market wants, how the market works and where the market's going. One only has to read the Harry Potter books, which are chock-a-block with brand name products, magical shopping malls, enchanting sales brochures and celebrity wizard endorsements, to see that JKR is very marketing savvy. She knows what her brand stands for, is cognizant of the most effective marketing strategies and has a fair idea of where she fits into the great marketing scheme of things. Rowling, admittedly, hasn't been trained as a marketer. Like Larry Ellison, Michael O'Leary, Donald Trump, Damien Hirst and what have you, she doesn't require formal qualifications to confirm her commercial credentials. Her sales figures speak volumes, literally. Rowling, furthermore, is only the latest in a long line of authorpreneurs – Charles Dickens, Mark Twain, L. Frank Baum, Edgar Rice Burroughs, Norman Mailer et al. – all of whom had an uncanny ability to sell themselves to the reading public. Few, however, have sold themselves as well as Harry Potter's handler.

Back story

The legend of J.K. Rowling has been worn smooth by countless retellings (e.g., Beahm, 2004; Kirk, 2003; Smith, 2001). Stranded on a delayed train to London, the penniless single mother had a vision – a vision involving an orphaned wizard with nasty stepparents, a magically mysterious school of witchcraft, and the eternal battle between good and evil. Harry Potter strolled into her life fully formed, and by the time she got to King's Cross, the settings, the protagonists, the plots and the entire seven-book series were firmly established in the aspiring author's mind (Rowling, 1997, 1998, 1999, 2000, 2003, 2005).

Turning this celestial vision into literary reality was rather less straightforward and, in keeping with the traditional 'struggling author' template, Rowling battled long and hard to bring her ambition to fruition. Suffering the privations of single motherhood and life on the dole while living in a freezing Edinburgh flat, she scribbled on napkins in a local coffee shop, typed the manuscript herself, received rejection after rejection from narrow-minded publishers who considered boarding school stories about trainee wizards hopelessly antiquated, and eventually got lucky with Bloomsbury. But not before her commissioning editor uttered the immortal line of hack-Hollywood dialogue, 'You'll never make money from children's literature, Jo!'

The first book, *Harry Potter and the Philosopher's Stone*, was released in June 1997. Only 2,000 hardback copies were published and there was little or no promotional support, much less media attention. But the public loved it. Word got round and sales took off. The second volume built on the buzz surrounding the first and by the time the third volume came out in 1999, a full-scale kiddie craze was unfolding. Came 2000, and the release of the fourth book, Harry Potter had the whole world in his hands. His grip tightened the following year, when the first live-action, big-budget, CGI-a-go-go movie was unleashed. The multiplexes imploded. A brand was born.

In the five years since 2001, Potterphilia has subsided somewhat. Instead of being a year-round, 24/7 phenomenon, as it was at the turn of the millennium, the hysteria is now largely confined to new book or movie releases. These days, Harry Potter is just another media franchise similar to *Star Wars*, *X-Men* or *Pirates of the Caribbean*, albeit a massive media franchise. Thus far, more than 300 million copies of the first six books have been sold, making Harry Potter the third biggest bestseller of all time after *The Bible* and *The Thoughts of Chairman Mao* (Brown, 2005). They have been translated into 120 different languages, including Icelandic, Serbo-Croat, Swahili and Ancient Greek. Four live-action movies have been made – the fifth is in production and scheduled for release on 13 July 2007 – and to date these have grossed $3.5 billion at the global box office. More than 400 items of tie-in merchandise, most notably DVDs, computer games, action figures and Potter-themed apparel, are currently available and, all told, is it estimated that the brand is worth $1 billion per annum, or thereabouts (*Sunday Times*, 2006).

Impressive as this is, it remains to be seen whether Pottermania will outlive its source material. The series is set to end in 2007, with the publication of the seventh and final volume, *Harry Potter and the Deathly Hallows*. However, the continuing movie franchise, Rowling's stated desire to write a *Rough Guide to Planet Potter* and, possibly, all sorts of spin-off serials featuring secondary characters (e.g., *Ron Weasley and the Spiders From Mars*, *Gilderoy Lockhart and the Love Potion Faux Pas*, *Hermione Granger's Guide to GCSE Revision*) are sufficient to ensure that the boy wizard will be around for some time to come, even as his original aficionados marry, mate and make their children read the books that rocked the world in the good-old days of the late-twentieth century.

Real story

The fundamental problem with the foregoing summary of Harry Potterism is that, although it conforms to the familiar fairy-story, rags-to-riches and-they-all-lived-happily-ever-after narrative template, it also occludes some of the hard facts about the franchise. As Rowling frequently makes clear, the much-recycled, PR-friendly, Caledonian-Cinderella story of the single mother struggling in an Edinburgh garret is not entirely true, though she was quite prepared to perpetuate it in the early days, before superstardom beckoned. Likewise, the legend that HP was an authentic, word-of-mouth phenomenon, an artefact of kiddie conversations, playgroup chit-chat, interparental interchange and unmediated, unmarketed, smells-like-teen-spirit *enthusiasm*, doesn't withstand close scrutiny.

The occurrence that really set the Rowling ball rolling was the sale of the American publishing rights for $105,000, a record sum for children's literature (Nel, 2001). This deal was done less than one month after the UK publication of the first Potter novel – before the schoolyard groundswell had time to build – and it triggered a great deal of US media interest in the no-name Limey author who'd won the literary lottery. Inevitably, this transatlantic buzz stimulated UK media interest and once Rowling's rags-to-riches story found its way into the papers, the Harry Potter craze really started in earnest.

Another factor that affected the early up-take – and again confounds the 'authenticity' thesis – was the influence of schoolteachers (Borah, 2002). One of the major ways in which 'word got out' about Harry was via the classroom. The first edition of the first book was published with the school library market in mind and what few promotional activities there were, were targeted at educators. The books were read aloud in class, kids were encouraged to write essays on the apprentice mage, or paint pictures, or make magic wands, or write fan letters to the author. Two anthologies of 'first generation' fan letters have been published (Adler, 2001; Moore, 1999), many of which allude tangentially to teachers' mediating role in the book buzzing process. It thus seems that teacher power was as important as pester power in the initial phase of the brand levitation process.

Much-recycled though it is, the grass roots, fan-led legend doesn't hold water. Harry Potter has always been beholden to marketing. Nowhere is this better illustrated than in the carefully orchestrated promotional activities that accompany the launch of each new title. As Brown (2005) explains, this begins with a countdown, where the days left to publication are ostentatiously deducted on dedicated websites and in window displays. Hints are then dropped about the storyline, character development and – hold the front page! – impending deaths. An unfortunate 'accident' usually occurs with a couple of weeks to go, when pre-release copies of the strictly embargoed novel are stolen, hijacked, discovered in dumpsters or go on sale in unnamed Wal-Marts in deepest West Virginia. Finally, the big day arrives: bookshops are opened at 1 min after midnight; theme parties in apt locations, such as King's Cross railway station, are thrown; and, most importantly, copious TV coverage of the unfolding first day frenzy is broadcast to the book-buying multitudes.

The key point about these OTT behaviours is not that they are crass or contrived. It is that they commenced way back in 1998 with the launch of the second novel, *Harry Potter and the Chamber of Secrets*. What's more, they have increased in intensity with each subsequent release and the steady accumulation of the boy wizard's audience. Each book has sold more than its predecessor and although the movies' worldwide grosses have fluctuated slightly, they have never fallen below $790 million, which represents a huge hit by conventional cinema standards, even when the massive marketing costs (of approximately $50 million per movie) are taken into account. In such circumstances, J.K. Rowling's anti-marketing outbursts seem, well, dubious at best and disingenuous at worst.

The triwizard iTribes

Now, none of this means that HP fandom is irredeemably inauthentic, much less a massive marketing imposture. There's no doubt that the boy wizard's aficionados are unfailingly fanatical, as the movie and book launch brouhahas bear witness. The teenage mage may owe more than many imagine to promotional log-rolling, kite-flying and pork-barrelling, but there's no denying that the HP tribe is enormous, enthusiastic and evangelical. Like most contemporary brand communities, moreover, it owes much to the world wide web (Kozinets, 1999, 2001). Indeed, there is an oft-repeated fable that Potter's sudden Stateside success was largely attributable to a little boy whose father worked for AOL at a time when AOL was middle America's ISP of choice and on-line was taking off, big time (Whited, 2002). At his son's insistence, the AOL executive set up a dedicated Harry Potter chatroom on the ISP homepage ... and the rest is history.

Similar to the freezing-garret fairy-story, this origin myth may or may not be true, but it can't be denied that the Internet is integral to HP fandom. The instantiations of this fandom come in many shapes and forms, however. These include copious tribute websites; innumerable on-line encyclopaedias; manifold role-playing games; any amount of fan art, including images aplenty of Draco Malfoy in bondage gear (see below), to say nothing of video mash-ups, Potter podcasts, photo galleries, discussion groups, trivia quizzes, interview archives and, inevitably, a smattering of virtual retail stores selling all manner of magical memorabilia – wands, broomsticks and wizarding outfits in S, M, L, XL and XXL (Waugh, 2005).

Perhaps the most remarkable manifestation of this cybertribalism is fanfiction (Lanier and Schau, 2006). These are stories written by fans using the Harry Potter characters, which are then posted on the web, where they are reviewed and discussed by the community at large. The sheer scale of the fanfic phenomenon is staggering. According to fanfiction.net, the principal clearing house for amateur literary endeavours, some 258,760 Harry Potter sequels are available on-line. This is an immense figure by any reckoning, but it is especially impressive when set against the stories generated by analogous literary figures. Fanfiction.net lists 72 sequels to *Inkheart*, 1,848 additions to the *Artemis Fowl* series, 587 extrapolations of *His Dark Materials* and even *Lord of the Rings*, with 38,165 posted parsings, doesn't come close to the Potter stockpile.

Fairly typical of the breed is *Harry Potter and the Ancient Runes*, by Raven Gryffendor. As yet unfinished, it contains 28 chapters, the first of which begins:

> It was a hot, sticky day in Little Whining, Surrey. The weather had been extremely pleasant since the beginning of summer. People could be seen in the streets talking away happily to each other, people in town centers could be seen shopping until they dropped and children could be heard playing endlessly until the break of dawn. Privet Drive was known for its loud, boisterous residents but it was far too hot for people to get all worked up and bothered today. Everyone had retreated to the safety of their homes, where there was less chance of them getting to dehydrated or sunburned. Well, everyone except a skinny teenage boy who thought it much safer to be outside, out of the way of his Aunt and Uncle. This way he didn't have to deal with them any more than he had to.

The accompanying reviews, unfortunately, have not been kind. 'This sucks!!' says Bob. 'I don't know if I like this story,' proffers Anonymous. 'I hate to be the reviewer that gives the bad review, but I am,' announces another Anonymous. So much for fanfic community spirit.

Its alleged faults notwithstanding, *Ancient Runes* is a fairly innocuous contribution to the Harry Potter canon. Others are much more ambitious. With the Harry Potter characters and Hogwarts setting as a starting point, these launch off in all sorts of creative directions. Some 'crossover' into other forms of fanfic – written by *Star Wars* or *Dr Who* or *Star Trek* or *Sherlock Holmes* enthusiasts, for example – where they date, mate and spawn many and varied literary miscegenations. This is a wonderland where Chewbacca and Hagrid finally meet and greet, where Yoda recognizes Dudley Dursley as his long lost son, where Albus Dumbledore is outed as a Time Lord, where Beam me up Scabbers is the order of the day and where Sherlock meets Hermione and seizes his opportunity to milk the line, 'Elementary my dear Watson'. It's also a wonderland where Harry Potter gets up to the sorts of things that aren't really suitable for adult audiences, let alone adolescents. Known as 'slash' fiction, this puts the perv into Impervious, the dung into Mudungus, the butt into Butterbeer, the arse into Parselmouth, the homo into Alohomora and does things with Engorgement Charms that you don't want to know about (Brown, 2005).

So outrageous has some Potterporn become, that a rating system, akin to the parental advisory guidelines in movies and music, has recently been introduced. Prompted by an inflammatory article in *The Scotsman*, which highlighted the adult – often flagrantly gay – character of some HP fanfic, the classification comprises six categories, ranging from K (suitable for most ages), through T (13 and older), to MA (mature adults only).

This fanfic corpus, in turn, has generated a secondary literature of its own. Apart from the inevitable academic interest and of course the ever-present MSTings – reviews in the jocular style of *Mystery Science Theater* – several celebrity fanfic authors now exist. The most high-profile of these is Cassandra Claire, who famously portrayed Harry's Hogwarts nemesis Draco Malfoy in leather bondage pants, an outlandish outfit he doesn't actually wear in the canonical works but is now widely considered his signature ensemble (Waugh, 2005). Hence the fetishistic fan art referred to earlier.

Get a life

When the HP iTribe is not penning pornographic paeans to Malfoy's chaps, or getting hot and bothered about the latest 'shipping' debate ('ships' are fantasy romantic relationships among the canonical characters), they're wrapped up in related RL activities. Live action role-playing games, or LARPs, are especially popular, not least among university students. The first wave of Harry Potter fans – the kids who were 11 when the first book about an 11-year-old boy wizard was published – are now at college and they've taken their wands, broomsticks, quidditch kits and gold lamé wizarding outfits with them. The games, which usually involve recreating scenes from the books according to complex Dragons and Dungeons-style rules, are played out across university campuses and analogous educational institutions worldwide, though they are particularly popular in Finland and Japan, where there's a long tradition of 'cosplay' (Anonymous, 2006).

Alongside LARPs, Harry Potter is the subject of numerous conventions, such as Nimbus 2003 in Orlando, Nimbus 2005 in Salem, Accio 2005 in Reading and Lumos 2006 in Las Vegas. These provide an opportunity for HP devotees to get together, tell stories, cast spells, exchange experiences, debate the books, buy or barter memorabilia, swan around in their expensively acquired outfits and, not least, listen to learned papers on profound Potteresque subjects like 'It's Not Easy Being Hermione', 'Muggles and Mental Health' and 'Love Potion # 9: Vice, Volition and Voldemort'. Don't ask.

Another thing aficionados often do, perhaps unsurprisingly since the Weird Sisters feature in the books and Franz Ferdinand played at the Hogwarts Yule Ball in the fourth movie, is groove to the latest musical sensation, a genre popularly known as 'wizard rock'. That is, nearly nü-metal bands who compose songs and release albums predicated on the Harry Potter phenomenon (Rose, 2005). The first such combo, Harry and the Potters, was formed in Boston in 2002. A duo, they play in costume (punkified school uniform), in character (Harry Year Four, Harry Year Seven) and in libraries, bookstores, pizza parlours and donut emporia up and down America's east coast (their tour bus is a silver minivan known as the Pottermobile). With three albums under their belt – a self-titled debut, *Voldemort Can't Stop the Rock* and *Harry and the Potters and the Power of Love* – their 30-song repertoire includes such instant classics as 'Wizard Chess', 'Save Ginny Weasley', 'Stick it to Dolores' and the spellbinding 'SPEW'. Almost inevitably, however, the wizard rock genre is getting increasingly competitive thanks to the arrival of rival bands like The Whomping Willows, Dobby and the House Elves, the Moaning Myrtles and, naturally, Draco and the Malfoys. No sign thus far of The Rowling Stones.

Be that as it may, the most obvious RL form of HP fandom, a theme park, remains unrealized. Given the size of the Harry Potter market, given bookstores' penchant for Potteresque theming – Ottakers even changed its name to Pottakers for the release of *Half-Blood Prince* – and given Rowling's own recreation of the Hogwartscape for her Edinburgh Castle bash (see below), a fully fledged theme park seems like the next natural step. However, the idea has never got beyond the discussion/speculation/cashflow calculation stage, primarily because the HP franchise-owner, Warner Bros, doesn't operate theme parks. There's a constantly circulating rumour, nevertheless, that Disney and Warner Bros are on the point of doing a deal, whereby Hogwarts would be integrated into the Magic Kingdom's ineffable attractions. It won't be too long, presumably, before Harryheads are happily cavorting on animatronic Ford Anglias, knock-em-dead Knight Rides, Forbidden Forest Adventures, Quidditch Pitch Battles, Firebolt Roller Coasters and Shrieking Shack Splash Downs. It doesn't take too much imagination, what's more, to work out the retail mix of the accompanying Potter Plaza, Hogsmeade Mall, or whatever they decide to call it (Table 12.1).

Table 12.1 The shopping mall that must not be named (likely tenant mix)

Housefurnishings	**Sports, pets, etc.**
Pottery Barn	Floo Locker
Erised Mirror Workshop	Seekers Sneakers
Crouch's Couches	Fawkes Fireworks
Dobbytat	Skeeters Beetles
	Humphrey's Boggarts
Apparel	St Brutus Sports Centre & Fitness Suite
Worm Tailoring	
Madame Maxine's Outsize Outfitters	**Food court**
Hext	Dunkin Dursleys
Crookshanks Shoes	The Leaky McBurger
Bagman's Hold-alls	Bludger King
T.K. Maxine	Pomfrey's Pomme Frites
	Happy Death Eater
Speciality goods	Snapelle Soft Drinks
Hermione's Secret	
Abercrombie & Filch	**Services**
Quirrell's Quills	Umbridge Orthodontics
Shrieking Radio Shack	Weasleys Weezing Wizards
Burns & Nobbles	Hagrid's Hair Care
	Volde Mortgages
Convenience goods	Portkey Cutting
Bertie Botts Grotto	
Martin Miggs Magazines	**Department stores**
Ollivanders Provender	Muggle Mart
Beauxbatons Bread & Pastries	Dementors Depot
Nearly Legless Nick's Liquor Store	You-know-who Haus

The auror, the auror

Clearly, the iTribe attracted to Harry Potter is nothing if not adhesive. The bond between author and audience is somewhat stickier, however. Uneasy is perhaps the best word to describe it. On the one hand, the HP brand community is an integral part of the Pottermarketing process, insofar as fans' willingness to stand outside bookstores at midnight, while television station reporters record their pieces to camera, is central to the publishers' pre-launch PR operation. It is the fans, furthermore, who provide the incredible, gee-whiz, hold-the-front-page sales figures that are integral to the accompanying press coverage – books sold, copies printed, first day receipts, etc. – and building the marketing momentum that's necessary nowadays in the cultural industries. They also organize and attend the tie-in parties, vote for Rowling in book-of-the-year awards, and basically do everything above and beyond the call of brand fan duty (Brown, 2005).

On the other hand, Harry's fans are often treated diffidently, not to say shabbily (Blake, 2002). The basic customer-centric values of mainstream marketing practice are not adhered to by Potter's handlers. Denial marketing rather than demand-responsive marketing is widely practised. As Dening (2001) notes, the fans are tantalized, teased and tormented during the pre-launch hoopla. More seriously, HP's legal representatives have been quick to quash any infringement of copyright law. School plays based on the boy wizard are forbidden. Tribute websites have received threatening cease-and-desist letters. Legitimate schools of witchcraft have been shut down by order of Warner Bros. Books about the phenomenon have been removed from sale at the request of my learned friends. And, incredibly, injunctions have even been served on Canadian school-kids who bought *Harry Potter and the Half-Blood Prince* from a local supermarket, which sold them ahead of time. Although the kids acted in good faith, they were barred from reading their own book prior to its official release date.

Interestingly, the edgy relationship between author and enthusiast features prominently in the books themselves. One of the most striking aspects of the Harry Potter novels is the frequency with which fans form part of the narrative. Less than three pages into the first book, the boy wizard's fame is being discussed. An otherwise unremarkable 11-year-old who lives with his unpleasant step-parents in quotidian suburbia, Harry is actually a superstar of the wizarding community and blessed with magical abilities beyond number. He is stared at, pointed out and feted by (some of) his new-found magical acquaintances. Come the second book, he has stalkers, autograph hunters, love struck admirers, celebrity role models and more. By the fourth and fifth books, however, the once-admired teenage thaumaturge has fallen from favour, stands accused of rampant egomania and is in serious danger of losing the plot. Even his best friends turn against him. Happily, the sixth book not only restores the reputation of the 'chosen one' but also puts the kid back in the picture. Sadly, he is surrounded by hangers on, false friends, jealous rivals and sycophants with an eye for a quick buck or several:

'Harry Potter, I am simply delighted!' said Worple, peering short-sightedly up into Harry's face. 'I was saying to Professor Slughorn only the other day, *Where is the biography of Harry Potter for which we have all been waiting?'*

'Er,' said Harry, 'were you?'

'Just as modest as Horace described!' said Worple. 'But seriously –' his manner changed; it became suddenly businesslike, 'I would be delighted to write it myself – people are craving to know more about you, dear boy, craving! If you were prepared to grant me a few interviews, say in four- or five-hour sessions, why, we could have the book finished within months. And all with very little effort on your part, I assure you. . .'

(Rowling, 2005, pp. 295–296)

Presumably, these characterizations of celebritude are reflections of Rowling's personal experiences, as are the innumerable references to amoral journalists, press intrusion, foul weather friends, life in the gilded goldfish bowl, threatening letters from illiterate cranks and, in an intriguing aside in the middle of the fifth book, the fundamental difference between long-term fans and bandwagon fans:

'Is that a Tornados badge?' Ron demanded suddenly, pointing to the front of Cho's robes, where a sky-blue badge emblazoned with a double gold 'T' was pinned. 'You don't support them, do you?'

'Yeah, I do,' said Cho.

'Have you always supported them, or just since they started winning the league?' said Ron, in what Harry considered an unnecessarily accusatory tone of voice.

'I've supported them since I was six,' said Cho coolly. 'Anyway . . . see you Harry.'

She walked away. Hermione waited until Cho was halfway across the courtyard before rounding on Ron.

'You are so tactless!'

'What? I only asked her if –'

'Couldn't you tell she wanted to talk to Harry on her own?'

'So? She could've done. I wasn't stopping –'

'Why on earth were you attacking her about her Quidditch team?'

'Attacking? I wasn't attacking her, I was only –'

'Who *cares* if she supports the Tornados?'

'Oh, come on, half the people you see wearing those badges only bought them last season –'

'But what does it *matter*?'

'It means they're not real fans, they're just jumping on the bandwagon –'

(Rowling, 2005, p. 208)

Regardless of the veracity of these representations or indeed the validity of Rowling's fan typology, JKR's relationship with her audience has changed through time. Broadly speaking, three phases of development can be discerned: *enthusiasm*, *exasperation* and *exploitation*. Prior to 2000, when Harry Potter fandom was still comparatively low-key, Jo was ready, willing and able to interact with her admirers. She was happy to participate in the personal appearances, media relations, meet-greet-and-autographs side of the writing business. So much so, that the end papers of the second novel are filled with reproductions of fan letters from satisfied customers:

> Dear J.K. Rowling
>
> I really enjoyed your book Harry Potter and the Philosopher's Stone. I know it all off by heart as I am reading it for the fourth time. Could you please tell me when the next Harry Potter book is coming out as I so want to read it.
>
> (Daniel Hougham)

> Dear Ms. Rowling
>
> My name is Fiona Chadwick and I am nine years old. I really like the book Harry Potter. My class and I are reading it as a novel. I think all the class are enjoying it to but the only thing wrong with it is that you can't put it down.
>
> (Rowling, 1998, npn)

The turning point, however, was the release of the fourth volume in July 2000, when Rowling's UK publishers organized a launch event at King's Cross Station. The media gathered en masse in the station forecourt, several children were hurt in the crush and the subsequent press coverage was uniformly negative (the book was duly dubbed 'Harry Potter and the Goblet of Hype'). Similar scenes were re-enacted in America and media intrusion rapidly reached intolerable levels, especially when details of JKR's failed marriage, strained familial relationships and alleged plagiarism of the work of another author, were splashed across the world's trash-talking tabloids (Smith, 2001). It was during this period that heavy-handed attempts were made to shut down Potter tribute websites, high walls were built around her home in Edinburgh, much to neighbours' annoyance, restraining orders were placed upon several mid-life-stricken stalkers and the author was battling with Warner Bros to ensure that the movie adaptations stayed true to the books. It is little wonder that the fifth book's portrayal of fandom – and the vicissitudes of celebritude – is unremittingly negative. Whatever else it is, *Harry Potter and the Order of the Phoenix* is an angry, exasperated book, arguably the least successful in the series (as JKR acknowledges).

In recent years, Rowling has moved beyond exasperation to what can best be described as exploitation. That is to say, she has learned to use her fan mandate. The launch of the fifth book, for instance, involved only one personal appearance, when JKR read extracts to 4,000 carefully selected Pottermaniacs in the Albert Hall. There were no prying press questions to answer, nor was she subject to the quixotic demands of obnoxious PR-types. To the contrary, she had turned the tables on the tittle-tattlers and, paradoxically, her refusal to play the promotional game – by communing instead with true fans – generated even greater media coverage than before. Way to go, Jo.

An even more effective strategy was employed when the sixth book release rolled round. This time, the official launch took place in the splendour of Edinburgh Castle, where Rowling's one and only appearance was in front of 40 hand-picked fans, who were there as representatives of the world's press. Carefully vetted newspapers had earlier organized tie-in competitions to select their 'official' cub reporters, whose copy was filed in the immediate aftermath of an audience with the queen of teen fiction. The event was duly covered by numerous television stations, the resplendent castle was exuberantly set-dressed for the night and the friends and family of the chosen few sat in the esplanade's serried bleachers, cheering everyone as they arrived.

Rowling's authorpreneurial exploitation of her fan mandate doesn't stop with biennial book launches. Her extensive charity work, most notably for single parents and MS sufferers, is guaranteed front-page, feature-article coverage as well as the undivided attention of decision-takers. When Joanne complained about the plight of caged schoolchildren in Eastern Europe (Rowling, 2006), steps were quickly taken to stop the barbaric practice. She is courted by politicians, what's more, not least the prime minister in waiting, Gordon Brown, though he let himself down badly with his single televised question 'where does Harry get his money from?' Evidently, he'd never read the novels, but given that Rowling's fanbase are likely first-time voters come the next general election, the wannabe PM wasn't going to let ignorance stop him currying favour with a key constituency. Indeed, had he perused Rowling's tongue-in-cheek treatment of the British prime minister in the very novel he was endorsing, Brown might have concluded that discretion was the better part of Voldemort (Rowling, 2005).

Another important aspect – perhaps the most important aspect – of the on-going relationship between HP's creator and HP cognoscenti is the R&D function that the fans increasingly perform. After six sizeable volumes, the Hogwartscape is so extensive that it's hard to keep track of who's who and what's what. More than 200 characters are in play and the list of places, spells and named magical activities is legion. However, in a superhuman act of wikiwizardry, www.the-leaky-cauldron.org keeps tabs on the ever-expanding cast list. Rowling herself uses this unofficial site to avoid slip-ups and also monitors the manifold HP theories, plot suggestions and inter-fan altercations on the web. Jo does so, reportedly, to reassure herself that no one has yet worked out how the series will end, though she has also expressed reservations about some of the racier fanfic and admits to being astonished by the shipping debates. JKR has even confessed to making anonymous postings on 'what'll happen to Harry?' discussions at Mugglenet.com. Apparently, her 'theories' about the boy wizard's fate were dismissed by wiser heads among the fanbase!

When good fans go bad

Amusing as it is to think of Rowling being rebuffed by rabid admirers, there is a dark side to this author-audience entanglement. Akin to her fictional hero's baneful bond with Lord Voldemort, the creator's creations have been affected by the fandom menace. The author's original plan for the seven-book series has been blown off course by her readership in general and the demands of the movie franchise in particular. There's no doubt, for example, that the shipping debates, especially those concerning the Harry/Ginny and Ron/Hermione entanglements, were incorporated into *Half-Blood Prince*. The denouement of the fifth book, furthermore, was transparently beholden to Hollywood, in as much as the climactic shootout in the Ministry of Magic read more like a GCI shopping list than a novel. The characters too seem to have taken on more and more of the idiosyncrasies of the actors who play them in the movies, though there's clearly a chicken-and-egg element to this. Most remarkably of all, the ending of the seventh book – the much-vaunted climax of the entire series, which was famously written at the very outset – has also been changed (Yeoman, 2006). As the first draft is unlikely ever to be made available, it is impossible to calculate the extent of this change. However, it's undeniable that the basic attributes of the Harry Potter product have been adjusted in light of customer response.

Viewed from a conventional marketing perspective, Rowling's behaviour is eminently sensible, exemplary even (Prahalad and Ramaswamy, 2000; Vargo and Lusch, 2004). She's moving from an entrepreneurial to a marketing mindset. The brand is being co-created with the assistance of enthusiastic consumers. The producer is responding to the consumer and the consumer is contributing to the production. At long last, the postmodern marketing millennium has arrived! Prosumers rule! Power to the paypal!

It's always hard to argue with sales figures, particularly when the sales figures stem from what is widely believed to be best marketing practice. It goes without saying that Rowling's embrace of the Potter iTribe has paid dividends where many maintain it really matters: the bottom line. It's undeniable that the sales of each successive volume have steadily increased, despite occasional lamentations about overexposure, and when the seventh customer-co-created book is unleashed, all previous records will doubtless disintegrate. Yet, it is also arguable that consumer input has adversely affected the Harry Potter series. Fans' insatiable desire for more stuff has convinced the author that bigger is better and the volumes since *Azkaban* have expanded alarmingly. The British edition of *Goblet of Fire* clocked in at 636 pages and *Order of the Phoenix* exceeded 700, which JKR has since admitted was way too much. As a consequence, *Half-Blood Prince* was somewhat slimmer, though at 607 pages it's not exactly a novella.

Set against the increase in the quantity of Rowling's words, there has been a significant decrease in their quality. There is a widespread sense that the incredible invention of the first three books has been lost and that, for all their bulk, the later episodes are a pale shadow of the earlier volumes. Most mainstream marketers, admittedly, will maintain that the customer is always right, that the sales figures speak for themselves, that the public gets what the public wants. This may be so, but it's also true to say that the customer is always right wing – conservative, reactionary, stuck-in-the-mud – that sales figures don't always speak the truth and that the public shouldn't always get what the public wants (Brown, 2004). This is especially so when we are talking about fandom, rabid fandom most of all. Whatever else they are, fans are notoriously conservative. They resist change. They inhibit innovation. They want more of the same. They not only venerate the object of their desire, they entomb it in aspic forever and ever, amen (Hills, 2002; Jenkins, 1992; Lewis, 1992).

Fans, furthermore, are atypical. True, they talk an awful lot; they really, really love the product; and they are nothing if not proactively evangelistic. But they are also self-selected. They are not representative, not even remotely. Their enthusiastically put views are hopelessly distorted, albeit hopelessly distorted in a direction marketers find congenial. Isn't it great to gather eager followers? Isn't it wonderful to co-create with our oh-so-articulate customers, as the marketing textbooks recommend? Aren't we the bees' knees of branding? The answer, in a nutshell, is NO.

Yes, Blanchard and Bowles (1998) urge us to attract raving fans. However, it's important to recognize that raving fans are just that. Raving. And their ravings should be treated with considerable caution and not a little scepticism. It is madness to cede control to enthusiastic amateurs, no matter how creative they appear to be, how keen they are to help, or how seductive their whispered sweet nothings. In saying that, I'm not suggesting that fans, enthusiasts, aficionados, cognoscenti or whatever we want to call them should be ignored. Far from it. Fandom is a good thing, by and large, as are happy-clappy, tell-the-world customers. But, just as fans shouldn't be ignored, they shouldn't be idolized either, much less worshipped or adored.

None of this means that we should revert to the passive, quiescent, stimulus-response model of consumers that once held sway within marketing thought. Nor is it a return to the 'cultural dupes' scenario beloved by crumbly cultural theorists of the Marxism-maketh-Man contingent. There's no question that today's consumers are wise to marketers' wiles and that they are ready, willing and able to engage with marketers as well-informed equals (Brown, 2004). The so-called 'troublesome consumer' is not a myth and today's marketers have to take this into account. Consumers may be increasingly fan-like in their relationship with the marketing system – the brandscape is littered with closely knit communities (Kozinets, 1999; Muñiz and O'Guinn, 2001) – but fans aren't passive dupes either. To the contrary, the fan culture literature shows that they are unfailingly fractious, strongly opinionated and, not least, extremely proprietorial (Hills, 2002). They have invested time, energy and financial resources. They have earned the right to be heard. They refuse to remain silent. They understandably expect their voices to be attended to.

This is certainly true of the Harry Potter brand community. Although it has given J.K. Rowling a powerful mandate to air her views on matters political and although politicians listen respectfully to the concerns of the iGeneration's Bob Geldof, Harry Potter's fanbase hasn't written Rowling a blank check. Her room for manoeuvre is really rather limited, as fans' willingness to criticize her contributions to the canon attest. The movies too are roundly condemned if they make an obvious mistake, as in the case of an erroneous inscription on a *Goblet* tombstone, which had world wide wizards up in arms. Likewise, a boycott of tie-in merchandise was mooted when many feared JKR was selling out to crass commercial interests. Warner's heavy-handed attempts to shut down tribute websites were met with considerable resistance and eventually circumvented. The fanfic community had to be pleaded with before its voluntary code of practice was introduced and Potterporn was confined to the top cybershelf. When Rowling mounted her anti-marketing hobby-horse by condemning advertisers' use of ultra-thin models, the readership was quick to condemn Jo's representations of obesity. Fat characters in the Harry Potter novels are unfailingly portrayed in an extremely negative light, Dudley Dursley especially. Mote and beam, JKR! Likewise, when Rowling urged her readers to support their local bookshop, rather than price-cutting chain stores and supermarkets, which are doing untold damage to the trade, many noted that the Harry Potter books are one of the supermarket chains' biggest loss-leaders and market share-grabbers. Put your own house in order, Jo!

When JKR oversteps the mark, in other words, the HP community clips her wings. Hegel's master-slave relationship is alive, well and teaching at Hogwarts. So powerful indeed has the slave become that it's calling the shots in the seventh and final volume. As previously noted, the original ending has already been changed and no one will be surprised if Draco Malfoy's wearing leather chaps when the series reaches its climax. Much as the fans adore Joanne Rowling, woe-betide her if she fails to meet audience expectations for the grand finale. The iTribes may not be revolting but they're definitely getting restless.

References

Adler, B. (2001). *Kids' Letters to Harry Potter From Around the World*. New York: Carroll & Graf.

Anonymous (2006). Cosplay, *Wikipedia* (accessed 3 August), www.wikipedia. org/wiki/cosplay.

Beahm, G. (2004). *Muggles and Magic: J.K. Rowling and the Harry Potter Phenomenon*. Charlottesville: Hampton Roads.

Blake, A. (2002). *The Irresistible Rise of Harry Potter*. London: Verso.

Blanchard, K. and Bowles, S. (1998). *Raving Fans: A Revolutionary Approach to Customer Service*. London: HarperCollins.

Borah, R.S. (2002). Apprentice wizards welcome: fan communities and the culture of Harry Potter, in Whited, L.A. (ed.), *The Ivory Tower and Harry Potter*. Columbia: University of Missouri Press, pp. 343–364.

Brown, S. (2004). O customer, where art thou? *Business Horizons*, **47** (4), 61–70.

Brown, S. (2005). *Wizard! Harry Potter's Brand Magic*. London: Cyan.

Brown, S. (2006a). Rattles from the swill bucket, in Brown, S. (ed.), *Consuming Books*. London: Routledge, pp. 1–15.

Brown, S. (2006b). *The Marketing Code*. London: Cyan.

Dening, P. (2001). Selling Harry Potter, *Irish Times Weekend*, 10 November, 1.

Frank, T. (1997). *The Conquest of Cool: Business Culture, Counterculture and the Rise of Hip Consumerism*. Chicago: University of Chicago Press.

Heath, J. and Potter, A. (2006). *The Rebel Sell: How the Counter Culture Became Consumer Culture*. Oxford: Capstone.

Hills, M. (2002). *Fan Cultures*. London: Routledge.

Holt, D.B. (2002). Why do brands cause trouble? *Journal of Consumer Research*. **29** (June), 70–91.

Holt, D.B. (2004). *How Brands Become Icons: The Principles of Cultural Branding*. Cambridge: Harvard Business School Press.

Jenkins, H. (1992). *Textual Poachers: Television Fans and Participatory Culture*. New York: Routledge.

Kirk, C.A. (2003). *J.K. Rowling: A Biography*. Westport: Greenwood.

Kozinets, R.V. (1999). E-tribalized marketing? The strategic implications of virtual communities of consumption, *European Management Journal*, **17** (3), 252–264.

Kozinets, R.V. (2001). Utopian enterprise: articulating the meanings of *Star Trek's* culture of consumption, *Journal of Consumer Research*, **28** (June), 67–88.

Lanier, C.D. and Schau, H.J. (2006). Culture and co-creation: exploring the motivation behind Harry Potter on-line fan fiction, *Paper presented at Consumer Culture Theory Conference*, Notre Dame, August.

Lewis, L.A. (ed.) (1992). *The Adoring Audience: Fan Culture and Popular Media*. New York: Routledge.

Moore, S. (1999). *We Love Harry Potter!* New York: St Martin's Griffin.

Muñiz Jr, A.M. and O'Guinn, T.C. (2001). Brand community, *Journal of Consumer Research*, **27** (March), 412–432.

Nel, P. (2001). *J.K. Rowling's Harry Potter Novels*. New York: Continuum.

Prahalad, C.K. and Ramaswamy, V. (2000). Co-opting customer competence, *Harvard Business Review*, **78** (January–February), 79–87.

Rose, L. (2005). Wizard rock, *Forbes*. 13 June, www.forbes.com.

Rowling, J.K. (1997). *Harry Potter and the Philosopher's Stone*. London: Bloomsbury.

Rowling, J.K. (1998). *Harry Potter and the Chamber of Secrets*. London: Bloomsbury.

Rowling, J.K. (1999). *Harry Potter and the Prisoner of Azkaban*. London: Bloomsbury.

Rowling, J.K. (2000). *Harry Potter and the Goblet of Fire*. London: Bloomsbury.

Rowling, J.K. (2003). *Harry Potter and the Order of the Phoenix*. London: Bloomsbury.

Rowling, J.K. (2005). *Harry Potter and the Half-Blood Prince*. London: Bloomsbury.

Rowling, J.K. (2006). My fight by J.K. Rowling, *Sunday Times News Review*, **5** (February), 1–2.

Smith, S. (2001). *J.K. Rowling: A Biography*. London: Michael O'Mara.

Sunday Times (2006). Harry keeps us spellbound, *The Sunday Times Rich List 101–250*, 26.

Vargo, S.L. and Lusch, R.F. (2004). Evolving to a new dominant logic for marketing, *Journal of Marketing*, **68** (January), 1–17.

Waugh, R. (2005). Mad about Harry, *Night and Day*, **10** (July), 24–27.

Whited, L.A. (ed.) (2002). *The Ivory Tower and Harry Potter*. Columbia: University of Missouri Press.

Yeoman, F. (2006). Hints of Harry's death put his fans in fear of The End, *The Times*, **1** (July), 8.

13

Inno-tribes: *Star Trek* as wikimedia

Robert V. Kozinets

Star Trek is dead; *Star Trek* has never been more alive. In May 2005, the two-hour season's finale of *Enterprise*, titled 'These are the Voyages' – was broadcast on Paramount's UPN network. Perhaps it should have been titled 'Those were the Voyages.' There would be no new *Star Trek* series from Paramount, although a film is tentatively in development. The cancellation broke 18 straight years of *Star Trek* series, with at least one, and sometimes two series airing at any time. Despair hit the fan community. Letter-writing campaigns were marshalled. Fans fought valiantly, but unsuccessfully, to save *Star Trek* yet again.

Yet *Star Trek* persists. Today, in apartment buildings, basements, living rooms and public parks in Virginia, Texas, Scotland and across the world, the fan base that sustained the series throughout its 40-year incarnation is producing new and professional-looking episodes of *Star Trek*. Although many of these new fan-made series are recapitulating familiar themes and characters, others are being used to take the series to uncharted new territories, to blend in alternatives lifestyles, meanings and identities that had long been excluded from the official *Star Trek* universe. By analyzing this phenomenon, its popular reception, and its implications for understanding the mutating variegations of contemporary consumer culture, I suggest that this phenomenon of fan production is an act of tribal reclamation with wide-ranging implications.

Tribal reclamation? This initial association of *Star Trek* communities with tribes is no mere throwaway b-school jargon. The analogy of fan consumers as nomadic tribal 'poachers' was aptly deployed by Henry Jenkins (1992) who developed it from Michel de Certeau's (1984) notions of reading as a poaching of the masses on the terrains of the elites. Jenkins (1992) studied female-centric fan communities and their variegated tastes, casting fans as a type of 'travelling' community with common but shifting interests in a variety of media properties. Like tribes, fan communities move among corporate landscape, occupying them ideologically and affectively, 'poaching' and appropriating ideas, myths and memes, living with them, making them their own, and moving on. I like the analogizing of fans as tribes because it casts the phenomenon of fandom (an insider term for fan community) in an emotional light that resonates with my own ethnographic experience. But let's be brutally honest about our metaphors here. Sure, it's trendy, but does the word 'tribe' really have relevance that stands closer scrutiny?

Affirmative, Captain. Consider the Pomo 'tribe' of California. They lived in much smaller groups (called 'bands') that stayed in relatively close proximity to one another and were bonded by filial loyalties of lineage and marriage. The Pomo were composed of many distinct bands of people, as many as 70 different bands. They were not a unified people in the sense of a group who were all socially linked or governed; on the contrary, they were extremely spread out and covered great patches of land. What linked the various bands of Pomo peoples in the Pomo tribe was the only thing that truly could link them: they often shared space [in Tuan's (1977) sense, they had intersecting frontiers but different geographical home bases], they shared a common language (actually they had seven different languages, but what they did share was enough linguistic elements to meaningfully communicate), and they shared a sufficient amount of rituals, practices and traditions that they recognized each other as members of the same culture (with much diversity and many regional variations). An imperfect but unavoidable intersection of place, language, rituals and material culture was the bases of their 'tribalness.'

Now, to *Star Trek* fans. When I moved among them (see Kozinets, 1997, 2001), fan clubs tended to contain under 100 members in number. Like the Pomo, they functioned as small social bands whose common interests overlapped, and whose members gathered sporadically but regularly with other bands that shared similar interests. Like a tribe, my local fan club in Toronto had a hierarchical structure with its own powerful Chief; we met regularly, and our meetings had an emotional, personal intensity in which there was a lot of support, friendship, and encouragement, and also a lot of jockeying for position, infighting and strife. In our fan club, there were smaller groups, families, groups of families and groups of friends who saw each other more frequently. *Star Trek* and science fiction played a part in but were not always central to that socializing; this was never a grouping devoted solely to *Star Trek*, but always to a wider pursuit of consumption interests in science fiction, space travel, fantasy and good quality alternative media fiction. The media tastes changed collectively with the TV and movie seasons; the tribe moved along; there are tribes that feed on many fertile grounds. The club had monthly get togethers and additional social events, such as group dinners and group movie nights.

The club I belonged to also interfaced with other *Star Trek* fan clubs in the area. We would often bring copies of our monthly newsletter to these other clubs as gifts, to share what our local tribe was doing. The Klingon tribe came over once and demonstrated a Klingon tea ceremony, some linguistic feats and some martial arts. We got together with some other local fan clubs and did charitable work at a food bank. Once a year all the local and regional tribes would gather at the big Toronto Trek convention – the major Canadian pow-wow and one of the big annual pow-wows – and would meet foreign members from strange and distant places like Australia, Wales, South Africa and Tennessee. Acting, drawing, singing, story telling, sharing, display, costuming, exhibits, meeting, trading and buying would occur at these festivals.

In organization, the *Star Trek* fan club system seems like the same network of concentric and overlapping circles that described Native American and other tribes (see Bacon-Smith, 1992) and seems also to share more than a few practices established by the tribal form. Just as smaller groups of Pomo tribal members gathered sporadically and regularly, so did *Star Trek* fan clubs in their engagements with Klingons. As larger tribal groups pow-wow, and cross-tribal groups met in large congresses, so did *Star Trek* tribes gather in their annual attendance of Toronto Trek and other conventions in the region. The clubs share the loose local–regional–global links of the tribal form, and the shared rituals, language and traditions that bind them. As the next section will explain, these rituals and systems have a strong basis in *Star Trek*'s history of innovative, hybridized institutional relationships: the tribal rights to feed on fertile grounds.

A brief history of *Star Trek*

Almost from its origins, *Star Trek* has been positioned in a contested terrain between fan's science fictional interests and multinational media conglomerates' need for profit. The series was created by Gene Roddenberry, a former Second World War pilot and LAPD officer who had previously written for numerous television series. Aware of the tribes of science fiction fans who gathered in reading clubs and at convention congresses, Roddenberry courted them at a time when it was far from common to do so. He approached them with *Star Trek* as if bearing a gift, a long-awaited quality science fiction television series. Many fans were enthusiastic and grateful – science fiction in the 1960s was largely a literary phenomenon rarely taken seriously in the media – and swore lifelong loyalty to *Star Trek* and fealty to its Creator.

'Gene saw humanity as an evolving species that was going to keep getting better and better. He believed the future was something to look forward to and that the exploration of space and the development of our quality of life were things mankind was going to focus on' (Berman, 1994, p. 2). That Roddenberry was an ideologue who consistently positioned himself as a secular humanist and peaceful utopian visionary added much to his credibility and built his status as an important Chief within the technologically utopian science fiction fan tribe – a leadership role that sustained him through lean years and led him back into the Promised Land of motion pictures and a successful new series.

The original *Star Trek* series lasted two unsuccessful seasons marked by dismal ratings and was then slated for cancellation by NBC. At 56 episodes filmed, the series would not have enough episodes to qualify for the second life of syndication and would thus have reached extinction. Roddenberry brainstormed and then barnstormed support for a letter-writing campaign to save *Star Trek*. He enlisted the support of prominent fans Bjo and John Trimble, among others, who professionalized and organized the fans' campaign. The ensuing campaign was unprecedented. *Star Trek* fans, some accounts claim as many as a million of them, wrote letters to NBC in 1968 begging them to give *Star Trek* another chance in what still stands as the largest act of fan activism in history. The fans took charge of the future of the series, deciding that it was worth saving. An overwhelmed NBC gave the show another season and then cancelled it for good but, its fate tied to the tribes', from syndication *Star Trek*'s phoenix ashes rose.

September 8, 2006 marked the 40th anniversary of *Star Trek*'s debut on 'NBC's peacocked airwaves' with the national airing of the first *Star Trek* episode, entitled 'The Man Trap.' Kirk, Spock and, crew now indelible members of the television pantheon and *Star Trek* is indisputably one of the most popular television series of all time. Backed by years of increasingly successful conventions, books and memorabilia sales, and continual letter writing to networks and studios, the franchise reincarnated on the big screen, beginning in 1983 with the successful premiere of *Star Trek*: *The Motion Picture*. This was followed by nine other movies, with the last, 2002s 'Nemesis' a box office disappointment that took in less than it cost to make.

By the year 2006, the original show was shown in 75 countries worldwide and in many of them is still being shown. There were five spin-off television series, three of them – *Star Trek: Deep Space Nine, Star Trek: Voyager* and *Enterprise* – created by Paramount studio producer Rick Berman, who had taken over the franchise from Roddenberry after the latter's death in 1991. All three series generated some degree of fan excitement along with disappointing ratings, poor reviews, and considerable amounts of fan hate mail.

Star Trek as wikimedia

Despite the failures of the newer series, the *Star Trek* franchise as a whole seems perfectly capable of surviving on little more than momentum. The number of devoted *Star Trek* fans worldwide is in the millions; a common estimate is 30 million people, but this is likely an understatement. Uncounted thousands of fans belong to the hundreds of *Star Trek* fan club organizations present in almost every country in the world. There are many different sub-tribes of *Star Trek* fans, whose orientation to the show is different: collectors, modelmakers, gamers, role players, filmers, writers, slashers, fan clubbers, actor fans, series fans, artists, dealers, tech-freaks, alien hackers, Klingons, Vulcans, Cardassians, Bajorans, and on and on. This prodigious fertility is a product of the complexity, multifacetedness, intertextuality, mystery, and openness of the original core text of the *Star Trek* series. These qualities work in concert with fans' own abilities, meaning systems, socio-historical situations, and disparate needs. The show offered various sketchily described aliens and their culture and fans filled in the blank spaces, inserting their own needs, desires and histories.

In the old days, fans would write fiction in the form of written text (for a fascinating history, see Hellekson and Busse, 2006). The fan effort that previously went into the production of printed written fiction ('fanfic') and convention organizing is now being channelled – and it even seems amplified – into efforts to create a stunning variety of *Star Trek*-based entertainment product. *Star Trek* fans create their own podcasts and radio broadcasts. They have produced animated series such as the humorous Finnish 'Star Wreck' and the Flash animation series 'Stone Trek' which hybridizes *Star Trek*'s world with that of The Flintstones. There are fan-made *Star Trek* music and rap videos, *Star Trek* novelizations, *Star Trek* protest trailers, and films – even a parodic *Mystery Science Theater 3000* version of the official (and reviled) *Star Trek V* feature film. This is a burgeoning enterprise existing in a legal vacuum. As Jenkins' (2006a, p. 255), emphasizing the role of fans, rightly notes, 'we might think of fan fiction communities as the literary equivalent of the Wikipedia: around any given media property, writers are constructing a range of different interpretations that get expressed through stories.'

We are in new conceptual terrain and lack terms to describe what has happened to *Star Trek* as a media property. *Star Trek* has gone native or, better, it has gone wiki – it is now 'wikimedia.' Fans add to *Star Trek* and correct one another just like Wikipedia encyclopaedia contributors add to the famously expansive universe of the online encyclopaedia. By the term 'wikimedia' I mean to describe a distinct media content form that has, either deliberately or unintentionally, gone open source and begun spawning new content through the efforts of non-profit, do-it-yourself, collaborative media creators acting outside of the structure of corporate, institutional organization or sanction. The existence and notioning of wikimedia has major implications for our understanding of contemporary consumer culture. But it is still almost entirely unexamined by academics. It also may have major implications for marketing strategy, as this chapter will only begin to unpack further on. The following section begins this undertaking by proceeding to the centrepiece of this chapter: a look at the production of new *Star Trek* episodes by fans.

Prosuming's final frontier

As Russ Belk and I have noted in numerous other articles related to videography in consumer and marketing research (e.g., Belk and Kozinets, 2005), technological and manufacturing advances in digital videocameras and digital video production and editing software have enabled amateur film-makers to create professional-looking videographic works that would have been prohibitively expensive even a decade ago. These technologies have freed up the art and craft of video making so that they are accessible to almost anyone with some ingenuity and access to a budget of a few thousand dollars. The increasing pervasiveness of Internet access and broadband connections has simultaneously made distributing these films easier than ever before. Fans had been making their own small-budget films for many years. But fan creations have reached new heights of professionalism and pervasiveness and, as in many other spheres, *Star Trek* fans are leading the way.

According to a recent article 'up to two dozen of these fan-made "*Star Trek*" projects are in various stages of completion, depending what you count as a full-fledged production' in countries such as Holland and Belgium (Hakim, 2006). And according to various FAQs posted on websites and quotations in various articles covering the phenomenon, Paramount, the studio that own the rights to *Star Trek*, has been tolerant and its executives have consistently declined comment on these developments. As long as fans do not sell or profit from their work (an established fan community standard), Paramount allows them to continue creating and distributing new episodes of *Star Trek*.

I must admit that when I began investigating this topic, I was sceptical about what I would see in these episodes. But as I began viewing them, in all of their diverse quality, I got a strange rush. Although they were far from perfect, these episodes had verve, style, humour – there was a freshness and a primal energy about all of them that came from their sheer authenticity as major undertakings presented as communal gifts. Other *Star Trek* fans posting on popular newsgroups seem to have related impressions.

> Matt: Disturbingly this is more or less as good as any TOS episode, though the acting is below the TOS [The Original Series] standard (some will ask if that's even possible), the effects, sound, and other production values are pretty good. Actually if these guys had studio backing I can't imagine why they couldn't make an entire new TOS series around the [Starship] Exeter [online series].
> (Posted on <alt.tv.star-trek.tos> 18 August 2003)

> Ron: I gotta say it. That was excellent. The first new TOS episode in what, 34 years? These people did a fantastic job. Someone at Paramount needs these guys. Considering the limits on their production I am amazed by how incredibly well this compares to real TOS and present production Enterprise. Thank you for the link.
> (Posted on <alt.tv.star-trek.tos> 18 August 2003)

I have dozens of other laudatory postings – nit-picking in places, but overwhelmingly grateful and exhilarated in tone. *Star Trek* is back and it's ours, they proclaim with pride. The U.S.S. Farragut (www.ussfarragut.com) and

Starship Exeter (www.starshipexeter.com) series are situated in the original, Classic, or TOS ('The Original Series') *Star Trek* universe, filmed in digital video on reconstructed sets (whose online descriptions ring with overtones of care, precision, and authenticity). The series feature starship space scenes rendered with exquisite special effects that surpass the original series, but introduce us to new starship crews composed of amateur actors, who act out new scripts penned by Hollywood unknowns. Fans write, film, edit, score, produce, and distribute these new episodes. Empowered by affordable new technologies and the mass distribution of the Internet, these new fan-made shows seek to play with the original format of the series, but not alter it in any material ways. But that same careful tendency to avoid rocking the starship is not universally present, as the next section attests.

Gays, grays, and ego plays

More than 40 original *Star Trek: Hidden Frontier* episodes have been produced and distributed by a group of fans in Los Angeles. Set in the time period of *Star Trek: Deep Space Nine*, what this show lacks in production values it makes up for in imagination and ambitious theming. The show is filmed against a green screen (which shows through as a greenish halo suffusing the actors' heads and bodies), and uses computer-generated backdrops and sets. But in terms of theme, *Hidden Frontier* goes where *Star Trek* has steadfastly refused to go: into the worlds of occult space mysticism and the portrayal of future gay culture. The following newsgroup excerpts present some fan responses to the series and its inclusion of these two themes.

> Charlie: Just in the last couple of days I had the chance to download the fan-produced series *Star Trek: Hidden Frontiers*. . . . The real problem is the science. For example they seem to have gotten Richard Hoagland for an adviser as they talk a great deal about Hyperdimensional Physics and show monuments in the Cydonia region of Mars (for more on this see http://www.badastronomy.com/bad/misc/hoagland/face.html). I don't mind sloppy science but I do mind pseudoscience being passed off as real science. A quick Google search on Hyperdimensional Physics will reveal a rich source of links for it. Unfortunately most appear to be UFO, Crop Circles, and mysticism sites. . . . The series does deserve a few brownie points for featuring an openly gay couple.

> Leonard: Frankly, I could have done without the 'openly gay' couple's spit-swapping scene however. It was totally overboard and gratuitous, and just ruins the suspension of disbelief for me completely to be reminded of the real world gay agenda of 'in your face', and 'we're here, we're queer, get over it' crap. Who really gives a fuck?
> (Exchange posted on <alt.tv.star-trek.enterprise> on 20 May 2005, editing for spelling and grammar errors and readability)

Charlie's gripe with the series is its use of occultish space references of 'pseudoscience' in place of legitimate 'real science.' Although it did feature telepathy, repeated visitations from godlike aliens, and a mystical Vulcan race, *Star Trek* also adhered to a conventional materialist viewpoint where astrophysics were concerned. In distinct contrast to *The X-Files* series, it did not feature or seek to intertextually relate with folk UFO and fringe space visitation and alien abduction lore (see Curran, 1985; Kozinets, 1997). The fan creators of *Hidden Frontier* have taken considerable liberties with *Star Trek*'s orientation by doing so. Their alien 'Grays' partake of the same legends of interplanetary visitations as have driven folk UFOlogy, Roswell crashes, Area 51, alien autopsy, and Project Blue Book/Majestic-12 Project government cover-ups, as depicted in popular works such as Whitley Strieber's (1987) *Communion* book series (see also Hopkins, 1997). UFO, crop circle, and mystically oriented websites are disdained by Charlie as unworthy of inclusion in the legitimate, real, true, authentic science universe of *Star Trek* – a statement that many fans would affirm. These are areas that *Star Trek*'s official productions have avoided, contaminated territory that would taint *Star Trek*'s aura of scientific legitimacy with weird occultish overtones.

Leonard's post is more concerned about another deviation from *Star Trek*'s 40-year-old norms. *Star Trek* staked its utopian reputation on egalitarianism and tolerance of diversity (see Kozinets, 2001). The original show featured Russian and Japanese officers working together with Americans in a peaceful future where Earthlings are united (in paramilitary extra-planetary pursuits). *Star Trek* featured the first interracial kiss on American prime-time television, and many of the show's themes were allegories on the immorality of racial intolerance and class differences. Sex was also ubiquitous in the original show, with Captain Kirk's interstellar conquests serving as the backdrop for many storylines. However, fans have long noted the omission of gay characters from the show; in *Star Trek*'s utopian, egalitarian future, gay or lesbian unions seem markedly absent. This absence is made all the more stark when compared with the homoerotic 'slash' fiction created by fans almost since *Star Trek*'s inception. Slash fiction romantically paired Captain Kirk with Mr. Spock ('Kirk/Spock' fiction was abbreviated to a simple slash; see Bacon-Smith, 1992; Jenkins, 1988; Penley, 1997).

Jenkins (1995) wrote about the 'Gaylaxians,' a community of gay, lesbian and bisexual science fiction fans who read *Star Trek* by looking for places to insert 'queer meanings' into the show's future vision, to identify gay themes and characters in the text, and to work actively (through protests such as letter-writing campaigns) towards their more overt inclusion (see also Geraghty, 2003). There have been intermittent letter-writing campaigns by gay and lesbian *Star Trek* fans for at least 17 years, and Gene Roddenberry at one point publicly promised an openly gay or lesbian character on the show. Yet the show never delivered, prompting *Star Trek*'s particular fans to speculate on all sorts of reasons why gays and lesbians have been excluded from humanity's paradisical future.

In an article for the *Columbia News Service*, Linda Rodriguez (2003) quotes Wayne Wilkening, the Chairman of the Boston chapter of the Gaylaxian Science Fiction Society as saying: 'All it would have taken [by *Star Trek*'s official producers to make gay fans happy] is an acknowledgment that same-sex relationships occur normally in the *Star Trek* universe. It [Hidden Frontiers' homosexual depiction] fits very well in the *Star Trek* universe; it treats homosexuality and gay characters as normal parts of the crew. It's positioned as it's OK socially, but that individuals still have to come to terms with how they feel about it.'

In contrast, aforementioned message poster Leonard patrols the borders of heterosexual propriety, classifying the unambiguous inclusion of affectionate gay characters as a 'spit-swapping scene'; the exchange of same-sex spit is viewed as far more offensive than the passionate but closed-mouth kisses for which Captain Kirk was famous. The same-sex kissing was 'totally overboard and gratuitous,' according to Leonard. It defies the reality of *Star Trek*, which requires 'suspension of disbelief' by drawing Leonard into the political same-sex rights assertions that drive Stonewall remembrances and Gay Pride days, and other expressions of GLBT rights, rights that he denigrates with the insulting designation 'crap.'

Death by canon, or the death of canon?

Aporia is a term meaning an impassable or insoluble contradiction, a paradox in a text's meanings. Ultimately, the fannish act of interpretation exists through the grace of the inherent aporia of the text; the text's openness begets the ambiguity enabling the tribe to settle into the space, but the settling of the ambiguity begets controversy and ideological turf wars. Should gay males be 'swapping spit' in the hallowed halls of starship corridors? Should a rigorously scientific show like *Star Trek* be linked with outlandishly occultish unreality such as alien abductions and crop circles?

Should *Star Trek* be used to critique *Star Trek*? Fans' already well-developed creative proclivity has now been married to abhorrence for manifestations of *Star Trek*. The fans hated, despised even, the ridiculous and confusing Shatner-directed fifth *Star Trek* movie, and many also were disgusted by the three most recent television series (particularly *Enterprise*). Their animosity creates considerable fan activity aimed at expunging the influence of this movie and these series and dissociating it from the official lore of *Star Trek*. That official lore, called 'canon' and described elsewhere in several texts (Jenkins, 1992; Jindra, 1994; Kozinets, 2001) is the body of work that fandom socially constructs and collectively agrees to consider the legitimate narrative of the culture of consumption. Think of it as analogous to various sects of the Jewish faith that consider the Old Testament, but not the Talmud or the Zohar, as their core text. And it is the constituent elements and control over that canon – and consequently over much of *Star Trek*'s fan-negotiated brand DNA – that is being drawn into ambiguous terrain and contested through *Star Trek's* descent/ascent into wikimedia.

Is it worth considering the implications of these fan creations? What indications of their impact upon *Star Trek's* brand and community do we have? Consider first that *Star Trek: Enterprise* – the last *Star Trek* television series – garnered an average audience of 3 million people in 2005 its final season, making it a dismal 150th among television series that year. This viewership was drastically depleted from its 2002 premiere episode that was watched by 12 million viewers. *Enterprise's* dismal ratings led pundits to speculate that *Star Trek's* social meanings were burnt out, used up, spent. The results prompted a lawsuit from affiliated videogame maker Activision alleging that the once proud *Star Trek* franchise had been allowed to stagnate and decay. As *Entertainment Weekly* writer Russo (2003) poignantly put it: 'Are things really this dire for the 37-year-old, multibillion-dollar-generating granddaddy of all entertainment franchises? . . . It's dead, Jim. Almost.'

Mr. Russo spoke too soon. Consider next this amazing fact. *Star Trek: New Voyages* is a fan-created series based in Ticonderoga, NY, that boasts that one of its episodes has been downloaded over 30 million times. The success of fan-made series such as *New Voyages* indicates that *Star Trek's* large and enthusiastic fan base continues to live long and prospect online for good material. Such an impressive number suggests the major impact that these productions can potentially have on the *Star Trek* brand.

The key informant for my dissertation informed me that in science fiction, filk, and *Star Trek* fandom 'egoboo is the coin of the realm.' Egoboo is a sense of ephemeral pleasure that comes from the public recognition of one's own efforts, the joy of seeing one's own name as author, or in the credits, spoken by others, celebrated as a creator, a maker, a player. It is a short form and expansion of the term ego boost. Significantly, this is a term that migrated from the science fiction community into the open source programming community – the term was a useful appellation of the motivation of both fans and open source programmers [according to Greenwald (1998) and others, there has been considerable overlap between *Star Trek* fans and high technology early adopters from the time of the Internet's inception]. Yet recent interviews and postings by the main force behind *Star Trek: New Voyages*, indicate that these fan actors are hoping for Paramount and the fans, at some point, to show them the money.

The continuing wikimediated voyages of starships Enterprise, Excelsior, Farragut, Intrepid, and others pose an exponentially enlarged opportunity for fan ego boosts (and if they can ever be monetized, for fan wallet boosting). *New Voyages* continues the five year mission of the U.S.S. Enterprise, with her crew of Captain Kirk, Mr. Spock, Dr. McCoy, and others, played by new (fan) actors with the as-yet unfamiliar names James Cawley, Jeffery Quinn, and John Kelley. With an audience of millions, these fan actors are elevated into a localized stardom. Stars from the series are now revered guests at the *Star Trek* conventions they once attended as fans. Moreover, the *New Voyages* series is so popular it has attracted the attention and support of original writers and actors from the television series. Screenwriter Dorothy Fontana, who wrote such original *Star Trek* classics as 'Tomorrow is Yesterday' and 'Journey to Babel' in the 1960s recently wrote a new episode for *Star Trek: New Voyages*. Walter Koenig, the actor who played Ensign Chekov in *Star Trek*'s original series has reprised his classic role, and George Takei, who played Lieutenant Sulu will star in another episode.

Imagine the possibilities of starring as your own role model in a new version of the show you loved as a child, working with original actors from that series. This is a fantastic bridge crossing the boundaries between fictional and real worlds. Like modern Eleusian rites or Macumba possessions, the participant enacts and embodies the god. In the following section, I broaden out from these phenomena to suggest and explore their implications through a theorization of 'inno-tribes,' where inno-tribes are different bands and tribes of consumers united in their novel creation of an expanded culture of consumption.

Star Trek fans as inno-tribes

The introduction of actual consumption into audience reception theory into cultural studies was a slow process. Sparked by Stuart Hall's (1980) theorization of consumers' decoding practices, David Morley embarked on a historic study of the reception of Britain's nationwide study and found, among other things, a pattern of oppositional and dominant readings of the television news show, depending partially on the social class situation of the audience member. Morley's protégé, John Fiske, was the pioneer of fan-based studies. He looked at the activities of television fans and found that, rather than the passive and brainwashed receptors they had been theorized to be, fans engaged in a variety of creative activities, such as decorating their rooms, writing letters, organizing into fan clubs, and creating scrapbooks.

In the past, this creativity was, much like the inner practices of Firat and Venkatesh's (1995) ostensibly 'active' consumers, largely relegated to symbolic acts of identity creation as well as the aforementioned individualistic room decoration and scrapbook making. Those days of mainly symbolic production are past. In his continuing landmark studies of fan productivity, Henry Jenkins exposes the levels and depth of fan co-creation (Jenkins, 1988, 1992, 2006a; see also Bacon-Smith, 1992; Penley, 1997).

It is with these understandings of tribalness, poaching, consumption and creation that I return to my original (Kozinets, 2001) conception of *Star Trek* fan community as a culture of consumption. I originally wrote that 'the term culture of consumption is used to conceptualize a particular interconnected system of commercially produced images, texts and objects that particular groups use – through the construction of overlapping and even conflicting practices, identities and meanings – to collectively make sense of their environments and orient their members' experiences and lives' (Kozinets, 2001, p. 68). I was very interested in what we could say about *Star Trek*'s material culture *and not the tribes it formed.* Subsequent scholars have almost uniformly cited the term 'culture of consumption' from my work, and used it instead *to refer to the groups of people themselves.* But my conceptualization foregrounded the material manifestation of mythic texts and memorabilia: 'commercially-produced images, texts and objects that particular groups use' and not the particular groups. I did this because I wanted to capture and permit an 'exploration of cultural heterogeneity not accorded to conceptions that privilege a shared system of meaning.' I was emphasizing a communal system that had flexible, contested and dynamic borders. Yes, the cultures were focused upon *Star Trek*, but there were so many different kinds of culture and so many different ways that they interpreted and consumed *Star Trek* that to call them 'a culture' was to obscure much of their diversity. Schouten and McAlexander (1995) earlier made a similar point about the variety of Harley-Davidson subcultures, and Martin, Schouten, and McAlexander (2006) hammered the point home in their wonderful ethnography of women Harley riders; Kates (2002) made a similar point about the 'protean' quality of gay men's communities.

The tribal analogy explicated earlier works well here, and is more parsimonious. Like the Pomo tribes of California, the different tribes of *Star Trek* share the same general territory (the *Star Trek* text) but may occupy entirely different parts of that vast landscape. Like those tribes, they may have several different languages, and a huge range of customs and rituals that are unique only to themselves, but they gather together, they share enough linguistic and symbolic material to communicate, they share some common customs, and they recognize one another as members of the same general tribe. For this chapter, we need to annex this conceptual territory further in order to specify the creative acts of these tribal forms.

Individual fans are certainly not all creative. Tribes are not all making digital films. Some, perhaps many, are happy to simply buy and consume commercial goods. Fan clubs are not necessarily in the business of creating new texts and objects (although they often do) and certainly not all are using *Star Trek* as wikimedia. The tribal form, however, does seem to follow the openness of the culture of consumption's interpretive field; the two are interlinked in my cultures of consumption conception. Institutional histories and structures of accommodation seem to also play an important role.

I wonder if it will muddy the water more than clarify it to suggest that we build a new definition based partly on an inversion of my earlier definitional lens. I am proposing that we focus on the particular bands and tribes of people who actively engage in the co-creative, producerly role that this chapter seeks to highlight demonstrates. In other words, what if we looked at the 'consumers' or 'prosumers' who collectively open up the source code of the culture of consumption (i.e., to turn media into wikimedia), go elbows deep into it, and add onto the culture of consumption? I call these bands of prosumers 'inno-tribes' and suggest that they are *prosumers who identify as the members of a particular group that collectively uses a culture of consumption – and whose 'use' includes the individual and collective construction of overlapping and even conflicting practices, identities, meanings, and also alternate texts, images, and objects.*

What this new definition and this chapter highlight is not merely the 'use' of that particular interconnected system of commercial images and objects – whether it is Coca Cola collectibles, pop art, old books, wine labels, or Battlestar Galactica – but the way that inno-tribe members construct practices, identities, meanings, *and also* alternative texts, images and objects. The culture of consumption is raw material for inno-tribes that then forms the basis for a new and more expansive culture of consumption. The material culture grows, expands, memetically transcribes, reproduces. This is similar to the 'archive fever' tendency noted by Derrida (1995): as the archive intertextually incorporates references to itself, the archive grows and expands. 'The archivist produces more archive, and that is why the archive is never closed' (Derrida, 1995, p. 68). That is also why the original *Star Trek* series is completely, totally alive, today; because it is constantly being (re)written. Inno-tribes contribute and share their new material culture with their own bands and across the congresses and pow-wows into the larger concentric circles of related consumer tribes. This realization has implications for our understanding of contemporary consumer culture and the ever-shifting ground of global intellectual property rights.

Considerations

Something terrible and ultimately irreconcilable happened when companies were given the power to control the creative, mythic, cultural images that ended up mattering so deeply to ordinary people. It happened because people could not stop caring about icons like Elvis, Mickey Mouse and Mr. Spock; that mythic linkage was not a choice. As much as anything cultural can be said to be hardwired into our being, the need to believe in myths, rally around rousing tales, and share iconic new stories is. Some corporate executives, however, have little time or patience for such matters. Boards and stockholders demand that they focus on profitability in the short, near short, and even-shorter terms. This focus and this motive can lead entertainment executives to find as many ways as possible to use brand and line extensions to expand their popular media properties' cultures of consumption – their interlocking system of texts, images and objects – and to offer them for sale, exchanging them with those who will pay, excluding others.

However, that stubborn populace cannot stop caring about icons like The Beatles, Cinderella and Captain Kirk, and some of them are right-brained, inspired and skilled. Others just can't afford the memorabilia, or don't like what is offered. That subset of the population writes their own fanfic, draws their own art, makes their own web pages, dubs mix tapes and sonic blends, casts groovy sculptures, and paint freaky wiccan pagan neocon New Age Book of Revelations versions of the core text. These creative individuals want to use the culture of consumption as their own playground, twisting it like plasticine to their own ends. Unlike corporate producers, they run on egoboo, and this means that the more people they distribute their work to, the bigger the egoboo, the better off they are. Egoboo means sharing is good. Profit motive means sharing is not so good.

I read these countercultural grassroots routines of building sharing networks and local gift economies in terms of institutionalized and technologically enabled 'grassroutines' that are developed in communal response to mass cultural narratives. In a wider sense they harbour an irony. Marketers seek to increasingly infiltrate consumers' and their communities' organic Word-Of-Mouth (WOM) networks; the techniques of WOM are very popular in the entertainment industry, especially in the post-Blair Witch Project viral marketing campaign fervour. However, consumer collectives counterbalance these efforts by assuming control over the means of myth making. The result is a truly new form of cultural production and counterproduction.

Corporate executives tend naturally to see this new product development as competition. *Star Trek*/Paramount/Viacom's executives certainly did – they cease and desist-lettered the online fan community into submission in 1996 and their original reception of many of the new fan-made film series, *New Voyages* included, was to have their lawyers send it more cease and desist letters. Why are fans making and giving away what we as a company are set up to manufacture, distribute and sell, they must have wondered (and what also may have crossed their minds is how in the world they are doing it for $70,000 an episode!)? They aren't in business to do that; we are. We've got (jumbo-sized) expenses. We developed it. We bought it. How can we let this happen?

But Paramount has let it happen, and in this strange fact lies the heart of our little mystery. This uncharacteristically charitable corporate parental acceptance suggests to me the notion of an 'invigoration strategy.' It goes something like this: by letting the series go feral, turning it into wikimedia, it will be invigorated by the energies of the fan community; they will make it their own, and recharge it with the evaporated meanings that the old series gained in syndication but that the new series lacks. This is the 'brand hijack' described by Wipperfürth (2005) but amplified and magnified. Here, the consumers are not simply engaging in WOM marketing that alters brand meanings, they are creating and distributing new products, as if brewing up a new and altered version of Pabst Blue Ribbon or Red Bull and serving it, or filming and exhibiting their own back story sequels of the Blair Witch Chronicles. There is a shared goal between the creative consumer and the cultural producer: both want to enlarge and expand the culture of consumption. However, their visions do not exactly converge in the manner of that expansion. The prosumer fan/band/tribe member customizes to a high degree, producing material that is of interest to him or her, or his or her band, and possibly other members of the wider tribe as well. This may not be what the cultural producer wants. And then there's the fact that they give it away (one could assume that there is a group of young people who are now being introduced to Kirk, Spock, and the *Star Trek* franchise through *New Voyages* and the online-distributed fan-made series; the 'original' may seem to them a pale copy).

There is another entertainment example of this invigoration strategy (Jenkins, 2006b). The BBC series *Doctor Who* was cancelled, went feral, offered a variety of direct-to-video and fan offerings, and returned to enormous success. In the *Doctor Who* story 'most of the key producers and writers [of the current successful series] are the fans who kept the series alive during the down period' (ibid.). Like *Star Trek*, *Doctor Who* had a history of novel institutional accommodation with fans and writer, even including special rights arrangements where some series' writers were entitled to own the rights on characters they had created (allowing some rich and institutionally-supported cross-pollination between writers' rights and fan community creations). Fan cinema of *Doctor Who* stretches back well before digital cinema days, and included casting a female doctor, something that the show's official producers have to this day refused to do. There is also the case of *Star Wars* digital fan films, in which a generation of young, aspiring film-makers is employing digital technology to 'remake' *Star Wars* on their own terms, and share it over the Internet (Jenkins, 2006a, p. 131). Brown, Kozinets, and Sherry (2003, pp. 28–29) argue that the impetus for this urge to remake *Star Wars* lies in fans' desire to create their own more authentic version.

Empowered by the group, enculturated and educated by fellow producers, spurred by dissatisfaction and hunger for authenticity, goaded by-in-group competition, and hankering for employable skill development, fans build a base of productive consumption. And operating under the 'caring-and sharing ethos of community' (Kozinets, 2002), they prefer to distribute their works through the gift economy. 'Like the older folk culture of quilting bees and barn dances, this new vernacular culture encourages broad participation, grassroots creativity, and a bartering or gift economy. This is what happens when consumers take media into their own hands' (Jenkins, 2006a, p. 132; see also Kozinets, 2001, 2002). In contrast, corporate executives wants to create content and colonize communities based on costs versus benefits, showing a profit to stakeholders. Capital investment exists to be exploited and sold as profitably as possible to consumers. There is an inherent conflict of interest between the inno-tribe, its members, the larger tribe made up of many bands, clans and sub-tribes, and the content-owning corporate executives who must somehow meaningfully manage the elements of this relationship.

Because the world of entertainment is so incredibly visible, and the Internet and media so pervasive, every inno-tribe like the *Star Trek* fan community increases the probability of more inno-tribes springing into being. And the examples are not limited to media products like television shows and motion pictures. An example in the technoworld is charted by Muñiz and Schau (2005) in their exploration of the Apple Newton community, a definite inno-tribe – who behave in ways startlingly similar to fan groups. Harley-Davidson is another (Schouten and McAlexander, 1995). Wipperfürth (2005) offers dozens of examples of the closely related, interesting, but less dramatic 'brand hijack' by committed consumers of the marketing campaigns of goods ranging from beer, beverages, and clothes to technology and cars.

Due to length constraints, I must leave largely unexplored this new relationship and its powerful implications for the changing face of consumer culture. The current Wikipedia entry on '*Star Trek* (fan made productions)' (2006) offers a concise history and then accurately notes that fan fiction has been one of the main battlegrounds in which the legal issues balancing a copyright owner's legal rights against consumers' use of that material has been fought. Moreover, '*Star Trek* has been at the forefront of the controversy' (ibid.).

In an age of Web 2.0 (see Treese, 2006) and Open Source Marketing (see Pitt, Watson, Berthon, Wynn, and Zinkhan, 2006), where the collective intelligence of prosuming consumers and emergent inno-tribes is being touted as the current techno-marketing imperative, what is the broader role of wikimedia in the marketing strategy handbook? Brands are increasingly experimenting with wikimediating concepts; they are opening up their content to consumer creativity. Recent, Chevy Tahoe allowed consumers to assemble their own 'Consumer Generated Advertising' from clips and titles (many consumers created intriguing 'subvertizing' criticizing the auto industry and spouting environmental messages; see Carducci, 2006). Converse took it all the way to becoming a 'wikibrand' in allowing consumers to create their own original twenty-three second wikiadvertising. But this path is fraught with peril.

What are the contested contours – legal, communal, social – of the relation between inno-tribes, cultures of consumption, and corporations? How are their conflicts settled? Is it true that media companies will need to share rights with increasingly powerful prosuming collectivities – allowing them to prosume so that they can also consume? What are the implications of the open sourcing of the multibillion-dollar *Star Trek* franchise for other entertainment properties and for brands and products in general? One of the key themes running throughout online fan accounts and media descriptions concerned if and how Paramount was 'allowing' fans to create and distribute this content. Will these 'invigoration strategies' allow marketers to manage the hijacking and poaching of their own brands, conjuring the feral enchantments of authentically auratic retro brands?

The truth is, *Star Trek* never really belonged to Paramount at all. From the moment Gene Roddenberry humbly came to the convention offering it as a gift, it belonged to the tribe.

References

Bacon-Smith, C. (1992). *Enterprising Women: Television Fandom and the Creation of Popular Myth*. Philadelphia, PA: University of Pennsylvania Press.

Belk, R.W. and Kozinets, R.V. (2005). Videography in marketing and consumer research, *Qualitative Marketing Research*, **8** (2), 128–141.

Berman, R. (1994). Roddenberry's vision, in *Farewell to Star Trek:The Next Generation: TV Guide Collector's Edition*. Toronto, ON: Telemedia, pp. 2–3.

Brown, S., Kozinets, R. V. and Sherry, J. F. Jr., (2003). Teaching Old Brands New Tricks: retro branding and the revival of brand meaning, *Journal of Marketing*, **67** (3), 19–33.

Carducci, V. (2006). Culture jamming: a sociological perspective, *Journal of Consumer Culture*, **6** (1), 116–138.

Curran, D. (1985). *In Advance of the Landing: Folk Concepts of Outer Space*. New York: Abbeville Press.

de Certeau, M. (1984). *The Practice of Everyday Life*. Berkeley, CA: University of California Press.

Derrida, J. (1995). *Archive Fever: A Freudian Impression*, trans. Eric Prenowitz. Chicago, IL: University of Chicago Press.

Firat, A.F. and Venkatesh, A. (1995). Liberatory postmodernism and the reenchantment of consumption, *Journal of Consumer Research*, **22** (December), 239–267.

Geraghty, L. (2003). Homosocial desire on the final frontier: kinship, the American romance, and Deep Space Nine's 'erotic triangle', *Journal of Popular Culture*, **36** (January), 441–465.

Greenwald, J. (1998). *Future Perfect: How Star Trek Conquered Planet Earth*. New York: Viking.

Hakim, D. (2006). Fans are flying the enterprise in final frontier for 'Star Trek', *New York Times*, 18 June.

Hall, S. (1980). Encoding/decoding, in Hall, S. et al. (eds.), *Culture, Media, Language*. London: Hutchinson, pp. 128–140.

Hellekson, K. and Busse, K. (ed.) (2006). *Fan Fiction and Fan Communities in the Age of the Internet*. Jefferson, NC: McFarland.

Hopkins, B. (1997). *Intruders*. New York: Ballantine.

Jenkins, H. (1988). Star Trek rerun, reread, rewritten: fan writing as textual poaching, *Critical Studies in Mass Communication*, **5** (June), 85–107.

Jenkins, H. (1992). *Textual Poachers*. New York: Routledge.

Jenkins, H. (1995). 'Out of the closet and into the universe': queers and Star Trek, in Tulloch, J. and Jenkins, H. (eds.), *Science Fiction Audiences: Watching Doctor Who and Star Trek*. London and New York: Routledge, pp. 237–265.

Jenkins, H. (2006a). *Convergence Culture: Where Old and New Media Collide*. New York: New York University.

Jenkins, H. (2006b). Personal email communication, 25 August.

Jindra, M. (1994). Star Trek fandom as a religious phenomenon, *Sociology of Religion*, **55** (Spring), 27–51.

Kates, S.M. (2002). The protean quality of subcultural consumption: an ethnographic account of gay consumers, *Journal of Consumer Research*, **29** (December), 383–399.

Kozinets, R.V. (1997). 'I want to believe': a netnography of the X-Philes' subculture of consumption, in Brucks, M. and MacInnis, D.J. (eds.), *Advances in Consumer Research*, Vol. 24. Provo, UT: Association for Consumer Research, pp. 470–475.

Kozinets, R.V. (2001). Utopian enterprise: articulating the meanings of Star Trek's culture of consumption, *Journal of Consumer Research*, **28** (June), 67–88.

Kozinets, R.V. (2002). Can consumers escape the market? emancipatory illuminations from burning man, *Journal of Consumer Research*, **29** (June), 20–38.

Martin, D., Schouten, J. and McAlexander, J. (2006). Claiming the throttle: multiple femininities in a hyper-masculine subculture, *Consumption, Markets and Culture*, 9, September: 171–205.

Muñiz Jr, A.M. and Schau, H.J. (2005). Religiosity in the abandoned Apple Newton brand community, *Journal of Consumer Research*, **31** (March), 737–747.

Penley, C. (1997). *NASA/Trek*. New York: Verso.

Pitt, L.F., Watson, R.T., Berthon, P., Wynn, D. and Zinkhan, G. (2006). The penguin's window: corporate brands from an open-source perspective, *Journal of the Academy of Marketing Science*, **34** (2), 115–127.

Rodriguez, L. (2003). Gay and lesbian Star Trek fans look online for satisfaction, on *Columbia News Service*, retrieved 7 July 2006, from http://www.jrn.columbia.edu/studentwork/cns/2004-05-03/783.asp.

Russo, T. (2003). Fallen star, *Entertainment Weekly*, July 25, 36.

Schouten, J.W. and McAlexander, J.H. (1995). Subcultures of consumption: an ethnography of the new bikers, *Journal of Consumer Research*, **22** (June), 43–61.

Star Trek (fan made productions) (2006). in *Wikipedia, The Free Encyclopedia*, retrieved 10 July 2006, from http://en.wikipedia.org/wiki/Star_Trek,_fan_made_productions.

Strieber, W. (1987). *Communion: A True Story*. New York: Beech Tree Books.

Treese, W. (2006). Web 2.0; is it really different? *NetWorker*, **10** (June), 15–17.

Tuan, Y. (1977). *Space and Place: The Perspective of Experience*. Minneapolis, MN: University of Minnesota.

Wipperfürth, A. (2005). *Brand Hijack: Marketing without Marketing*. New York: Portfolio.

14

Seeking community through battle: understanding the meaning of consumption processes for warhammer gamers' communities across borders

David J. Park, Sameer Deshpande, Bernard Cova and Stefano Pace

Introduction

In his pioneering article, Cova (1997) examines how people form bonds through consuming products and experiences in a postmodern society. He suggests individuals form 'tribes' through these consumption processes. Each tribe contains unique social and interpersonal dynamics, which are often related to the shared product or brand thus forming what Muñiz and O'Guinn (2001) name a 'brand community'. This chapter explores tribe and brand community concepts within a gaming context by examining meanings inherent to consumption processes for US and French participants of a battle re-enactment game titled Warhammer. To date, very little consumer culture research has examined gaming communities from this perspective.

This chapter will first examine literature on consumption tribes indicating how various approaches define and influence consumption scholarship with notions of community. We then contextualize Warhammer via gaming literature to describe the game's unique traits, which enable complex consumption experiences for enthusiasts. After this discussion, the results from our comparative analysis of consumption experiences are presented, and a discussion is initiated on the limitations of using postmodern concepts of tribe and brand community. We also highlight the importance of engaging these concepts with a poststructural perspective. We argue our results situate and synthesize the Warhammer gaming community in between postmodern and poststructural approaches, which suggests a rethinking is needed in terms of describing consumption experiences.

Warhammer gamers constitute a unique social group that share specific experiences resulting from the manner in which the role-playing game is designed and played. In order to better understand the study of experiential meanings during consumption processes between US and French Warhammer gamers, literature on consumption tribes helps to create a context in which to reference these processes.

Consumption tribes

A tribal approach to consumption practices (Cova and Cova, 2002) analyses consumer groups through consumption experiences and cultural patterns rather than by demographic features such as age, gender or by psychographic features such as attitudes, opinions and interests. As Thompson and Troester (2002) point out, this approach to understanding consumers emphasizes aspects of social and interpersonal dynamics, similarities or differences in rituals and the emotional relationship that consumers experience with the brand, event and others in the community. Arnould and Price's (1993) river rafters or Celsi, Rose, and Leigh's (1993) skydivers may or may not resemble their demographic characteristics, but they share meanings attached to the experience of skydiving or river rafting. In the river rafting trips undertaken in the Colorado river basin, the tribe enacts activities in a certain sequence, which resembles a notion of sacred rituals for the participants. As a result, they exchange a shared expectation of satisfaction. Similarly, skydivers get involved in activities such as dirt-dive choreography, the ascent, the exit, the free fall, and under canopy. The divers are well acquainted with these rituals and share similar motives.

Mountain men share a fantasy consumption experience of a historic primitive ritual in the Rocky Mountain American West (Belk and Costa, 1998), while natural health seekers share a common value system that manifests wellness-oriented consumption outlooks and practices, which are nourished and shared among the tribal members (Thompson and Troester, 2002).

Each of these groups has a very specific need that is satisfied through consumption experiences. As Belk and Costa (1998, p. 218) describe for mountain men, 'participation in the fantasy world offers a special opportunity for transformative play, while reinforcing a romanticized set of beliefs'. Similarly, the dramatic white water river rafters experience 'absorption and integration', 'personal control', 'joy and valuing', and a 'newness of perception and process' as described by Celsi et al. (1993). Such an understanding of needs among tribal members sought through various activities is critical in the process of understanding the ways in which individuals consume games, products, or experiences.

Other researchers such as Schouten and McAlexander (1995) describe communities formed around specific brands. Here, similar to high-risk experiences such as skydiving, tribes are formed around shared consumption experiences of a commercial product. Schouten and McAlexander (1995) describe the consumption experience of Harley-Davidson motorcycle owners and analyse the social structure, dominant values and symbolic behaviours that represent this subculture. Similar tribes exist around media programmes such as *X-Files*, *West Wing* and *Star Trek*.

Somewhat similar to Schouten and McAlexander (1995), Muñiz and O'Guinn (2001, p. 412) define brand community as a 'specialized, non-geographically bound community, based on a structured set of social relationships among admirers of a brand'. Such a community provides identity to its members, and is surrounded around a brand that is commercially marketed, most often in mass media. The authors suggest there are three core markers of community; (1) members have a shared sense of belonging to the community, (2) members share rituals and traditions, (3) members feel a sense of moral responsibility towards each other (Muñiz and O'Guinn, 2001, p. 413).

This study adopts Muñiz and O'Guinn's (2001) conceptualization of brand community in its comparative analysis of US and French Warhammer tribes. Although Warhammer is more than a specific brand *per se*, the name does define a commercial product and gaming experience for members of a particular community. Before describing our results, it is important to note how Warhammer and other similar games can cultivate and create unique experiences for enthusiasts.

Warhammer

Forget the power of technology, science and common humanity. Forget the promise of progress and understanding, for there is no peace amongst the stars, only an eternity of carnage and slaughter and the laughter of thirsting gods.

(Warhammer, 2001)

Warhammer is a tabletop game that requires space to accommodate figurines and additional items such as small trees or hills. In order to participate, players need a basic start-up kit with a small army and an extensive rulebook. The army consists of various figurines that resemble different creatures. Each figurine has distinct characteristics and values that affect the manner in which the game is played. In addition, each figurine is used to compete with other participants' armies through various spells and 'battlefield' scenarios. Competition is regulated through extensive rules, which determine how figurines or armies defeat others through the accumulation of 'damage scores'.

According to the rulebook, these scores increase when players are able to defeat their opponents during various battle scenarios. Other than the club scene, there is also a thriving Warhammer online community at web addresses such as http://www.dawnofwargame.com/homepage.php that tend to focus on science fiction rather than a medieval period battlefield.

Figure 14.1 A Warhammer battlefield.

Warhammer belongs to a more than 30-year old lineage of fantasy role-playing games (FRPGs) that have transfixed young males for decades. FRPGs are characterized by 'fantasy personas' (Waskul and Lust, 2004, p. 343) gamers enact and play on a battlefield while negotiating rules and outcomes with the game master (Fine, 1983). FRPGs can also be considered a conduit where the social world is uniquely assigned by each gamer (Fine, 1983). Sometimes referred to as a 'leisure subculture' (Fine, 1983, p. 237), FRPGs have been conceived as a caricature of social life (Coleman, 1989) since gamers share an experience, a social structure, common activities, norms and values (Fine, 1983).

Mathews (1997) aids the discussion of FRPGs by contrasting fantasy literature with science fiction, utopian fiction and satire. He notes these three literature forms are more or less based on certain logical and scientific explanations. Fantasy literature defies this scientific logic. FRPGs, especially those based in the medieval period, tend to follow this pattern. FRPGs also differ from other games since 'the game is not competitive, has no time limits, is not scored, and has no definitions of winning or losing' (Waskul and Lust, 2004, p. 336). Instead, players have flexibility to work with the rules and outcomes and are required to cooperate to overcome an environmental challenge. Fine (1983, p. 233) argues such cooperation 'provides an opportunity for the development of collective sociability'. Since players are required to enact fantasy characters, these games end up 'more like games of mimicry than chance or competition' (see Caillois [1958] 2001 in Waskul and Lust, 2004, p. 336).

Warhammer enables collective sociability and mimicry with its use of various miniatures on a 'battlefield' (Figure 14.1). Besides the figurines in the start-up kit, there are several different kinds of figures with distinct characteristics and values that can be additionally purchased. In addition, extensive rules apply to the game. According to the rulebook, scores increase when players are able to defeat their opponents during various battle scenarios.

Like other fantasy games such as Dungeons and Dragons, Warhammer requires players to take on personas of fictitious characters to create life on a medieval period battlefield. What differentiates Warhammer from other FRPGs is that these gamers do not just enact the characters, they meet together to create the figurines, as well as the rest of the battlefield. This heavy investment of time, physical and mental energy, and ability to control the game in order to display the artefacts of self-expression makes Warhammer unique. Such a heavy commitment to the game also results in an intense emotional attachment.

Although small but growing (DeRenard and Kline, 1990), additional literature on FRPGs also connects social and cultural aspects of gaming. Starting from a seminal work on Dungeons and Dragons gamers by Gary Alan Fine (1983), with a more recent followup by Waskul and Lust (2004), and other games in online versions (see Diablo II by McBirney, 2004), these studies tend to focus on the cultural aspects of games and the gamers. There have also been studies focusing on gamers' psychological makeup and social behaviours in comparison to non-gamers (Douse and McManus, 1993; Lancaster, 1994).

Understanding gaming brand community: a case of warhammer gamers in the US and France

In order to gain a greater understanding of cross-border consumption processes for Warhammer enthusiasts, we conducted a total of 24 in-depth interviews in Marseilles, France and Madison, Wisconsin (USA), as well as collected data via naturalistic inquiry during a three week period.[1] Our participants were overwhelmingly male and were quite similar to other FRPG gamers. For example, Fine (1983) describes Dungeons and Dragons gamers as 'young and unmarried college graduate males who often read science fiction, fantasy and history' (p. 47). Fine (1983) argues that the content of the game, and the nature of recruitment into this subsociety make it unattractive for women.

Adolescents, similar to some subcultures, often form worlds of their own through these games, which are different from their adult contemporaries. The medieval context of FRPGs is especially attractive since it allows gamers to form an enclave away from logic and scientific reasoning of the adult world. McBirney (2004) considers this experience as an opportunity to escape from reality. In Mathews' (1997, p. 1) words, 'fantasy enables us to enter worlds of infinite possibility. The maps and contours of fantasy are circumscribed only by imagination itself. The breathtaking sweep of its scope can be awesome and even frightening'. In sum, the game's structure allows participants to be creative and imagine various war scenarios, as well as fabricate the miniatures that are involved in the game.

Several consumption themes evolved from the interviews and observations in the US and France. In terms of 'socialization' as a theme, both American and French Warhammer gamers socialize a lot among themselves when they play, however, they are less likely to hang out together outside of the game environment. We found this theme to reveal an interesting contradiction in the nature of their socializing. The American gamers feel a sense of being looked upon as outcasts by the outside world due to their interest in Warhammer. On the other hand, French players seem to face a certain sense of opposition from mainstream society for their indulgence in an imaginary game with figurines now that they are young adults. Nonetheless, these perceived societal perceptions do not prevent Warhammer enthusiasts from continuing to socialize in the game room.

When the socialization consumption theme of American and French Warhammer gamers is compared with gaming literature, certain similarities and differences become apparent. The peculiar form of socialization among Warhammer gamers confirms previous gaming studies. Davis (1983) suggests gamers exhibit lower scores on feelings of sympathy and concern for others, while Fine (1983, p. 44) notes they have relatively high levels of aggression and may appear more introverted in nature. On the other hand, gamers report

---

[1] Details on this study have already been reported in Cova, Pace, and Park (forthcoming). We summarize those findings there.

themselves to be more imaginative (Holmes, 1981). In addition, they are more likely to describe themselves as scientific and prefer to play with computers and read, rather than visit the cinema, theatre, concerts, or attend parties (Douse and McManus, 1993).

American Warhammer enthusiasts also hold a strong attraction to violent imagery when they describe the various aspects of the game. They are also interested in reading violent books and watching violent TV shows and movies. For French informants, violence seemed less relevant. What interests the French more is the opportunity to regress to a medieval era that may be best experienced by imagination. On the other hand, both American and French informants experience a sense of accomplishment after investing time and effort in painting and assembling warrior replicas, as well as when they win over more experienced players and thus master the game. However, French informants experience accomplishment more from clever strategic moves than any other activity.

In addition, Warhammer gamers feel a sense of accomplishment from personally creating figurines, which can be considered a form of an extension of the self (Waskul and Lust, 2004). Moreover, FRPGs can become challenging due to the demands on the gamers to play with three intersecting roles of 'persona, player and person' (Waskul and Lust, 2004). Persona is the imaginary character that the gamer has to enact. Embodied presence through this character is challenging, demanding, but satisfying, since the success for the gamer depends on the success of the character (Fine, 1983). Here the personal creation of the objects and the creative manner form the basis of self-extensions. They also help gamers increase their efficacy (Fine, 1983).

As American informants became more experienced, their focus moved towards winning the game rather than on other aspects such as painting. Thus, with experience, informants become more competitive, which can overshadow their need for socializing and the easy-going environment. French counterparts on the other hand were less concerned about winning and more about enjoying the various facets. American gamers were often competitive to satisfy their urge to win the battle, while the French felt less of a sense to win and more of a desire to experience the game itself. Since Warhammer demands more commitment of time and energy than other games, it may cultivate an augmented feeling of competitiveness. To place these differences in an FRPG context, FRP studies highlighted the non-competitive nature of FRPGs, which seems to be more consistent with the French players. FRPGs are considered more of a leisurely activity demanding cooperation (Fine, 1983), which is a distinctive feature from other games.

Finally for American informants, consuming Warhammer enabled them to imagine and create various war scenarios, and different historical periods to thus 'transfer' them back in time. In addition, the figurines created a conduit for the players to enter into a different reality through their fictitious names and physical forms. The French similarly enjoyed the opportunity to escape into another universe, but the emphasis was more on creativity through escapism and the interesting experience. Warhammer enthusiasts' interests paralleled the interests of other FRP gamers in this respect (Douse and McManus, 1993; Fine, 1983).

Warhammer community: in between postmodernism and poststructuralism

The postmodern approach to consumption has contributed to the renewal of the understanding of consumer collectives by putting into play two closely related concepts: tribes of consumption (Cova and Cova, 2002) and brand communities (Muñiz and O'Guinn, 2001). Cova and Cova (2002, p. 602) define a consumption tribe as being 'a network of heterogeneous persons – in terms of age, sex, income, etc. – who are linked by a shared passion or emotion; a tribe is capable of collective action, its members are not simple consumers, they are also advocates'. Cova and Cova (2002) also contrast a consumption tribe with a 'segment', defining the latter as 'a group of homogeneous persons – they share the same characteristics – who are not connected to each other; a segment is not capable of collective action, its members are simple consumers' (p. 603). Muñiz and O'Guinn (2001, p. 412) define a brand community as 'a specialized, non-geographic bound community, based on a structured set of social relationships among admirers of a brand'. In the postmodern approach, consumers are seen as uprooted ('non-geographic') and isolated from previous structures ('heterogeneous persons' who do not 'share the same characteristics') which used to give them stable identities. Rigid categorization based on the political–economic organizational forms of class, gender, and other distinctive categories such as age or geography are replaced by a more complex or organic structure (Maffesoli, 1996) based on shared experience, common ethos and passion.

However, the poststructural approach to consumption argues that whereas postmodernity has brought on fragmentation, this does not mean that master categories such as nation, class, gender, sexual preferences, generation, religion and stage of life are no longer of central importance to the organization of society and consumption. Indeed, Holt (1997) emphasizes the sociohistorical context in which all consumer collectives are formed: (1) people can understand and thereby consume the same product or brand in many different ways according to the categories they belong to; (2) consumer collectives are mainly based on a shared interpretation of consumption practices thus indicating that a similar set of cultural frameworks or tastes are applied to the act of consumption. In the same vein, Thompson and Troester (2002) maintain that their results on the natural health microculture, in addition to Holt's findings, suggest that reality may be far less anarchic than is believed by postmodern marketers.

In addition, both the postmodern perspective and poststructuralist theories (especially, Holt, 1997) argue that postmodern consumers have multiple affiliations and divergent consumption patterns. While Maffesoli (1996) and Cova and Cova (2002) view tribes as volatile and independent of societal structure,

Holt (1997) emphasizes how consumer collectives are always connected to a socio-historical context.

The poststructural and the postmodern approaches reach a synthesis through the tribe concept (see Figure 14.2). Postmodernism advocates both a free expression of the self and the return to one's local roots. Among these roots, there is the cultural heritage of a subject drawn from the local society to which he/she belongs. Poststructuralism, on the other hand, considers the cultural heritage as a point of aggregation for individuals that cannot be discarded. Consequently, the postmodern and poststructural approaches share a common ground: the cultural heritage is an origin for the poststructural theory, while it is an aim for the postmodern subject. In order to return to her/his own roots, the subject employs a tribe. This seems to be a postmodern and poststructural move at the same time.

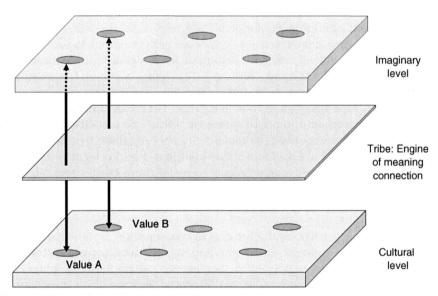

Figure 14.2 Postmodern and poststructural views.

Referring to Figure 14.2, from a poststructural perspective the subjects would move exclusively on the first level, which represents cultural values rooted in society. The subjects' behaviour would be dictated by these values through internalized personality traits and/or external bonding influences. The higher level in the figure represents imagination, which is a system of imaginary values created by the constellation of tribes to which the subject belongs (Cova and Cova, 2002). It is not a realm of fantasies, but a parallel and rich universe often described by literature on communal consumption. This universe has its own rules – sometimes more detailed than 'real' ones – but is freely chosen by subjects. The tribe acts as a connector between the two levels.

Through the tribal rituals (postmodern) one freely chooses to live some cultural facets of his or her society (poststructural). 'Trekkers' (Kozinets, 2001) for example, draw their core values and utopias (such as universalism, tolerance for variety, spirituality) from the real society discourse (the first level), where these values are real issues, either affirmed or challenged. Then they live these values in the imaginary level of the TV series *Star Trek* through the rituals, language garments and gatherings of the tribe.

Our study of Warhammer enthusiasts in France and the US suggests individuals form bonds with each other based on consumption processes inherent to the game. They resemble a tribe described by Cova (1997), which exemplifies the synthesizing of poststructural and postmodern approaches. The meaning of Warhammer is suspended between the postmodern imaginary level (Cova and Cova, 2002) created by the Warhammer constellation of communities and the rooted structural meanings drawn from the local cultures. The tribal dimension lies in between, which influences the meanings attached to the game. The tribe is the postmodern engine which connects imaginary meanings and cultural meanings, thus giving the subject the poststructural freedom to refer to his or her cultural heritage without being bounded by it.

On the one hand, young and unmarried college graduate males over-whelmingly crowd this tribe. On the other hand, it highlights the co-existence of geographically organized sub-tribes within the Warhammer community that allocate different meanings to the brand according to the culture they belong to. Competitiveness, for instance, distinguishes US and French gamers. Competition is drawn for the local US culture, where this cultural facet is probably more salient than in France. This cultural facet is re-lived in the imaginary level of Warhammer through the ritual of battles at the tribe level. The cultural value of competitiveness is freely picked up by the US subject from his culture and used in the tribe.

The local cultures show similarities and thus the global nature of the Warhammer experience, but at the same time they reflect sufficient differences that create the uniqueness of each culture. Consequently, it may be possible to discern certain logic of cultural consistency with regard to what type of collective affiliations a consumer makes: age, gender, and geography matter for individuals in affiliating to the Warhammer community.

The synthesizing of postmodern and poststructural views also allows us to take into account the evolution that a community commonly undertakes. Individuals are first attracted by the similarities they share with other members, which are not related to the passion of the gaming community. One starts to play chess in a group of chess players, for instance, attracted by peers that do the same, not only by the game itself. Then the community evolves and the profile of individuals achieves a more heterogeneous nature. Once the new entrant develops chess competencies, he/she starts to play with different opponents: older or younger, from the same country or from abroad. A similar evolution is observed in the development of a religious cult, where the cult attracts people by leveraging on the similarities between the group and the potential new entrant. The experienced sense of belonging is often the first step to enter the group. Then the common passion starts to have more relevance. In the Warhammer case, some of the subjects may be new entrants of the group, attracted by the 'structural' commonalities shared with the members in other contexts: same university, same age, or same lifestyle. During later stages however, one can expect that the subject would feel part of the group also with individuals of differing profile. We believe this discussion will serve as a starting point to begin rethinking consumption processes within both postmodern and poststructural approaches.

Conclusion

The purpose of this chapter was to examine similarities and differences between Warhammer gaming tribes in the US and France, as well as position our results within postmodern and poststructural approaches to consumption. In doing so, we first examined literature on consumption tribes noting how various approaches define and influence consumption scholarship with notions of community. We then contextualized Warhammer via gaming literature to describe the game's unique traits, which enable complex consumption experiences for enthusiasts. After this discussion, we then presented the results from our comparative analysis between French and US Warhammer gamers' consumption experiences. We finally argued our results situate and synthesize the Warhammer gaming community in between postmodern and poststructural approaches, which suggests a rethinking is needed in terms of describing consumption experiences.

References

Arnould, E.J. and Price, L.L. (1993). River magic: extraordinary experience and the service encounter, *Journal of Consumer Research*, **20** (June), 24–46.

Belk, R. and Costa, J. (1998). The mountain man myth, *Journal of Consumer Research*, **25** (December), 218–240.

Caillois, R. [1958] 2001. *Man, Play and Games*. Chicago: University of Chicago Press.

Celsi, R., Rose, R. and Leigh, T. (1993). An exploration of high-risk leisure consumption through skydiving, *Journal of Consumer Research*, **15** (September), 1–21.

Coleman, J.S. (1989). Simulation games and the development of social-theory, *Simulation and Games*, **20** (2), 144–164.

Cova, B. (1997). Community and consumption: towards a definition of linking value of products and services, *European Journal of Marketing*, **31** (3), 297–316.

Cova, B. and Cova, V. (2002). Tribal marketing: the tribalization of society and its impact on the conduct of marketing, *European Journal of Marketing*, **36** (5/6), 595–620.

Cova, B., Pace, S. and Park, D. (forthcoming in 2007). Global Brand Communities Across Borders: The Warhammer Case, *International Marketing*

Review's Special Issue on "Contemporary Thinking, Topics and 1 International Branding".

Davis, M.H. (1983). Measuring individual differences in empathy dence from a multidimensional approach, *Journal of Personality and Psychology*, **44**, 113–126.

DeRenard, L.A. and Kline, L.M. (1990). Alienation and the game Dungeo and Dragons, *Psychological Reports*, **66**, 1219–1222.

Douse, N.A. and McManus, I.C. (1993). The personality of fantasy game players, *British Journal of Psychology*, **84**, 505–509.

Fine, G.A. (1983). *Shared Fantasy: Role-Playing Games as Social Worlds*. Chicago: The University of Chicago Press.

Holmes, J.E. (1981). *Fantasy Role Playing Games*. New York: Hippocrene Books.

Holt, D.B. (1997). Poststructuralist lifestyle analysis: conceptualizing the social patterning of consumption in postmodernity, *Journal of Consumer Research*, **23** (March), 326–350.

Kozinets, R.V. (2001). Utopian enterprise: articulating the meanings of Star Trek's culture of consumption, *Journal of Consumer Research*, **28** (June), 67–88.

Lancaster, K. (1994). Do role-playing games promote crime, Satanism, and suicide, among players as critics claim? *Journal of Popular Culture*, **28** (2), 67–79.

Maffesoli, M. (1996). *The Time of Tribes: The Decline of Individualism in Mass Society*. London: Sage.

Mathews, R. (1997). *Fantasy: The Liberation of Imagination*. New York: Twayne Publishers.

McBirney, K. (2004). Nested selves, networked communities: a case study of Diablo II: Lord of Destruction as an agent of cultural change, *Journal of American Culture*, **27** (4), 415–421.

Muñiz Jr., A.M. and O'Guinn, T.C. (2001). Brand community, *Journal of Consumer Research*, **27** (March), 412–432.

Schouten, J.W. and McAlexander, J.H. (1995). Subcultures of consumption: an ethnography of the new bikers, *Journal of Consumer Research*, **22** (June), 43–61.

Thompson, C.J. and Troester, M. (2002). Consumer value systems in the age of postmodern fragmentation: the case of the natural health microculture, *Journal of Consumer Research*, **28** (March), 550–571.

Warhammer (2001). retrieved 15 January 2001 from: http://www.warhammer. net

Waskul, D. and Lust, M. (2004). Role-playing and playing roles: the person, player, and persona in fantasy role-playing, *Symbolic Interaction*, **27** (3), 333–356.

Part V

Tribes as entrepreneurs

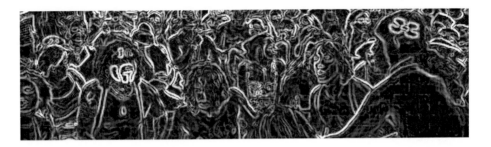

15

'Gothic' entrepreneurs: a study of the subcultural commodification process

Christina Goulding and Michael Saren

Introduction

The 'new dominant logic of marketing' switches the view of firms as the principal economic producers and value creators to one in which customers are actively engaged in the value creation and marketing process (Normann and Ramirez, 1993; Vargo and Lusch, 2004; Wikström, 1996). This chapter examines how subcultures play an important role in enabling consumers to act proactively and productively in the market as entrepreneurs. Subcultures have often been conceptualized as the catalyst for counter-hegemonic strategies of resistance (Kellner, 1995); however, they are also cultures of consumption which involve consumers as innovators in the active creation of markets along with the development of products and services to meet the needs of these markets. This chapter reports some of the research which we have conducted into the 'Gothic' subculture, a micro-community that emerged from the punk rock generation of the late 1970s and continues to flourish. Based on our findings, we propose two inter-related concepts which are relevant to this book. These are the tribal entrepreneur, and the subcultural commodification process.

The following section provides a brief review of the background to our research on the Goth community, following which we draw on this to illustrate the entrepreneurial Goth and the concept of the subcultural commodification process.

The research background

The 'Gothic' subculture is more than a fashion culture – it is a micro-community that emerged from the punk rock generation of the late 1970s which continues to flourish today, all be it in a number of re-fashioned incarnations. Goth is a subculture closely associated with the wearing of black, an interest in the 'darker' side of life and death, a particular musical aesthetic and, in the UK at least, with the cult and sexuality of the vampire.

For 2 weeks of the year, one in April, the other at the end of October, the quiet fishing town and seaside resort of Whitby in the North East of England is taken over by over 2,000 Goths. The town is the place where Goths of all persuasions get the opportunity to congregate at the Whitby Goth Festival which celebrated its 10th anniversary in 2003. Whitby on face value may seem an incongruous location to hold a venue that attracts individuals the width and breadth of the country and even as far away as Australia and the US. However, its significance becomes clear when linked to the vampire myth. It was while living in Whitby that Bram Stoker penned his novel 'Dracula', in which the aristocratic vampire's arrival in Britain occurs in Whitby, thereby immortalizing the abbey and Victorian graveyard which stand high above the town. For this reason, the place of Whitby represents a kind of spiritual home for Goths and that is why we chose it as the site for our research (Figure 15.1).

Goth is not a homogenous culture and a sense of theatre is created and enhanced by the diversity of costumes and looks embraced by the different factions. For example, even in the day vamp Goths can be seen patrolling the street, the men in top hats and tails reminiscent of Gary Oldman's Dracula, the women in tight bodices, bustled dresses, feather-trimmed hats and black lace parasols. The Romantics nostalgically clad in Byronesque, flowing velvet coats and lace-ruffled shirts contrast with the pale faces, jet-crimped hair and black street garb of the Punk Goths. Cyber Goths, on the other hand, introduce some colour in the form of red and black striped leggings, whilst still retaining the black in the form of long leather coats and 4 in. thick metal soled boots. However, it is after dark that Goths really come into their own at the two main venues which are packed to capacity with Vampire Goths intermingling with Cyber Goths, Punk Goths, and those who adopt a form of fancy dress 'anything goes' approach. The music with its heavy almost Wagnerian bass blares well into the early hours until the Goths retire, some on foot, others in hearses!

Figure 15.1 Victorian costumes.

The research methods

It is salient to note that the authors are not Goths and prior to this study had no first hand experience of the Gothic subculture. As consumer researchers our initial interest was triggered by our past research into subcultures and identity and the supporting props and materiality which enabled their existence. Consequently, rather than define the parameters of the research before entering the field, we adopted a theory building approach in order to allow the data to generate concepts (Glaser and Strauss, 1967) and ideas. The general aim of the research was to develop grounded data driven insights into the experience of being part of the Gothic subculture from a consumption perspective.

Prior to the October Festival in 2004 we contacted the organizer Jo Hampshire who was responsible for initiating the first and subsequent bi-annual events which have continued to grow over the last 10 years. We explained our interests and asked for her assistance in recruiting informants. She invited us to design and submit a poster detailing who we were, what the research was about and contact addresses. These posters were then distributed at all the pre-events and were displayed throughout the duration of the festival at all the major venues. Jo also provided us with passes allowing access to all areas and all events which enabled us to engage in participatory observation in addition to collecting data by way of the interview method.

Data collection consisted primarily of a quasi-ethnographic approach involving immersion in the setting and context of the experience (Arnould, 1998; Arnould and Wallendorf, 1994) through participatory observation of events and activities, including retail locations, band venues and dance nights. Observations were written up in the form of memos, and photographs were taken over a seven day period. In addition, the posters generated a great deal of interest and we were contacted by an initial six respondents who agreed to be interviewed about their experiences. These interviews lasted over three hours each and took the form of the individuals telling 'their' stories. This resulted in a snowball effect whereby we were introduced to others who also agreed to talk to us. In total we interviewed 14 Goths face to face in considerable depth. However, in order to ensure balance, we also undertook an analysis of Gothic websites and chat rooms such as Gothic/Punk, where individuals publish their own stories, experiences and issues of interest or concern regarding the scene.

Data collection and analysis were simultaneous consisting of an inductive, interactive process between data collection, preliminary analysis, idea gener-ation, further data collection and more focused questioning, in keeping with the grounded theory tradition of theoretical sampling and constant comparison (Glaser and Strauss, 1967). Following on from this we were contacted via email by a number of people who had seen the poster and were keen to participate. The time gap allowed us to reflect further on the data collected at the site, refine our ideas and construct a more structured interview schedule which we conducted by email with new respondents. This was also delivered to the original group who were asked to reflect, adjust anything they felt was not right and add to their original narratives. Several themes emerged from the data which had explanatory power in relation to understanding the experience of being a Goth. One of these was the evolutionary process that Goth has undergone since its inception in the early 1980s. This eventually led us to conceptualize this phenomenon in terms of the subcultural commodification process which charts the evolutionary changes in structures, people, meaning, materiality, commodification and eventually its appropriation by the mainstream.

The stages of subcultural commodification

The following represents our analysis of the three main stages of the commodification process which we posit. These stages can be summarized as: (1) rebellion (2) fragmentation and (3) commodification.

Stage 1: rebellion

The Gothic subculture emerged out of the dying embers of Punk Rock in the early 1980s at a London nightclub called the 'Bat Cave'. An anonymous author of a tribute posted on the Goth/Punk website describes the characteristics of the Goths in those formative years as: 'pale-faced, black-swathed, hair-sprayed night dwellers who worshipped imagery, religious and sacrilegious, consumptive poets and all things spooky. Their bands included "Sex Gang Children", "Specimen" and "Alien Sex Fiend"; post-punk doom merchants who sang of horror-film imagery and transgressive sex' (Brandon Lee Tribute). These individuals saw themselves as outside of the mainstream but bound together by common passions, interests and mutually shared activities (Wenger, 1999). However, whilst regarded as outsiders, they welcomed this segregation and saw participation as a form of rebellion against the mundane, as suggested by Naythe, an 'Elder' Goth who has been on the scene since it started:

> The scene was a backdrop that encouraged Goth's music and style towards the unique, thus an incentive for the imaginative macabre misfits who shunned the dull light of the mainstream.

One might argue that Goth, in the early days was an ordered whole, with each part of the subculture fitting together in a homological style (Arnett, 1993). Essentially homology constitutes the fit between the values and lifestyle of the group, the subjective experience of its members and the musical forms in which it expresses its concerns (Arnett, 1993; Willis, 1978). At this stage in the development of the subculture it is possible to draw on the work of the neo-Marxist cultural theorists such as Kellner (1995), Hebdidge (1979/1997), Frith (1996) and Willis (1978, 1990) who conceptualize subcultures as pockets of collective, ritualized resistance or rebellion. Certainly early Goths displayed elements of conscious counter-hegemonic strategies for rebelling, not necessarily against the dominant hierarchies of control, but against the homogenized culture of commodities that was and is mainstream consumer society; again to quote Naythe:

> There was a time when no one in this subculture resembled anyone else; whether the form of expression was audio, visual or tactile. At that stage of the game, being Goth was equated with being a reject, freak and outcast by the rest of society. If we're honest it still is to a degree. But no one could accuse us of not trying to make the effort to be as far outside of the cultural norm as possible in appearance, music and attitude. We were the masters of the idiosyncratic.

However, as in the case of so many other subcultures, there was a gradual adoption process by new members who did not necessarily share the original motives of the innovators (Goulding, Shankar, and Elliott, 2002). According to Hebdidge (1979/1997) this adoption process usually occurs when what was once considered deviant becomes familiar and marketable, giving rise to a process of recuperation which has two characteristic forms. The first is the commodity form where there is a conversion of subcultural signs such as music and clothes into mass-produced objects. The second is the ideological form, or the labelling or redefinition of what was once considered deviant. Whilst this does not necessitate entry into the mainstream, it does open the doors for the second stage of development which is characterized by fragmentation.

Stage 2: fragmentation

Fragmentation is a concept which has been recognized as endemic to the contemporary 'geographies' of consumption (Clarke and Purvis, 1994; Firat and Schultz, 1997). Firat and Venkatesh (1995, p. 253) define fragmentation as 'literally, the breaking up into parts and erasing of the whole, single reality into multiple realities, all claiming legitimacy and all decoupling any link to the presumed whole'. Fragmentation consists of a series of inter-related ideas, the breaking down of markets into smaller and smaller groups and correspondingly, the proliferation of a greater number of products to serve the increasing segments. Goth has evolved and fragmented in terms of music and fashion. Labels applied to the various musical genres now include 'original Goth', 'mellow Goth', 'metal/industrial Goth', 'experimental/folky/occult Goth' and 'new Goth' (Figure 15.2).

Similarly fashions range from simple black tee-shirts and black jeans or bondage trousers associated with what are now called 'Cyber Goths', to the Victorian and Edwardian costumes constructed from velvet and lace and worn by the 'Romantics' and 'Vampire Goths'. This in itself does not reflect the eclecticism of Goth. Add to this pirates, nuns, devils, 1920s flappers, men dressed as women, women dressed as men, and some so totally androgynous as to be indistinguishable and the picture becomes more representative of the reality of the Goth scene as it stands today, as Laura, a 22-year-old Goth comments:

> Goths use lots of sensuous material like velvet and lace, PVC and leather for clothing – I suppose it's quite decadent and redolent of an image. The velvet and lace is more a Romantic image, whereas the PVC and leather are taken from the S&M fetish scenes, so props are all part of portraying your image. The Victorian crowd accessorize with top hats, black lace parasols and canes, whereas the cyber crowd sometimes wander about with what look to be paint-ball, or radar guns. Hair also defines the kind of impression you're going for, though there are crossovers. Generally you have the long black flowing hair, which is often accentuated with hair extensions, be they permanent, or removable. This kind of look you'd see with the

Figure 15.2 Retail display.

Romantic/Victorian look. The dreaded look is much more symbolic of the cyber crowd, with wool braids and dreads. More recently, the cyber crowd have been seen a lot more with plastic and foam tubing as extensions. The cyber element of Goth is quite exciting in that people are always trying out new materials in different ways to keep the futuristic look fresh.

This diversity is seen as a welcome progression, as Chris a 24-year-old male Goth illustrates:

I like the various strands of Goth. Subcultures can become stagnant if everyone holds the same beliefs, musical leanings and taste in clothes, so Goth is very much more vibrant because of its diversity. You can have people who verge on liking dance music, mixing with heavy metallers with no clash of personalities.

Fragmentation even extends to gender and acts as an enabler for what Butler (1994) terms the performance of gender, as Becky, a 21-year-old female Goth explains:

> I get the impression that a lot of Goths are well-educated and very tolerant people, probably because they are often on the receiving end of intolerance and abuse for one reason or another. I would say that the majority have been on the social fringes for much of their lives and thus are probably more open to similarly minded people, so sexuality isn't even an issue for most. Goth men do experiment a lot with feminine clothing and identity, and I think this is because the Goth aesthetic is effeminate, bordering on the androgynous. The physicality of a lot of Goths allows for this. To generalize I would say that Goths tend to the extremes of physical appearance – they're either really skinny, or really big, so they do have more opportunity to play about with clothes – the asexual, and the voluptuous looks. I think that the cyber look on a lot of Goth men is great, but it demands the wearer to be skinny, whereas the Victorian look is great on the bigger busted and bellied – what good is a corset if there's nothing to put in it?

At this stage the commodity becomes the key defining signifier of group membership and affiliation for the various factions within the subculture. This occurs as individuals strive to construct and maintain their identities through the tangible and symbolic resources available to them (Elliott and Wattanasuwan, 1998; Sarup, 1996). At some point, the equality and levelling process characteristic of the formative stage gives way to the development of hierarchies, based largely on the 'look', commitment to the group and knowledge of the subculture, as Clinton a 23-year-old male Goth notes:

> It's a bit like the 'Animal Farm' motto really. There is equality, yet there is a hierarchy too. I would say that anyone could be a Goth if they wanted to and there is not much within the culture to prevent a person of any colour or creed from doing so. Yet there is a hierarchy and this is very much to do with personal participation. You'll find that the Goths 'higher up' are the ones who make the most effort with the scene and with their image. For example, I like the fangs and the whole vampire look, but I didn't just want a pair that stuck over your teeth. I searched the yellow pages until I found a dental technician who would make them so they sat on a plate which was hidden. They took months to make and cost around £350, which was a hell of a lot cheaper than if a dentist had made them.

Such props, as Clinton's fangs constitute a form of what Thornton (1996) in her reworking of Bourdieu's (1984) cultural capital, terms 'subcultural capital'. Here the theme of 'who I am is constantly redefined through perceived contrast to others' (Thompson and Haykto, 1997, p. 21) through the commodification of image, or as Firat and Venkatesh (1995, p. 52) comment:

> In customizing oneself to (re)present marketable (self) images, the consumer is interacting with other objects in the market to produce oneself ... consumption is increasingly becoming a production process, goal orientated and purposeful.

At this stage the values, beliefs and lifestyles of the original core community give way to those of what Maffesoli (1996) terms the 'neo-tribe' or temporary group where solidarity is based on appearance and form. This is usually the catalyst for the final stage, which is commodification and appropriation by the mainstream.

Stage 3: commodification

From the consumption side, commodification comes from a concern of the consumer not with the concrete and specific use-value of a product, but with the price that a product will fetch on the market (Lash, 1990). Today the Gothic subculture is well served by a burgeoning retail and leisure industry. In Whitby there are numerous shops dedicated to Goth and the festivals also play host to retailers drawn from the length and breadth of the country who come to set up stall in the foyers of the two main locations (Figure 15.3).

On sale here are products as wide ranging as custom made fangs, coffins, corsets, bondage gear, leather, PVC clothing, feathered masks, wigs, records

Figure 15.3 Merchandising.

and CD's and custom made jewellery. There are even souvenirs such as book markers and light bulbs fashioned in the shape of crucifixes (Figure 15.4). The Goth scene has now become a hyperreal environment (Eco, 1987). A blurring of different genres, where commodities have become the defining core of the subculture. To quote Lash (1990, p. 48) 'Commodification also means as Marx underlined in the section on commodity fetishism, the power of things over people and the importance attributed to commodities in capitalism as opposed to human beings.' Drawing on the work of Baudrillard, Bertens (1995) comments that consumption as a system of meaning is no longer organized along the lines of needs or pleasure, but rather as a system of signs which appear to be a particular mode of transition from nature to culture. Today, the Gothic subculture is a culture of consumption which has moved beyond individual creativity to a two-sided system of production and consumption. According to Baudrillard (1990), 'image makers have opened up a Pandora's box of illusions, treatments and enhancements which have obliterated the division between reality and unreality' (Rojek and Turner, 1993, p. xi).

Figure 15.4 Wigs.

In essence the raw energy or the original life force of the subculture is gradually being replaced by the reification of symbols and products as the mainstream recognize the lucrative potential of what was once considered deviant and marginal. This is not necessarily the desired outcome for all, and particularly for those who were around at the birth of the scene. To return to the 'Elder' Goth Naythe:

> How can our scene continue to develop and thrive when everywhere you look the same themes resound without the cutting edge or distinctive flare that made it exceptional? I fear that Goth has succumbed to the boredom of mainstream homogenization, where what is alien and unacceptable to the majority can be transformed by marketing into the latest and greatest product, once it's been reupholstered for television and the everyday consumer. Example: The Kodak commercial where the painted up teen Goth girl takes morbid, but artsy, pictures and displays them in class for the snide titillation of her judgmental peers. In the rear of the classroom, a boy dressed in black smiles at her in approval. Makes you want to gag? It should.

Lash (1990) suggests that the narratives and information we consume, the melodies and songs we hear and the images we see, come in increasingly commodified form. Today Goth has entered the mainstream with High Street stores selling heavily bejewelled crucifixes as accessories and Gothic style 'evening' wear. Gothic bands such as 'Evanescence' have reached number one in popular music charts and even hard core Gothic metal bands such as 'Ramstein' have their own website and shop selling everything from tie-pins to sweat shirts. Add to this Goth calling cards for marketing directors and the ability to purchase over the net, as one flyer offered, 'one stop shopping for vampires', and it is easy to see that Goth is now big business. The effect of this diffusion is accessibility and even respectability on the part of new entrants who bring with them their own preconceptions making the experience a two-way process of appropriation. Entrepreneurs flourish and the marketing machine moves into action. The result of this is that the original innovators are either forced out or exit in disgust to find new sites to express their individuality; to leave Sam and Naythe with the last word:

> Sam: Don't get me wrong. Most of my friends are on the scene and when I go to our local club I almost always have a good time. But there's something there now that wasn't there before, a kind of edge that fashionability seems to have given it, which perverts the inclusiveness and permissiveness and turns them into something that leaves a bitter taste in my mouth. You probably know what I'm talking about. Every club has at least one of them, and probably a little clique of them. They've got lots of names: Fashionistas, Matching-Black Supremists, Goth Supremists, whatever. Just that small group of people who feel the need to ignore the principal ideas of 'Gothdom',

i.e. that deviance isn't evil and we should be accepted for what we are, and instead try to turn the scene into one great long beauty contest come fashion show . . . Goth supremists judge people on looks and clothes. Isn't that what mundanes do to Goths all the bloody time?

Naythe: Those of us who don't fit into the current stereotyped ideal are in turn harassed, ridiculed, ignored and ostracized by people in the very group that we once sought refuge in. Just look around you at things you may have seen, perhaps experienced. Waif-thin sub-urbanites who've decided to latch onto something cool enough to piss off their parents' mock Junoesque girls as fat while criticising any boy sleeker and prettier. Teenaged/early twenty something new-comers have informed elder Goths who've been on the scene since before it was termed Goth that they are too old for this and it's time they grew up. There is an unnerving bigotry in the scene resulting from the need to perpetuate a specific ideal: Uber-Goth. Couple with ignorance personal insecurity, malice and fear, it all adds more fuel to the fire which proves that Goth has exploded into the mainstream. . . It's enough to make an Elder like me slash my wrists down the centres rather than bungling the effort by cutting across.

Some conclusions and implications

The subcultural commodification process

The concept of Product Life Cycle (PLC) has a well-established place in the marketing literature as a means of analysing the adoption, diffusion and decline of products and services (Gatignon and Robertson, 1985; Rogers, 1962). According to the PLC, all products eventually die, as emphasized by Levitt (1960) and typically products develop through four stages in their life – intro-duction, growth, maturity, decline. During their life they adapt, are improved, developed and spread more widely amongst consumers. PLC theory also shows that products do not remain the same, for different parties involved, during their lifetime. Products are constantly changing as producers adapt and develop them (product innovations), find better ways of producing them (process innovations) and as different consumers use them in different ways and view them in different ways (resignification) (Saren and Tzokas, 1998).

Similarly, subcultures of consumption follow a life cycle during which the people, products and symbolic meanings alter over time as the subcul-ture undergoes a process of commodification. Ultimately there is a diffusion process whereby the subculture-derived products, fashions, lifestyle and ser-vices find their way into more mainstream culture. This has been recognized – although not explicitly stated in these terms – by, for example, Schouten and McAlexander (1995) who talk about the adoption of the bikers' 'core' prod-uct, the Harley Davidson, by 'weekenders'. Similarly, Goulding et al. (2002)

described the commodification of 'rave' as it moved from an illicit underground movement to the global multi-million dollar industry it is today. Likewise, the Gothic subculture has evolved from an underground movement populated by a relatively small number of similar minded individuals to a heavily consumption based activity which has fragmented and spread across Europe and the US. Consequently, the notion of a subcultural commodification process of evolution, anomalous to the PLC, offers a framework for identifying the changing needs and activities of the subcultural consumer and the accompanying proliferation of an industry from both within and around the subculture which emerges to serve these wants and needs.

The sublime object of class struggle

The study of subcultures has long held a fascination for social and cultural commentators, largely influenced by the Frankfurt School with their focus on the industries of commercially driven mass-produced culture. These critical theorists with their emphasis on 'high' culture versus 'low' culture denigrated mass-popular culture as inferior and ideologically debased (Horkheimer and Adorno, 1972). In this view, the main function of the 'culture industries' was to create passive, unquestioning, conformist workers whose needs could be met through the consumption of intellectually and aesthetically inferior offerings, such as cinema and popular music. In the UK, cultural studies as an academic discipline emerged in the 1960s at the Centre for Contemporary Cultural Studies at Birmingham University. Within this group subcultures were conceptualized as the catalyst for counter-hegemonic strategies of resistance employed by (predominantly) working class, male, youths, in their attempts to construct and assert meaningful identities as a way of resisting social and cultural forms of domination (see for example, Kellner, 1995 on 1950s Teddy Boy gangs; Hebdidge, 1979/1997 on the Mods of the 1960s and Frith 1980, 1997 on Punk Rock). This work remains highly influential today. The title of Hall and Jefferson's (1976) *Resistance Through Ritual* sums up the theoretical focus running through most of the papers which have as their basis, social class, sub-ordination, and collective ritualized resistance through the creation and maintenance of subcultural, style based activities.

Our study of Goths shows how much contemporary subcultures have changed. It is no longer possible to define them simply on the basis of social class, age or gender. Nor can we understand them in terms of the oppressed using the only strategies of resistance open to them to strike a blow against the dominant hierarchies of control.

On the contrary we must recognize and devote more attention to the fragmented, multi-ethnic, multi-class, non-gendered, and transitory nature of what might be termed 'postideological' or 'postmodern' subcultures (Bennett, 1999).

The evolutionary nature of subcultures

Despite the materiality that underpins, supports and defines the very existence of many subcultures, it is only over the last decade that consumer researchers have woken up to the realization that analysis of consumer behaviour at such micro-levels can add to our understanding of product use, brands and shared symbolic meaning (Goulding et al., 2002; Kates, 2002; Kozinets, 2001, 2002; Miklas and Arnold, 1999; Schouten and McAlexander, 1995). This is despite the fact that subcultures may be defined as sites of praxis, ideologically, temporally, and socially situated where fantasy and experimentation give way to the construction, expression and maintenance of particular consumption identities. As this chapter has attempted to demonstrate subcultures can also be viewed as cultures of consumption which involve innovators and the creation of markets and products and services to meet the needs of these markets. Consequently groups that may appear marginal or deviant initially are worthy of examination as many others, like Goths, may undergo a process of commodification and ultimately diffusion into mainstream consumer society. As our analysis of Goth has shown, these micro-communities may start off as rebellious collectives, but eventually evolve, fragment and grow as consumer collectives, markets and entrepreneurial businesses. Values, beliefs and forms of expression change, as do the symbolic meanings and the nature of the commodities used to support and maintain the subculture.

Our studies of the Goth community show little evidence of it being a manifestation of a class struggle, on the contrary, there is more evidence to suggest that it is a conscious reaction against 'mundanity' or the homogenization of contemporary consumer society. Goth is an interesting case of study which defies traditional subcultural classifications. Rather than just working class, it attracts members from across the social spectrum. Rather than a youth culture it consists of members of all ages, young and old. Rather than male dominated, it embraces individuals regardless of gender or sexuality and interestingly, is one of the first subcultures to actively privilege the feminine. Moreover, Goth, it might feasibly be argued is a subculture of consumption which produces and nurtures proactive entrepreneurs as well as passive consumers. It is based on the commodity form and its influence has been far reaching in terms of music, style and dress. Our argument is that marketers can learn lessons from the creativity and innovation shown by these new entrepreneurial communities and there is value in analysing the progression from the 'margins to the mainstream'. The concept of a subcultural commodification process offers a framework for charting developments in subcultural evolution.

References

Arnett, J. (1993). Three profiles of heavy metal fans: a taste for sensation and a subculture of alienation, *Qualitative Sociology*, **16** (4), 423–443.

Arnould, E. (1998). Daring consumer-oriented ethnography, in Stern, B. (ed.), *Representing Consumers: Voices, Views and Visions*. London: Routledge.

Arnould, E. and Wallendorf, M. (1994). Marketing oriented ethnography: interpretation building and marketing strategy formulation, *Journal of Marketing Research*, **31** (November), 484–504.

Baudrillard, J. (1990). *Cool Memories*. London: Verso.

Bennett, A. (1999). Subcultures or neo-tribes: rethinking the relationship between youth, style and musical taste, *Sociology*, **33** (August), 599–614.

Bertens, H. (1995). *The Idea of the Postmodern: A History*. London: Routledge.

Bourdieu, P. (1984). *Distinction: A Social Critique of the Judgement of Taste*. London: Routledge and Kegan Paul.

Brandon Lee Tribute at http://www.altculture.com/aentries/g/gothic.shtml last accessed 12/12/03.

Butler, J. (1994). Gender as performance, *Radical Philosophy*, **67** (Summer), 32–39.

Clarke, D. and Purvis, M. (1994). Dialectics, difference and the geographies of consumption, *Environment and Planning A*, **26**, 1091–1110.

Eco, U. (1987). *Travels in Hyper-reality*. London: Picador.

Elliott, R. and Wattanasuwan, K. (1998). Brands as symbolic resources for the construction of identity, *International Journal of Advertising*, **17**, 131–144.

Firat, F.A. and Venkatesh, A. (1995). Liberatory postmodernism and the re-enchantment of consumption, *Journal of Consumer Research*, **22** (3), 239–267.

Firat, A. and Schultz, C. (1997). From segmentation to fragmentation: markets and marketing in the postmodern era, *European Journal of Marketing*, **31** (3/4), 183–207.

Frith, S. (1980/1997). Formulism, realism and leisure: the case of punk, in Gelder, K. and Thornton, S. (eds.), *The Subculture Reader*. London: Routledge.

Frith, S. (1996). *Performing Rites*. Oxford: Oxford University Press.

Gatignon, H. and Robertson, T. (1985). A propositional inventory for new diffusion research, *Journal of Consumer Research*, **11** (March), 849–868.

Glaser, B. and Strauss, A. (1967). *The Discovery of Grounded Theory*. Chicago: Aldine.

Goulding, C. Shankar, A. and Elliott, R. (2002). Working weeks, rave weekends: identity fragmentation and the emergence of new communities, *Consumption, Markets and Culture*, **5** (4), 261–284.

Hall, S. and Jefferson, T. (eds.) (1976). Resistance through Ritual: youth subcultures in post-war Britain. London: Routledge.

Hebdidge, D. (1979/1997). Subcultures: the meaning of style, in Gelder, K. and Thornton, S. (eds.), *The Subcultures Reader*. London: Routledge.

Horkheimer, M. and Adorno, T. (1972). *Dialectic of Enlightenment*. New York: Seabury.

Kates, S. (2002). The protean quality of subcultural consumption: an ethnographic account of gay consumers, *Journal of Consumer Research*, **29** (3), 383–399.

Kellner, D. (1995). *Media Culture*. London: Routledge.

Kozinets, R.V. (2001). Articulating the meanings of Star Trek's culture of consumption, *Journal of Consumer Research*, **28** (1), 67–88.

Kozinets, R.V. (2002). Can consumers escape the market? Emancipatory illuminations from burning man, *Journal of Consumer Research*, **29** (1), 20–38.

Lash, S. (1990). *Sociology of Postmodernism*. London: Routledge.

Levitt, T. (1960). Marketing myopia, *Harvard Business Review*, **34** (4), 45–56.

Maffesoli, M. (1996). *The Time of the Tribes: The Decline of Individualism in Mass Society*. London: Sage.

Miklas, S. and Arnold, S. (1999). The extraordinary self: gothic culture and the construction of the self, *Journal of Marketing Management*, **15** (6), 563–576.

Normann, R. and Ramirez, R. (1993). From value chain to value constellation: designing interactive strategy, *Harvard Business Review*, July–August, 65–77.

Rogers, E. (1962). *Diffusion of Innovation*. New York: Free Press.

Rojek, C. and Turner, B. (1993). Regret Baudrillard, in Rojek, C. and Turner, B. (eds.), *Forget Baudrillard*. London: Routledge.

Saren, M. and Tzokas, N. (1998). The nature of the product in market relationships: a pluri-signified product concept, *Journal of Marketing Management*, **14**, 445–464.

Sarup, M. (1996). *Identity, Culture and the Postmodern World*. Edinburgh: Edinburgh University Press.

Schouten, J. and McAlexander, J. (1995). Subcultures of consumption: an ethnography of the new bikers, *Journal of Consumer Research*, **22** (1), 43–62.

Thompson, C. and Haytko, D. (1997). Consumers' uses of fashion discources and the appropriation of countervailing cultural meanings, *Journal of Consumer Research*, **24** (Summer), 15–42.

Thornton, S. (1996). *Club Cultures: Music, Media and Subcultural Capital*. Cambridge: Polity Press.

Vargo, S.L. and Lusch, R.F. (2004). Evolving to a new dominant logic for marketing, *Journal of Marketing*, **68** (January), 1–17.

Wenger, E. (1999). *Communities of Practice: Learning, Meaning and Identity*. Cambridge: Cambridge University Press.

Wikström, S. (1996). The customer as a co-producer, *European Journal of Marketing*, **30** (4), 6–19.

Willis, P. (1978). *Profane Culture*. London: Routledge and Kegan Paul.

Willis, P. (1990). *Common Culture*. Buckingham: Open University Press.

16

Marketing, prosumption and innovation in the fetish community*

Roy Langer

'Marketing research apparently has a blind spot with regard to the all too obvious and many examples of fetishism, even if it is situated in mainstream culture'

(Trudy Barber, 2004)

Introduction

This chapter draws on three streams of consumer research to understand the fetish community in Denmark. Starting with Hirschman and Holbrook's seminal articles on hedonistic consumption (Hirschman and Holbrook, 1982; Holbrook and Hirschman, 1982), a (still) growing body of research has addressed the linkages between experiential consumption, emotions, social

*This chapter is based on two previous conference papers by the author (Langer, 2003a, b).

relations and identity work. These linkages appear as tribes, life mode, and brand communities and cultures of consumption (Cova and Cova, 2002; Firat and Dholakia, 1998; Kozinets, 2001; Muñiz and O'Guinn, 2001). Other studies have examined communities as diverse as skydivers, bikers, mountain men, ravers and roller skaters (Belk and Costa, 1998; Celsi, Randall, and Leigh, 1993; Cova and Cova, 2001; Goulding and Shankar, 2004; Goulding, Shankar, and Elliott, 2002; Schouten and McAlexander, 1995).

Other streams of research that inform this chapter are studies of symbolic consumption (Belk, Wallendorf, Sherry, 1989; Schouten, 1991); consumers' self-conceptions and body image (Thompson and Hirschman, 1995); consumer spectacles (Kates, 2000); and fashion discourses, cultural meanings and self-identity (McCracken, 1986; Thompson and Haytko, 1997). The final piece of the interpretive lens is derived from research that has emphasized sexuality and emotional appeals in contemporary consumer culture, especially as it is reflected in advertising and marketing communication (Reichert and Lambiase, 2003, 2006; Schroeder, 1998; Schroeder and Borgerson, 2003).

This study, therefore, seeks to bring together these different streams of research in an attempt to understand the emergence of the fetish brand community, which both encapsulates hedonic and symbolic consumption in relation to sexuality, body image and identity work; and the cultural meanings expressed in fashion and other products and services. I attempt to outline why it is important to analyse the cultural symbolism of brand communities in order to understand which identities brands provide to their consumers. I also seek to illustrate why a historical understanding of how particular brand communities have emerged is important in order to understand tribal marketing.

I first define the fetish community based on traditional understandings of fetishism developed in different academic disciplines and fields of study. I argue that such traditional definitions are still relevant for our understanding of the emergence of the fetish community, but that recent research on brand communities and fetishization enables a more nuanced understanding of the community. I then present findings from textual, ethnographic and netnographic research on the fetish community *ManiFest Copenhagen*. In what follows, I discuss the role of marketing in the fetish community with a particular focus on the concept of innovation. The final section discusses implications for future marketing practice and research.

Defining the fetish brand community

When defining fetishism, we have to distinguish between three traditional understandings of the term: anthropological, Marxist and psycho-analytical. In an anthropological perspective, fetishism refers to the idolized worship of transcendental and divine magic represented by Gods, ghosts, forces of nature or other constructs. Brosses (1760) was the first to define a fetish as a cultural object that affects its worshippers, because they believe the object has occult, mystical and magic energy.

The Marxist concept of commodity fetishism refers to an inauthentic state of social relations in complex capitalist market systems, where social relationships are confused with their medium, the commodity. Introduced by Marx (1867) in the opening chapter of *Das Kapital*, it links the anthropological understanding of fetishism to social theory by transforming religious artefacts to what he perceives as secularized ideological beliefs in commodities in capitalist society.

The psycho-analytical understanding of fetishism was developed by Binet (1887), who used the term to refer to a predominant or an exclusive sexual interest in inanimate objects (such as boots or panties), materials (such as fur, leather or rubber), parts of the human body (such as foots or hair) and practices (such as tattooing and body modifications). Such fetishism was perceived as abnormal, sick and perverse, and became incorporated into the sexological classics by Krafft-Elbing (1886) and Freud (1905, 1927). Freud viewed fetishism as a sexual perversion stemming from males' childhood trauma regarding the 'Oedipus Complex', castration fear and the splitting of the Ego (Lowenstein, 2002).

These three traditional understandings of fetishism can contribute to our understanding of the emergence of the fetish community as a social entity and why members of this community identify with fetishized objects. However, in recent research in marketing, advertising and consumption studies the concepts of *brand community* and *fetishization* can also inform our understanding of the emergence of this community.

The concept of brand community stresses the connection between product identity and culture, as it refers to a community of consumption that emerges on the basis of attachment to brand(s). Muñiz and O'Guinn (2001, p. 413) define a brand community as an enduring self-selected group of actors sharing a system of values, standards and representations that recognizes bonds of membership with each other. Brand communities are defined as fairly stable social entitities that are liberated from geography, are explicitly commercial and are informed by a mass-mediated sensibility in which the local and the mass converge. Brand communities do not need to be in opposition to mainstream culture, can include a multitude of consumers who can be both committed to the brand and the group.

The concept of fetishization in visual consumption culture (Schroeder and Borgerson, 2003; cf. Schroeder, 2000) identifies liminality, blackness and decontextualization as significant qualities of fetishist consumption. Liminality denotes the conceptual and ontological divide between nature and culture, as fetish clothing is usually worn tight and inscribes the wearer with its liminal qualities. Blackness refers to an exoticized identity and sexualized fascination with 'the other' due to black skin's exoticization in the Western (Caucasian) world. Finally, decontextualization refers to the eroticization of consumer products.

The origins of the fetish community can be dated back to the 1970s, when punk appeared as an anti-fashion including sadomasochistic gear, corsets, straps and chains, rubber and PVC, fishnets and plastic stilettos in a 'bricolage' outfit. This anti-fashion combined elements and images of prostitution and fetishism; and it both exploited and manipulated sexual clichés and gender roles as symbols of rebellion (Steele, 2001, p. 166). Hence, the emergence of the fetish community was heavily drawing on traditional understandings of fetishism, as reflected by the anthropological and psycho-analytical perspectives on fetishism. But rather than just adopting this inter-pretation of fetishism, the punk movement translated, re-interpreted the term and re-introduced it in opposition to mainstream ideology and aesthetics.

The institutionalization of the fetish community started in the early 1980s in London. Today, it is an international community circulating around a variety of fetish brands, including fetish clubs, fairs and events; fashion producers; print magazines; Internet websites; body and performance artists; models and musicians (Figure 16.1).

Fetish Product Category	Fetish Brands
Fashion and accessories	DeMask, Skin Two, Blackstyle, House of Harlot, Vex
Fairs and party events	London Fetish Fair, Black and Blue Ball (New York), Rubber Ball (London), Europerve (Amsterdam)
Clubs	Torture Garden (London), AlterEgo (Miami), KitKaKlub (Berlin), A Nuit Elastique (Paris), Club Sin (Montreal), ManiFest (Copenhagen)
Magazines	Atom Age, Skin Two, Marquis, Dressing for Pleasure
Websites	www.ukfetish.info, www.manifestfetishclub.com, www.londonfetishscene.com
Photographers	Barbara Behr, Eric Kroll, Helmut Newton, John Willie
Performance artists	Fakir Musafar, Midori, The Enigma
Musicians	Carlos Peron, Era
Models	Dita von Teese, Delilah Knotty, Bianca Beauchamp, Peter Holmes

Figure 16.1 Fetish brands in different product categories.

Members of the fetish community gather around these brands, define their own identities through consumption of these brands and transcend geo-graphic limitations through frequent use of media. In fact, media use plays an integrated role in both fetish consumption and community interaction. But membership to this community also goes beyond individual consumption of brands or mediated interaction, as it also includes the participation in and contribution to social events, such as fetish parties, fairs and clubs.

Besides clothing items as the most important idolized objects, also body modifications and sexual rituals, events, parties and performances play an important role in fetish consumption. Although fairly stable, the boundaries of the fetish community to other consumption communities on the dystopian darker side of life – such as Goth, Cyberpunk and BDSM communities – are permeable and fluid.

The emergence of a powerful and still growing industry with strong brands can in itself be interpreted as commodity fetishism in a Marxist sense, which to some degree weakens – but does not eliminate – initial anthropological and psycho-analytical interpretations. This is supported by a simultaneous inclusion of fetish objects into mainstream consumption culture. Schroeder and Borgerson (2003) have described how images and artefacts of the punk movement became incorporated into mainstream culture by Haute Couture designers and idols in the music industry. Others have described the almost omnipotent fetishization in movies, consumer magazines, the Internet and videogames (cf. Reichert and Lambiase, 2006).

However, the inclusion of fetishism into mainstream culture and consumption could only facilitate the transformation of the fetish community from being in opposition to it to being a brand community that reflects commodity fetishism. This process was not imposed on the community by clever marketers, and it certainly did not mean that the original connotations of rebellion and opposition to mainstream culture disappeared. But the emergence of the fetish community as a brand community would have been unthinkable, if this process would not have been constantly fuelled and inspired by the subculture itself.

Futurologist Alvin Toffler coined in his book *The Third Wave* (1980) the term prosumer, in which he predicted that the role of producers and consumers would blur and merge. He anticipated that consumers would take part in production and marketing processes, in particular when developing and specifying design requirements. More recently, authors of *The Cluetrain Manifesto* noted that 'markets are conversations' with the new economy 'moving from passive consumers . . . to active prosumers' (Levine et al., 2000).

In the fetish community, such a symbiotic relationship between marketers and consumers indeed exists, as the founding stories of companies addressing the community demonstrate. The London-based commercial publisher, fetish fashion and event producer *Skin Two* started in 1983 in a cellar in Soho as an underground fetish club that soon began to grow. In 1984, *Skin Two Magazine* was founded – today one of the biggest commercially produced community publications sold around the world. The company also arranges the annual *Skin Two Rubber Ball Weekend* – one of the world's most famous fetish events, and has expanded into clothing production, movie distribution and a wide range of other fetish-related business activities.

The growth of this company would have been impossible without innovative ideas and creative inspiration from community members. Community members were and are the best marketers and ambassadors of the company, and they are innovators both in a narrow sense as product developers and in a broader sense as cultural producers (Venkatesh and Meamber, 2006). They are content providers for fetish media, posing as models in their creative outfits. And they are product developers and designers, who by presenting their home-produced fetish clothes at fairs, parties and in clubs provide new ideas and inspiration to commercial fetish fashion producers – they are prosumers in the true sense of the word. A company like *Skin Two* is, therefore, engaged in symbiotic relationships with community members by serving the needs of the members of the fetish brand community, by assisting in the socialization of new members and by facilitating communications between members of the community.

I have now defined the fetish community as a brand community that offers its members different identities drawing on three different interpretive perspectives on fetishism. I have described how the emergence and development of this community was facilitated by the fetishization of mainstream consumption culture and by prosumption within the community. In the following sections, I seek to substantiate this definition and description by reporting the results of a long-term study of the fetish club *ManiFest* in Copenhagen, Denmark.

Methodology

As it is one of the main objectives of this analysis to offer 'thick descriptions' (Geertz, 1973, p. 10) of the fetish community, an interpretive and interdisciplinary approach has been applied. My study draws on sociology, anthropology, ethnography, communication studies, individual and social psychology, as well as a variety of accessible data sources, data collection and interpretative methods (Elliott and Jankel-Elliott, 2003, p. 215).

The choice of the Danish fetish club *ManiFest* [translation: Manifesto; but also a pun in Danish language meaning Mani(ac)-Party] was convenient and based on easy access to locations, observational opportunities, textual, visual and virtual data. Denmark, as a country, is also what might be called an extreme case as it has very liberal and relaxed attitudes to sex and gender emancipation. Data collection included participant observation data from fetish clubs, fetish parties and fetish fairs, textual and visual data from e-zines, magazines, flyers and web pages, and interview data from open-ended and semi-structured qualitative interviews with members of the fetish community in Denmark conducted from 1997 to 2002.

The methodology applied was based on involvement with consumers resembling an anthropology of consumption (Sherry, 1995) that can be defined as ethnomarketing or marketing ethnography (Arnould and Wallendorf, 1994). The analysis of empirical data was based on qualitative content analysis through meaning condensation (Kvale, 1996, p. 193), discourse analysis (Elliott, 1996) and netnographic analysis (Kozinets, 2002; Langer and Beckmann, 2005).

Finally, Bakhtin's work on medieval carnivals (Bakhtin, 1984) was applied in the interpretation of the empirical data. In *Rabelais and His World* (ibid.), Bakhtin describes the carnival as a social institution, where people are organized in a way that defies their usual socioeconomic and political organization in everyday life: everybody is equal and engages in a form of free and familiar contact with others despite of the barriers of heritage, property, profession or age. Costumes and masks are devices to cause increased awareness to the individuals' sensual, material, bodily unity and community.

Though Bakhtin in his analysis referred to medieval carnivals, his perception of carnivals can serve a sense making interpretive frame for the fetish parties of our time. Participants in carnivals live two lives: an official life, monolithic, serious and subjugated to a strict hierarchical social order based on family background, educational level, income, gender, profession, age or else. They perceive this official life as being full of dogmatism, sub-ordination and rigidity due to existing social rules and norms. The second life at the carnival is the opposite: free and unrestricted, full of obscenity and pleasure, blasphemous laughter, familiar and even intimate contact with everyone. Carnival participants celebrate bodily excess, ridiculing and inverting the hierarchies of their first life. In this respect, the consumption of fetish carnivals is both symbolic consumption of consumer spectacles in order to re-define identities and hedonic experiential consumption emphasizing emotional and erotic appeals, as described in the introductory section of this chapter. The fetish club as carnival expresses a destabilization of official worldviews, even though participants follow or even share them in their first lives. Both lives are legitimate, but both are – at least for most participants – also clearly separated from each other in terms of time and space.

ManiFest: a fetish carnival

ManiFest is a registered association with members drawn from the fetish community in Denmark and the rest of Scandinavia. Anybody interested can become a member in exchange for a small annual fee. It was founded in 1998, although annual fetish parties with open access to non-members have been organized in Copenhagen since 1995. With about 1,400 members, it is the largest organized fetish community in Northern Europe, and it co-operates with local and international fetish fashion shops, performers and clubs.

Members of *ManiFest* come from all generations and age groups, although the majority is aged between 20 and 40. Like in other brand communities, *ManiFest* members have diverse social, educational and professional backgrounds, but such differences are not detectable and are hidden behind the second skin of fetish clothing or are rendered unidentifiable through nudity.

ManiFest organizes between seven and nine fetish parties annually, each of them having between 200 and 600 participants and each of them lasting for no more than 6–7 hours at locations, which only members of the community are allowed to access. Hence, *ManiFest* parties are generally separated from first life in both time and space. This separation is also, so to speak, manifested in a very strict dress code, although participants do not have to dress according to the specific topics for each party, such as 'Girl Power', 'Bondage' or 'Gothic Vampire Empire'. However, as illustrated below, there are certain other rules members of *ManiFest* have to adhere to (Figure 16.2).

(Un-)covering the skin at fetish parties is an expression of freedom from official norms and values, 'a special type of communication impossible in everyday life', with 'special forms of marketplace speech and gesture, frank and free, permitting no distance between those who came in contact with each other and liberating from norms of etiquette and decency imposed at other times' (Bakhtin, 1984, p. 10). *ManiFest* parties are a contemporary Western version of

ManiFest membership card

The Fetish tribe is not without any rules that members of the tribe have to respect. Rules in *ManiFest* are defined as follows:

> All are welcome, but we do have some demands and rules: 'Everyone must perform a good and respectful behaviour towards others. Everyone must follow our dresscode: Leather, PVC, Latex, Rubber, Drag, Trans, Erotic Lingerie and extreme sexual expression. You will not be admitted if you do not comply with the dresscode. No streetwear, cotton, blue jeans, etc. . . . *ManiFest* encourages passionate flirt, extreme desire and open playfulness. Many members love to look and show off, and to enjoy sex and fetish play in front of others. It is of course totally up to each individual, whether you want to look or not – or if you want to show off and play. Freedom, desire and mutual respect are important keywords for *ManiFest*. Failure to comply with written or unwritten rules, can lead to banishment from *ManiFest*.'

Moreover, the tribe also protects its' members by having formulated a clear policy for photography:

> 'Photography is not allowed at *ManiFest*! This is to respect many of our members' wishes for anonymity and discretion. If, on rare occasions, *ManiFest* is photographing for our homepage or other media, displays will be posted at the entrance, and no one will be photographed against their wishes.'

Other rules include that a 'No' in response to an invitation to activity is a 'No', and that a 'No' has to be accepted without any further discussion; that the play- and darkroom is reserved for couples only until 2 a.m., smoking restrictions and that contributors to the web-based *ManiFest*-guestbook have to use language and tone that is not insulting, harsh or vulgar and are restricted from using the guestbook for commercial advertising purposes.

Source: www.manifest.eu

Figure 16.2 Membership rules of *ManiFest Copenhagen*.

carnivals expressing the universal phenomenon of ritual liminality (Falk, 1995, p. 98). This is also declared in the welcome words on *ManiFest*'s homepage:

> *ManiFest* is a lustful alternative to the everyday mainstream culture, with all its sexual double-standards, hypocrisy and superficiality. We celebrate freedom, flirtation, hedonism and ecstasy. We *ManiFest* our inner selves, our hidden fascinations and sensual visions.

Joining the fetish community enables members to reclaim and regain possession of their bodies, as the body has become commoditized to such an extent, that even legal, ethical, political and social questions have been raised about the body as an individuals' property (Benson, 2000, p. 251). One member comments on this:

> I really enjoy not obeying all the norms and rules for good taste. We are all like puppets on strings in our everyday life. *ManiFest* is one of the last resorts, where you can escape from the rat race – at least for some hours.

When asked, why they had become members of *ManiFest*, many of the informants explain that friends had invited them. Others point out that fetish parties are less violent and more exiting than ordinary clubs, while others place great emphasis on socializing with likeminded people, with whom they share aesthetic and sexual preferences. Like in other communities of consumption, social interaction is important. A fetish party consists of at least two parts: the pre-party with a limited number of friends and the main party. At the pre-party, friends meet in some private place to help each other with dressing up, to listen to music and to talk. Others meet for dinner in a restaurant or for a drink in a bar. One member of the fetish community recounts the importance of the pre-party:

> I sometimes think the pre-party is even more fun than the party itself. It's just so great to see all my friends around and talk about what might happen tonight. We are chatting and joking and are really getting close.

However, what makes the fetish community distinctive and different from other communities is the fetish carnival itself. The carnival is – in the case of *ManiFest* – held at different locations and venues. The venues always have a large dance floor, a bar, a dark room and various sites, which are equipped with pillories, a St. Andrew Cross and other equipment. Some members bring their own personal equipment – such as whips, crops, collars, chains, ropes – to the party, others do not. Some use this equipment, others do not; some participate in sexual activities in public, others just watch; and others go only to dance or socialize in the bar area. However, sexual arousal and fantasies – referring to the second and psycho-analytical conceptualization of fetishism – play some role for most members of the community.

All participants have in common that they both wear and feel attracted to fetish clothing. While some members arrive in full fetish dress at the venue, others go, after arrival, to a dressing room to change clothes or to shine up their outfit. Jeans and other clothes made of cotton are strictly banned; and black is the predominant colour all over. This supports Schroeder and Borgerson's fetish theory about the symbolic connotation of blackness, referring to exoticized identities and erotic fascination with 'the other'. Some participants also wear clothes in other colours; red (the colour of life, heat, romance, passion and love) or white (the colour of innocence and light). But these clothes are still made of leather, rubber, PVC or similar tight-fitting materials. This supports another and even more important aspect of Schroeder and Borgerson's fetish theory, namely the aspect of liminality. Tight-fitting fetish clothing transcends the important cultural and psychological divide between culture and nature, outside and inside, public and private, work and pleasure. It is also exactly this aspect of liminality based on fetish clothing that, in a Bakhtin perspective, constitutes the difference between the everyday lives and fetish carnivals.

Decontextualization as the third aspect of Schroeder and Borgerson's fetish theory is also supported. Although there are a few more males than females at most of the parties, there is no serious gender disparity in the community. Traditional gender role divisions are blurred. Genderbending – the playful re-definition of gender roles – is popular among a considerable number of participants. Women are dressed like men and vice versa; women dance and play with each other – as do some of the men. This decontextualiztion leads to sexual and gender empowerment in form of increased control over sensual experience and sexual self-presentation. For instance, a female community member declares in *ManiFest*'s guestbook: 'I am looking for the man in leather trousers and naked body, about 30–35 years. . . Our agreement is still valid: you are MINE at the next party!'(Figure 16.3).

However, members of the community also express diverse self-identities. Whereas some of them regard themselves as 'kinky pervs' outside or at the margins of mainstream culture ('I am not a part of society, here is my society', one member declared), others are more interested in gaining legitimatization of their aesthetic and sexual preferences ('I really think that *ManiFest* – and also media reporting about the parties – contributes to more tolerance in society', another members said). Such different perceptions indicate a tension between subculture and mainstream culture. One of the original co-founders of *ManiFest* comments on this tension as follows:

> We are constantly fighting against becoming part of mainstream culture – against being just another party event. If we are going to loose the 'icebreakers', we can close immediately. On the other hand, we are not going to make it financially, unless we are not able to attract more and new members. It really is a dance on a rope. . .

This dance on a rope is even emphasized by the fact that not all members share the same aesthetic preferences. Ongoing controversies about which music should be played at the parties reflect different music tastes. The Danish Goth community, for example, has established their own events, where they can be on their own and gather around their own preferred music. These events are sometimes overlapping in terms of event dates with *ManiFest* parties. Also the Danish gay community arranges their own events, resulting in that homosexuals, transvestites and other gay groups participate in *ManiFest* parties infrequently, partly because of prejudices and intolerance about bi-, trans- and homosexuality among some fetish community members.

Manifest Copenhagen: Voices of experience

The open-access website of *ManiFest* is a major instrument to keep the community together. Here, photos from previous parties and performances are published and here, members of the community such as Rubberqueen, Fetishchick, Barbiesissyslut, Sir Rubberduck, GetNaked, Mona Lisa, Bunnybarbie (tv), Silkguy, Miss StrapOn and Silverclaw and visitors from Sweden, Norway, Ireland, Italy, Germany and other countries discuss community issues, inform about interesting events in Denmark and abroad, and report their experiences – as the examples below illustrate:

- 'To those of us who are interested in genderbending, drag, gender-identity – next week there is a Queer-festival: http://www.queerfestival.org.'
- 'Ekstra Bladet (Danish tabloid) publishes on Fridays a theme series of articles about sex. . . Last Friday it was about fetishism, and unfortunately they blended modern fetish play and parties with a century old Freudian perspective on it... You can both read the article about fetish as illness and my two responses to the authors here: . . .'
- 'Like last year, we offer to arrange a dinner in the restaurant Schefflers, while participating in the German Fetish Ball in Berlin. Write to Stig, if interested.'
- 'Preparty! We have been reading a posting from the couple "Ebonylust" and think you sound like somebody we would like to invite to our manifest preparty. We are 10–20 rubber-adults, who meet for dinner in a restaurant before the party. Please write, if you would like to join us.'
- 'Thanks to Stig & Co for a wonderful party last Saturday – and thanks to Louise for pleasant company – you forgot one of your shoes in my car.'
- 'Can't we prohibit smoking at *ManiFest*? I actually know somebody, who does not come any longer, because he can't stand this smoking hell. What is the distribution of smokers and non-smokers in *ManiFest*'
- 'It just can't be right that people get access, although they do not live up to our dresscode and that some just come by in order to watch us. We are not animals in a zoo!'
- 'By the way, I hereby inform you that one member has received one year of suspension after Saturday. There have been repeated complaints from different guests who felt plagued by his offensive behaviour. Let me emphasize that all guests shall behave politely and with respect to each other – and let me know, if somebody has problems in doing so. Best regards, Stig'
- '*ManiFest* supports the victims of the Tsunami in South East Asia with 20 Danish Crowns for each paying guest tomorrow. You are welcome to give an extra donation – all the money goes in full to one of the major aid organizations.'
- 'Dear Stig, I am so grateful that you arrange these parties!'

Figure 16.3 Community member voices on the *ManiFest* website.

Marketing and innovation in the fetish tribe

Marketers to the fetish community are constantly facing the risk of getting detached from the community, if members loose the feeling of exclusivity due to commercialization and commoditization. If the community moves too far to the much mainstream, the most innovative members might disappear. Hence, tribal marketers face challenges that are unlike those of the mass marketers, where one of the main goals of marketing is to increase the number of consumers. In tribal marketing, this is not necessarily the case, as tribal members do not want to be approached as if they were ordinary mass audiences and because members want to feel different from the mass.

Another important issue is innovation in the community. Barber (2004, p. 145) states: '[W]e have to stop and consider how sexually unanticipated uses of technology are being developed by users themselves.', and argues that deviation, fetishism and sexuality could prove to be fundamental factors in creativity and innovation, as they might give birth to unanticipated uses and technologies.

Authors studying innovation processes (cf. Prahalad and Ramaswamy, 2000; von Hippel, 2001) support this argument; Von Hippel (1988, 2005) emphasizes the importance of lead users for marketing, as lead users face needs that will become general in a marketplace months or years in the future. Referring to product development in the community of windsurfers and other communities, von Hippel (2005, p. 4) argues that 'many of the products lead users develop for their own use will appeal to other consumers too and so might provide the basis for products manufacturers would wish to commercialize'.

The implications for tribal marketers are obvious. As Cova and Cova (ibid., p. 600) propose, marketing to communities should be seen as 'the activity of designing and launching of products and services destined to facilitate the co-presence and the communal gathering of individuals in the time of the communities'. They suggest that tribal marketers should focus on customer–customer relations instead of focusing on customer–company relations; that tribal marketers should regard the organization as supporting these relations; that what the company does, its products, services and servicescapes, are there to support the link between customers; that a tribal approach to marketing relies on rituals and cult places instead of loyalty cards, bulletin boards and bonus-programmes; and that tribal marketing should seek to build effect instead of cognitive loyalty.

As we have seen, exactly this is happening in the fetish community: many of the marketers emerged from within the community and remain active members of the community. Their primary marketing task is to create events where the members of the community gather, in particular websites, concept-shops, fetish fairs and fetish parties and that all support and exhibit other products and services offered. Even in cases, where producers of fetish fashion and media products and services do not organize such gatherings themselves, they are closely related to and support others who organize such events. Also, marketers must be aware of the complexity of the different identity giving functions of the different understandings of fetishism to community members described earlier in this chapter.

When talking about innovations we must, however, distinguish between fundamental/radical and incremental innovations, as well as we must distinguish between innovations perceived on individual and on community level. Fundamental and radical innovations stemming from innovative lead users might be of importance with regard to product development at the community level, and eventually these may diffuse into mainstream culture. Incremental innovation, however, is evolutionary innovation with lower degrees of uncertainty and risk. In practice, incremental innovation is taking place on an individual level, for instance if a community member develops her own outfit. Here, marketers can encourage community members by supporting the legitimacy of moving one step further on an established trajectory.

Indeed, for the case of the fetish community the diffusion of fetish artefacts into popular mainstream culture and fashion is a two-edge sword, as it both increases the social and cultural acceptance of what previously had been regarded as deviant, and at the same time endangers the strong sense of exclusivity among community members. In response, fetish marketers have in co-operation with members of the fetish community developed a number of strategies.

First, there exist hierarchies within the community, as event organizers, performance artists and innovators/lead users are idolized and worshipped by other community members. The exclusivity of the exclusive can be facilitated by marketers. *Second*, community growth can provoke a further diversification of the community into sub-branches and chapters, and eventually even to the separation of certain subgroups from 'mainstream' fetish culture. This potentially endangers the existence of the community, as this process most often will drain away the innovators. In response, marketers seek to establish closer relationships with such innovators and lead users by offering them tangible and intangible privileges. *Third*, communities develop certain restrictions in terms of access to the community or to particular activities and events within the community. This strategy has been successfully applied for decades, for example by the music industry, where only insiders and the chosen few were allowed backstage-access or participation in pre- and after-parties.

Conclusions

If Maffesoli (1996, p. 77) was thinking of the fetish community, he explains that in communities, actors (producers) and spectators (consumers) are one and the same:

> [A]esthetics is a way of feeling in common. It is also a means of recognizing ourselves. Parva esthetical? Be that as it may, the hodge-podge of clothing, multi-hued hairstyles and other punk manifestations act as a glue; theatricality founds and reconfirms the community. The cult of the body and other games of appearance have value only inasmuch as they are part of a larger stage in which everyone is both actor and spectator.

The fetish community is a brand community or postmodern tribe, characterized by hedonistic, symbolic and experiential prosumption of consumer spectacles and fashion that involve identity work, body images, sexuality, emotional appeals and social relations. This community emerged out of rebellion against mainstream culture, drawing heavily on traditional anthropological and psychoanalytical understandigs of fetishism. These original understandings are still identity giving for many members of the community, although the fetishization of mainstream culture as well as the emergence of brands within the community also created in commodity fetishism in this subculture of consumption.

Based on Schroeder and Borgerson's fetish theory, blackness, decontextualization and – most important – liminality have been identified as the main characteristics of symbolic fetish expressions. Drawing on Bakhtin, liminality also explains the critical divide between culture and nature, outside and inside, public and private, work and pleasure, as expressed at fetish carnivals, where participants temporarily step into second lives that are fundamentally different from their first lives; that is, their ordinary everyday lives in mainstream culture. At fetish carnivals, members of the community invert the social order of their official lives by engaging in bodily excess and disrespect to social hierarchies. They escape – temporarily – in the attempt to subvert the rigidity of suppressive social norms and values. But at the same time, they still consume products and brands.

The tension between the different understandings of fetishism and understanding the critical divide between everyday life and fetish carnivals is of importance for marketing and innovation. These tensions and this divide separate alternative and exclusive subculture from mainstream culture, tribal marketing from mass marketing, the fetish community from the fetishization of mass consumption.

Tribal marketing seeks to establish close relations between marketers and the community. The marketing organization does not primarily produce products and services to consumers, but it first of all supports and facilitates tribal prosumers and innovators in the community. But the tensions between subculture and mainstream culture also create limits for growth, as overt commercialization is an existential threat to the community. Hence, the most important task for tribal marketers is to keep the *status quo* between exclusive subculture and mainstream culture alive. Future tribal marketing research might address how such a balance between subcultures of consumption and mainstream consumption can be established and maintained.

Acknowledgements

I would like to thank Stig and members from *ManiFest Fetish Club Copenhagen* for their co-operation and support for this research.

References

Arnould, E. and Wallendorf, M. (1994). Market-oriented ethnography: interpretation building and marketing strategy formulation, *Journal of Marketing Research*, **XXXI**, 484–504.

Bakhtin, M. (1984). *Rabelais and His World*. Bloomington, IN: Midland-Indiana University Press.

Barber, T. (2004). Deviation as key to innovation: understanding a culture of the future, *Foresight*, 6/3, 141–152.

Belk, R.W., Wallendorf, M. and Sherry Jr., J.F. (1989). The sacred and the profane in consumer behavior: theodicy on the odyssey, *Journal of Consumer Research*, **16** (1), 1–38.

Belk, R.W. and Costa, J.A. (1998). The mountain man myth: a contemporary consuming fantasy, *Journal of Consumer Research*, 25/2, 218–240.

Benson, S. (2000). Inscriptions of the self: reflections on tattooing and piercing in contemporary Euro-America, in Caplan, J. (ed.), *Written on the Body; The Tattoo in European and American History*. Princeton, NJ: Princeton University Press, pp. 234–254.

Binet, A. (1887). Le fétichisme dans l'amour, *Revue Philosophique*, **24**, 143–167.

de Brosses, C. (1760). *Du culte des Dieux Fétiches ou Parallèle de l'ancienne Religion de l'Égypte avec la Religion actuelle de Nigritie*, Introduction, Paris, 5–17, downloaded on 31st October 2006 at: http://www.psychanalyse-paris.com/811-Du-culte-des-Dieux-Fetiches.html

Celsi, R.L., Randall, L.R. and Leigh, T.W. (1993). An exploration of high-risk leisure consumption through skydiving, *Journal of Consumer Research*, **20** (1), 1–23.

Cova, B. and Cova, V. (2001). Tribal aspects of postmodern consumption research: the case of French in-line roller skaters, *Journal of Consumer Behaviour*, **1** (1), 67–76.

Cova, B. and Cova, V. (2002). Tribal Marketing. The tribalisation of society and its impact on the conduct of marketing, *European Journal of Marketing*, **36** (5–6), 595–630.

Elliott, R. (1996). Discourse analysis: exploring action, function and conflict in social texts, *Marketing Intelligence and Planning*, **14** (6), 65–68.

Elliott, R. and Jankel-Elliott, N. (2003). Using ethnography in strategic consumer research, *Qualitative Market Research*, **6** (4), 215–223.

Falk, P. (1995). Written in the flesh, *Body and Society*, **1** (1), 95–105.

Firat, A.F. and Dholakia, N. (1998). *Consuming People. From Political Economy to Theaters of Consumption*. London: Routledge.

Freud, S. (1905). Three Essays on the Theory of Sexuality, *Standard Edition*, **23**, 275–278.

Freud, S. (1927). Fetishism, *Standard Edition*, 147–157.

Geertz, C. (1973). *The Interpretation of Cultures*. New York, NY: Basic Books.

Goulding, C. and Shankar, A. (2004), Age is just a number: 'rave' culture and the cognitively young 'thirty something', *European Journal of Marketing*, **38** (5–6), 641–688.

Goulding, C., Shankar, A. and Elliott, R. (2002). Working weeks, rave weekends: identity fragmentation and the emergence of new communities, *Consumption, Markets and Culture*, **5** (4), 261–284.

Hirschman, E.C. and Holbrook, M.B. (1982). Hedonic consumption: emerging concept, methods and propositions, *Journal of Marketing*, **46**, 92–101.

Holbrook, M.B. and Hirschman, E.C. (1982). The experiential aspects of consumption: consumer fantasies, feelings, and fun, *Journal of Consumer Research*, **9** (2), 132–140.

Kates, S.M. (2000). Sex and the city: production and consumption of the Sydney gay and lesbian mardi gras, in Schroeder, J. and Otnes, C. (eds.). *Proceedings of the 5th Conference on Gender, Marketing, and Consumer Behavior*, Provo, UT: Association for Consumer Research, 33–34.

Kozinets, R.V. (2001). Utopian enterprise: articulating the meanings of star trek's culture of consumption, *Journal of Consumer Research*, **28** (1), 67–88.

Kozinets, R.V. (2002). The field behind the screen: using netnography for marketing research in online communities, *Journal of Marketing Research*, **39**, 61–72.

Krafft-Elbing, R. von (1886). *Psychopathia Sexualis*, 12th ed. (1965), New York: Putnam.

Kvale, S. (1996). *InterViews: An Introduction to Qualitative Research Interviewing*. London: Sage.

Langer, R. (2003a). First or second skin? The rise of fetish consumption culture, in Smith, S. (ed.). *Proceedings of the Ninth Cross Cultural Research Conference*, Montego Bay/Provo, UT, 14–18 December 2003.

Langer, R. (2003b). SKIN TWO: (un)-covering the skin in fetish carnivals. *Proceedings of the European Association for Consumer Research Conference*, Dublin, 5–7 June 2003.

Langer, R. and Beckmann, S.C. (2005). Sensitive research topics: netnography revisited, *Qualitative Market Research – An International Journal*, **8** (2), 189–203.

Levine, R., Locke, C., Searls, D. and Weinberger, D. (2000). *The Cluetrain Manifesto*. Cambridge, MA: Perseus Publishing.

Lowenstein, L.F. (2002). Fetishes and their associated behavior, *Sexuality and Disability*, **20** (2), 135–147.

Maffesoli, M. (1996). *The Time of the Tribes. The Decline of Individualism in Mass Society*. London: Sage.

Marx, K. (1867). *Das Kapital. Kritik der politischen Ökonomie, Bd I: Der Produktionsprozess des Kapitals*, 1962, Berlin: Dietz Verlag, Marx-Engels-Werke Band 23.

McCracken, G. (1986). Culture and consumption: a theoretical account of the structure and movement of the cultural meaning of consumer goods, *Journal of Consumer Research*, **13** (1), 71–84.

Muñiz, A. and O'Guinn, T. (2001). Brand community, *Journal of Consumer Research*, **27** (4), 412–431.

Prahalad, C.K. and Ramaswamy, V.K. (2000). Co-opting customer competence, *Harvard Business Review*, 78/1, 79–87.

Reichert, T. and Lambiase, J. (eds.) (2003). *Sex in Advertising. Perspectives on the Erotic Appeal*. Mahwah, NJ: Lawrence Erlbaum.

Reichert, T. and Lambiase, J. (eds.) (2006). *Sex in Consumer Culture. The Erotic Content of Media and Marketing*. Mahwah, NJ: Lawrence Erlbaum.

Schouten, J.W. (1991). Selves in transition: symbolic consumption in personal rites of passage and identity reconstruction, *Journal of Consumer Research*, **17** (3), 412–425.

Schouten, J.W. and McAlexander, J.H. (1995). Subcultures of consumption: an ethnography of the new bikers, *Journal of Consumer Research*, **22** (2), 46–61.

Schroeder, J.E. (1998). Consuming sexuality: a case study in identity marketing, in Fischer, E. and Wardlow, D. (eds.), *Gender, Marketing and Consumer Behavior*. San Francisco, CA: San Francisco State University, pp. 27–40.

Schroeder, J.E. (2000). *Visual Consumption*. London: Routledge.

Schroeder, J.E. and Borgerson, J.L. (2003). Dark desires: fetishism, representation, and ontology in contemporary advertising, in Reichert, T. and Lambiase, J. (eds.), *Sex in Advertising: Perspectives on the Erotic Appeal*. Mahwah, NJ: Lawrence Erlbaum Associates, 65–89.

Sherry Jr., J.F. (1995). *Contemporary Marketing and Consumer Behavior: An Anthropological Sourcebook*. Thousand Oaks, CA: Sage.

Steele, V. (2001). *The Corset. A Cultural History*. New Haven and New York: Yale University Press.

Thompson, C.J. and Haytko, D.L. (1997). 'Speaking of fashion: consumers' uses of fashion discourses and the appropriation of countervailing cultural meanings, *Journal of Consumer Research*, **24** (1), 15–42.

Thompson, C.J. and Hirschman, E.C. (1995). Understanding the socialized body: a poststructuralist analysis of consumers' self-conceptions, body images, and self-care practices, *Journal of Consumer Research*, **22** (2), 139–153.

Venkatesh, A. and Meamber, L.A. (2006). Art and aesthetics: marketing and cultural production, *Marketing Theory*, **6** (1), 11–39.

von Hippel, E. (1988). *The Sources of Innovation*. New York, NY: Oxford University Press.

von Hippel, E. (2001). Innovation by user communities: learning form open–source–software, *MIT Sloan Management Review*, **42** (4), 82–86.

von Hippel, E. (2005). *Democratizing Innovation*. Boston, MA: MIT Press.

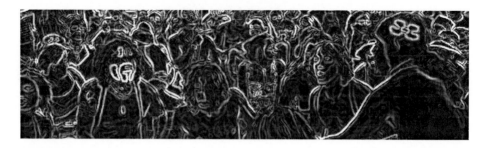

17

The war of the eTribes: online conflicts and communal consumption

Kristine de Valck[1]

Introduction

Since the quick rise of the Internet in the 1990s, the concept of the virtual community has attracted considerable attention from marketers. This interest is usually fuelled by the idea that virtual communities form 'unified fronts' that represent single homogeneous market segments. Different from traditional segmentation marketing that is based upon common consumer characteristics like age, gender and income, virtual communities of consumption allow for direct marketing actions based upon specific consumer interest, in the manner of placing banner advertisements for Bordeaux wine in a community of Bordeaux wine lovers. Moreover, virtual communities are considered attractive because of their many-to-many marketing potential: the consumption and brand enthusiasts that gather in virtual communities to exchange information and experiences do not only feed each other's loyalty and devotion, but they also serve as

[1] The author likes to thank the editors and two anonymous reviewers for their helpful comments on a previous version of this chapter.

important advocates by informing and influencing fellow consumers that look for advice (Kozinets, 1999).

What underlies this interest is the premise that community embodies a set of voluntary, social, and reciprocal relations that are crowned with a strong 'we-feeling' (Muñiz and O'Guinn, 2001). Community stands for a sense of fellowship, family, and custom, as well as bounding together by understanding, consensus, and language (Fernback and Thompson, 1999). Indeed, research efforts have made apparent that the three core components of traditional community can often also be found online, that is, consciousness of kind, shared rituals and traditions, and a sense of moral responsibility (cf. Bagozzi and Dholakia, 2002; Kozinets, 2001; Muñiz and O'Guinn, 2001; Muñiz and Schau, 2005). How marketers can benefit from the communal spirit and social bonding within communities has been highlighted by various ethnographies of consumer cultures that have put the shared practices and consumption meanings of the community members central stage (e.g., Celsi, Rose, and Leigh, 1993; McAlexander, Schouten, and Koenig, 2002; Schouten and McAlexander, 1995). Although attractive, this notion of community is incomplete. The extant literature on consumer cultures has underexposed the tensions, rivalries, and diversity that are also an inherent aspect of communities (Harrison and Jenkins, 1996; Kozinets, 2001). As a result, marketers that embark on a virtual community adventure in the hope to build or attract a group of like minded, unanimous consumers may be surprised by the outright wars that they encounter.

That we find persistent discord within virtual communities is not evident. In his theory of social systems, Parsons identified functional prerequisites that must be satisfied for any system to survive or maintain equilibrium with respect to its environment. The functional prerequisite for the social system (being one of the components of the general social system) is integration. Action for this component system includes the coordination of individuals and groups, and the bonding of members of society by means of values and normative constraints (Parsons and Shils, 1951). Thus, one of the key aspects of a 'real' community is having to deal with and resolve conflict. Thereby, the community relies on subsystems of loyalty, morality, polity (e.g., courts, police), and economy (e.g., contracts, property rights) (Perdue, 1986). However, in an online environment that is characterized by low entry and exit barriers, virtual communities lack sufficient means to oblige their members to integrate in the system, and be loyal to it. If a member does not agree with the group norm, the easiest option is to leave the virtual community and join one that is more similar in beliefs and behaviour, thus circumventing conflict. In this respect, Fernback and Thompson envisioned that '[n]ew communication technologies can both draw people together into cohesive communities of interest, and further atomize them as they retreat deeper into tribalism' (1999, p. 4).

In contrast to Parsons' modernist point of view in which social systems focus on stability and order, postmodernists have introduced the idea of a tribalized society. Tribes are considered unstable, small-scale, affective, and not fixed by any of the established parameters of modern society (Cova and Cova, 2002;

Maffesoli, 1995). They form, disperse, and reform as something else on the waves of temporary shared emotions and passions. Indeed, many virtual communities meet these tribal characteristics. Alon, Brunel, and Schneier Siegal (2005), for example, describe the life cycle of a community of expectant mothers. These women form cohesive online support groups organized around due dates. They may come from all walks of life, having not much more in common that the upcoming emotional life experience of child bearing. The focus of group interactions is not static, but changes over time; sometimes giving precedence to individual needs, other times serving group needs. After birth, these communities tend to slowly dissolve, or reform around new emotions linked to, for example, breastfeeding, children's diseases, or combining work with care.

Kozinets (1999) is the first to point out that virtual communities of consumption that are seemingly united groups, in fact represent multitudes of tribes; 'all of which have aspects in common, and important – sometimes crucial – points of differentiation' (Kozinets, 1999, p. 258). These points of differentiation lead to split-offs. It is not uncommon, for example, that members of the first hour don't recognize themselves anymore in the spirit of the matured community and restart another online group that is only open for a select few (e.g., the Well versus Howard Rheingold's Brainstorms community). It is true that split-offs are facilitated by the ease with which new online groups, forums, rooms, and blogs can be created. Nevertheless, split-offs also require drive, decision, and action power: without (a) leader(s) and a clear vision of what the new community will constitute, members hesitate to leave what is known for what is unknown. Even if alternative, existing communities are available, many members consider the costs of switching too high: it takes time and energy to get acquainted with any community's environment, its written and unwritten codes of conduct, the other members, as it takes time and energy to build one's online reputation (e.g., Kozinets, 1999; Walther, 1995). Therefore, members will linger, despite their differences. The result: tensions, and sometimes warfare.

The aim of this chapter is to analyse these tensions to understand what are the axes of warfare within virtual communities. A three year netnography of forum discussions within a virtual community dedicated to food consumption has not only given insight in the core tensions and how they are played out, but also in the manners in which community members overcome their tensions and reunite in commonality. With this insight, we can start to develop a more comprehensive understanding of the concept of the virtual community that includes the idea of conflict next to the idea of commonality. Implications for marketers are discussed in the final section.

Netnographic study

The virtual community that served as the focal site of investigation is organized around culinary matters (www.smulweb.nl). It was initiated in 1998 by an independent company that developed online community concepts for third parties. In 2004, the community has been sold to a large Internet portal. The community counts more than 160,000 registered members, attracting around 30,000 unique visitors per month. Its main topics of interest are recipes, restaurants, food products, kitchen utensils, dieting, and wine. The community provides theme pages, member pages, discussion forums, chat rooms, and databases for articles, reviews, and recipes.

In order to study the interaction dynamics between community members in the discussion forums, I have applied the method of netnography, thereby following the guidelines developed by Kozinets (2002). I made my entrée in the community and started informal observation of the forums in September 2000. I reviewed a range of member contributions, conducted in-depth interviews with members and administrators, and participated in an offline community gathering. After three years of knowledge building, I intensified my monitoring by systematically reviewing all topics discussed in the forums in 2003. In several rounds, I made a purposeful selection of 53 discussion threads for further analysis. The total research volume amounted to 3,161 postings generated by 82 distinct contributors, the majority of which belong to the group of core community members that are dedicated to the topic of interest, and daily involved in social and informational exchange (cf. Kozinets, 1999).

The conclusions are based on an iterative content analysis (Glaser and Strauss, 1967; Spiggle, 1994). My interpretation of the data has been constructed through continuously moving between individual postings, chunks of postings, entire discussion threads, and the emergent understanding of the complete data set (cf. Thompson, 1997). The evolving netnography has been posted in its entirety to the community to elicit member feedback. In total, 16 members (active discussants and lurkers) reacted. All reactions were positive and affirmed the analysis and interpretation.[2]

Findings

The netnography of the discussion forums has been guided by three questions: What are the core tensions? How are these tensions played out? And how are they overcome? The analysis has revealed three axes of tension, which can be classified according to the community level at which they occur: (1) tensions among the core members who challenge each other's expertise, (2) tensions between the core members and the larger community about appropriate practices and norms, and (3) tensions within the community as a whole caused by differing lifestyles and related consumption behaviours. These tensions are addressed in the following paragraphs by means of examples that highlight

[2] The netnography has been conducted as part of my dissertation research: de Valck, K. (2005), *Virtual Communities of Consumption: Networks of Consumer Knowledge and Companionship*. Rotterdam: Erasmus Research Institute of Management, RSM Erasmus University/Erasmus School of Economics. Available online: http://hdl.handle.net/1765/6663. Only part of the findings are presented in this chapter.

the tactics of warfare. Finally, I will discuss how the community members cease-fire and make peace.[3]

Who is the best?

The forum discussions contain a lot of information about food products, food preparation, kitchen utensils, and specific recipes. The participants pose and answer culinary questions, and they give each other explanations and background information. In short, they share knowledge. From the existing marketing literature we know that people engage in knowledge-sharing communication for reasons of benevolence, that is, they truly want to help others (e.g., Fitzgerald Bone, 1992). However, knowledge is also shared to experience feelings of prestige (e.g., Dichter, 1966). In many discussion threads, examples of both sides can often be found simultaneously. The forum participants exchange information, but at the same time, by showing what they know, they articulate conceptions of culinary expertise. Moreover, they constantly challenge and put each other's culinary expertise to the test. The result: subtle warfare about who is the ultimate expert, like in the following example about potato preparation.

Potatoes are a core element in the Dutch cuisine. Van Gogh's famous painting 'The Potato Eaters' (1885) exemplifies the historical importance of the potato as the main nutrition for the ordinary Dutch man in the nineteenth century. But to date, potatoes are still a major part of the daily dinner of many forum participants. Even though the potato seems a simple food product, the Dutch discern many aspects regarding its preparation. Although we would assume that there are more complicated things to prepare (and thus to establish expertise by discussing it), it is exactly the simplicity of the potato that lends it for distinguishing between ordinary and superior cooking qualities. Forum discussants try to outdo each other, for example, by summing up all the ingredients they use to prepare mashed potatoes:

> I prepare mashed potatoes with milk, butter, pepper, salt, nutmeg, and a spoonful of mustard (Brenda); I always use freshly boiled potatoes, mash them by hand with a pestle under while adding splashes of milk until I get a smooth substance. Instead of mustard, I frequently use grated cheese, which is very tasteful (Betty); I prepare mashed potatoes in various ways: with cheese, with fresh herbs, sometimes I mix the boiled potatoes with celeriac and add some yogurt, with garlic, onions or ham cubes, sometimes I mash sweet potatoes, and sometimes I prepare mashed potatoes with a crispy layer in the oven (Rachel).

It is clear that the discussants are not simply sharing recipes, but that they are showing off their expertise to turn an ordinary potato into a fabulous dish. In similar kind of discussions, forum participants usually first make clear that

[3]Member quotes are translations of the original postings that were written in Dutch. All names are pseudonyms.

they live by the heightened norm established by the core group of community experts so as to distinguish themselves from the ordinary cook. Then, they try to establish superior expertise within ranks by giving further details about their special method, or by questioning the special method of someone else:

> Every once in a while I make fries using fresh potatoes and a machine to cut the potatoes. I bake them in two rounds, first to cook them and then to make them crispy (Betty); Do you still have such an old-fashioned machine to cut fries? I think my father still owns one, but if I make fries I cut them by hand into the perfect size fries (Alice); This potato cutter caused me muscle aches. And half of the potatoes turned into flakes. I cut them myself; this is a perfect job during the time needed to heat the fat (real bovine fat). I bake them first at 160° Celsius and I bake them off at 180° Celsius (Brenda).

In this example, the norm is to make French fries only 'once in a while' with 'fresh potatoes' and to bake them 'in two rounds'. Alice and Brenda point out to Betty that true experts are supposed to know that potato cutters don't produce perfect fries; handcraft does. Finally, by explicating the type of fat and the exact temperatures that are used, Brenda tries to establish herself as the expert of the experts. It is clear that this match to be recognized as head of the tribe is played with vigour, causing tensions between the contestants.

Us and they

The core members not only challenge each other; as a group, they challenge the practices and norms of others that deviate from their own high standards. These standards are actively negotiated by discussing issues such as 'what is a good cook?', 'what is a healthy diet?', 'dressed-up dishes or back to basics?', and 'is pizza junk food or not?' Negotiations about these issues are elaborate and sophisticated. Particular situations in which norms may vary are described in detail and extensively deliberated. Often times, forum discussants tell stories about a relative, friend, neighbour, or colleague whose cooking or eating behaviour they disapprove of. Usually they do so to show to the other members that they themselves know the 'right' norms, and adhere to them.

Defining in-group and out-group boundaries does not only occur with regard to non-community members, the core members also set themselves apart within the community. Tension arises, for example, from the different attitudes concerning the contribution of recipes to the community's database. Ideally, core members would like a database that only contains self-concocted recipes, but this is hardly feasible given that most recipes are variations of existing ones. The next best thing is to submit only recipes that one has tried out and adjusted to her personal taste. Finally, if a recipe is copied from a cookbook or culinary magazine, core members agree that the source should be mentioned. However, the majority of recipes that are submitted do not apply to these standards. Especially, since the creation of a top 100 of most active recipe contributors, the quantity of submissions has increased (more than a thousand recipes per member is no exception), whereas the quality has decreased, because recipes are copied over and over again with only minor, or no, adjustments.

There is no policy regarding copying practices, and the administrators don't exert control over the submissions. Thus, it is up to the core members themselves to propagate their norm. Since many recipes are copied from within the community's database, they have a personal stake in this, namely to protect their own original submissions. The following quotes illustrate the various tactics that are used to set other members straight. The vocabulary reflects that emotions rise high.

> I think that copying a recipe from a cookbook is not as bad as copying-and-pasting each other's recipes. Stealing like this passes the limit (Mary); It is a scandal when members steal from one another. I mean when they steal recipes or even entire self-written articles (Linda); I especially cannot stand it when they copy each other's recipes and put them on their own personal SmulWeb page. If I encounter such a person I always send a message to those who submitted the recipe last and ask them if they knew that the recipe has already been submitted before (Patricia); For some time I have been busy tracking copies. There is only one word for people who copy entire websites – they are THIEVES (Harry); I think a scaffold [publicly announcing that a recipe has been copied] is a fair punishment and maybe the only thing that really works. Members who behave in this way do not deserve any protection, because they know that what they do is wrong, and it might serve as a warning for others (Rachel).

Members who have been the target of the rule enforcers refute:

> Only the SmulWeb administrator can oblige the members to mention the source of their recipes, not one or several other members. What happens now, checking recipes and leaving messages in guest books about so-called illegal copying of recipes, I really find offending (Helen); I think they have nothing better to do! Please, leave us alone (Ellen).

What happens here is a tribal fight over territory. The core members, who are highly involved in the community and its topic of interest, feel they can claim the terrain and define the rules. However, due to the expansion of the community, their sacred ground is invaded by other tribes that live by other rules. Being outnumbered by the others, the core group can do nothing but accept or leave. For the moment, they have mainly retreated to certain areas of the community. In the long run, they might leave altogether. One of the core members puts it into words like this:

> Of course all members may decide for themselves what to do with their membership: one likes to submit 5000 recipes, the other likes to

annoy the forum, again someone else likes to hip hop from one guest book to the other and leave a cute illustration. [. . .] I think everyone agrees that SmulWeb has defeated its object of being a good recipe database. It has become a chat box and website full of illustrations; the topic of cooking is trivial. Personally I don't like this development, but it offers a lot of entertainment and recreation to a lot of people. [. . .] If the ratio cooking versus other topics worsens, then I might leave the community. I won't just stay to participate in the forum [. . .]. The good contacts that I have built up within SmulWeb will continue to exist even when I am no longer a member (Rachel).

Clash of cultures

In this community of culinary lovers, most members agree that fresh produce is preferable over ready-made products. The pro-fresh norm is set by recurring statements that the preparation of fresh mayonnaise, soup, mashed potatoes, etc., is not difficult, and that the taste is so much better than that of the pre-processed variants. Although there is general agreement about the pro-fresh norm, members differ in their attitude towards ready-made products. Some forum discussants, who claim that they always prepare everything fresh, put on a strong anti-ready-made discourse. In their opinion, 'bon-vivants' and 'idealistic and passionate cooks' will never opt for ready-made products. This discourse evokes feelings of inferiority with those who do use pre-processed and canned foods. One of them states: 'I feel like the worst cook ever. I think I should start a homepage with the title culinary barbarian' (Sharon). The frustration of 'culinary barbarians' is illustrated by the following quotes:

I really don't believe that you always use fresh produce and nothing else. [. . .] I use canned foods and pre-processed products and that is considered by some a deadly sin (Nicole); I don't believe anything of these always-everything-fresh stories. [. . .] I don't use ready-made products regularly, but I shall never say NEVER (Rachel); I am honest: I also cook with ready-made mixes and I really don't know what is against it? Yes, of course I am also not highly talented in culinary matters (Sharon); But you are very honest, and honesty lasts. [. . .] Everyone uses canned foods and pre-processed products, but they are just afraid to admit it (Tony).

The accusation of dishonesty is further reflected in the vocabulary of members who 'dare to say' or 'dare to be open about' the fact that they use ready-made products.

Instead of a direct attack on the strong advocates of the pro-fresh norm, forum participants also put up resistance by justifying and contextualizing their usage of ready-made products. It is often mentioned that in today's households of busy kids and working parents, there is limited time and energy for cooking. One forum participant puts it like this: 'Preparing fresh mashed potatoes for a family of five is neither easy nor quick' (Rachel). In these cases, cans and mixes are seen as a 'solution'; they can be easily kept in storage and efficiently prepared, also by teenagers and less culinary skilled partners. Preparing everything fresh obviously requires not only time and energy, but also knowledge and skill as one participant acknowledges: 'I don't know on top of my head how I should prepare all the things that I buy in pre-processed form, like pesto and mayonnaise' (Mary). However, few admit outright that they lack expertise. Many participants present an image of themselves that implies they would make everything fresh, *only if* they had, for example, more time, or a kitchen large enough to store all the necessary equipment.

The debate about fresh versus ready-made products is in essence a debate between members with different lifestyles. In the first place, members differ in their level of culinary involvement. Statements such as: 'I do cook, but not wholeheartedly' (Neil), and 'I prefer eating over cooking!' (Amy) make clear that not all community members are passionate cooks. Some just like to talk about food, others are hobby chefs, but there are also members for whom cooking is like a religion, as expressed in the following quotes:

> I've always had an interest in cooking, but it has never become a fanatical hobby. [. . .] I simply don't have time, nor feel like spending half my days in the kitchen (Betty); It pisses me off when 'spending a lot of time in the kitchen' and 'always being a responsible cook' is beatified (Rachel); That's putting things on their heads. I put a lot a time and love into cooking and that's why I joined this community. I am a member of this community, because everything revolves around food or it should be like that. And to my delight, I do spend half the day in my kitchen (Brenda).

Not only differing levels of culinary involvement play a role in the tension between community members. Also their diverging background in terms of age, education, income, profession, and family situation cause conflict. This is exemplified in a discussion about nouvelle cuisine.[4] After a denigrating description of 'haute cuisine' by a forum participant, a nouvelle cuisine lover replies: 'I am fed up with this bullshitting about Nouvelle (not Haute) Cuisine. Everyone just

[4]Culinary philosophy dating back to eighteenth century France, revived and redefined in the 1970s. In 1973, Henri Gault wrote a manifesto summing up the 10 commandments of the nouvelle cuisine: (1) reduced cooking times, (2) new utilization of products, (3) reduction of choice on menus, (4) less use of refrigeration, (5) use of advanced technology, (6) ban on obsolete cooking principles, (7) banishment of brown and white sauces, (8) application of knowledge about dietetics, (9) aesthetic simplicity of presentation, and (10) invention. The movement attracted a lot of admirers, but also a lot of critics. The last group was specifically critical about the fashions, mannerisms, and trickery that also attached themselves to this movement: miniscule portions, systematic under cooking, inopportune marriages of sugar, salt, and spices, excessive decoration, and ridiculous names of dishes (Davidson, 1999).

points to the three peas instead of discussing the quality of the 100 g of fish or meat. Probably the quality is not recognized' (Alice). Another discussant adds that people who mention the three peas and tell the story about going to a snack bar afterwards obviously have never eaten in an exclusive restaurant. The reaction to this comment perfectly illustrates the perceived distinction: 'Well, I am just a simple farmer, who celebrates going to the McDonald's once a year. Excuse me for insulting the renowned Michelin star restaurant visitors!' (Brian).

The tension comes down to a distinction between forum participants who are able and willing to buy expensive (i.e., exclusive, high quality) products and ingredients, and the ones who cannot afford it, or who are not willing to pay more for products that have good enough, cheaper (ready-made) alternatives. Thus, it is a matter of differing affluence and preference. In the forum discussions, participants who buy expensive products and ingredients like to express their appreciation of the food they can prepare with it. This triggers perceptions of 'snobbism' and 'showing off' by the participants who do not buy expensive products and ingredients. Especially when discussants proclaim that they are passionate cooks *and* propagate expensive, high quality food as the only right choice, the other camp feels downgraded and excluded. One discussant voices her frustration about this in the following way:

> Sometimes I feel I don't belong here. I get the feeling that people want to outdo each other. When I read how easily people talk about buying things and preparing food and showing how good he or she is . . . bah. In the beginning I really looked up to the SmulWeb members and I thought 'well, these are all very elite people', but by now I think they behave like that, in the end they are ordinary people as well. I would like to have a peek in their lives to see how it really is (Sharon).

Celebrating similarities

The three axes of tensions that have been highlighted in the previous paragraphs suggest that the virtual community under study is full of competition, debate, and contrasts. However, despite the many differences between the members, there are also important similarities that result in feelings of commonality. Many discussion threads are joyful accounts of recognition and identification with respect to cooking and eating habits. These discussions often refer to the past; participants recount, for example, how they learned to cook. By exchanging stories about first cooking experiences and culinary tutors, the forum participants heighten their sense of similarity and community. These stories function as signs of a shared initiation ritual that has been the starting point for an increasing interest in culinary matters, and that has eventually resulted in membership of the same community. In a similar vein, forum participants share stories about the excellent cooking qualities of their (grand-) children, who have taken after them with respect to their interest in culinary matters. Also these narratives function as community builders.

By representing culinary interest as a quality that is inherited, the discussants portray an ongoing life cycle that secures the continuous existence of the community: they share an interest and passion not only with each other, but also with cooks of the past and the future.

Constructing a shared past and future that reinforces community spirit is one way to overcome nowadays' personal and situational differences, confessing secret passions is another. Community members are united in their love for food. In celebrating this similarity, forum participants go as far as engaging in self-disclosures about behaviour that they probably hide from others, that is, they tell each other about how and when they indulge in eating. In western society this kind of behaviour is often stigmatized; if you cannot control your food intake you are presumed to have an eating disorder or an addiction. Thus, within the community, feelings of delight for indulging in eating exist next to feelings of guilt. The fact that they are 'amongst each other', however, induces many happy exchanges of secret passions: snacking at night is one example.

> It is not that I wake up at night and engage in indecencies, but eating late at night and then really gross, yes, that I do. Just now, 1.30 A.M., I have ripped open the filet américain and ate it with sweet-and-sour (Kevin); I am often awake at night for my work and sometimes I get a real hunger attack. Then I stuff myself with everything I can lay my hands on (Tony); We call it the kick of a voracious appetite and if it happens at night I just dive into the kitchen. It doesn't happen too often, but if it does we don't shun a large steak with mushroom sauce (Susan); I always have sea-snails in the freezer and I love to eat them at night when I yearn for some food (Brenda); I just satisfied my night hunger with a pile of macaroons, and my all time favorite cheese for at night is farmers' cheese with holes in it (Emma).

Discussion

In contrast to the many accounts exemplifying the positive characteristics of virtual communities (i.e., strong member ties, mutual support, unifying rituals, shared meanings and practices, etc.), this chapter has shown that this is but one side of the story. The other side tells of competition, conflict, and clashes. Virtual communities that are organized around broadly defined consumption activities do not form one 'happy family'. Although united at one level in their interest for the consumption activity, community members vary greatly in their passion, preferences, and practices. This leads to the formation of tribes that each have their own totem within the community.

The obvious implication for marketers is that the community does not form one single homogeneous target group, but that it can be segmented into multitudes of subgroups or 'tasteworlds' (Kozinets, 1999, p. 258). The difficulty here is that these segments are not stable. In line with the realm of thoughts of the neo-tribalists, community members constantly reorganize themselves into tribes that can be delineated by topic or taste, but also by 'good old-fashioned' consumer characteristics. The formation and reorganization of tribes is expressed by means of discourse. Thus, depending on the topic of discussion, community members belong to one tribe or the other. The fact that these tribes are no stable, clear-cut segments also explains why virtual communities more frequently have to cope with warfare instead of split-offs; members that strongly agree on one level might fiercely dispute on another, making the axes of schism less apparent.

Although this virtual tribalism complicates the marketer's job, it also aids it. Groups of people tend to define themselves most strongly opposite to other groups: 'we are what they are not, and vice versa' (cf. Bourdieu, 1979). This explains the recent interest of consumer researchers for inter-tribal conflicts (e.g., Hickman and Ward, 2007). These conflicts contain a wealth of information about the value systems that drive consumer behaviour (cf. Thompson and Troester, 2002), because it is specifically when community members are faced with competition about what is the 'right' or 'ultimate' norm, that they pronounce these (differing) value systems most articulately. The analysis of conflicts *between* tribes, thus, is relevant to gain a sharper insight in the particularities of the shared consumption meanings and practices that bind a community and set it apart from others. However, conflicts *within* tribes reveal the dynamics by which shared consumption meanings and practices are defined: they reveal which meanings and practices are really shared, which simply co-exist, and which are actually disputed, thus helping the marketer to better define the nuances of communal relationships.

For community members, intra-tribal conflicts function as social and identity markers on two levels: (1) the compound of the virtual community, and (2) the larger context of real life (RL) society. Within the first, members need to determine where they stand relative to the other members with regard to their expertise about the community's topic of interest, as well as their objective and orientation of participation (i.e., informational, recreational, relational, or transformational – Kozinets, 1999). Based on the outcome of the assessment, they develop a set of roles and a network of interpersonal attraction, which serves to differentiate them from 'the others' within the community (cf. Hare, 1962). As we have seen in the SmulWeb case, community members compete with each other on a personal level over who is the ultimate expert. In a community of over 160,000 members, and a core group of 100–200 members, it is difficult to claim that position. To differentiate themselves from each other, many community members put forward one particular aspect of their expertise that makes them stand out (e.g., hands-on knowledge about a rare regional cuisine, in-depth knowledge about the million variations of one specific dish). On a group level, community members divide themselves in an endless number of tribes (e.g., core versus periphery, ready-made versus fresh), because allies will help them to accomplish their individual and sub-group goals (e.g., 'freeing' the community of non-original recipes, or convincing oneself that serving pasta with a ready-made sauce is not detrimental to your health).

Community members also need to determine where they stand relative to the other members with regard to RL characteristics (demographics, socio-economic profile) that play an important role in interactional processes. Virtual communities represent a unique form of consumer networks, because of the heterogeneity of their member databases. Within SmulWeb, we find a large variety of members that diverge in terms of age, education, income, national-ity, household and professional situation, living standards, etc. In a RL culinary community, for example, a cooking club, culinary society, or wine course, it is not likely that people from such diverging backgrounds would come together due to geographical, practical and ideological barriers. These differences are the cause of tensions and conflict. However, they are also the motor of the com-munity's interaction processes. By describing and explaining their motivations and behaviour, consumers actively learn from and influence each other. In this respect, it is noteworthy that participants in the offline community gatherings diverged little in background. Presumably, barriers of social status (education, income, etc.) that only pop up in the online community when certain topics are discussed, become too apparent and insurmountable when people meet offline. Online tensions might rise high, but community members find ways to strike a balance by alternating negotiations and fights with celebrations of their similarity: interest in the general topic. The relative anonymity of the computer-mediated environment, and the fact that members can leave the community whenever they want, contributes to an open atmosphere that even results in confessions and disclosures about behaviour that is normally hidden from public scrutiny. In RL, people tend to uphold their decorum; online, amongst people that share and understand their passions, members let go of this decorum and bond with each other by confiding secret habits and rituals.

Marketers that want to exploit virtual communities as management tools need to deal with the dynamics of conflict and communal consumption. As much as members' 'togetherness', conflict needs to be accepted as an inherent part of community life. In the end, marketers will find shared practices and consumption meanings are as informative as the ones that are internally dis-puted when it comes to discovering new market opportunities, ideas for prod-uct innovation, and positioning and communication strategies (cf. Kozinets, 1999). However, community managers should also guard against too much conflict. Warfare that lasts too long and that puts too much stress on members' differences might undermine the community spirit. The solution to temper online conflicts should not so much be sought in establishing a polity system as in RL society, although communities can benefit from a clear code of con-duct and its enforcement. Instead, managers should benefit from the fact that cyberspace can be easily extended with the addition of a server. It is import-ant to allow members to form subgroups around preferred 'totems' in separ-ate 'territories' within the community platform, so as to avoid split-offs that will end informational and influential tribe-to-tribe interactions. Such places of retreat are not only beneficial to calm heated war spirits, but in the end they might also serve as the ready-made target tribes that a lot of marketers were looking for in the first place!

References

Alon, A., Brunel. F. and Schneier Siegal, W. (2005). Ritual behavior and community life-cycle: exploring the social psychological roles of net rituals in the development of online consumption communities, in Haugtvedt, C.P. Machleit, K. and Yalch, R. (eds.), *Online Consumer Psychology: Understanding How to Interact with Consumer in the Virtual World*. Hillsdale, NJ: Erlbaum.

Bagozzi, R.P. and Dholakia, U.M. (2002). Intentional social action in virtual communities, *Journal of Interactive Marketing*, **16** (2), 2–21.

Bourdieu, P. (1996 [1979]). *Distinction: A Social Critique of the Judgment of Taste*, trans. by Nice, R. Cambridge, MA: Harvard University Press.

Celsi, R.L., Rose, R.L. and Leigh, Th.W. (1993). An exploration of high-risk leisure consumption through skydiving, *Journal of Consumer Research*, **20** (June), 1–23.

Cova, B. and Cova, V. (2002). Tribal marketing: the tribalisation of society and its impact on the conduct of marketing, *European Journal of Marketing*, **36** (5/6), 595–620.

Davidson, A. (1999). *The Oxford Companion to Food*. Oxford: Oxford University Press.

Dichter, E. (1966). How word-of-mouth advertising works, *Harvard Business Review*, November–December: 147–166.

Fernback, J. and Thompson, B. (1999). Virtual communities: abort, retry, failure?, Available online: http://www.well.com/user/hlr/texts/Vccivil. html

Fitzgerald Bone, P. (1992). Determinants of word-of-mouth communications during product consumption, in Sherry, J.F. and Sternthal, B. (eds.), *Advances in Consumer Research*, 19. Provo, UT: Association for Consumer Research, pp. 579–583.

Glaser, B.G. and Strauss, A.L. (1967). *The Discovery of Grounded Theory*. Chicago, IL: Aldine.

Hare, P.A. (1962). *Handbook of Small Group Research*. New York, NJ: Free Press of Glencoe.

Harrison, T. and Jenkins, H. (1996). Appendix A: interview with Henry Jenkins, in Harrison, T. (ed.), *Enterprise Zone*. Boulder, CO: Westview, pp. 259–278.

Hickman, T. and Ward, J. (2007). The dark side of brand community: intergroup stereotyping, trash talk, and schadenfreude, in Fitzsimons, G.J. and Morwitz, V.G. (eds.), *Advances in Consumer Research*, 34. Provo, UT: Association for Consumer Research.

Kozinets, R.V. (1999). E-tribalized marketing?: the strategic implications of virtual communities of consumption, *European Management Journal*, **17** (3), 252–264.

Kozinets, R.V. (2001). Utopian enterprise: articulating the meanings of Star Trek's culture of consumption, *Journal of Consumer Research*, **28** (June), 67–88.

Kozinets, R.V. (2002). The field behind the screen: using netnography for marketing research in online communities, *Journal of Marketing Research*, **39** (February), 61–72.

Maffesoli, M. (1995). *The Time of the Tribes: The Decline of Individualism in Mass Society*. London: Sage Publications.

McAlexander, J.H., Schouten, J.W. and Koenig, H.F. (2002). Building brand community, *Journal of Marketing*, **66** (January), 38–54.

Muñiz Jr., A.M. and O'Guinn, Th.C. (2001). Brand community, *Journal of Consumer Research*, **27** (March), 412–432.

Muñiz Jr., A.M. and Schau, H.J. (2005). Religiosity in the abandoned Apple Newton brand community, *Journal of Consumer Research*, **31** (March), 737–747.

Parsons, T. and Shils, E.A. (1951). *Toward a General Theory of Action*. Cambridge, MA: Harvard University Press.

Perdue, W.D. (1986). *Sociological Theory: Explanation, Paradigm, and Ideology*. Palo Alto, CA: Mayfield Publishing Company.

Schouten, J.W. and McAlexander, J.H. (1995). Subcultures of consumption: an ethnography of the new bikers, *Journal of Consumer Research*, **22** (June), 43–61.

Spiggle, S. (1994). Analysis and interpretation of qualitative data in consumer research, *Journal of Consumer Research*, **21** (December), 491–503.

Thompson, C.J. (1997). Interpreting consumers: a hermeneutical framework for deriving marketing insights from the texts' of consumers' consumption stories, *Journal of Marketing Research*, **34** (November), 438–455.

Thompson, C.J. and Troester, M. (2002). Consumer value systems in the age of postmodern fragmentation: the case of the natural health microculture, *Journal of Consumer Research*, **28** (March), 550–571.

Walther, J.B. (1995). Relational aspects of computer-mediated communication: experimental observations over time, *Organization Science*, **6**, 186–203.

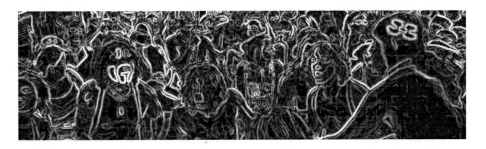

18

Brand communities and their social antagonists: insights from the Hummer case

Marius K. Luedicke and Markus Giesler

A brand community constitutes a form of postmodern tribe that connects consumers on the basis of a trademark. These 'structured sets of social relations among admirers of a brand' (Muñiz and O'Guinn, 2001, p. 412) inspire consumer culture theorists for theoretical exploration as much as marketing practitioners for financial exploitation. While marketing managers are collecting experiences on how to influence the initiation and ideological configuration of 'their' brand communities, researchers are investigating the social fabric of 'Gemeinschaften' (Tönnies, 1957) such as subcultures of consumption (e.g., Schouten and McAlexander, 1995), brand communities (e.g., Muñiz and O'Guinn, 2001), or postmodern tribes which consume (e.g., Cova, 2003) that evolve, for instance, around brands of vehicles, technology products, celebrities, sports or television shows. Following Schouten's and McAlexander's (1995) groundbreaking ethnography of the Harley-Davidson subculture, consumer culture theorists have elicited numerous influences of brand-related social groupings on individual and communal identity projects (Arnould and Price, 1993;

Belk, 1988; Elliott and Wattanasuwan, 1998; Holt, 2002; Peñaloza, 2001) including social distinctiveness (Schouten and McAlexander, 1995), socioeconomic refuge (Kozinets, 2001), brand-related spiritualism (Muñiz and Schau, 2005; Schouten and McAlexander, 1995), shared risk (Celsi, Rose, and Leigh, 1993), and family ties (Arnould and Price, 1993; Moisio, Arnould, and Price, 2004).

As these insightful studies were exclusively concerned with illuminating the inside structures of various forms of consumption-centred tribes (Maffesoli, 1996), they have largely remained silent on the role of involved, proactive social environments that irritate and inspire these social formations from outside their boundaries. Salient exceptions from the typical marginalization of these influences are Muñiz and O'Guinn's concept of 'oppositional brand loyalty' (p. 420) that describes a powerful social mechanism that leverages consciousness of kind through definition of a commonly rejected brand, and Kozinets' use of 'stigma' (2001, pp. 73ff) that explains the relationship-deepening defamation of devoted fans of the *Star Trek* television series by advocates of the mainstream.

Our research seeks to enhance existing knowledge on the boundary conditions of brand communities by asking whether and to what extent proactive social environments matter for brand communities. To this end, we sought an extreme context of study that would be expected to reveal a broader range of distinctions and practices than an 'ordinary' brand community. We identified and consequentially studied community surrounding the Hummer brand of vehicles, a brand that is uniquely situated within an emotionally supercharged context of cultural, legal, economic, ecological and social imbalances. As this explosive combination evokes unprecedented emotional outbursts and practices among Hummer owners and their antagonists, it nicely illuminates the extreme forms of outside community influence. In order to better understand their mutual irritations, we employed a blend of ethnographic and netnographic methods to create a multi-perspective account of the ideologies, communications, and behaviours of both community members and antagonists.

The subsequent report on this research is organized as follows. First, we introduce the analytical framework that we have used instead of classic sociological perspectives for observing brand communities as distinctive, dependent, and ephemeral social systems. Next, we explain our research method and define the character of the Hummer brand and the related communities that constitute our empirical context of study. Then, we show and discuss the Hummer brand community's means of distinction, reproduction, and reflection that emerged from our data. We conclude the chapter with answers to our research question and suggest implications for consumer culture theory on marketplace cultures (Arnould and Thompson, 2005).

Analytical framework

A 'brand community' as introduced by Muñiz and O'Guinn (2001) is a 'specialized, non-geographically bound community, [that is] based on a structured set of social relations among admirers of a brand' (p. 412). A 'postmodern tribe' (Maffesoli, 1988) or 'tribe which consumes' (Cova and Cova, 2001), instead, is 'a group of individuals who are not necessarily homogenous (in terms of objective social characteristics), but are inter-linked by the same subjectivity, the same emotions ("affectual tribes") and capable of taking collective action, short lived but intense' (Cova, 2003). Whereas both constructs are concerned with theorizing 'Gemeinschaft' (Tönnies, 1926), brand community is the more exclusive concept. Accepting a postmodern condition (Firat and Venkatesh, 1995) and a neo-archaic, affectual re-tribalization of contemporary Western societies (Maffesoli, 1988, 1996), we appreciate brand communities as specific forms of tribes that connect people deeply, enduringly, and rationally through continued communal consumption of trademarked products (cf. Cova and Cova, 2002; Kozinets, 1999).

Three properties conceptually constitute a brand community (Muñiz and O'Guinn, 2001): *Consciousness of kind* (Gusfield, 1975) embraces intrinsic connections felt among members (Tönnies, 1957; Weber, 1922) and an internal 'collective sense of difference from others not in the community' (Muñiz and O'Guinn, 2001, p. 413). *Rituals and traditions* 'perpetuate the community's shared history, culture, and consciousness' (p. 413) through celebrations of the brand's history, sharing of stories, and symbolic behaviours (McCracken, 1986). A *'sense of duty or obligation* to the community as a whole, and to its individual members' (Muñiz and O'Guinn, 2001, p. 413, italics added) ensures community coherence and the integration of new members.

These 'core community communalities' (ibid.) provide a useful framework for understanding some of the key coherence mechanisms of brand communities. Yet, at the same time, they conceptually factor out the outside catalysts that may speak to, influence, and even provoke the community. For the purpose of better understanding the dialectical processes among brand community members and their proactive social antagonists, we thus require two key conceptual shifts: First, to move the classical conceptual focus away from analysing communalities towards scrutinizing distinctions. Second and consequentially, to turn away from single-perspective ethnographic accounts towards a multi-perspective study which also includes the ideologies and practices of non-owners, antagonists, and others in the social environment of the community.

The notion of 'distinction' that we turn our attention to has widely been used in sociology for conceptualizing relations of socioeconomic class (Weber, 1962), taste (Bourdieu, 1984), or complexity (Simmel, 1890). Only recently have sociologists borrowed from research on cybernetics (von Foerster, 1979), math (Spencer-Brown, [1969] 1999), and cognitive psychology (Maturana, [1974] 1999, 1987; Varela, 1979) to better anchor functional differentiation theories of society (Luhmann, 1995; Parsons, 1971). Adopting a radical constructivist epistemological view, the above researchers came to accept that not only psychic and organic systems, but also self-referential social systems sustain themselves on the basis of culturally resonant distinctions (Giesler, 2003). Applying these insights to the study of brand communities, we conceptualize communities as matrices of multi-faceted, meaningful distinctions that are perpetually co-created, interpreted, and negotiated among people with the brand as an anchor for community and controversy.

In sum, this framework of analysis inspires for studying brand communities as distinctive, dynamic, socially embedded phenomena and opens up for including outside realities into the focus of research. With this concept in mind we next approach the following empirical context.

The Hummer case

Source: Own illustration.

The Hummer brand marks a class of sport utility vehicles by General Motors that has inherited its aesthetics and functions from the AM General army truck 'High Mobility Multi-Purpose Wheeled Vehicle,' short 'HUMVEE'. Mostly national television reports of the gulf and Iraq wars showing soldiers driving or some even losing their lives in Humvees, brought fame to the brand as an national icon for military and patriotic achievement. Inspired by Arnold Schwarzenegger, AM General introduced a civilian version of the Humvee under the name of 'HUMMER' the distinguished rugged appearance of which quickly became favoured by affluent movie and sports celebrities. Inspired by the unique vehicle and again by Arnold Schwarzenegger who drove up at the Golden Globe awards in the first civilian Hummer ever built, General Motors bought the Hummer brand in 1999 and soon after introduced the 'HUMMER H2' sport utility vehicle. The vehicle shown in the picture above became one of the most controversial vehicles in the US. The extravagant, sporty, aggressive looking, and fuel-inefficient luxury truck was more affordable and visible on North American roads than the AM General Hummer. Due to its high raised front bumpers, the limited rear view, its poor gas mileage, and a tax loophole that allowed business owners to deduct the vehicle from their taxes, the Hummer H2 inspired unprecedented amounts of social noise among the North American public. It attracted fascination, longing, and sympathy as much as open conflict, insults, and violence among owners and non-owners.

The spectrum of social forms around the Hummer brand reaches from core brand community members over the large general public to proactive Hummer haters. Hummer enthusiasts join a great variety of independent local and national Hummer Clubs. The largest of this kind and the only GM-accredited formal community is 'The Hummer Club Inc.', a privately governed non-profit organization the goal of which is 'to promote the safe use and enjoyment of Hummer vehicles in a family-oriented atmosphere; promote information exchange among members (. . .) hold and sponsor events (. . .) encourage land use consistent with the guidelines set forth by the Treat Lightly! organization (. . .)' (Hummer Club Inc. website, http://www.thehummerclubinc.com [2006/10/2006]).

In the middle of the spectrum, the majority of North Americans admire the brand and envy owners, are indifferent towards it, or perceive the vehicles and their owners as distasteful, irresponsible, or ridiculous people.

At the core antagonists' side, we find communal activity but not a full-blown Anti-Hummer community (cf. Thompson and Arsel, 2004). These antagonist communal forms include, for instance, the popular website http://www.fuh2.com that was listed second by google.com under the keyword 'hummer h2' and in October 2006 held more than 3,600 pictures of consumers exposing their middle fingers to Hummer vehicles all over the planet, and the female activist organization 'Code Pink: Women for peace' that organizes anti-Hummer demonstrations and offers Hummer protest material on its website.

To obtain a tenable idea of the central discourses that evolve around the brand, we sought to create an account of the Hummer owners' community and the relevant social environments that largely contribute to Hummer brand meaning in various unique ways. We used a combination of phenomenological interviews (Thompson, 1997), netnographic data (Kozinets, 2002), and archival data. In detail, we first searched the Internet for relevant information such as Hummer fan- and hate-pages, web-logs, owners clubs, online discussion forums, mailing lists, news reports and corporate commercials. We then conducted phenomenological interviews of 50–150 min in length, each with five key protagonists and antagonists of the community, including AM General marketing staff, two highly involved members of The Hummer Club Inc. (one male, one female), a leading web forum contributor, and the owner and webmaster of the Hummer hate page www.fuh2.com (email interview). In parallel, we studied the less involved public meanings of the brand by interviewing visitors to the 2005 North American Auto Show in Detroit. Twenty-three interviews of 15–25 min in length were conducted with 48 people of

Asian-American, African-American, and Caucasian origin. The sample included 34 male and 14 female informants, five of which were adolescents. Respondents were asked about their opinions, feelings, particular relationships and communicative contributions to the HUMMER brand. About half of our respondents tended towards disliking the vehicle, whereas the other half rather admired the brand. All persons that we interviewed had seen or even driven a Hummer prior to the Auto Show. The archival data that we used included, among other things, two monographs on Hummer as well as frequent newspaper reports, magazine articles and television appearances. Throughout the entire project, a research homepage provided a virtual home for the research that offered a project overview, participant legal information, web links, guestbook, and the researcher's contact information. In the next section, we present empirical evidence of the relationships among Hummer owners and their social counterparts.

Empirical evidence

> At HUMMER our customers can't be labelled by colour, gender or creed. HUMMER is a mindset. A mindset of daring, self-assured, entrepreneurial people who see HUMMER as being a reflection of themselves – unique.
>
> (Randall Foutch, GM)[1]

> The [HUMMER] H2 is the ultimate poseur vehicle. It has the chassis of a Chevy Tahoe and a body that looks like the original Hummer; that is it's a Chevy Tahoe in disguise. The H2 is a gas guzzler. Because it has a gross vehicle weight rating over 8,500 lbs, the US government does not require it to meet federal fuel efficiency regulations. Hummer isn't even required to publish its fuel economy (owners indicate that they get around 10 mpg for normal use). So while our brothers and sisters are off in the Middle East risking their lives to secure America's fossil fuel future, H2 drivers are pissing away our 'spoils of victory' during each trip to the grocery store.
>
> (Jason, none, forum)[2]

These key statements of GM employee Randall Foutch and Hummer opponent Jason amply illustrate that the Hummer brand community evolves around

---

[1] Except for official corporate statements and news reports, the identities of the informants of this study have been concealed to protect privacy. The brackets behind the quotes – for example (Susan, H1, email) inform about the informant possessing an H1, an H2, both and H1 and H2, no Hummer, or that ownership status is unknown to the authors. The data source includes web, forum, interview, and email.

[2] All informant quotes in this chapter are cited in original idiom, including spelling and grammar. Where necessary, clarifications have been added in rectangular brackets.

an extraordinarily distinct and controversial consumer product. The adapted war vehicle Hummer H1 and the redesigned sport utility vehicle Hummer H2 are appreciated for their safety, capability and physical appearance, whereas opponents criticize those same properties as dangerous, ecologically irresponsible, and intimidating. Some supporters of the brand communicate their admiration of the 'King of off-road' (Tim, n/a, forum) in various personal and mediated forms, whereas some critics voice their dislike in online forums, public demonstrations, driver affronts, or even vandalism.

In our study, 'Hummer brand community' includes people who communicate about and socialize around their consumption of Hummer products, whereas 'social environments' means owners who do not socialize, General Motors' marketing professionals, the media, the anonymous uninvolved social observers and the various Hummer antagonists. However, of key interest to our study are the discourses among the core community members and the most devoted Hummer antagonists as they best reveal how a brand community differentiates, why it attracts opposition, and if and how extensive protest influences the community. Using micro-level data within the above conceptual framework, this section first delves into the functional, aesthetic, political, and social distinctions that the community uses for differentiation. Then it demonstrates the ways in which the community reproduces itself within its social environments. Finally and most importantly, it unveils the key coping and reflection strategies emergent in the community.

Distinction

Hummers are advertised by General Motors as being 'like nothing else'. There is no doubt among the informants of this study that this is true, yet, for diametrically opposite reasons. This section examines how the Hummer brand and the systems of meaning that evolve around it differentiate in the societal context by illuminating the functional, aesthetic, political, and social distinctions that are perpetuated by owners and non-owners of the brand.

Functional distinctions

Functional distinctions are concerned with the physical utility of Hummer products. For the Hummer brand community and its environments, the distinctions between safety and threat as well as capability and subordination are predominant. Hummer drivers are convinced they possess the safest consumer vehicle on North American roads. This belief is equally inspired by size and weight as well as by the presumed capabilities of the vehicles. Although most Hummer owners have never got 'off Highway 101 and (. . .) over Mount Tam' (sfgate.com, 12/29/2002), trust in these characteristics is nevertheless frequently articulated. Hummers are, for instance, considered to be a 'family insurance policy' (ibid.) or even a must for any responsible head of the family.

Consider the statement of Hummer role model Arnold Schwarzenegger, who owns several H1 and H2 vehicles:

> I want a big SUV because I have four children and to protect the family.
>
> (A. Schwarzenegger, cited at CNN.com, 22 September 2003)

For non-owners, however, this feeling of safety turns into a feeling of threat, as road safety is perceived as relative. H2-owners Ray and Stephen, who drove H1s in the Army, provide reasons for these feelings:

> Id rather be the one that survives the impact with the small car then the poor schmuck treehugger that i run over. Id rather pay the money for the gas then have to worry about some dumbass in a rice rocket blowing through a light and hitting me in the side.
>
> (Ray, H2, forum)

> If you are driving a big truck and got this little Honda civic ahead of you, your first thought is: I am just gonna run him over.
>
> (Stephen, none, interview)

The other central functional distinction separates capability from subordination. At the national events of The Hummer Club Inc., the off-road capability of both H1 and H2 vehicles is frequently contested and celebrated. Among the members of the Hummer brand community there is little doubt about the superior capability of Hummers. In the urban realm, capability, and dominance materialize quite differently. Owners such as Brian contribute tales of heroic potency that are readily confirmed and criticized by outside contributors such as Jason:

> This weekend will be taking the H2 out to the sticks [. . .] to get some peace and quiet away from the city and all those tiny, wimpy vehicles that are always getting stuck in my grill and between the little groves in my tires.
>
> (Brian, H2, web)

> The H2 is a death machine. You'd better hope that you don't collide with an H2 in your economy car. You can kiss your ass goodbye thanks to the H2's massive weight and raised bumpers. Too bad you couldn't afford an urban assault vehicle of your own.
>
> (Jason, none, forum)

Aesthetic distinctions

Aesthetic distinctions are concerned with the appeal of the products to the human senses (cf. Postrel, 2003). The central aesthetic differences cover the range from fascination to intimidation. Surprisingly, the data unveiled that, although about half of the informants largely reject Hummers, they are nonetheless intrigued by the vehicles' bold aesthetics. Marc, who has driven a

Hummer once, argues against the vehicle, but with his body language and the way in which he reports on his experience he still cannot conceal his fascination with the H2 over the course of the interview:

> I've driven one, I don't like it. It's too big. It is very intimidating for people in front of you if you come up very high on behind, they scatter. [Feels like you are saying.] Get the hell out of the way.
>
> (Marc, none, interview)

Hummer owners agree that the public feedback they receive on the looks of their vehicles is '99 per cent positive' (Peter, H2, interview). Our Detroit sample, however, shows that the percentage of people saying that they dislike the vehicles is dramatically lower. In the following quote, Jonathan reports on the conspicuousness of the products as positive, whereas Nathalie expresses her negative feelings of intimidation and fear, both of which are central to the appeal of Hummers:

> We get waved to by children like we are driving a fire truck. People are constantly asking us to sit in, look in & even feel it.
>
> (Jonathan, H2, email)

> It's a very intimidating looking vehicle. It's just the size and shape of the vehicle.
>
> (Nathalie, none, interview)

Political distinctions

Political distinctions mark Hummer-related communications that revolve around the prevailing distinction of freedom versus responsibility. Occasionally, the Hummer brand community gets involved in political discourses. When it comes to justifying purchases, owners refer, for instance, to liberal ideals and the dictum of free economic choice. Consider Rick's typical statement:

> The good thing about marketing economy is that you can vote with your dollars and if I choose to purchase a vehicle that is less efficient . . . that is my choice.
>
> (Rick, none, interview)

Opponents vehemently condemn opinions such as the above for ignoring the environmental and social effects of such a consumption choice. In web forum discussions, participants draw on cultural resources such as American patriotism, national pride, political and local affiliations, job and literacy hierarchies, gender differences, and even the Iraq Wars to support their arguments. Political statements that refer to excessive gas consumption in times of controversial US engagements in oil-producing eastern countries include: 'Driving a Gas Guzzler is not patriotic,' 'I drive a. . . WEAPON OF MASS CONSUMPTION' (bumper sticker), or 'Soldiers die in their HUMMERS, so you can play Soldier too!' (demonstration billboard) (Authors unknown, n/a, web).

Social distinctions

Social distinctions, as they are noticed and enjoyed by many Hummer drivers, are deeply embedded in various societal discourses, and continuously fueled by numerous contributors. Outside informants Rick and Nathalie, for instance, summarize the two primary social effects of Hummers as 'consumption symbols' (Belk, 1988, p. 152):

> Like it or hate it, it gets you noticed.
>
> (Rick, none, interview)

> If you see a HUMMER, you automatically don't think of a lower class individual.
>
> (Nathalie, none, interview)

In addition to the symbolic effects of perceived functional superiority, aesthetic extravagance, and political affiliation, Hummer vehicles are culturally associated with American cultural stereotypes of masculinity, athleticism and economic success.[3] These associations are largely fueled by the archaic military heritage of the vehicles, the number and presence of athletes and movie stars conspicuously consuming Hummers (about 60 celebrities were known in 2005 for driving Hummers), and the above-average prices of the products.[4] Arnold Schwarzenegger, the most famous member of the Hummer brand community, personifies for most informants the social distinctions of the brand. As Nathalie summarizes: '[I can] picture him being the Terminator coming out of the HUMMER. Totally see those two together' (none, interview).

The Hummer brand community uses these social distinctions extensively. Tom (H2, web), for instance, impresses potential real estate customers with his H2; the tall blonde H1 driver Susan irritates men ('women will drive by and give me a thumbs up, and guys will mumble and say grrrr, it's a women driving a HUMMER!' (Susan, H1, interview)); Peter (H2, interview) enjoys the attention ('Every time we drive out on the streets we turn heads.'); and Ronny simply likes to show off ('I like taking the kids and wife places and park up front so everyone can see!! That's the best part is when other kids look and hit there moms and dads and say look!! My kids like it tooo!!' (Ronny, H2, web)).

---

[3] For an account of the underlying American ideology of manhood see Holt and Thompson (2002).

[4] HUMMER H1 vehicles start at $112,000. H2s begin at $55,000.

While especially the adolescent informants of this study largely support and enjoy the feeling of social superiority, critics confront the owners with rationalized arguments:

> According to Bradsher, internal industry market research concluded that S.U.V.s tend to be bought by people who are insecure, vain, self-centered, and self-absorbed, who are frequently nervous about their marriages, and who lack confidence in their driving skills.
>
> (Malcom Gladwell, www.gladwell.com)

The importance of social distinctiveness is perceived differently among the Hummer brand community and the less involved, less communally oriented owners. The urban H2-fractions of the Hummer brand community cherish the showiness and social attention as key characteristics of the brand. The core members of the Hummer Club Inc., instead, seem to be more attracted by the vehicle's off-road capability and the family and fun orientation of the club. However, independent of individual attitudes the above particularities of the Hummer brand inspire social environments to pay attention and feed their opinions back to the community.

Reproduction

The interpretive framework of this study conceptualizes the aesthetic, political, and social distinctions of the Hummer brand community as socially constructed through ongoing discourses. This section details the Hummer brand community's particular communicative means for developing and reproducing these distinctions. Attention is focused on communication and interaction between community protagonists as well as communication and interaction with the social environments.

Among its members, the Hummer brand community employs personal forms of communication, such as club events and mediated ones, such as club magazines, web pages, mailing lists and online forums. Members of The Hummer Club Inc., for instance, meet for the 'Chile Challenge' or the 'Death Valley HUMMER Happening' to pursue and share their off-road passion with other members. This is where Muñiz and O'Guinn's (2001) core community communalities can be observed most readily. As social relationships are the core constituent of the Hummer brand community, these events play an important role for reproducing and updating shared meaning, for retaining old members, attracting new ones, and deepening social ties among owners, spouses, friends, children, club board members, representatives of the manufacturers, and guests (cf. McAlexander, Schouten, and Koenig, 2002; Muñiz and O'Guinn, 2001; Schouten and McAlexander, 1995). In the online realm, sharing knowledge about parts, repairs, tuning, events and off-road tips are predominant communications. Glorious roadside stories that are shared over the Internet contribute to the reproduction of the perceived capability and superiority of the Hummer vehicles.

Communicating distinctiveness to the social environments is equally central for the Hummer brand community. Aside from corporate advertising for the vehicles, Hummers have attracted extensive media attention. As of early 2005, Hummer vehicles have been featured in at about 60 movies (e.g., Gone in 60 s), 13 music videos (e.g., Britney Spears in a pink H2), 40 TV-shows (e.g., CSI: Miami), 12 video games (e.g., Area 51), 6 books (e.g., Padgett, 2004) and 12 non-GM commercials (e.g., McDonalds). With the exception of the Britney Spears video, these contributions to the Hummer discourse helped sharpening Hummer as distinct, sporty, aggressive, testosterone brand. Community protagonists also personally engage in reproducing a positive image of the Hummer brand community. Two varieties of individual contribution are predominant in our data, compensation and exploitation. Being concerned with compensating negative outside images, protagonists highlight the Hummer brand community's positive ethics and social responsibility by using, for instance, the distinctiveness of and fascination with Hummer to support their local communities. The Rocky Mountain News reports:

> Volunteers wearing Santa hats with 'H2' stitched on them smiled as they drove through Medved's Wheat Ridge service center to load trunks with toys [that were later given out to needy children].
> (Jennifer Miller, Rocky Mountain News, 20 December 2004)

Similarly, GM and The Hummer Club Inc. use the vehicles' distinctive features to promote initiatives such as 'stars after school,' the environmental organization 'Tread Lightly!' and the 'Sierra Club'.

Consumers such as Ronny, on the other hand, are instead mainly interested in conspicuously exploiting the physical and social features of the Hummer brand to support their individual identity projects. Following Arnold Schwarzenegger, who is quoted saying 'I needed a vehicle that matched the expressiveness of my personality' (Padgett, 2004, p. 91), many Hummer owners show off their vehicles to reflect the style and meaning of their possessions onto themselves (Belk, 1988; Holt, 2002). The Hummer brand community can leverage these efforts, for instance, by offering gatherings in public places. Consider this invitation of the H2 Club Chapter New York:

> East Coast Dinner at NY TIMES SQUARE . . . 43rd & 44th @ ABC Studios Bldg. Time: 6:30 pm, Trucks from all over are welcome. With the approval of the NYPD, we're going meet at NY Times Square at 6:30 sharp to meet, compare, and take pictures. About an hour later, the crew will depart to 'Tao Asian Bistro' for dinner and fun . . . Make sure you bring your cameras!
> (H2 Club Chapter New York, web)

The social opposition to the Hummer brand community reproduces itself as well. Informants agree that opposition usually forms spontaneously on the road but there are also planned events by social activist organizations such as 'Code Pink' or networks such as the 'Earth Liberation Front.' In public spaces, Hummer owners are frequently insulted, yelled at or cut off. Peter, for instance, reports that his vehicle was keyed once and spat on several times:

> I have people yell obscenities and when we come to a four way stop they . . . well . . . 'you and your god-damn HUMMER, get out of my way' . . . you know. (. . .) We get flipped off about once every two weeks.
>
> (Peter, H2, interview)

Organized protests materialize in street demonstrations such as the 'Code Pink' anti-Hummer demonstrations on Earth Day 2003, where participants produced placards with slogans such as 'How many lives per gallon?' or 'BIG HUMMER little brain' in front of Hummer dealerships. Testing the extreme, the Earth Liberation Front burned several Hummers being displayed at a California dealership and spray-painted slogans such as 'Fat, Lazy Americans' (Associated Press, 08/22/2003) on the walls.

On the netnographic site, various web pages and online forums invite and communicate H2 protest. A popular hate-page presents more than 1,600 individually submitted and commented photographs of people making obscene gestures at H2 vehicles. The owners of the page recently started selling T-shirts and baseball caps with the web address and a popular picture on them.

In summary, the Hummer brand community and its antagonists both reproduce using personal and mediated, spontaneous and organized, online and offline forms of communication. In doing so, each contribution refers to and reproduces the opposite side as well.

Reflexivity

Reflexivity conceptualizes the particular means by which social systems make sense of and react to internal and external communication. Thus far, findings have unveiled that the fundamental distinctions of off-road capability versus environmental irresponsibility, positive attention versus selfish vanity and social superiority versus excessive consumption are used and reproduced by the Hummer brand community and its social environment. Data also supports the existence of immediate interaction between the Hummer brand community and its social environment. This section explores whether this interaction affects the Hummer brand community and if so, how this interaction manifests itself.

In spite of high gas expenditure and ecological criticism, the environmental effects of Hummer consumption are not openly discussed by the Hummer brand community. On the contrary, the Hummer brand community considers itself environmentally responsible:

> We [The HUMMER Club Inc.] have a large percentage of the population with discretionary income. They do what is environmentally correct: join the Nature Conservancy, or the Sierra Club, or Land Trust. (. . .) [it's like they are saying] 'I am giving money to these groups, therefore, it's ok.'
>
> (Susan, H1, interview)

By displaying environmental consciousness and showing responsible behaviour on off-road tracks, the community frames itself as ecologically conscious. In a similar vein, gas-guzzler accusations against urban drivers are ignored or countered with reference to freedom of choice:

> Peoples' concerns are that it burns too much gas and it's bad for the environment. There are a lot of reasons . . . It's just a matter of opinion.
>
> (Peter, H2, interview)

Arnold Schwarzenegger, being harshly criticized during his campaign for backing environmental policies as Governor of California and driving Hummers at the same time, reacted in the same fashion. Instead of accepting the argument and parting with his Hummers, he chose to support a GM initiative for developing sustainable engines. Followed by the media, he occasionally drives an hydrogen-fueled H2 through California (Padgett, 2004).

Partial acceptance of the stigma of selfish vanity inspired Hummer owners and clubs to engage in charitable activities. Susan (H1, interview), for instance, entertains physically challenged children by offering them rides in her H1. Jason (H1/H2, interview) holds guest lectures at a business school to inform prospective leaders about the benefits of the public private partnership of The Hummer Club Inc., and a Colorado Hummer dealer cooperates with the Department of Human Services and the Colorado State Foster Parents Association to deliver Christmas gifts to foster children.

Allegations of overconsumption are based on the fact that the Hummer is a vehicle, which exceeds most customers' needs. The Hummer brand community reacts to these charges in various ways. The programme 'HUMMER Owners Prepared for Emergency (HOPE),' for instance, is a Hummer brand community-initiated cooperation which has emerged between The Hummer Club Inc., GM, and the American Red Cross. HOPE membership allows Hummer owners to provide transportation for Red Cross workers and their supplies to reach emergency sites that 'are not accessible with normal vehicles' (Morris, 2004). The programme has three key impacts on the perceived meanings within the Hummer brand community. First, it responds to intimidation allegations by depicting HOPE members as (national) security supporters rather than as a menace. Second, it signals to the social environment that the vehicles are a useful and necessary enrichment to society rather than an excessive luxury. Third, the programme enhances the original distinction of functional superiority by adding altruism and moral superiority to the set of relevant distinctions. HOPE membership constitutes further pride, as owners become entitled to assist the drivers of less capable vehicles in the case of an emergency.

When it comes to reasoning against their detractors, the arguments of the Hummer brand community are manifold. Usually, the Hummer brand community simply frames protests categorically as envy, as there is no other acceptable way of rationalizing certain threats. Consider the following text by Jack posted on the most salient anti-H2 web forum:

> The shame of all of the 'people' who have so much negativity to say about the H2 either are just totally jealous, or can't make enough money to afford one, two or more! Maybe these 'people' should not have 'Partied' so much in College, if they ever went to college? . . . And by the way – Fuck you ALL!! That are Jealous of a Vehicle – Period!!!!
>
> (Jack, H2, forum)

Another reflexive strategy that was frequently observed in interviews is accusing opponents of insufficient knowledge about the true capability, utility, and gas mileage of Hummers. The following quote exemplifies such an argument that was fought online between a member of the US army who drives a HUMVEE professionally and an owner of a H2 sport utility truck:

> Hey Peter let me just be the first to say (edit) your H2. I don't need it to dog it. I drive an H1 almost everyday. Its called Army. Your Hummer is a sissy truck. It is for rich girls that want to feel like they are special and older guys that can't afford the insurance on a Porsche. I flip off everyone I see on the road.
>
> (Cliff, n/a, forum)[5]

Discussions that emerge from contributions such as Cliff's draw on a host of cultural resources, including the Army, slavery, Al Quaeda, or political affiliations. They provide insights into the depths of passion that both sides share about the Hummer, yet on diametrically opposite sides.

The existing tensions often result in informants feeling more rather than less attached to their Hummers. Jonathan summarizes this strengthening effect as follows:

> People actually try and cut us off on the freeway. We have been cussed at, yelled at, given the thumbs down for 'killing children' (not sure

---

[5] The forum administrator edited this submission.

what that was about). Six times in the last three months people have tried to steal a parking spot from us when we were waiting first. (. . .) This only makes me want to drive a Hummer more. Why be like everyone else, when you can make a statement and cause much hooplah everyday!

(Jonathan, H2, email)

In summary, the findings of this section illustrate how the Hummer brand community inspires, uses, and reproduces the social discourses that it is unable to escape (cf. McCracken, 1986). According to the above data, the Hummer brand community employs *six discursive strategies* in responding to outside stimuli.

Positive feedback is silently consumed, eagerly responded to, or actively reinforced. The community tends to react with benevolence to positive feedback. For some parts of the Hummer brand community, the positive attention that Hummers attract and socializing around the product is a core motivation for purchase. Some owners, who fear that the product's distinctiveness is fading due to its broader diffusion, regain attention by extensively tuning their vehicles or showing them off in conspicuous downtown Hummer convoys.

In reacting to outside threats, the Hummer brand community reacts with ignorance, rationalization and recontextualization. Outside allegations that are of no interest to the community or even entirely question its legitimacy are largely ignored. The Hummer-owning mother of young children, for instance, overlooks the allegation of overconsumption as she views herself as doing what responsible mothers should do. When antagonistic arguments can be rationalized within the interpretive framework of the core distinctions, the brand community self-referentially reframes them to fit the accepted meaning. For instance, Hummer owners typically frame protests categorically as envy.

The most sophisticated interpretive strategy of the Hummer brand community is the recontextualization of accusations. The Hummer Club Inc. initiated HOPE programme, for instance, can be viewed as such a recontextualized response. By establishing cooperation between Hummer owners and the American Red Cross, the community responds to the most salient allegations by depicting HOPE members as (national) security supporters rather than a menace. It also signals to the social environments that the vehicles are a useful and necessary value to society rather than an excessive luxury, and it enhances the original distinction of functional superiority by adding owners' altruism and moral superiority. Recontextualization strategies are favoured when the brand community has no other means of reacting to a relevant outside argument than through remote compensation. Protagonists of the Hummer brand community typically do not give up on their vehicles and community affiliation due to opposition, but they do donate to environmental organizations to balance their (environ-) mental account (Thaler, 1985). With these discursive strategies of selective blindness, the brand community reduces social complexity by banning certain interpretations and encouraging others (cf. Glasersfeld, 2003; von Foerster, 1979).

Discussion

In the above section, we explored the role of antagonistic social environments for a community of Hummer owners that constitute a true brand community in the sense of Muñiz and O'Guinn (2001) and with its social periphery also a consuming tribe in the sense of Cova (2001). Grounded in a social-constructivist interpretive framework, we inquired into the ways in which the Hummer brand community and its active social environments discursively construct, situate, and transform one another.

Our study unveiled a group of ideological distinctions that signify the ideological foundations of the Hummer brand community. These distinctions are 'off-road capability versus environmental irresponsibility,' 'positive attention versus selfish vanity,' and 'social superiority versus excessive overconsumption.' Together with the physical symbolism of the branded products, we found these ideological distinctions to constitute a powerful set of cultural resources that provide individuals and groups with rich topics for discussion, reasons to socialize and argue, and ideologies to identify with. The bivalent distinctions and their ongoing reproduction though brand-related communication also provide critics with material to perpetuate the opposite ideology, organizing protests, and taking aim at the community's foundations. By addressing, for instance, the 'ultimate off-road vehicle' (GM) openly as an 'ultimate poseur vehicle' (Jason, none, forum), antagonists involve the community in an ongoing dispute about the predominant meaning of the brand, its owners and the owner community.

In summary, our study unveiled the following key insights: In the Hummer context, consumers utilize the brand as a cultural resource composed of a set of functional, economic, aesthetic, and ideological distinctions that inspire vivid interactions among people (Arnould and Thompson, 2005; Holt, 2002). Drawing on and constrained by the distinctions that the brand and the respective communication offers, consumers creatively develop their particularly refined ideologies. We find devoted Hummer lovers on one end of the spectrum and passionate, even violent antagonists on the other. In the middle, owners, observers, and companies negotiate the predominance of the brand's prevalent meaning while being largely uninvolved in communal forms. Towards both extremes of admiration and antagonism, community building has been observed more frequently (Kozinets and Handelman, 2004; Muñiz and Schau, 2005; Thompson and Arsel, 2004). Establishing favourable ideologies around the brand in their rituals and traditions, members of the Hummer Club Inc. evolve a sense of belonging and moral responsibility.

On the antagonist side, in contrast, communication rather resembles the conceptual form of an emotional tribe that is interested in oppositional Hummer-related ideology (Cova, 2003). Contributions to the antagonist discourse are centralized in online forums (e.g., www.fuh2.com) that hold single submissions and brief discussions rather than recurrent community-building conversations. Only eventually does protest manifest itself in anti-Hummer activities such as the CodePink activism. Signs of a protest community in the negative sense of Muñiz and O'Guinn (2001) have not been found yet.

Our data suggests that members of the Hummer brand community who are frequently involved in communal activities, such as club meetings and off-road events, seem concerned by outside protest in a different way to individual owners. Active brand community members such as Jason feel better supported by their kind who frequently confirm the shared ideological positions and are secure in the positive use and fascination of Hummers. This group of owners seeks collective experiences and general social acceptance of their pastime so that they engage in recontextualizing the protest that they encounter rather than ignoring it.

Individualistically oriented owners such as Peter and Arnold Schwarzenegger, instead, prefer to pursue showiness and instant gratification of their selves through the public attention that they receive. The lack of peer-group reconfirmation and focus on socially reconfirmed 'cool' leads more frequently to the response strategies of ignorance and rationalization.

By deciding to proliferate a certain set of meanings, the Hummer brand community not only passively evokes, but also knowingly accepts antagonism. For instance, maintaining the passion for off-road driving with gas-guzzling trucks, with the knowledge on the valid arguments of environmentalists, or abiding with showy, heavy vehicles with high bumpers in spite of the anger of mothers worried about the safety of their children.

How does the antagonistic context matter to the community? Focusing on the Hummer brand community's internal perception of outside references, we found a strong awareness of both friendly and oppositional responses. In order to sustain, members develop strategies for enjoying and leveraging positive feedback as well as ignoring protest, circumventing it, or finding creative ways of reframing evil as good and good as evil. The establishment of the HOPE programme is only one salient example of transformative processes within the community in the face of rising protest.

As the Hummer brand is an extreme case of controversy, our above observations of the Hummer brand will not exactly reflect the modus vivendi of other brand communities with their environments. Only a few brand communities and consuming tribes encounter headwinds as blatant as reported here. Yet, for our goal of understanding outside social influences on consumer communities, the study of this peculiar context holds an array of valuable insights for less controversial communities, all of which are also elements within their particular social matrices of meanings. Hence, referring back to our research question, we conclude that social environments not only matter for brand communities, but also are crucial counterparts for the reproduction and transformation of the distinct messages that communities need for their successful perpetuation. This study has also demonstrated the usefulness of our alternative analytical framework for inquiring into brand community-related discourses from multiple perspectives in order to derive relevant knowledge on ideological distinctions and cultural co-creation mechanisms concerning brands.

In summary, our study has shown that proactive social environments hold both curses and blessings for brand communities. Curses, as at their most influential, outside influences are capable of both evening out the brand's distinctions through commodification of the exclusive into the mainstream (Holt, 2002) and of overbalancing the antagonists' side in such a way that neither marketers nor customers can successfully contrast the brand and its communities against the winning social condition; and blessings, as less hostile social environments can inspire and leverage the distinctiveness of a brand and its communities in a productive way, if and as long as the negotiated distinctions resonate strongly enough somewhere in the societal matrix.

References

Arnould, E.J. and Price, L.L. (1993). River magic: extraordinary experience and the extended service encounter, *Journal of Consumer Research*, **20** (1), 24–46.

Arnould, E.J. and Thompson, C.J. (2005). Consumer Culture Theory (CCT): twenty years of research, *Journal of Consumer Research*, **32** (4), 868–883.

Belk, R.W. (1988). Possessions and the extended self, *Journal of Consumer Research*, **15** (2), 139–168.

Bourdieu, P.-F. (1984). *Distinction: A Social Critique of the Judgement of Taste*. London, UK: Routledge and Kegan Paul.

Celsi, R.L., Rose, R.L. and Leigh, T.W. (1993). An exploration of high-risk leisure consumption through skydiving, *Journal of Consumer Research*, **20** (1), 1–23.

Cova, B. (2003). Analyzing and playing with tribes which consume, *Finanza, Marketing e Produzione*, **XXI** (1), 66–89.

Cova, B. and Cova, V. (2001). Tribal aspects of postmodern consumption research: the case of French in-line roller skaters, *Journal of Consumer Behavior*, **1** (1), 67–76.

Cova, B. and Cova, V. (2002). Tribal marketing: the tribalisation of society and its impact on the conduct of marketing, *European Journal of Marketing*, **36** (5/6), 595–620.

Elliott, R. and Wattanasuwan, K. (1998). Brand as symbolic resources for the construction of identity, *International Journal of Advertising*, **17** (2), 131–145.

Firat, F.A. and Venkatesh, A. (1995). Liberatory postmoderism and the reenchantment of consumption, *Journal of Consumer Research*, **22** (3), 239–267.

Giesler, M. (2003). Social systems in marketing, in Darach Turley and Stephen W. Brown (eds.), *European Advances in Consumer Research*, Vol. 6. Valdosta, GA: Association for Consumer Research, pp. 249–256.

Glasersfeld, E.v. (2003). An introduction to radical constructivism, http://www.umass.edu/srri/vonGlasersfeld/onlinePapers/html/082.html [2004/10/27].

Gusfield, J.R. (1975). *Community: A Critical Response*, Oxford: Blackwell.

Holt, D.B. (2002). Why do brands cause trouble? A dialectical theory of consumer culture and branding, *Journal of Consumer Research*, **29** (1), 70–90.

Holt, D.B. and Thompson, J.C. (2002). Man-of-action heroes: how the American ideology of manhood structures men's consumption, http://ssrn.com/abstract=386600 [2004/10/11].

Kozinets, R.V. (1999). E-tribalized marketing?: the strategic implications of virtual communities of consumption, *European Management Journal*, **17** (3), 252–624.

Kozinets, R.V. (2001). Utopian enterprise: articulating the meanings of Star Trek's culture of consumption, *Journal of Consumer Research*, **28** (1), 67–89.

Kozinets, R.V. (2002). The field behind the screen: using netnography for marketing research in online communities, *Journal of Marketing Research*, **39** (1), 61–73.

Kozinets, R.V. and Handelman, J.M. (2004). Adversaries of consumption: consumer movements, activism, and ideology, *Journal of Consumer Research*, **31** (3), 691–704.

Luhmann, N. (1995). *Social systems*. Stanford, CA: Stanford University Press.

Maffesoli, M. (1988). *Le temps des tribus*. Paris: Méridiens Klincksieck.

Maffesoli, M. (1996). *The Time of the Tribes: The Decline of Individualism in Mass Society*, Thousand Oaks, CA: Sage.

Maturana, H.R. [1974] (1999). The organization of the living: a theory of the living organization, *International Journal of Human–Computer Studies*, **51** (2), 149–168.

Maturana, H.R. and Varela, F.J. (1987). *The Tree of Knowledge: A New Look at the Biological Roots of Human Understanding*. Boston: Shambhala.

McAlexander, J.H., Schouten, J.W. and Koenig, H.F. (2002). Building brand community, *Journal of Marketing*, **66** (1), 38–54.

McCracken, G. (1986). Culture and consumption: a theoretical account of the structure and movement of the cultural meaning of consumer goods, *Journal of Consumer Research*, **13** (1), 71–84.

Moisio, R., Arnould, E.J. and Price, L.L. (2004). Between mothers and markets: constructing family identity through homemade food, *Journal of Consumer Culture*, **4** (3), 361–384.

Morris, M. (2004). Everything HUMMER, Azimuth, 2004 (Feb), pp. 17–18.

Muñiz, A.M.J. and O'Guinn, T. (2001). Brand community, *Journal of Consumer Research*, **27** (4), 412–432.

Muñiz, A.M.J. and Schau, H.J. (2005). Religiosity in the abandoned apple Newton brand community, *Journal of Consumer Research*, **32** (4), 737–748.

Padgett, M. (2004). *HUMMER – How a Little Truck Company Hit the Big Time, Thanks to Saddam, Schwarzenegger and GM*. St. Paul, MN: MBI Publishing Company.

Parsons, T. (1971). *The system of modern societies*. Englewood Cliffs, NJ: Prentice-Hall.

Peñaloza, L. (2001). Consuming the American west: animating cultural meaning and memory at a stock show and rodeo, *Journal of Consumer Research*, **28** (3), 369–397.

Postrel, V.I. (2003). *The Substance of Style: How the Rise of Aesthetic Value is Remaking Commerce, Culture, and Consciousness*, 1st ed. New York, NY: HarperCollins.

Schouten, J.W. and McAlexander, J.H. (1995). Subcultures of consumption: an ethnography of the new bikers, *Journal of Consumer Research*, **22** (1), 43–62.

Simmel, G. (1890). *Über sociale Differenzierung: Sociologische und psychologische Untersuchungen.* Leipzig: Duncker & Humblot.

Spencer-Brown, G. [1969] (1999). *Laws of Form – Gesetze der Form*, 2nd ed. Lübeck: Bohlmeier.

Thaler, R. (1985). Mental accounting and consumer choice, *Marketing Science*, **4** (3), 199–215.

Thompson, C.J. (1997). Interpreting consumers: a hermeneutical framework for deriving marketing insights from the texts of consumers' consumption stories, *Journal of Marketing Research*, **34** (4), 438–456.

Thompson, C.J. and Arsel, Z. (2004). The Starbucks brandscape and consumers' (anticorporate) experiences of glocalization, *Journal of Consumer Research*, **31** (3), 631–642.

Tönnies, F. (1926). *Gemeinschaft und Gesellschaft, Grundbegriffe der reinen Soziologie*, 7th ed. Berlin: K. Curtius.

Tönnies, F. (1957). *Community and Society (Gemeinschaft und Gesellschaft)*, in Charles P. Loomis (ed. and trans.), East Lansing: Michigan State University Press.

Varela, F.J. (1979). *Principles of Biological Autonomy.* New York: Elsevier/North-Holland.

von Foerster, H. (1979). Cybernetics of cybernetics, in Krippendorff, K. (ed.), *Communication and Control in Society*, New York: Gordon and Breach, pp. 5–8.

Weber, M. (1922). *Wirtschaft und Gesellschaft*, Tübingen: J.C.B. Mohr (P. Siebeck).

Weber, M. (1962). *Basic Concepts in Sociology.* Secher, H.P. (trans.), London: Peter Owen.

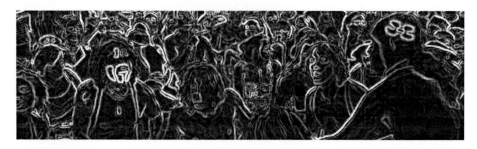

19

New consumption communities and the re-enabling of 21st century consumers

Isabelle Szmigin, Marylyn Carrigan and Caroline Bekin

The production consumption balance

An essential element of marketing exchange is the involvement of the consumer. Yet this exchange can be described as one of captivity for the consumer dependent on the hegemony of the dominant marketing process (Gramsci, 1998). The rhetoric of relationship marketing is one of consumer centrality, yet power remains in the hands of the supplier (Szmigin, 2003), and cultural alienation ensures inclusion based on exchange. The marketing process also alienated the consumer from production; industrial capitalism has meant that people are estranged from the creation of goods. The end of the last century, however, saw an increasing interest and concern in the nature of production of consumer goods and in turn this has led to the evolution of a range of behaviours including downshifting (Schor, 1998) and boycotting (Friedman, 1999), the latter often related to the mode and nature of production. Typically, such consumer behaviour and especially boycotting has been seen as anti-marketing (Garrett, 1987; Voight, 2000) yet from a consumer research perspective it can be viewed as re-enabling the consumer. Rather than characterizing boycotters or others as being outside the mainstream and therefore 'flawed consumers' (Bauman, 1998), it is more appropriate to examine the conceptual development of the consumer in relation to both marketing and the exchange system where alternative consumer behaviours may be seen as part of an enabling process.

This chapter examines the development of movements that question the supremacy of marketing. It explores the practical presentation of such movements through data from participant observation, depth interviews, websites, print documents, broadcast material and conversations with participants in what are termed New Consumption Communities. New Consumption Communities are presented as beneficial in terms of consumer re-enablement as they offer alternative ways to engage in consumption and negotiate with the market place. Four distinct case studies are presented throughout the text in order to diversely illustrate the conceptualizations in this chapter. The first of these is Garstang Fairtrade town, which, at a public meeting in 2000 voted to become the pioneer fair trade town in the UK. Garstang is a small (population over 4,000) historic market town between Preston and Lancaster in England. The second community is Ithaca Hours, a US-based trading system community founded in 1991. Participants of Ithaca Hours are merchants and residents in or around Ithaca, NY. The principle behind Ithaca Hours is particularly important to the notion of exchange; Ithaca Hours is a form of currency used by participating local businesses and individuals that directly relates to use value in terms of the direct labour an Hour is worth. The value of each Hour equals an average hourly wage of the area. This process was seen by members as reclaiming commoditization because generally work would be worth the same amount regardless of what that work was. Hockerton Housing Project (HHP) in Nottinghamshire is the UK's first ecologically sound, energy-efficient, earth-sheltered housing complex, launched in 1998. It was built by five resident families who produce 100 per cent of their own wind energy, grow organic food, and have their own sewage, water collection, and filtering systems. Members are committed to a community business that comprises guided tours, educational and specialist workshops. HHP considers itself a best practice example and catalyst for sustainable living. Finally, Futurefarms is a UK-based community cooperative formed in 2004 in Martin, Hampshire. Its eight founding members reside separately and in the parish. Their aim is to produce as much of their daily food as possible on local land. The non-profit cooperative was set up in a response to members' concerns with food mileage, detrimental to the environment and indicative of the (lack of) relationship between producer and consumer.

Reconnecting consumption and production

The twentieth century saw consumption overtaking production. Brands became central to this consumption process, consumed for what they stood for, and for the development and bolstering of our self-identity (Holt, 2002). Branding is still the dominant image creator with consumers supposedly able to distinguish themselves through the brands they buy. As the century wore on a number of issues arose which led to a refocusing on production. Issues such as BSE, genetic modification, food miles, and the dominant role of multiple retailers in the supply chain became public issues of production as well as consumption. Such issues are particularly salient to Futurefarms members:

> The idea is to produce the food locally because when you go and buy food in a supermarket so often it's come from you know, even thousands of miles away and also to produce food which we know where it's come from. We know what's happened to it, because there have been so many food scares and BSE and you hear terrible stories about chickens injected with protein from unspecified sources and you . . . but none of that's on the label, so we just want to produce food where we know what's gone into it.
>
> (Janette, Futurefarms)

> You pick up a cabbage in a shop and there're no holes in it. I think, 'Why didn't the caterpillars eat this? What's wrong with it?'
>
> (Susanne, Futurefarms)

Ironically suppliers require us to be involved in the production process while being excluded from any real control in it. Self-service, which started with supermarkets and petrol stations, now requires us to assemble our own furniture, collect money from ATM machines, and issue our own books in libraries. But what awareness do we have of our role in the production process? Slater suggests that the central issue is about how we relate to things in modern life and that once we lose the connection and control of that connection we move into a state of alienation and distance (Slater, 1997). Of course there have been examples to show that the process of production is considered an attribute. In its development the Body Shop used three key values, the non-exploitation of animals in product testing; the payment of fair wages with provision of good working conditions in manufacture, and environmental responsibility through recycling packaging. Similarly, the growing market for organic produce has, as well as a concern for the quality of the food in terms of taste and product safety, a production concern to do with the planet's environmental degradation and its genetic diversity. This is highlighted, by Nick, a HHP Member:

> If you go to a pub or a restaurant you get that ratchet pile of vegetables which is always the same. You get the carrots, the peas and the mange touts, and some bleached cauliflower . . . there's hardly any taste difference between them. That is the issue with a lot of bought vegetables. They look good, but . . . our vegetables come in

every shape and size, sometimes they look a bit mangy but the taste is completely different.

(Nick, HHP)

Re-enabling the consumer

A reconnection with the mode and means of production inevitably brings us to Marx. In Fine's (1984) review of Marx's 'Das Capital', he made clear that Marx viewed the need to produce and consume as integral to human nature. In particular Marx wanted a revealing and explanation of social relations and organization of production, and as Fine puts it 'To distinguish people's possible relations with the physical world from those induced with it and other people' (1984, p. 18). According to Marx, the worker is detached from the product and its production process, 'but the view of this situation is distorted. The capitalist is subject to the control of exchange and profit-making. For both, it appears that things exert this control, and not the social relations of production peculiar to capitalism' (Fine, 1984, p. 26). To Marx, the objectification of things produced under capitalism or, in other words, the loss of legal ownership over the product of one's own work (Bocock, 1993), coupled with people's estrangement from one another and the commoditization of goods, could have major consequences to individuals' sense of worth and self-concept. Importantly, Marx believed that production was more than a means to life but rather contained the potential for self-realization and advancement (Lee, 1993), 'As individuals express their life, so they are, what they are, therefore, coincides with their production, both with *what* they produce and with *how* they produce' (Marx and Engels, 1974, p. 42). As Lee has suggested, this production has a 'metaphysical kernel', an essence of its creation and its social and historical context (1993, p. 5), and of course central to Marx's view of production under capitalism was the objectification of value resulting in an impoverished realization of human activity. With one or two exceptions as noted above, the Western consumer has for some time effectively been alienated from all aspects of the metaphysical kernel of production; today's exchange values having failed to signal any ethically and culturally relevant attributes which may inform true use value. The communities discussed here challenge these conditions by either producing some of their own foods and utilities (i.e., Futurefarms and HHP) or by purchasing positively through fairly traded choices (i.e., Garstang) or in the case of Ithaca Hours reclaiming commoditization through managing exchange differently to the market. The return to local people may vary; while for some the system provides an important source of financial support, for others it is primarily a way of meeting others in the community. Importantly, people find that their spending is inevitably redirected locally. The kinds of services bought include plumbing, carpentry, electrical work, childcare and food. Restaurants and entertainment venues take the Hours as well as stores and farmers markets. Community suppliers thrive and feel less threatened but members argue that this does not produce an isolationist community.

A renewed interest in and understanding of existing and potential relations within production processes and their impact on labour value and consumer value is as necessary now as it was in the nineteenth century; more so even as the impact of structures, relations, and choices are affecting people across continents, within their own lands and across generations. It might be argued that the recent increase in concerns over the risks in consumption (Schlosser, 2001) coupled with a rise in ethical considerations in purchasing (Klein, 2000) represents a fundamental re-orientation in the relationship between the buyer and supplier and production and consumption. However, producers are quick to capitalize on consumers' anxieties; they are only too aware of new attributes that can be used to enhance their brands, exemplified, for example, by the pro-liferation of organic goods in multiple retailers. It is also significant that again supermarkets are muscling in on these alternative consumption communities by holding farmers' markets in their car parks and foyers (La Trobe, 2001). Nonetheless, it is important to acknowledge that alternative consumer communities may also take advantage of mainstream marketing techniques in order to advance their interests. Both Futurefarms and HHP are business-oriented; HHP is already able to employ two community members full-time due to the income generated by their educational business. Similarly, while Fairtrade towns promote ethically traded goods, they do so within the existing marketing system.

Whether consumers can and will take action to reclaim production is a point argued in a number of areas. On the one hand there are those who believe that consumer knowledge and power will drive the behaviour of the retailers and regulators (Kahn and McAllister, 1997), while others question the extent of consumer knowledge, power, and indeed interest (Fine and Leopold, 1993; Holt, 2002). Cook, Crang, and Thorpe (1998, p. 166) have argued against the 'blunt dichotomy between either a knowledgeable and hence powerful, or ignorant and hence manipulated, consumer'; rather, they say there is evidence for both positions. In fact there has been evidence of much consumer interest. In a seminar on the need for marketing reform, Smith (2004) presents longitudinal and representative data collected across the last three decades, which shows that almost half of US consumers have a high level of concern not about *what* is being marketed, but about *how* things are marketed to them. Although they acknowledge the usefulness and necessity of marketing, it is the intrusiveness of the marketing process and the lack of consumer inclusivity that troubles these mainstream consumers. This represents a real consumer interest in marketing practice, and acts as a warning for marketing to abdicate some of its power in the producer–consumer relationship.

Consumers have attempted to work both within and without the dominant marketing process. It has perhaps been inevitable that concern for the production process has often been expressed by middle class, income rich, time poor individuals; they may be well placed to afford supermarket organic produce and least best placed to spend time sourcing goods from a range of suppliers. However, the communities in this chapter show that members can have very diverse backgrounds, and that the interest and engagement in the production of their own goods is time-consuming often requiring lifestyle adaptations.

Concern has been expressed over the inevitable inconsistencies, for example, that those who buy ethically traded coffee may be paying for it from a purse produced by an exploited third world workforce (Strong, 1997). The problem with this argument is that it presupposes people can immediately work outside the bounds of the existing system with perfect information. Consistency is not a pre-requisite for the re-enabling of people and often ethical choices can work against each other, forcing consumers to prioritize their concerns. Having said that, there are groups and individuals who are proactively moving the enabling process forward. Some clearly have vested interests to pursue; the Farmers Market Movement is both allowing local producers to operate outside of the supermarket supply chain and potentially increase their profits, but they are also re-engaging consumers with the nature of production in terms of how, when, and where their food is produced. Previous research has suggested that important attributes for consumers of such markets include the enjoyable experience of getting to know the stallholders, availability of information on the products, opportunities to taste prior to purchase and that by using the market, support is being given to the local producers (Young and Holden, 2002). The FreeCycle Network (free cycle. org) consists of groups around the world enabling people to access and redistribute goods for free. Largely managed over the Internet it allows people to 'recycle' unwanted items with no money exchange.

Conceptualizing new consumption communities

Re-engaging production and consumption does not imply an overthrow of that exchange process. There is, however, an important shift taking place which may have significant implications for both producers and consumers and for the hegemonic position of marketing and particularly branding. Essential to this is the development of alternative consumption communities which reveal the inadequacies of the existing system as well as offering alternative modes of consumption and thinking to a diverse range of people.

We present a first stage in conceptualizing the development of this re-enabling process. We suggest that a movement, which has developed over time but gained particular momentum over the last century, is in turn leading to the development of New Consumption Communities which undermine 'the tyranny of the normal' (Bowring, 2000) and the dominance of marketing values. This conceptualization presents the coexistence of the dominant branding position with the resistance of boycotting and anti-branding producing a re-enabling of consumers in some form of community mode (Figure 19.1).

This conceptualization does not represent a shift from one position to another *per se*; branding remains the dominant paradigm of the market. Rather it is fluid with each element developing and coexisting historically. Also this consumption circle reveals the shifting balances in power between the consumer and supplier.

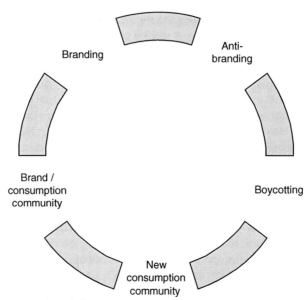

Figure 19.1 The consumption circle.

A closer look at the consumption circle

Branding

In a world where use value has effectively been replaced by sign value, the rise and rise of the brand has hardly been surprising. Holt (2002) presented the development of branding as establishing the legitimacy of marketing in presenting a value proposition to the consumer. Interestingly, he also suggests another principle was at work at the same time, what he refers to as 'P.T. Barnum hucksterism' (2002, p. 80), which saw consumers as dupes who would buy inflated claims. Now branding, he says, is used by consumers as a 'cultural resource' allowing a form of expressive culture, implying that consumers are using brands rather than vice-versa. This approach is supported by others who suggest that it is consumers who are the final arbiters and if they don't like the brand it will wither and die (Economist, 2001). But this argument is simplistic; brands are not about a one-to-one relationship of equal parity but rather about mass marketing an idea that will allow us to feel we are expressing ourselves, even if we are only doing the same as thousands of others. The buttress of mass marketing is that consumers simply cannot be bothered to investigate and resist the lure of the brand; there will always be a vast body that are probably happy or at least not dissatisfied with the status quo.

Boycotting

Boycotting aims to achieve certain objectives through urging consumers to refrain from selective purchase (Friedman, 1999). Boycotting is frequently aimed directly at the company rather than its high profile brands, often concerned with issues external to the marketplace such as human and animal rights and the environment. Boycotting behaviour has always had a degree of selectivity; it has tended to be specific to certain areas of activity and is primarily focused on the whole company. It is less about enabling consumers and more about disabling companies, as a central plank of action is withdrawing support for the company through taking away patronage. There is, however, an important community aspect to the action, as a rationale for boycotting put forward by Garrett (1986) is that while large companies may ignore the complaints of individuals a collective voice is harder to dismiss.

Anti-branding

The anti-branding movement which at least partly developed from the 'NoLogo' (Klein, 2000) phenomenon has been more generally damaging to the hegemony of marketing than boycotting, in that it was highly visible and also came at a time when the Internet had developed into a useful basis of conversation between people with similar concerns. Partly as a result of the impact of the Internet these conversations also helped to develop communities of like-minded people less limited by age, geography, economic, or social status. We recognize that use of the Internet has an economic dimension although access has become more generally available in public places such as libraries. The Internet has been particularly important as a source of information transfer and it is significant that it generated a range of different types of site and information exchange from consumer advice on how to complain (e.g., www.howtocomplain.com, www.complainer.co.uk, etc.) to dedicated sites reviewing and revealing the behaviours of a range of corporations (e.g., www.corpo ratewatch.org.uk). Much of the Internet activity can be termed anti-branding, although it is not essentially anti-consumption. Corporate Watch's 'What's wrong with supermarkets'? while attacking the large multiple retailers also positively campaigns for example, for incentives to localize food production and retailing including covered food markets, through directed funding from Regional Development Agencies and tax incentives to small local traders and trading schemes. Similarly, Wyecycle, a community business in the southeast of Britain, attacks supermarkets in its list of '10 ways to create a better world' but its primary focus is on the reduction of waste through a range of initiatives based around recycling and re-reusing. By pointing out and exploring alternatives to the status quo this anti-branding movement gave the incentive to groups to begin to consider more fully alternatives that might work for them. They effectively paved the way for communities that were based on positive consumption decisions that are here termed New Consumption Communities.

New consumption communities

Marx suggested that alienation is not the only route for humans but that it is the result of the economic, social, and political institutions which are part of capitalism (Bocock, 1993). The alienation of modern consumer capitalism has been well documented; branding, while ostensibly allowing people to express their identity may be little more than a temporary opiate. People are, however, a creative species able to work in a cooperative manner and we should also consider ways in which alienation might change or lessen in light of consumers' responses to the experience of estrangement.

A conceptual framework for understanding new consumption communities

The development of New Consumption Communities may be compared to the classification developed by Hirschman (1970) as categories of consumer response to corporate behaviour. He suggested three potential responses: exit (refusal), voice (complaint) and loyalty (patronage in the hope of change). We have refined this for the twentyfirst century into the following to reflect the conceptualization developed above.

Exit

'Exit' can be viewed as the refusal to consume, or the active boycott of particular brands. There are several examples of exit among the four New Consumption Communities exemplified throughout this chapter. At Garstang, for example, exit meant eschewing the purchase of non-Fairtrade bananas and chocolate; at Futurefarms it meant not shopping at supermarkets:

> I dislike them on a number of grounds. I'm a stroppy old bloke basically and I dislike being told what to do and any commercial shop exists to try and make you buy their produce and if anyone is trying to influence me psychologically then I'm usually aware of it and I resist it. So I dislike that side of it, I dislike the way we are led to believe they treat the producers of their produce.
>
> (Mark, Futurefarms)

At HHP Nick exemplifies exiting through his choice of clothing, but highlights some of the complexities and in particular the difficulty of putting principles over fashion and value as far as his teenage daughter is concerned:

> Well, we still buy clothes, we've got a teenage daughter, but I think, yes, what I try and do is resist buying just for fashion. I still like to look smart, but I think the key thing is not just buy extra clothes just because you want. . . You're bored with the other fifteen shirts and pairs of jeans. . . Thinking about the implications of that, my daughter bought a pair of jeans last week in Newark and she was very pleased that she'd got them for ten pounds. So being a right old

bore of a dad I said, well they look very nice Rebecca, but at ten pounds . . . That is incredibly good value but somebody has had to make it for a very low pay rate. So there is an ethical issue, so just to remind her that some of those cheap clothes – and there's an awful lot now – there's a cost somewhere. Somewhere in the world someone is sitting in a sweatshop being paid very little and in very poor conditions . . . I'd say she's at that point where she just doesn't want to know about those things . . . that's difficult.

(Nick, HHP)

Exit is at the heart of the principle behind Ithaca Hours. There is an important resistance aspect to the Ithaca Hours concept in terms of opposition to supremacy of the dollar in exchange systems:

We printed our own money because we watched Federal dollars come to town, shake a few hands, then leave to buy rainforest lumber and to fight wars. Ithaca Hours, by contrast, stay in our region to help us hire each other. While dollars make us increasingly dependent on multinational corporations and bankers, Hours reinforce community trade and expand commerce that is more responsive to our concern for ecology and social justice.

(www.geocities.com/rainforets/7813/ccs-ithi.htm)

In our email discussion with Ithaca participants we found this feeling supported by users:

I loved going to locally owned businesses and exchanging the money and knowing the money would keep circulating locally, meaning that we would all be supporting each other.

(Laurie, Ithaca)

Voice

In the context of the New Consumption Communities framework 'Voice' represents complaint through lobbying, demonstration or the support of particular consumerist groups. In all the communities, 'Voice' also meant advocating their own causes as well as that of other groups. Members of Garstang had to form a steering group in order to initiate the process of transforming Garstang into a Fairtrade town. The activists involved in Garstang originated from the Garstang Oxfam Group, but they quickly identified a way of getting the local community involved through chocolate. To persuade churches, schools and traders to use and/or sell Fairtrade products the Oxfam Group invited people to a special meal featuring Fairtrade chocolate and banana pancakes. Alliances were also built up with local farmers and organizations that agreed to sell or use Fairtrade goods displaying a special window sticker. A major success of Garstang has been its continued ability to attract attention to a range of community consumption issues. During Fairtrade fortnight 2002 they developed the theme of bringing the producer and consumer closer together with an event 'Garstang and Ghana – why do their farmers get a raw deal?' Garstang has built up strong links with Ghana, the town being twinned with Ne Koforidia. In this way Garstang are trying to educate and develop a broader understanding of the fate of small communities and small producers across the globe, not only within their own locality, highlighting a reconnection with production especially in relation to chocolate and coffee production and consumption.

All members of Futurefarms demonstrated a deep interest and drive to encourage others to become more involved with the Futurefarms project. In fact, for Nick, the idealizer of the project, taking part in the New Consumption Communities research project meant an opportunity to publicize the project's aims and developments. At HHP constant work is put into maintaining a network of visitors and supporters while Ithaca Hours maintains an online community while also articulating its willingness to disseminate its principles:

> We replace dependence on imports. Yet our greater self-reliance, rather than isolating Ithaca, gives us more potential to reach outward with ecological export industry.
>
> (www.geocities.com/rainforets/7813/ccs-ithi.htm)

Positive choice

'Positive choice' means the patronage of alternatives in the hope of change; the decision to seek alternatives to traditional consumption, for example, buying bulk non-branded and Fairtrade goods, using farmers markets and credit unions. This is the most significant feature of these communities, and all participants frequently demonstrated and cited their positive choices. At Garstang, suppliers as well as customers had to select Fairtrade, and at HHP positive choice is everywhere from building materials through to grocery shopping. The houses have been built to maximize natural insulation and minimize landscape impact. They retain warmth and need no artificial heating; internal temperatures vary between 18°C and 23°C throughout the year. The project's site has two artificial water lakes, one of which is used for tap water storage (the reservoir) and the other for fish and swimming. Rainwater is collected throughout the land and from the roofs of the houses. Water treatment is done without the use of chemicals and the site currently uses wind and solar energy sources. In order to offset some of the harm incurred from developing the site, over 3,000 new native trees have been planted on their land. Nick emphasizes that their lifestyle is about making positive choices rather than being deprived:

> This isn't about trying to live a very Spartan life, but there are ways you can . . . There's an approach which has less of an impact,

so . . . Okay, maybe we ought to spend a little bit more from shops which we know have got a more ethical purchasing policy. Fairtrade goods are an example, but perhaps it's getting a little over done now. But the principle is good . . . Buying local produce, trying to support local employment, local farmers, etc . . . So there are things that one can do . . . We do some bulk-buying. We purchase quite a lot of stuff from Suma, who are wholesalers, cooperative . . . They supply a lot of organic, fairly traded products . . . Items from toilet rolls through to walnuts and dates and so on.

(Nick, HHP)

Louise also articulated her thoughts on positive choices:

I think consumers are extremely powerful. One person can buy Fairtrade and organic products etc. and then that makes companies get on that bandwagon if they want to make money. And then companies change their ways of being, and then governments change. . . But I also think that governments and companies need to do more anyway.

(Louise, HHP)

Ithaca Hours support the community in a number of ways including providing new businesses with cash loans. Individuals found Hours helped to manage consumption:

I have given my children Ithaca Hours to use to purchase snacks, assured that the Hours would neither be stolen at school nor could my children use the Hours for purchases other than snacks at the local bakery – they can't be used at McDonalds etc.

(Sue, Ithaca)

The making of positive choice over trying to escape the market is well articulated by Nick from Futurefarms:

I can't do all of this on my own because I have to earn a mortgage, money type of salary and I have to work elsewhere, and I think a lot of us are, you know. It's modern, it's modern isn't it, and we can't escape that. I don't want to retreat back into a pioneer sort of, you know, Nova Scotia sort of dig the earth thing. I just want to be able to use technology, I'm not frightened of that, and do it together on a scale that I would not be able to manage myself.

(Nick, Futurefarms)

Other members discussed how they had adopted a seasonally oriented approach to food consumption since the project started, while Susanne was not prepared to reject the supermarket if it met her criteria:

> I like to get some shopping in Waitrose in Salisbury. They deliver out here and it's cheaper to give them a fiver for one lorry to come round to loads of people than it is to drag the old Landrover into town, and they're . . . I have never known such a big shop with such a good fresh food thing. All their salads and stuff are local, you know . . . And it even says the county where it's come from and you can go up to the assistant and say, 'Excuse me', and they know all about it. If somebody said to me, 'Where's the best place to get fresh local vegetables?' I'd send them to Waitrose.
>
> (Susanne, Futurefarms)

While shopping at a supermarket goes against the grain for other Futurefarms members, for Susanne it represented a positive and acceptable alternative.

It is important to highlight that an explanation of community as expressed through consumption has been developed by Muñiz and O'Guinn (2001). While their notion of brand community is wedded to well known consumer brands, we have not rejected the contribution it makes. They suggest the notion of a brand community as being those supporters and endorsers of particular consumer brands. In particular they refer to a 'consciousness of kind" evident in the brand communities they investigated; citing Cova (1997) they say that "the link is more important than the thing'. Muñiz and O'Guinn (2001) suggest there is a shared component among those in brand communities which includes a consciousness of kind or collective sense of connection, shared rituals and traditions and a sense of moral responsibility.

While Muñiz and O'Guinn were looking specifically at mainstream brands, their findings particularly in relation to how consumption can bring people together to form 'this consciousness of kind' seems particularly relevant to this chapter. In the case of the New Consumption Communities concept, the support of brands is arguably replaced by the support of particular actions in order to minimize certain issues which result from production disconnected consumption. All four communities expressed consciousness of kind, shared traditions and rituals, and responsibility toward other group members. In fact, all members of Futurefarms highlighted the new sense of community in the previously socially disconnected parish as the most beneficial aspect of the project, while HHP's Nick argued that food production and self-building played major roles in creating bonds in the beginning of their community. Although in Garstang Fairtrade also created the opportunity for a group of people to get together, at Ithaca some seemed more sceptical about how much Hours had actually helped the community come together.

Conclusions

In this chapter we have outlined some features of the existing hegemonic marketing exchange processes. Returning to Marx as a key informant on the structure of the market we have questioned the continued existence of the exchange process and why it has prevailed. Branding remains a dominant paradigm of twentyfirst century marketing offering as it does an ephemeral but still significant sign value in the process of exchange in mass markets. More recently, the dominance of the marketplace in its current form has come under attack, with groups not only re-conceptualizing the exchange process but also developing alternative modes of exchange and consumption. This is not to suggest that consumer resistance has only developed at the end of the twentieth century; indeed evidence suggests otherwise (e.g., Brobeck, 1997; Forbes, 1987). However, it was not until the later part of the twentieth century that production and exchange processes came increasingly under scrutiny with the increased potential to facilitate a sense of community between resistant consumers. We have presented this in a non-linear continuum showing the development from boycotting through to what we have termed New Consumption Communities. These communities are varied in nature and philosophy and we do not suggest that there is any consistency in their approach. Indeed we would argue that this is a positive benefit coming as it does as a reaction to the notion of mass marketing with an overall lack of self-reflexivity about its societal impact. These communities are all, however, questioning the supremacy of marketing and business more generally as represented by large brands and multinational corporations. The groups we have examined in depth are localized and concerned with their communities and with those that may be affected by our consumption. They tend not to be inward looking but concerned about others, the environment and the developing world. Increasingly, though, New Consumption Communities will be groups of like-minded people communicated through the Internet. There are already many good examples of these such as Freegans.org and Freecycle.org.

Some will argue that this is little more than tokenism and realistically no small community-based activity is likely to threaten the existing power of major retailers and indeed the global marketing system. Clearly, the exchange process and indeed branding still appear safe as new generations grow up to sample the joys of creating their identity through shopping. However, the New Consumption Communities are making contributions both in themselves and in the effect that they are having on the existing status quo. We have already mentioned the impact of organic goods and the resistance to genetically modified food. Recycling is finally becoming a mainstream activity in Britain as more and more councils recognize that they have a duty to consider the long-term effects of waste disposal, and multiple retailers are stocking Fairtrade products. This assimilation into the mainstream may not be what is ultimately required to undermine the dominance of the existing marketing process but it may be a sign to indicate the impact that New Consumption Communities can have. And as outlined above this may well be part of the development.

Importantly, the New Consumption Communities examined in this chapter view their activities not as resistance to mainstream production and exchange, but as positive alternatives that can complement and have a positive impact on society and exchange relations. The bigger picture, however, is to do with how sustainable these communities can become, how inclusive and available to all, how accessible both geographically and economically. Their purpose is not to replace the scale and scope of marketing but to form a credible choice.

References

Bauman, Z. (1998). *Work, Consumerism and the New Poor*. Buckingham: Open University Press.

Bocock, R. (1993). *Consumption*. London: Routledge.

Bowring, F. (2000). Social exclusion: limitations of the debate, *Critical Social Policy*, **20** (3), 307–330.

Brobeck, S. (1997). *Encyclopaedia of the Consumer Movement*. Santa Barbara: ABC-CLIO.

Cook, I., Crang, P. and Thorpe, M. (1998). Biographies and geographies: consumer understanding of the origins of foods, *British Food Journal*, **100** (3), 162–167.

Cova, B. (1997). Community and consumption: towards a definition of the linking value of product or services, *European Journal of Marketing*, **31** (Fall/Winter), 297–316.

Economist (2001). Who's wearing the trousers? 9.8.2001, **360** (8238), 26–28

Fine, B. (1984). *Marx's Capital*, 2nd ed. London: Macmillan.

Fine, B. and Leopold, E. (1993). *The World of Consumption*. London: Routledge.

Forbes, J.D. (1987). *The Consumer Interest: Dimensions and Policy Implications*. London: Croom Helm.

Friedman, M. (1999). *Consumer Boycotts: Effecting Change through the Marketplace and Media*. London: Routledge.

Garrett, D.E. (1986). Consumer boycotts: are targets always the bad buys? *Business and Society Review*, **58**, 17–21.

Garrett, D.E. (1987). The effectiveness of marketing policy boycotts: environmental opposition to marketing, *Journal of Marketing*, **51**, 46–57.

Gramsci, A. (1998). *Selections from the Prison Notebooks*, edited and translated by Hoare, Q. and Nowell Smith, G. London: Lawrence and Wishart.

Hirschman, A.O. (1970). *Exit, Voice and Loyalty*. Cambridge, MA: Harvard Press.

Holt, D. (2002). Why do brands cause trouble? *Journal of Consumer Research*, **29** (June), 70–90.

Kahn, B.E. and McAllister, L. (1997). *Grocery Revolution. The New Focus on the Consumer*. Reading, MA: Addison-Wesley.

Klein, N. (2000). *NoLogo*. London: Flamingo.

La Trobe, H. (2001). Farmers' markets: consuming local rural produce, *International Journal of Consumer Studies*, **25** (3), 181–192.

Lee, M. (1993). *Consumer Culture Reborn: The Cultural Politics of Consumption.* London: Routledge.

Marx, K. and Engels, F. (1974). *The German Ideology.* London: Lawrence and Wishart.

Muñiz, A.M. and O'Guinn, T.C. (2001). Brand community, *Journal of Consumer Research,* **27**, 412–432.

Schlosser, E. (2001). *Fast Food Nation.* London: Allen Lane Penguin Press.

Schor, J. (1998). *The Overspent American: Upscaling, Downshifting, and the New Consumer.* New York: Basic Books.

Slater, D. (1997). *Consumer Culture and Modernity.* Cambridge: Polity Press.

Smith, J.W. (2004). Consumer resistance to marketing, *Does Marketing Need Reform?* Boston, MA: Bentley College Seminar Series, retrieved 1 May 2006, from http://atc3.bentley.edu/resources/markreform/presentation.htm#

Strong, C. (1997). The problems of translating fair trade principles into consumer purchase behaviour, *Marketing Intelligence & Planning,* **15** (1), 32–37.

Szmigin, I. (2003). *Understanding the Consumer.* London: Sage

Voight, J. (2000). The consumer rebellion, *Adweek,* Jan 10, 46–50.

Young, J. and Holden, C. (2002). *NW Consumer Direct Initiatives – Farmers' Markets & Farm Outlets.* Northwest Food Alliance in Collaboration with Myerscough College.

20

Internationalization of a craft enterprise through a virtual tribe: 'Le Nuvole' and the pipe-smoker tribe

Stefano Pace, Luciano Fratocchi and
Fabrizio Cocciola

Introduction

The literature on communities (Cova and Cova, 2002; Kozinets, 1999; Muñiz and O'Guinn, 2001; Schouten and McAlexander, 1995) traditionally focuses on well-known brands (for instance, Salomon, Apple, and SAAB) and widespread activities. However, Small–Medium Enterprises (SMEs) and even craft companies can also leverage the tribal phenomenon, and a single entrepreneur may even gain a competitive advantage over larger organizations. In fact, the individual craftsperson can participate in the life of a community and gain a legitimate position within it, while this is not possible for an institution.

On this assumption, the present study investigates the relationships between tribal marketing and the virtual internationalization of craft enterprises, that is foreign expansion via the Internet. We illustrate the case of Maurizio Tombari, an Italian fine briar pipe manufacturer who is an active member of the virtual tribes of pipe-smokers and collectors. Through membership of the community, Tombari has gained a leading reputation as a pipe artist and a significant level of internationalization.

Our investigation has two main aims:

1 To show that tribal marketing is a new means of internationalization for craft enterprises. Moreover, this approach seems to be peculiar to craft enterprises and SMEs and provides them with a competitive advantage over larger companies.
2 To apply tribal marketing theory to craftspeople and entrepreneurs, and so contribute to the advancement of the theory.

Tribal marketing and virtual internationalization

Tribal marketing

'I'm celebrating the end of three days of pure hell looking for it with a bowl of Stonehaven in a Ser Jacopo Maxima blast.' Which mysterious ritual hides behind this celebration? What complicated technique does this statement refer to? Posts like this are strange to non-*connoisseurs* of the pipe-smoking world, while they are common knowledge to members of communities that gather online to celebrate pipe-smoking and share 'glorious' experiences like the one quoted above. These aggregations represent a new internationalization opportunity for micro-enterprises.

Social consumption is acknowledged as an autonomous object of study, rather than a moderating variable for a subject's consumption. 'To make it simple: community is a consumer behaviour term' (O'Guinn and Muñiz, 2005). Communities of consumption are variously called: consumption sub-cultures, brand communities, tribes (Cova and Cova, 2002; Maffesoli, 1996). They all share consumption (be it under the form of a preference for a brand, a generic product, an activity) as the aggregating core and the notion that 'the link is more important than the think' (Cova, 1996; Cova, 1997; Cova and Cova, 2002). While some differences can be found in the definitions of these concepts, the three typical features identifying a community are consciousness of kind, rituals and traditions, and moral obligation (O'Guinn and Muñiz, 2005).

The tribal and communitarian consumption phenomenon is particularly significant for the Internet. In the past, only territory and kin-based ties were the ascriptive (i.e., not voluntarily chosen by the subject) features that characterized membership of a community and its existence. Transportation and telecommunication systems then broadened the concept of community, showing that the concept is persistent and merely changes its form of expression (Kollock, 1999; Prandelli and Verona, 2002; Wellman, 2001). The Internet adds a new dimension to the concept of community by allowing people to gather regardless of their physical location (Hagel and Armstrong, 1999). The sense of community solicited by the Internet is shown by the co-operation typical of online groups (Kollock, 1999), co-operation that is almost surprising, as it would seem to be discouraged by the 'wild' and free land of the web. Another example from the Internet (in the sense of a natural platform for groups) is the collective actions often promoted by cybernauts on specific topics regarding consumption or social issues (Mele, 1999).

Kozinets (1999) deals with 'e-tribalized marketing' targeting communities that form on the web. These tribal groups are 'more active and discerning' (Kozinets, 1999, p. 252) and compel marketers to relinquish the one-to-one approach typical of modern marketing and assume a posture which is aware of consumption as social behaviour, rather than individual behaviour in its own right or individual behaviour affected by a social environment.

The literature on tribal marketing generally focuses on large companies and their significant marketing effort in trying to keep apace with a tribe, for example, Salomon, Nike and Harley-Davidson. The tribes studied are quite large and involve large numbers of consumers – even though not the mainstream – that justify the investment made by the company. Actually, by its own definition, tribal marketing would prefer a more personal relationship between the organization offering a product and the tribe. The firm should enter the tribe carefully and share the same language, emotions and rites. Obviously, an organization cannot be a full member of the tribe, since it is not a person. In this chapter, we propose the idea that an individual entrepreneur can exploit the tribal marketing approach better than a large company and leverage tribe membership to promote the internationalization of the firm.

Virtual internationalization of SMEs

The effects of the Internet on company internationalization are still debated and far from obvious. With respect to firms of any size, Petersen, Welch, and Liesch (2002) note that Internet-based strategies may reduce one of the most significant barriers to foreign market expansion, that is the uncertainty connected with managing business activities abroad. Other authors (Bakos, 1997; Barua, Ravindran, and Whinston, 1997; Lal and Savary, 1999) emphasize the opportunities offered by the Internet in considerably reducing search costs for both customers and firms. At the same time, however, Petersen et al. (2002), dispute that the Internet may facilitate the process of creating, transferring and retaining knowledge. This is a quite important aspect, since knowledge dramatically affects a business's market expansion abroad. Overall, the effects of the Internet on the foreign expansion of a company vary considerably and are not necessarily positive.

The evaluation of the Internet's potential for SME internationalization is even more difficult and disparate (Fariselli, Oughton, Picory, and Sugden, 1999; Hofacker, 2001; Poon and Swatman, 1999; Rockwell, 1998). While a good number of studies confirm the usefulness of the Internet for SMEs, a comprehensive theory explaining the effects of the technology on foreign market penetration is still in its infancy. Various factors would appear to facilitate SME internationalization via the Internet: interactivity in the communication and distribution processes (Chaston and Mangles, 2002), the decreasing significance of intermediaries in internationalization strategies, and the weaker role of economies of scale (Quelch and Klein, 1996).

SMEs operating in niche segments may be aided by the Internet, as had been recently confirmed by research on so-called 'regional products' that are 'associated spatially with a geographical area and culturally with the latter's customer or modes, with a minimum permanence in time or history [. . . and have] particular qualitative characteristics which differentiate [them] from other products' (Caldentey and Gómez Muñoz, 1977, p. 77). For this type of high-quality and niche product, the company's size is almost insignificant for the success of virtual internationalization, which is rather tied to the skills related to web marketing (Cardilli, Cocciola, Fratocchi, Giustiniano, and Presutti, 2004) and to the new environment (Giustiniano, 2002). Since web marketing is renewed by the tribal phenomenon, SMEs should recognize the new skills required, above all the capability to leverage virtual communities.

To sum up, resorting to the Internet will represent a step forward for SMEs in conquering foreign markets only if the conditions for the development of 'dedicated' organizational skills within the firm are met. Therefore, use of the Internet may allow SMEs to expand their market niches by increasing the critical mass of potential buyers at an international level. This is mainly possible if the web is used as a means of aggregating geographically dispersed individuals associated by specific common interests.

Virtual internationalization of craft enterprises

Among SMEs, craft enterprises represent a further peculiar field that is little studied, despite the fact that their economic relevance for many countries is significant. Craft enterprises usually do not follow the usual steps in their internationalization processes. They expand into foreign markets by developing and exploiting extant networks. This process is consistent with the view that the network of relationships drives internationalization. It might even be unrelated to any formal strategic reasoning and pulled by the network itself (Johanson and Mattson, 1988; Johanson and Vahlne, 1990). The network takes the form of a personal set of relations for entrepreneurs. For small companies, and even more for craft activities, the concept of network is based on personal contacts and relationships (Aldrich and Zimmer, 1986). Informal relations, conversations, and personal ties form a 'know-who' that is as relevant as the traditional 'know-how' (O'Donnell, Gilmore, Cummins, and Carson, 2001). A personal network is known to help the creation and support of small businesses in different forms, for example, information-sharing, expansion of the entrepreneur's contacts, encouragement, motivation, self-confidence and ideas (O'Donnell et al., 2001). Given the importance of personal networks, then, it can be expected that they might also drive the internationalization process.

The almost explosive international growth of some small and micro businesses questions the broadly accepted model of a longer process based on many stages from limited commitments in a nearby foreign country to 'greenfield' investments in distant areas (Johanson and Vahlne, 1977). Today's reality presents rather small companies defined as 'born global'. They are usually companies (often high-tech start-up firms) that from their foundation refer to a global rather than a domestic market. An explanation of this phenomenon is in the network view. The network can help entrepreneurs to leapfrog the common steps in the internationalization process.

In this context, in which the personal network represents a boost to the entrepreneur's activity and expansion, communities, specifically virtual communities, can multiply the network effects on the internationalization of a craft enterprise. The typical features of a community provide an ideal environment for the expansion of the activity, while the sense of reciprocity and solidarity, the sense of kind, and the common passion can drive the internationalization process. This effect is further encouraged by the very nature of virtual communities that aggregate subjects from different countries who otherwise would not have the opportunity to gather.

Internationalization can be reactive, in the sense that entrepreneurs react to changes encouraging them to go abroad, for example, saturated domestic patterns or declining sales. A form of reactive internationalization is through the virtual network. In this case, the craftsperson is embedded in a community that can pull him/her towards foreign markets, even if the business does not have a clear strategic approach to internationalization or a proactive stance.

A key feature of craft enterprises is the core role played by entrepreneurs. Their skills, both professional and personal, directly affect the success of the business and its internationalization. The craftsperson can be typified in different personal categories and approaches to business and life (Fillis, 2004). In particular, the 'idealist' is an artist with an uncompromising view. The work is done for artistic purposes and not really for customers. Reputation is the key driver for the idealist.

Craftspeople can create a new network of personal contacts by becoming members of virtual communities related to their business. In this community, they can leverage their reputations. Reputation is a key competence in a virtual community. An e-commerce platform such as eBay bases its success on the development of a feedback system allowing users to rate each other. On a more personal level, the reputation of a member in a virtual community can be assessed, and it becomes the main resource for the member. An 'idealist' craftsperson can gain a high reputation within a community regardless of any business goal. Through this reputation, the craftsperson is able to receive orders and then expand the business. Unsolicited orders – orders not directly raised by entrepreneurial marketing actions – are in fact one of the main sources of business for a craftsperson (Fillis, 2004). The virtual community phenomenon can multiply the typical effects of internationalization in craft enterprises.

At the same time, the craft enterprise can be more fragile in its success compared to larger firms. This is due to a lack of resources and to the fact that the fate of the business is anyway linked to the personal experiences.

All these facets can be found in the case that follows: Le Nuvole, a craft enterprise producing briar pipes.

The virtual tribe of pipe-smokers and 'Le Nuvole': a small workshop becomes international

Research methodology

The method followed is that of case study research (Yin, 1994). The case is that of 'Le Nuvole', a small craft workshop in Central Italy, founded and managed by Maurizio Tombari, and specializing in fine briar pipes. We collected documentary data and information through personal interviews with Tombari. We supplemented the data with direct observation of the dynamics of virtual groups attended by Tombari, using the netnography methodology devised by Kozinets (2002). Together with an expert in the field, we also visited W.Ø. Larsen in Copenhagen (Denmark), one of the most famous tobacco and pipe shops in the world.

Figure 20.1 Maurizio Tombari at work.

The craftsperson and his business idea

Le Nuvole is a case of 'niche' tribal marketing empowered by the Internet. Maurizio Tombari is an Italian pipe craftsman from Pesaro (central Italy) (Figure 20.1).

In 1996, he established 'Le Nuvole' (The Clouds – the name derives from the firm's slogan: 'Pipes, like clouds, unrepeatable and light in weight'), a small workshop specializing in fine briar pipes. Each pipe is handcrafted exclusively by Tombari, while his wife Stefania is responsible for the design of some collections (Figure 20.2).

Figure 20.2 A pipe by Tombari.

Tombari can be described – in the classification introduced earlier – as an 'idealist'. He considers his work first as an art, then as a business, and does not think much about the market. He would prefer a well-made pipe to a well-done business transaction. Personal artistic considerations play a major role in business decisions. Tombari would not consider eBay as a good outlet for his pipes, since he feels such a solution would be too commercial for a real work of art. eBay would seriously hamper the value of 'Le Nuvole' collections and Tombari's reputation.

Two years after the foundation of the company, Tombari opened the website www.pipe.it in order to exhibit and sell his fine pipes.

Right from the beginning, the website was not a traditional e-commerce venture. Tombari has been able to insert himself and his business into a small tribe of luxury pipe *connoisseurs* and collectors. He has not limited his marketing actions to a well-designed website and user-friendly transaction systems, as traditional e-marketing teachings would suggest. The most important part of his online presence is his participation in the virtual tribes of pipe-lovers and connoisseurs. By posting his messages in newsgroups and interacting with tribe members, Tombari has developed a notable reputation within the tribe, and his pipes have become a recognized brand. This is a completely different approach to the traditional advertising through banners.

The success of Tombari's business as a result of his web presence is significant for a craft workshop. Pipe.it receives on average 17,000 contacts per year without any advertising or mailing lists. According to Tombari, search engines such as Google are the main source of traffic to Le Nuvole website. The second source is virtual communities of pipe-smokers.

Although Tombari does not sell his pipes on eBay, there is a good deal of discussion about the products on the site. Tombari has remained loyal to the personal craftsmanship of his pipes, without any concession to industrialization. He continues to realize the entire manufacturing process without any employees. Consequently, the waiting list for a pipe from 'Le Nuvole' is so long that delivery can be after many months.

The most significant figure of this success is the notable level of internationalization reached by such a small workshop. At the beginning, 85 per cent of the total production was delivered to US customers, 4 per cent to European countries, 10 per cent to Italy, and the remaining 1 per cent was sold in the rest of the world (generally English-speaking countries). This data would define Le Nuvole as a case of instant internationalization, that is an internationalization occurring very quickly and without following the usual stages (Figure 20.3).

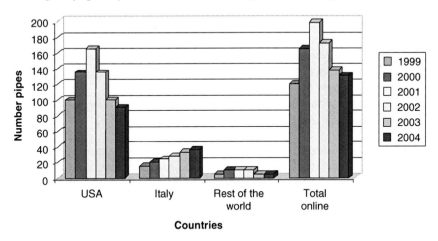

Figure 20.3 Online sales by country (Le Nuvole data).

After 2001, however, sales in the USA rapidly dropped. According to Tombari, this performance is explained by the following elements:

- the increase in Euro/US dollar exchange rate which had a dramatic impact on EU exports;

- the increasingly restrictive laws on smoking;
- the impact of 11th September 2001.

This drop confirms another feature of micro-companies in the international arena, that is their vulnerability.

If asked to explain why his business was so successful internationally, at least prior to the introduction of the Euro, Tombari does not indicate any definite strategic paths that he followed. This corresponds to international expansion driven by the network. In Tombari's view, his next possible market could be, for instance, the Far East. In this respect, it is interesting to note that the idea arose through an acquaintance from Taiwan who happened to know the Tombari family. This friend would offer translations.

The virtual tribe of pipe-smokers

A pipe is a relatively uncommon object in the habits of most people, and it can be considered an example of niche behaviour. This elitist character makes a pipe a 'cult' object able to generate passion and aggregate around it a tribe. Since pipe-smokers and collectors are not so numerous, the Internet is the ideal place to gather enthusiasts in a virtual tribe. At present, the Internet hosts a constellation of different tribes on pipe-smoking. One of the most popular newsgroups focused on this passion is alt.smokers.pipes, in which Tombari takes part. The group is listed in the Google search engine (the most comprehensive database of Usenet newsgroups of the web) and, as the name suggests, it is devoted to pipes and everything is associated with them. People posting to alt.smokers. pipes usually do not post to other groups, indicating that their online presence is motivated only by the specific topic. Moreover, cross-posting (i.e., posting the same message to two or more newsgroups) is infrequent. These two characteristics confirm the existence of a dedicated and closed group of people investing time online exclusively to discuss and follow their passion.

This group presents the typical characteristics defining a community (Muñiz and O'Guinn, 2001):

1 *Consciousness of kind*: A pipe-smoker is aware of being a member of a group of well-defined connoisseurs. Various meaningful personages and characters, and through them a quite distinctive type of person, are evoked by pipe-smoking. The fictional Sherlock Holmes, for instance, is a symbol of intellectuality, acuteness, and intelligence. He is depicted as a pipe-smoker, particularly during the most demanding mental efforts in the course of his investigations. This is an example of the pipe as an identity marker.
2 *Rituals and traditions*: Smoking a pipe is a ritual that distances this activity from cigarette smoking. The rite is ceremoniously sub-divided into the filling of the pipe, the burning of tobacco, the inspiration and all the associated gestures. Pipe-smoking is a traditional rite rooted in the past. Moreover, the parts of a pipe and the kinds of tobacco constitute a technical jargon that only connoisseurs know and understand.

One of the rituals of the newsgroup is dedicating a 'bowl' (i.e., the part of the pipe containing the tobacco) to an event or personage. For instance, a member in one of his posts dedicated a bowl to a passed-away musician. Fellow smokers (including Tombari) joined him in this virtual ceremony. It is the highest sign of respect and honour in the tribe. Another bowl was offered to celebrate the birth of a member's daughter. It is usual to read posts like the following honouring a deceased person *'I'm going to let them know that ASP [Alt.Smokers.Pipes] has hoisted a "bowl of remembrance" in his honor. I know they'll just love it!'*.

The ritual of collective, virtual pipe-smoking is even more interesting, given the fact that pipe-smokers usually smoke alone. The typical pipe-smoker is a meditative man contemplating life with a bowl of fine tobacco. Pictures posted by some members show men smoking serenely and alone, and these pictures are praised by the others as an appropriate rendition of the spirit of pipe-smokers.

Other pictures show famous or unknown men smoking their pipes alone. These pictures, together with the texts, define what smoking pipes means and form the sub-culture of the tribe.

3 *Moral obligation*: Answering questions (regarding tobacco blends, for instance) is 'morally due' in the tribe. Tombari even praises his competitors, as is customary in the community. The sense of community is strongly evident when something unpleasant unrelated to the strict topic of the community happens to a member. This occurred when one of the members of alt.smokers.pipes decided to reveal a serious disease, unrelated to pipe-smoking and thus even more personal, to the fellow pipe-smokers. The expressions of support received by the other members form one of the longest threads in the community. A similar although much less serious case happened when Tombari injured one of his hands working on a piece. A member of the community spread the news and the whole community aggregated to send its best wishes to Tombari.

4 *Language*: The jargon used in the newsgroup is quite complex as is expected for such a subject. Pipes have a rich typology: Egg, Tulip, Liverpool, Canadian, Lovat, Blackpool, and many more. The single parts of a pipe have precise names: stem, shank, bowl, heel, bit. Only a connoisseur is familiar with this language.

Some of the members put signatures at the end of their posts that identify them as real pipe connoisseurs. For instance, the signature *'Astleys 109 in a Le Nuvole dublin'* probably means (the jargon is rather complex for non-experts) that the writer is smoking a certain type of tobacco in Le Nuvole pipe (Tombari's brand) made of a specific kind of wood.

The community also exhibits some opposition towards the 'rest of the world', and opposition is often a trait defining communities. The contrast sometimes expressed by the pipe community is with the excessively strict smoking laws. Moreover, pipe-smokers historically divide themselves into fans of the English tradition (the Dunhill brand) and those who follow the Danish school.

Tombari is a regular member of the newsgroup which he considers the most significant virtual community for pipe-smokers ahead of MSN Pipes. Rather than a mere seller of pipes, Tombari is recognized as a participant, an artist and a lover of pipes. His posts show expertise and his pipes are considered works of art. Being familiar with the tribe and a legitimate member, Tombari can also post messages concerning new pipes. These postings are like ads, but they are accepted by the tribe as a part of the discussion and considered as an update on Tombari's current production. He solicits and receives comments, and the new collections shown to the most loyal fans prompt technical feedback and suggestions.

We have counted almost 500 postings by Tombari since the end of 1998. His contributions vary, he provides or receives suggestions, makes jokes and participates in other typical community exchanges, but only a minor part of the postings is devoted to the introduction of new collections. Moreover in such cases, the post is dutifully tagged as 'AD' (advertisement), in accordance with the group's 'netiquette' which does not tolerate advertising by companies.

Many pipe-lovers have their own website dedicated to their passion and these websites are linked to each other to form a so-called web-ring. The ring to which pipe.it belongs has 290 affiliated websites. The participation of pipe.it in the web-ring is almost paradoxical in a traditional e-marketing perspective. In a standard approach, a site should insulate itself from the competition and avoid reference to other external sites. It is not imaginable, for instance, for Yahoo to advertise or even refer to Google, a direct competitor. In the case of pipe.it, the tribal rules prevail – with the mentioned benefits in terms of commercial revenues – and the site openly refers to other members of the ring, including e-commerce sites. Theoretically, these links might distract a prospective pipe.it customer, but in the tribe culture the links show the visitor that the site is within a tribe, that it is a legitimate member and respects the tribal rules, and is thus worthy of a purchase. A 'closed' site exhibiting just its own products and without links to other sites would not have the same effect, since it would be considered a vendor, rather than a tribe member.

Proposing a typology of virtual communities

Tombari's experience probably would not be replicable in other types of community. We can distinguish four types of virtual communities along two axes (see Figure 20.4).

First, the number of posts per member measures the degree of community activity on a scale from lively to 'dormant'. Second, there is the concentration of the discussion, whether it is limited to few members dominating much of the discussion or extended to many participants who enrich the debate. The discussion concentration ratio can be measured as the percentage of the

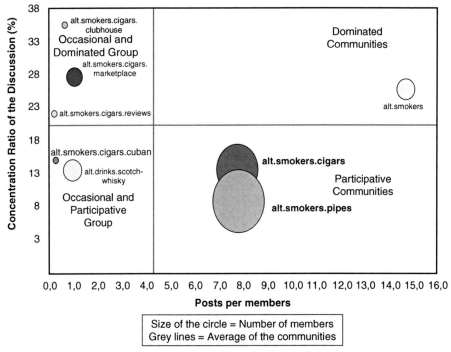

Figure 20.4 A taxonomy of virtual communities (*Source*: Our Elaboration).

total number messages posted by the top 10 posters. The community in which Tombari participates (alt.smokers.pipes) can be defined as a participative community. The activity is high (a high posts/members ratio) and the discussion is open to anyone, not limited to just a few very active members (low discussion concentration ratio). Moreover, the number of members (the size of the circles in the figure) is high. These three parameters show that alt.smokers.pipes is actually a 'healthy' community where Tombari's internationalization efforts can be successful. Other forms of community might be too dominated by a few members (upper part of the figure) and this would hamper the discussion and link the development of the craftsperson's reputation to a small group of people. Other communities might be 'dormant' with only a small number of posts per member.

By spontaneously selecting alt.smokers.pipes as his discussion arena, Tombari had a sound entrepreneurial idea and entered the right environment to further his artistic and commercial internationalization aims.

Conclusions

In this study, we have tried to investigate the relationships between tribal marketing and virtual internationalization in craft enterprises. More specifically, our aim was to understand if craft enterprises might improve their virtual presence on a global scale by basing their Internet strategies on the concept of tribe and the tools of tribal marketing. To this end, we analysed the experience of an Italian craftsperson operating in the pipe-smoking industry and selling all of his products mainly abroad though his website.

Among the main conclusions, we can note that:

- The Internet may have a dramatic power to aggregate people who share a passion for a niche activity or product and who are spread around the world. Their aggregation is not a simple quantitative demand, but takes the form of a tribe with its 'lively' features.
- The concept of tribe is at the same level as that of entrepreneur and craftsperson. A craftsperson is a creative person who lives a passion and transforms this into a business idea. This passion pushes the craftsperson to share ideas and emotions with other individuals sharing the same interest, thus forming a tribe. From this sharing and participation, commercial transactions also emerge. In this respect, it is clear that large companies do not have the same appeal and possibilities as an individual operator.
- As a corollary to the above point, the opposition and counter-power often expressed by communities against corporations (Cova and Carrère, 2002; O'Guinn and Muñiz, 2005) may also be explained by the fact that a firm is not an individual who can share emotions with fellows. A company cannot play on this pitch. Consequently, craft enterprises may gain a competitive advantage over large firms.
- E-marketing is renewed by the tribal marketing applied to the Internet. E-marketing has known two stages: the first where e-marketing and e-commerce overlapped and websites were considered mere showcases to offer products, and a second stage, in which communities were taken into account as a social phenomenon also generating commercial consequences (Hagel and Armstrong, 1999; Prandelli and Verona, 2002; Sawhney, Prandelli, and Verona, 2003; Sawhney, Verona, and Prandelli, 2005). In this second stage, websites hosted communities or leveraged extant communities from the outside. Experiences like that of Le Nuvole show that communities can be experienced from the inside, and this may introduce a new stage in e-marketing, at least regarding the e-marketing activities for craft enterprises.
- Recent internationalization theories basing foreign expansion on the network concept are confirmed and personal networks have gained particular weight. The distinction between business and personal networks is blurred in the case of craft activities, so giving fresh insights into further studies about networks.
- To be a viable channel of internationalization, a community should probably present clear involvement of members and openness in participation, but without any overwhelming presence of just a few members. We have proposed a taxonomy to provide an easy measure of the 'health' of a virtual community for an entrepreneur's purposes.

Any case study is vulnerable to the critique of not having strong external validity. However, the small size of these phenomena compels us to focus on one case of excellence and the single-case study design. Moreover, case study is particularly suitable for those exploratory studies which aim is to explore a new theory, as here with a new approach to internationalization for craft enterprises.

Naturally, the case of 'Le Nuvole' is not a recipe for doing good business. 'Le Nuvole' confirms that limitations in resources – typically affecting small organizations – can hinder further expansion and harm previous advantages. The advantage can easily be lost as a result of effects (such as moves in currency exchange rates) that larger organizations can more easily sustain. A craftsperson can establish some safeguards for his/her business through a more professional and business-wise management approach. However, these safeguards would affect the artistic and creative nature of the craft enterprise, the real source of its success. This trade-off between business and art would appear to be a weak point in craft enterprises when profits and sustainability are at stake.

References

Aldrich, H. and Zimmer, C. (1986). Entrepreneurship through social networks, in Sexton, D. and Smilor, R.W. (eds.), *Art and Science of Entrepreneurship*. Cambridge, MA: Ballinger Publishing Company, pp. 3–23.

Bakos, Y.J. (1997). Reducing buyer search costs: implications for electronic marketplace, *Management Science*, **43** (12), 1676–1692.

Barua, A., Ravindran, S. and Whinston, A.B. (1997). Efficient selection of suppliers over the Internet, *Journal of Management Information Systems*, **13** (4), 117–137.

Caldentey, A.P. and Gómez Muñoz, A.C. (1977). Typical products, technical innovation and organizational innovation, *Proceedings of the 52nd EAAE Seminar Typical and Traditional Productions: Rural Effect and Agro-industrial Problems*, Parma, 19–21 June, pp. 77–88.

Cardilli, G., Cocciola, F., Fratocchi, L., Giustiniano, L. and Presutti, M. (2004). The role of competences in the virtual internationalization process in of SMEs, *Paper presented at the 31st Annual Conference of the Academy of International Business*, UK Chapter, University of Ulster, Belfast, 23–24 April.

Chaston, I. and Mangles, T. (2002). E-commerce in small UK manufacturing firms: a pilot study on internal competencies, *Journal of Marketing Management*, **18** (3), 341–360.

Cova, B. (1996). The post-modern explained to managers: marketing implications, *Business Horizons*, **39** (6), 15–23.

Cova, B. (1997). Community and consumption: towards a definition of linking value of products and services, *European Journal of Marketing*, **31** (3), 297–316.

Cova, B. and Carrère, V. (2002). Les communautés de passionnés de marque: opportunité ou menace sur le Net? *Revue Française du Marketing*, 4/5, 119–130.

Cova, B. and Cova, V. (2002). Tribal marketing: the tribalisation of society and its impact on the conduct of marketing, *European Marketing Journal*, **36** (5/6), 595–620.

Fariselli, P., Oughton, C., Picory, C. and Sugden, R. (1999). Electronic commerce and the future for SMEs in a global market-place: networking and public policies, *Small Business Economics*, **12** (3), 261–276.

Fillis, I. (2004). The internationalizing smaller craft firm: insights from the marketing/entrepreneurship interface, *International Small Business Journal*, **22** (1), 57–82.

Giustiniano, L. (2002). SMEs, the Internet and internationalization processes: a critical analysis, in Giustiniano, L., Guido, G. and Marcati, A. (eds.), *SMEs, International Markets and the Internet: Opportunities and Challenges*. Roma: Luiss Edizioni, pp. 64–98.

Hagel III, J. and Armstrong, A.G. (1999). *Net Gain, Expanding Markets through Virtual Communities*. Boston: Harvard Business School Press.

Hofacker, C.F. (2001). *Internet Marketing*. New York: John Wiley & Sons.

Johanson, J. and Mattsson, L.G. (1988). Internationalisation in industrial systems: a network approach, in Hood, N. and Vahlne, J.E. (eds.), *Strategies in Global Competition*. London: Croom Helm, pp. 287–314.

Johanson, J. and Vahlne, J.-E. (1977). The internationalization process of the firm – a model of knowledge development and increasing foreign market commitments, *Journal of International Business Studies*, **8** (Spring/Summer), 23–32.

Johanson, J. and Vahlne, J.-E. (1990). The mechanism of internationalisation, *International Marketing Review*, **7** (4), 11–24.

Kollock, P. (1999). The economies of online cooperation: gifts and public goods in cyberspace, in Smith, M.A. and Kollock, P. (eds.), *Communities in Cyberspace*. London: Routledge, pp. 220–239.

Kozinets, R.V. (1999). E-tribalized marketing?: the strategic implications of virtual communities of consumption, *European Management Journal*, **17** (3), 252–264.

Kozinets, R.V. (2002). The field behind the screen: using netnography for marketing research in online communities, *Journal of Marketing Research*, **39** (February), 61–72.

Lal, R. and Savary, M. (1999). When and how is the Internet likely to decrease price competition? *Marketing Science*, **18** (4), 485–503.

Maffesoli, M. (1996). *The Time of the Tribes*. London: Sage.

Mele, C. (1999). Cyberspace and disadvantaged communities: the Internet as a tool for collective action, in Smith, M.A. and Kollock, P. (eds.), *Communities in Cyberspace*. London: Routledge, pp. 290–310.

Muñiz Jr., A.M. and O'Guinn, T.C. (2001). Brand Community, *Journal of Consumer Research*, **27** (March), 412–432.

O'Donnell, A., Gilmore, A., Cummins, D. and Carson, D. (2001). The network construct in entrepreneurship research: a review and critique, *Management Decision*, **39** (9), 749–760.

O'Guinn, T.C. and Muñiz Jr., A.M. (2005). Communal consumption and the brand, in Mick, D.G. and Ratneshwar, S. (eds.), *Inside Consumption: Frontiers of Research on Consumer Motives*. London: Routledge, pp. 252–272.

Petersen, B., Welch, L.S. and Liesch, P.W. (2002). The Internet and foreign market expansion by firms, *Management International Review*, **42** (2), 207–221.

Poon, S.P.H. and Swatman, P.M.C. (1999). An exploratory study of small business Internet commerce issues, *Information and Management*, **35** (1), 9–18.

Prandelli, E. and Verona, G. (2002). *Marketing in Rete. Analisi e decisioni nell'economia digitale*. Milan: McGraw-Hill.

Quelch, J.A. and Klein, L.R. (1996). The Internet and international marketing, *Sloan Management Review*, **38** (3), 60–75.

Rockwell, B. (1998). *Using the Web to Compete in a Global Marketplace*. New York: John Wiley & Sons.

Sawhney, M., Prandelli, E. and Verona, G. (2003). The power of innomediation, *MIT Sloan Management Review*, **44** (2), 77–82.

Sawhney, M., Verona, G. and Prandelli, E. (2005). Collaborating to create: the Internet as a platform for customer engagement in product innovation, *Journal of Interactive Marketing*, **19** (4), 4–17.

Schouten, J.W. and McAlexander, J.H. (1995). Subcultures of consumption: an ethnography of the new bikers, *Journal of Consumer Research*, **22** (June), 43–61.

Wellman, B. (2001). *The Persistence and Transformation of Community: From Neighbourhood Groups to Social Networks*. Report to the Law Commission in Canada. Toronto: Wellman Associates.

Yin, R. (1994). *Case study research: Design and methods*, 2nd ed. Beverly Hills, CA: Sage Publishing.

Index

Entries in *italics* denote films and publications.